Genocide's Aftermath

⚖ METAPHILOSOPHY

METAPHILOSOPHY SERIES IN PHILOSOPHY

Series Editors Armen T. Marsoobian and Brian J. Huschle

The Philosophy of Interpretation, edited by Joseph Margolis and Tom Rockmore (2000)
Global Justice, edited by Thomas W. Pogge (2001)
Cyberphilosophy: The Intersection of Computing and Philosophy, edited by James H. Moor and Terrell Ward Bynum (2002)
Moral and Epistemic Virtues, edited by Michael Brady and Duncan Pritchard (2003)
The Range of Pragmatism and the Limits of Philosophy, edited by Richard Shusterman (2004)
The Philosophical Challenge of September 11, edited by Tom Rockmore, Joseph Margolis, and Armen T. Marsoobian (2005)
Global Institutions and Responsibilities: Achieving Global Justice, edited by Christian Barry and Thomas W. Pogge (2005)
Genocide's Aftermath: Responsibility and Repair, edited by Claudia Card and Armen T. Marsoobian (2007)

Genocide's Aftermath:
Responsibility and Repair

Edited by

Claudia Card
and
Armen T. Marsoobian

First published in *Metaphilosophy* 37, nos. 3–4 (July 2006), except for "Genocide and Social Death," by Claudia Card, and "Epilogue: Reconciliation in the Aftermath of Genocide" by Armen T. Marsoobian.

BLACKWELL PUBLISHING
350 Main Street, Malden, MA 02148-5020, USA
9600 Garsington Road, Oxford OX4 2DQ, UK
550 Swanston Street, Carlton, Victoria 3053, Australia

First published 2007 by Blackwell Publishing Ltd

Library of Congress Cataloging-in-Publication Data

Genocide's aftermath: responsibility and repair/edited by Claudia Card and Armen T. Marsoobian.
   p. cm.
  Includes bibliographical references and index.
  ISBN 978-1-4051-4848-1 (alk. paper)
  1. Genocide–History. 2. Genocide–Moral and ethical aspects. 3. Genocide–Government policy. 4. Genocide–Prevention. I. Card, Claudia. II. Marsoobian, Armen.

HV6322. 7.G487 2007
304.6′63–dc22   2006036028

Set in Times
by Macmillan India Ltd
Printed and bound in Great Britain
by TJ International, Padstow, Cornwall

For further information on Blackwell Publishing, visit our Web site:
www.blackwellpublishing.com

CONTENTS

NOTES ON CONTRIBUTORS

Mohammed Abed is in the final year of his Ph.D. studies in the Department of Philosophy at the University of Wisconsin—Madison. His research interests are in normative ethics and political philosophy. In particular, his doctoral thesis is a study of political violence and the limits of obligation. His research extends to a range of other topics in these areas, including theories of reparative justice and other issues in international ethics. He has also completed work on Islamic and Jewish naturalism in the medieval period.

William Bradford (Chiricahua Apache) serves as general counsel and United Nations ambassador for the Miami Tribe of Indians of Indiana. He has published more than twenty books and articles in the fields of international law, law of indigenous peoples, and laws of armed conflict, and he is a leading authority on the subject of remedies for historical injuries suffered by indigenous peoples. He is a graduate of Harvard Law School and holds a Ph.D. in international relations from Northwestern University.

Claudia Card is the Emma Goldman Professor of Philosophy at the University of Wisconsin. She is the author of *The Atrocity Paradigm: A Theory of Evil* (2002), *The Unnatural Lottery: Character and Moral Luck* (1996), and *Lesbian Choices* (1995) and the editor of many books, most recently *The Cambridge Companion to Simone de Beauvoir*. She is currently a senior fellow at the Institute for Research in the Humanities (Madison, Wisconsin), where she is writing another book on evil and an introduction to feminist philosophy.

Nir Eisikovits, an Israeli attorney, earned his Ph.D. in legal and political philosophy from Boston University in 2005. His research focuses on the moral and political dilemmas arising in postconflict and transitional settings. His recent scholarly publications include "Forget Forgiveness: On the Benefits of Sympathy for Political Reconciliation" (in *Theoria*) and "Moral Luck and the Criminal Law" (in *Law and Social Justice*, edited by Joseph Keim Campbell et al.). He is assistant professor of philosophy at Suffolk University in Boston and a fellow at the International Institute for Mediation and Historical Conciliation.

Jean Jansem (born Semerdjian), whose work appears on the cover, was born in 1920 in the Armenian quarter of Seuleuze (Susurluk), Turkey. He was forced to leave his homeland for Greece and then Paris. He studied at the Ecole des arts décoratifs de Paris and attended the "Grande Chaumière" workshop in Montparnasse. He has had major exhibitions in Europe and the United States, and two museums in Japan are devoted solely to his art. Considered a leading exponent of the School of Paris, he was made chevalier of the French Legion of Honor in 2003. His series of paintings entitled *Massacres*, from which the cover painting is taken, is permanently exhibited at the Armenian Genocide Memorial in Yerevan, Armenia. He is represented by Galerie Matignon, 18 avenue Matignon, 75008 Paris, gm.matignon@wanadoo.fr.

Haig Khatchadourian is emeritus professor of philosophy at the University of Wisconsin—Milwaukee. He has also taught at a number of other American universities and universities in the Middle East. In addition to numerous articles in American and European journals, he is the author of nine books of philosophy and a volume of poetry. He is a member of the International Academy of Philosophy and a fellow of Britain's Royal Society for the Encouragement of Arts, Manufactures, and Commerce (FRA).

Karen Kovach is assistant professor in the Department of Family Medicine and director of the Biomedical Ethics Program at Mercer University School of Medicine. She received her doctorate in moral philosophy from the Graduate School of the City University of New York. Much of her research has focused on social aspects of moral life. She is currently working on some questions concerning individual moral responsibility and the Holocaust.

Armen T. Marsoobian is professor and chair of philosophy at Southern Connecticut State University. He is editor in chief of the Blackwell journal *Metaphilosophy* and has coedited four books: Justus Buchler's *Metaphysics of Natural Complexes* (1990), *Nature's Perspectives: Prospects for Ordinal Metaphysics* (1991), *The Philosophical Challenge of September 11* (2004), and *The Blackwell Guide to American Philosophy* (2004). He has published articles in aesthetics and American philosophy, and his current work deals with philosophical issues arising from genocide.

Larry May, Ph.D., J.D., is professor of philosophy at Washington University in St. Louis. He is just finishing a trilogy: *Crimes Against Humanity* (Cambridge, 2005), which won awards from the American Society of International Law and the North American Society for Social Philosophy; *War Crimes and Just Wars* (Cambridge, forthcoming in

2007), which won an award from the American Philosophical Association; and the manuscript "Aggression and Crimes Against Peace," which includes material published here.

Marina A. L. Oshana is associate professor of philosophy at the University of Florida. Her research focuses on issues in personal autonomy and moral responsibility and, more recently, self-identity. Her publications include "Autonomy and Free Agency," in *Personal Autonomy*, edited by James Stacey Taylor (Cambridge, 2005), and "Ascriptions of Responsibility," *American Philosophical Quarterly*, volume 34, no. 1 (January 1997). She has just completed her first book, *Personal Autonomy in Society* (forthcoming from Ashgate).

Rodney C. Roberts is a descendant of the African peoples who were enslaved at the Somerset Place plantation in Creswell, North Carolina. He was a 2005–2006 Fulbright lecturer and research scholar in the Department of Philosophy, University of Cape Town, South Africa, and is currently assistant professor of philosophy at East Carolina University. His primary research interest is in the conceptual analysis of injustice and related ideas, and in the development and application of normative injustice theory. He is the editor of *Injustice and Rectification* (Peter Lang, 2002).

Ernesto Verdeja is assistant professor of government at Wesleyan University. He is the author of articles in *Res Publica, Constellations, Contemporary Political Theory,* and *Contemporary Politics,* as well as a chapter on trials and truth commissions in *Genocide, War Crimes and the West,* edited by Adam Jones. He is currently completing a book manuscript on reconciliation in the aftermath of political violence, and his research interests are in contemporary political theory, genocide and political violence, and reconciliation and transitional justice.

Stephen Winter is currently completing his doctoral work in political theory at St. Catherine's College, Oxford. He has an M.A. from Dalhousie University in Halifax and a B.A. (Honours) from the University of British Columbia.

Bill Wringe is assistant professor of philosophy at Bilkent University, Ankara. He has published articles on justifying the punishment of war crimes, on the ethics of humanitarian intervention, and on basic needs and collective obligations. He also writes on some areas of analytic philosophy of mind.

1

INTRODUCTION:
GENOCIDE'S AFTERMATH

CLAUDIA CARD AND ARMEN T. MARSOOBIAN

The twentieth century has been indelibly marked as the century of genocide, and the twenty-first continues to perpetuate this dark legacy. One of the first modern genocides of this period was perpetrated by the Ottoman Turks against the Armenians; the most recent is being perpetrated by the government of Sudan upon the non-Arab inhabitants of Darfur. The term itself, "genocide," was coined by the Polish American jurist Raphael Lemkin to capture the peculiarly heinous mass killings of both the Jews in Europe from 1942 to 1945 and the Ottoman Armenians from 1915 to 1923. We now see much of modern history through the lens of genocide. This collection of essays brings together timely pieces that probe a variety of issues arising from the aftermath of genocide. We have chosen the title "Genocide's Aftermath: Responsibility and Repair" because we believe that an understanding of how to attribute responsibility for genocide and how to repair the evils perpetrated in genocides are two of the central moral tasks of philosophers. Much has been written by historians, sociologists, and psychologists in chronicling the causes, circumstances, and consequences of particular genocides. As philosophers we are primarily concerned with a conceptual understanding of the nature of genocide and how this understanding makes moral demands upon us to respond to genocide—to respond not only in the above terms of clarifying how we attribute responsibility for genocide and how we may engender its repair but also in the most important sense of what we as individuals and as nations should do to prevent genocide.

A range of issues are raised in the ensuing essays. In examining these issues, the authors make numerous references to historical instances of genocides and crimes against humanity. This historical backdrop both illustrates and tests the philosophical claims made in these essays. We begin this collection with Claudia Card's "Genocide and Social Death," an essay that originally appeared in 2003 but is included here in a revised form.[1] Card argues that social death is central to the evil of genocide (whether the genocide is

---

[1] Claudia Card, "Genocide and Social Death," *Hypatia* 18, no. 1 (2003): 63–79.

homicidal or primarily cultural); it is the dimension of social death that distinguishes genocide from other kinds of mass murder. Loss of social vitality is loss of identity and thereby meaning for one's existence. Seeing social death at the center of genocide takes our focus off body counts and loss of individual talents, directing us instead to mourn losses of relationships that create community and give meaning to the development of talents. Card's essay also serves as an excellent introduction to the current state of the philosophical literature treating genocide. Card disentangles the controversies that surround such issues as the degree of intention or foreseeability behind actions that have led to mass death of the sort that took place during the European colonization of the Americas. She also responds to possible counterarguments to her thesis from those who would point to the social vitality of cultures that once were the targets of genocide. The flourishing of post-Holocaust Jewish culture in the diaspora and Israel cannot simply be taken as evidence that social vitality is of secondary importance. Card points out that such refutations often ignore important distinctions by shifting the argument away from the victims of genocide: "The question . . . should not be simply whether the traditions survived but whether individual Jewish victims were able to sustain their connections to those traditions." Although Card does not take up the implications of this counterargument for revisionist or denialist genocide pseudo-scholarship, the implications are clear. Deniers of the Holocaust have pointed to the survival of Jewish culture as evidence for the "exaggerated" claims concerning the events in Europe during the 1940s. The same has been true with regard to the Turkish government's campaign to deny the Armenian genocide. Two of the following essays, those of Mohammed Abed and Bill Wringe, respectively, explicitly take up Card's concept of social death and further expand upon its implications.

Abed's "Clarifying the Concept of Genocide" probes the adequacy of the standard definition of genocide as codified in the 1948 U.N. Convention on the Prevention and Punishment of the Crime of Genocide. Further developing Claudia Card's notion that social death is the distinctive harm of genocide, Abed provides a compelling argument for the position that most cases of ethnic cleansing count as genocides. In identifying the features that make a group susceptible to the harm of genocide, he highlights the importance of the territorially bounded nature of cultures. The consequences of removing from their historical lands groups whose cultures are territorially bounded meet the standard of cultural death that is a central component of social death. This is particularly relevant given the fact that some commentators have tried to distinguish ethnic cleansing as somehow a lesser evil than genocide. The reservation system for American Indians, the township and "homeland" systems for black South Africans, and the collectivization of peasant farming communities by Stalin are some obvious historical examples that would have to be rethought given the argument Abed presents. His argument would also elevate what happened in the former Yugoslavia to a level of genocide comparable to what happened in the Holocaust to Jews from central and eastern European Jewry and in the genocide of Armenians from central and eastern Anatolia.

The essays of Karen Kovach, Marina A. L. Oshana, Bill Wringe, and Stephen Winter raise a number of interrelated issues. Kovach and Oshana treat issues related to intergenerational and vicarious responsibility for genocidal acts. In her "Genocide and the Moral Agency of Ethnic Groups," Kovach gives an account of the "ethnic identity group" as a way of understanding the "collective" nature of groups who victimize and of those who are victimized. Her claim is that while mere membership in an ethnic identity group is not sufficient for assigning blame or moral responsibility for the collective actions of that group, the "moral alignment" of oneself with that group does have implications for individual responsibility. Aligning oneself with an ethnic group entails a particular sort of relationship with the *idea* of that group as a collective agent whose collectivity rests on a shared ancestry. If one acts out of this understanding of one's relationship to the group, then one shares in the moral culpability of that group. This is a culpability that may also have implications for future generations of that ethnic group.

Oshana in her essay "Moral Taint" takes up the issue of vicarious and, by implication, intergenerational responsibility for historical acts of genocide or crimes against humanity. She argues that one can be morally compromised by one's ethnic heritage. Moral taint captures this sense of moral compromise. Tainted parties can thus be vicariously responsible for acts of genocide through their association with a particular ethnic group. While this does not reach the level of legal or direct moral responsibility, it does place a moral burden on such individuals. Atonement is the appropriate moral response to the shame of this moral burden. Needless to say, the short summary given here does not capture the nuanced and carefully crafted argument of this fascinating essay.

Wringe in his essay "Collective Action and the Peculiar Evil of Genocide" takes up the clarification of the concept of genocide and the thorny issue of distinguishing it from other instances of mass murder. While agreeing with Card that the harm of social death plays a significant role in characterizing genocides, he claims that we should not downplay the collective action that is peculiar to genocides. Wringe attempts to accommodate both the intentions of the perpetrators and the suffering of the victims of genocide. Central to his argument is the notion that the individual perpetrators of genocidal acts must be aware to a certain degree that they are participating in a collective project. Although there is no collective subject in a metaphysical sense, there are individual participatory intentions in a collective project. While individual acts of murder may well be evil, the peculiar evil of genocide requires a sense of participation in collective evil action.

The account that Wringe provides is especially illuminating when applied to actual cases of genocide. The type of collective action varies across actual cases. We recognize that genocides require collective actions, often by vast numbers of perpetrators. If we look at three historical cases of genocide, the Holocaust, the Rwandan genocide, and the Armenian genocide (although Wringe does not discuss the Armenian case in his essay), we see three cases of collective action. All three involved central coordination, though in varying degrees. With regard to the Holocaust there was a high degree of central coordination; we are all aware of the death camps and the machinery of the Final Solution. In the case of Rwanda there was a lesser degree of control. There was both explicit and direct involvement by Hutu elements of the government, the military, and militias armed by the government. There was also a high degree of civilian mob-inspired participation that took the form of neighbors killing neighbors. The Armenian genocide included perpetrators ranging from the military, the gendarmerie, and armed criminal elements, some from the local Kurdish population and others consisting of relocated Turks who themselves were victims of ethnic wars in the Balkans. On the model of collective action that Wringe proposes we could have varying individual intentions, but so long as they contributed to the evil of social death, they would still count as genocidal.

Different perpetrators may even formulate this collective project in different terms. Perpetrators act individually but with participatory intentions. Their actions contribute in some manner to a collective project—whether it be the Final Solution or the answer to the Armenian Question. What makes this approach especially attractive is that even though the individual perpetrator needs to have some sort of awareness of the collective project, he does not need to be aware of the scope and dimensions of the project. This may at times facilitate the recruiting of greater numbers of perpetrators. One might not be aware of the other participants in the genocide or be aware of their roles. Full mutual recognition need not be evident. For instance, those Kurds who took advantage of the situation of the deportation of the Armenians by robbing and raping the "relocation columns" of women, children, and the elderly were not centrally coordinated from Istanbul, nor were they vaguely aware of the dimensions of what was taking place. Yet under Wringe's approach they were just as much joint participants in the genocide as was the Committee of Union and Progress cabinet in Istanbul.

Winter in his essay "On the Possibilities of Group Injury" defends the notion that there is a philosophically viable notion of "group injury that is both grounded on ethical individualism and not 'simply' reducible to individual interests." Both Winter and Wringe reject as metaphysically dubious the notion of collective subjects or, in Winter's words, "group minds or ghostly collectives." The notion of group injury that Winter presents is based upon what he dubs "the comprehensive account of group interests." He sets out and defends five conditions for the existence of group interests. A mere summary of these conditions and their supporting arguments would not do them justice. Suffice it to say, he provides an intriguing way of parsing out the individual and collective nature of the harms inflicted in genocides and crimes committed against collectivities. Winter's notion of group injury, while extensionally broader than the injuries inflicted in genocides, does have advantages for discussions of genocide and of how repair must work both on the individual and on the group level.

The next three essays, by Rodney C. Roberts, Haig Khatchadourian, and Ernesto Verdeja, respectively, deal with compensation and reparations. Roberts rejects what he calls "the standard interpretation" of rectificatory compensation (sometimes referred to as reparations) shared by many philosophers. This is the view that individuals who have been wrongfully harmed should be compensated for those harms by being "placed in the position they would have been in had the injustice never occurred." The idea of being restored to some status quo ante, labeled "the counterfactual conception of compensation," leads to a number of problematic consequences that would make compensation impossible. Placing his argument in the context of American enslavement of Africans and the moral claims for compensation by descendents of slaves, Roberts demonstrates that the counterfactual conception undermines any reasonable talk of compensation. This conception contends that one cannot "really" be restored to one's prior status, so why bother trying. Or worse still, one's very existence as a descendent of slaves is dependent upon the harm of slavery having occurred in the first place, so such descendents should be "grateful" rather than be compensated. Roberts effectively exposes these fallacies and proposes a positive conception of rectificatory compensation that acknowledges the continuing harm perpetrated on the descendents of slaves. His argument can be applied by extension to other cases in which descendents of atrocities and genocides have called for some form of compensation, whether they be American Indians, diasporan Armenians, or black South Africans.

Khatchadourian provides a moral justification for a system of compensation and reparation drawing upon the work of a number of philosophers. He distinguishes the concept of reparative justice from the broader notion of compensatory justice by highlighting the fact that the former requires that there be a wrong committed on the part of the party that owes the reparation. Compensatory justice does not require such a wrong—for instance, in cases where society compensates individuals for accidents or natural disasters. An important first step in any system of reparatory justice is the injurer's acknowledgment of the injury she has caused. When such acknowledgment is not forthcoming and in its place a pervasive and systematic denial of injury is claimed on the part of the injurer, the failure of the system of reparatory justice is complete.

Khatchadourian takes the example of the Turkish denial of the Armenian genocide as his prime illustrative case. What is most egregious in this particular case is not the lack of acknowledgment but the active and systematic campaign of denial on the part of successive Turkish governments through political, economic, and diplomatic pressure and state-supported scholarship denying the genocide. Khatchadourian writes: "When a sovereign society denies its wrong, the injured parties are not only forced to continue to bear the *costs* of their injury but are also *denied recognition* as human beings equal in dignity and worth." He singles out the example of the work of Justin McCarthy, one of the few non-Turkish historians who have actively denied that a genocide of Armenians took place in the period 1915–1923. McCarthy has taken the logic of blaming the victims to the extreme of claiming that there was a reverse genocide of Turks by Armenian revolutionaries. In response to the work of another Armenian genocide denier, the Holocaust scholar Deborah Lipstadt has written: "Denial of genocide strives to reshape history in order to demonize the victims and rehabilitate the perpetrators, and is—indeed—the final stage of genocide" (Lipstadt 1996).[2]

Verdeja in his essay "A Normative Theory of Reparations in Transitional Democracies" details the advantages of a five-part approach to repairing the damage in a country in which one group of citizens, through the mechanisms of government, committed atrocities against another group. Focusing on the Latin American nations Guatemala, El Salvador, Peru, Argentina, Chile, and Brazil, Verdeja's concern is with how reparations can strengthen the transition to democracy. These are societies in which victims and victimizers must live together and be committed to the goal of establishing equitable liberal democratic institutions. Much of the violence committed in these countries was of a political as opposed to a strictly genocidal nature, even when ethnic groups were involved, as was the case with the Indians of Guatemala and Peru. Still, Verdeja's approach is valuable for other countries in which ethnic violence occurred, such as Rwanda and South Africa. Central to Verdeja's five-part approach is the notion of an official apology and reparations to the victims of atrocities. Such apologies "publicly reaffirm victims' moral worth and dignity" and at the same time force society to "reconceptualize its sense of 'we'" to include victims as equal citizens. Reparations also strengthen public trust in the government institutions that may have been implicated in the crimes and undermine the "justificatory narratives given by perpetrators." Finally, reparations may engender "public debate around a critical interpretation of history, one that calls for a careful reconsideration that eschews monumental, unreflective understandings of the past."

---

[2] For a balanced treatment of the campaign of Armenian genocide denial see chapter 6, "Epilogue: The Geopolitics of Memory," in Donald Bloxham, *The Great Game of Genocide: Imperialism, Nationalism, and the Destruction of Ottoman Armenians* (Oxford: Oxford University Press, 2005).

Verdeja points out that Latin American countries have gone down this road of apology and reparation to varying degrees. In the bigger picture of the twentieth century, we can see in the case of Germany, where there were few victims left to reincorporate into its citizenry, the chief benefit has been the strengthening of German democracy and a highly successful reconciliation with Germany's victimized neighbors. Japan has been a different story. The Nanking and Korean atrocities have never been repaired or even officially been recognized in any significant fashion. Some would say that Japan has yet to "eschew [its] monumental, unreflective understanding of the past." The history of the United States with regard to the decimation of the American Indian population has undergone a significant critical revision in the course of the past fifty years, though no official apology or reparations have been made (see William C. Bradford's essay in this collection). Unfortunately, modern-day Turkey has chosen the path of official denial of the Armenian genocide and has actively suppressed any critical historical examination of the events that surrounded the birth of its republic (see the latter section of Khatchadourian's essay in this collection). Questioning the Kemalist "monumental history" of Turkey has been cause for imprisonment until recently, though the threat today is still quite real.[3]

Larry May's essay "Prosecuting Military Leaders for War Crimes" displays both philosophical insight and a wealth of knowledge regarding international law. May uses the particular case of Croatian General Tihomir Blaskic, whose conviction by the International Criminal Tribunal for Yugoslavia (ICTY) for war crimes was subsequently overturned on appeal, to examine the legal basis upon which military and political leaders can be held responsible for violations of international humanitarian law. It is often the case that the actual acts of atrocity are carried out by lower-ranking soldiers under the command of individuals who deny direct command responsibility for those acts. A paper trail is often hard to find in such conflict situations. May contends that leaders, not the minor players, such as the foot soldiers, should be the primary focus of war crimes prosecutions because of their knowledge of the "criminal enterprise" of ethnic cleansing or genocide. This is what he means when he claims that the *mens rea* (guilty mind) component of criminal liability should be key in the war crimes and crimes against humanity prosecutions of military and political leaders.

---

[3] Orhan Pamuk, the Nobel Prize-winning Turkish novelist (of, for example, *My Name Is Red* and *Snow*) was charged in late 2005 for "insulting the Republic" under the newly passed Turkish penal code article 301/1 for making the following statement in a February 6, 2005, interview with the Swiss newspaper *Das Magazin*: "Thirty thousand Kurds and a million Armenians were killed in Turkey. Almost no one dares speak but me, and the nationalists hate me for that." Cited in the Penn American Center Web site www.pen.org/page.php/prmID/1014 (accessed 5 July 2006).

May skillfully leads us through the details of the ICTY trial chamber's decision and the appeals court's reversal in the Blaskic case to show that the better approach would have been based on the use of a joint-enterprise liability theory. In this approach negligence plays the central role in holding leaders responsible for the acts of their subordinates. A precommitment to the joint enterprise, whether the enterprise was criminal or not, extends a sense of willfulness (the willfulness necessary for mens rea) to the causal chain of events undertaken by members of this enterprise. A commander's claims of ignorance as to the actions of his troops would hold little legitimacy on this view if he was aware ahead of time that unsupervised miscreants in his units were capable of such atrocities. In the specific case of Blaskic, May writes:

> If the general was part of a joint enterprise, whereby some people in the joint enterprise put miscreants into positions where they could terrorize camp prisoners and other civilians, and where not properly supervising these miscreants was part of the plan, then when the miscreants are in fact not supervised it certainly no longer looks like simple negligence based on thoughtlessness. And even if it truly is thoughtless, it still looks as though the precommitment counts in allowing us to disregard the thoughtlessness and hold Blaskic strictly liable nonetheless.

There are some important conceptual similarities between May's approach and that of Wringe's notion of joint participatory intentions. Often members of the leadership in genocidal regimes try to muddy the line of command between themselves and the agents on the ground who commit the atrocities. Whether it is the Sudanese government using Arab "Janjaweed" militias to kill the black Sudanese of Darfur systematically or Turkish Interior Minister Talât using the irregular, paramilitary *Teşkilat-i Mahsusa*, or Special Organization, to organize the genocidal deportations of the Armenians out of Anatolia, the intention is to create a certain degree of deniability for the leadership.

In "Rethinking the Legitimacy of Truth Commissions: 'I Am the Enemy You Killed, My Friend,'" Nir Eisikovits provides a justificatory argument for the moral importance of the truth-commission approach to reconciliation between enemies. Truth commissions have been criticized for being undemocratic and for not providing the justice demanded by the victims of crimes against humanity. Taking South Africa's Truth and Reconciliation Commission as his paradigm case, Eisikovits surveys a variety of justifications given for its work. He proposes an alternative justification based upon Adam Smith's notion of sympathy—"the ability to project oneself imaginatively into the circumstances in which others operate and to view the world from their perspective." Eisikovits sees sympathy as central to political and social reconciliation. Two conditions are necessary in order to achieve sympathy: detailed exposure to the particular circumstances of the other, and the motivation to seek such an exposure. Eisikovits calls the latter "political generosity." This is a generosity that most importantly needs to be displayed by the victors in conflict situations. Unfortunately, political generosity is a virtue that has often been lacking once bitter racial and ethnic conflicts have ended. Rather, victor's justice has often sown the seeds of future ethnic conflict.

William C. Bradford's essay "Acknowledging and Rectifying the Genocide of American Indians: 'Why Is It That They Carry Their Lives on Their Fingernails?'" has a twofold purpose. First, it sets out the evidence for recognizing as genocide the treatment of American Indians in the course of the more than three hundred years of U.S. history. Unfortunately, for many Americans this is a hidden genocide. Bradford provides a compelling historical account of the many sorry dimensions of this genocide. Second, using this historical foundation, he proceeds to lay out and critique three existing theories of justice that seek to redress the harms of the genocide. As an alternative Bradford proposes what he calls justice as indigenism. This approach requires a profound rethinking of the premises underlying our relations with indigenous populations. The details of this theory and its application cannot be easily summarized, but its core conception rests on the reality that American Indians and non-Indians are two peoples who are forced by a common history to live in the same geographic home. While the two are interdependent, the basis for reconciliation must start from the acknowledgment that American Indians form a sovereign, independent nation. Without this acknowledgment and the strong sense of self-determination it entails, redress would only amount to a form of paternalism. Based on this recognition, Bradford proposes seven concrete steps (acknowledgment, apology, peacemaking, commemoration, symbolic compensation, land restoration, and reconciliation) that are necessary to achieve true reconciliation. Bradford believes that once such a reconciliation is achieved the United States will be strengthened as a nation and will have a stronger moral voice in dealing with the rest of the world, especially in its endeavors to punish and prevent genocides.

We hope that the thought-provoking essays that follow will provide an important contribution to the ever-growing philosophical scholarship on genocide, and that in some small measure they will provide the wisdom necessary for preventing genocide.

Reference

Lipstadt, Deborah. 1996. "Armenian Genocide," letter to *Princeton Alumni Weekly* 96, no. 4 (April 17).

2

GENOCIDE AND SOCIAL DEATH

CLAUDIA CARD

This essay develops the hypothesis that social death is utterly central to the evil of genocide, not just when a genocide is primarily cultural but even when it is homicidal on a massive scale. It is social death that enables us to distinguish the peculiar evil of genocide from the evils of other mass murders. Even genocidal murders can be viewed as extreme means to the primary end of social death. Social vitality exists through relationships, contemporary and intergenerational, that create an identity that gives meaning to a life. Major loss of social vitality is a loss of identity and consequently a serious loss of meaning for one's existence. Putting social death at the center takes the focus off individual choice, individual goals, individual careers, and body counts and puts it on relationships that create community and set the context that gives meaning to choices and goals. If my hypothesis is correct, the term "cultural genocide" is probably both redundant and misleading—redundant if the social death present in all genocide implies cultural death as well, and misleading if "cultural genocide" suggests that some genocides do not include cultural death.

1. What Is Feminist about Analyzing Genocide?

The question has been asked, What is feminist about this project?[1] Why might one publish it in a book of feminist philosophy? The answer is both simple and complex. Simply, it is the history behind the project and the perspective from which it is carried out, rather than a focus on women or gender, that make the project feminist. Some of the complexities are as follows.

The evil of genocide falls not only on men and boys but also on women and girls, typically unarmed, untrained in defense against violence, and often also responsible for care of the wounded, the sick, the disabled, babies, children, and the elderly. Because genocide targets both sexes, rather than being specific to women's experience, there is some risk of its being neglected in feminist thought. It is also the case that with few exceptions (such as Schott 1999; Card 1996 and 1997) both feminist and

---

[1] This question was raised by anonymous reviewers of an earlier draft of this essay.

nonfeminist philosophical reflections on war and other public violence have tended to neglect the impact on victims. Philosophers have thought mostly about the positions of perpetrators and decision-makers (most of them men), with some feminist speculation on what might change if more women were among the decision-makers and if women were subject to military conscription. The damage of war and terrorism is commonly assessed in terms of its ruin of individual careers, body counts, statistics on casualties, and material costs of rebuilding. Attention goes to preventing such violence and the importance of doing so, but less to the experience and responses of the majority of victims and survivors, who are civilians, not soldiers. In bringing to the fore the responses of victims of both sexes, Holocaust literature stands in sharp contrast to these trends. Central to Holocaust literature is reflection on the meaning of genocide.

Women's Studies, in its engagement with differences among women, has moved from its earlier aim to train a feminist eye on the world and all kinds of issues (such as evil) to the more limited aim of studying women and gender. I return here to the earlier conception that recognizes not only the study of women, feminism, or gender, but also feminist approaches to issues of ethics and social theory generally, whether the word "feminist" is used or not. My interests move toward commonalities in our experiences of evil, not only commonalities among women differently situated but commonalities shared with many men as well. Yet my lens is feminist, polished through decades of reflection on women's multifarious experiences of misogyny and oppression. What we notice, through a feminist lens, is influenced by long habits of attending to emotional response, relationships that define who we (not just women and girls) are, and the significance of the concrete particular.

Centering social death accommodates the position, controversial among genocide scholars, that genocidal acts are not always or necessarily homicidal. Forcibly sterilizing women or men of a targeted group, or forcibly separating their children from them for reeducation for assimilation into another group, can also be genocidal in aim or effect.[2] Such policies can be aimed at or achieve the eventual destruction of the social identity of those so treated. It may appear that transported children simply undergo change in social identity, not that they lose all social vitality. That may be the intent. Yet, parents' social vitality is a casualty of children's forced reeducation, and in reality transported children may fail to make a satisfying transition.

---

[2] Unlike Native American families whose children were forcibly transported for reeducation in the United States, many Jewish families during the Holocaust sought to hide their children in gentile households. Loss to the children of Jewish social vitality was hardly the responsibility of their families' decisions to do this but rather the responsibility of those whose oppressive measures drove families to try to save their children in this way.

The Holocaust was not only a program of mass murder but also an assault on Jewish social vitality. The assault was experienced by hidden children who survived as well as by those who died. Hitler's sterilization program and Nuremberg laws that left German Jews stateless were parts of the genocide, not preludes to it. Jews who had converted to Christianity (or whose parents or grandparents had done so) were hunted down and murdered, even though one might think their social identities had already changed.[3] This pursuit makes a certain perverted sense if the idea was to extinguish in them all possibility of social vitality, simply on grounds of their ancestral roots. Mass murder is the most extreme method of genocide, denying members of targeted groups any degree or form of social vitality whatever. To extinguish all possibility of social vitality, child transportation and reeducation are insufficient; it may be necessary to commit mass murder or drive victims mad or rob them of self-respect, all of which were done to Holocaust victims.

Although I approach genocide from a history of feminist habits of research and reflection, I say little here about the impact of genocide on women and girls as opposed to its impact on men and boys. I would not suggest that females suffered more or worse than males. Nor am I especially interested in such questions as whether lifelong habits of care giving offer survival advantages to segregated women. (Evidence appears to be that no one survives without others' care and help.) My interest here is, rather, in what makes genocide the specific evil that it is, what distinguishes it from other atrocities, and what kinds of atrocities are rightly recognized as genocidal. Feminist habits of noticing are useful for suggesting answers to these questions.

2. Genocide, War, and Justice

Genocide need not be part of a larger war, although it commonly is. But it can be regarded as itself a kind of one-sided war. Precedents for regarding one-sided attacks as wars are found in the idea of a "war on drugs" and in the title of Lucy Dawidowicz's *The War against the Jews* (1975). If genocide is war, it is a profoundly unjust kind of war, perniciously unjust, an injustice that is also an evil.

John Rawls opened his first book on justice with the observation that justice is the first virtue of institutions as truth is of systems of thought. No matter how efficient and well arranged, he wrote, laws and institutions must be reformed or abolished if they are unjust (1999, 3). Like critics who found these claims overstated, even Rawls noted that although "these propositions seem to express our intuitive conviction of the

---

[3] An example well known to philosophers is Edith Stein, student of and later assistant to Edmund Husserl. Her doctoral dissertation on the topic of empathy was originally published in 1917 (Stein 1964). She became a Catholic nun but was nevertheless deported to Auschwitz from her convent in the Netherlands.

primacy of justice," "no doubt they are expressed too strongly" (4). Not all injustices, even in society's basic structure, make lives insupportable, intolerable, or indecent. Reforms are not always worth the expense of their implementation. Had Rawls made his claim about abolishing unjust institutions in regard to *pernicious* injustices, however, it would not have been controversial: laws and institutions must be abolished when they are evil.

Not all injustices are evils, as the harms they produce vary greatly in importance. Some injustices are relatively tolerable. They may not impact people's lives in a deep or lasting way, even though they are wrong and should be eliminated—unjust salary discriminations, for example, when the salaries in question are all high. An injustice becomes an evil when it inflicts harms that make victims' lives unbearable, indecent, or impossible, or that make victims' deaths indecent.[4] Injustices of war are apt to fall into this category. Certainly genocide does.

3. The Concept of Genocide

"Genocide" combines the Greek *genos* for race or tribe with the Latin *cide* for killing. The term was coined by Raphael Lemkin (1944), an attorney and refugee scholar from Poland who served in the United States War Department. He campaigned as early as the 1930s for an international convention to outlaw genocide, and his persistence resulted in the United Nations Genocide Convention of 1948. Although this convention is widely cited, it was not translated into action in international courts until the 1990s, more than forty years later. The first state to bring a case to the World Court under the convention was Bosnia-Herzegovina in 1993. It was not until 1998 that the first verdict interpreting that convention was rendered, when the Rwanda tribunal found Jean-Paul Akayesu guilty on nine counts for his participation in the genocide in Rwanda in 1994 (Orentlicher 1999, 153). The United States did not pass legislation implementing ratification of the 1948 genocide convention until 1988 and then only with significant reservations that were somewhat disabling (Lang 1992, 1:400). Such resistance is interesting in view of questions raised during the interim regarding the morality of U. S. conduct in Vietnam. By the time the United States ratified the convention, ninety-seven other U. N. members had already done so.

The *term* "genocide" is thus relatively new, and the Holocaust is widely agreed to be its paradigmatic instance. Yet Lemkin and many others find the *practice* of genocide ancient. In their sociological survey from ancient times to the present, Frank Chalk and Kurt Jonassohn (1990) discuss

---

[4] For elaboration, see Card 2002, which includes chapters on war rape and on terrorism in the home. There is not a chapter on genocide, although genocide figures throughout as paradigmatic of atrocities.

instances of apparent genocide that range from the Athenians' annihilation of the people of the island of Melos in the fifth century B.C.E. (recorded by Thucydides) and the ravaging of Carthage by Romans in 146 B.C.E. (also listed by Lemkin, as the first of his historical examples of wars of extermination) through mass killings in Bangladesh, Cambodia, and East Timor in the second half of the twentieth century (Chalk and Jonassohn 1990). Controversies are ongoing over whether to count as genocidal the annihilation of indigenous peoples in the Americas and Australia (who succumbed in vast numbers to diseases brought by Europeans), Stalin's induced mass starvation of the 1930s (ostensibly an economically motivated measure), and the war conducted by the United States in Vietnam.

The literature of comparative genocide that Peter Novick calls "comparative atrocitology" (1999) so far includes relatively little published work by philosophers. Here is what I have found. Best known is probably Jean-Paul Sartre's 1967 essay, "On Genocide" (Sartre 1968), written for the Sartre-Russell International War Crimes Tribunal, which was convened to consider war crimes by the United States in Vietnam. In 1974 Hugo Adam Bedau published a long and thoughtful essay "Genocide in Vietnam?" (Bedau 1974, 5–46), responding to Sartre and others who have raised the question of whether the United States was guilty of perpetrating genocide in Vietnam. Bedau argues for a negative answer to that question, relying primarily on intent as an essential factor in genocide. His view is that the intent of the United States in Vietnam was not to exterminate a people, even if that was nearly a consequence. Berel Lang's essay "The Concept of Genocide" (1984/85) and the first chapter of Lang's book *Act and Idea in the Nazi Genocide* (1990) are helpful in their explorations of the meanings and roles of intent in defining "genocide."

Other significant philosophical works include Alan S. Rosenbaum's anthology *Is the Holocaust Unique? Perspectives on Comparative Genocide* (1996), which discusses the Nazi assault on Jews and Romani during World War II, the Atlantic slave trade, the Turkish slaughter of Armenians in 1915, and Stalin's induced famine. Legal scholar Martha Minow (1998) reflects philosophically on measures lying between vengeance and forgiveness taken by states in response to genocide and mass murder. Jonathan Glover's *Humanity: A Moral History of the Twentieth Century* (2000), in some ways the most ambitious recent philosophical discussion of evils, includes reflections on Rwanda, Stalin, and Nazism. The Institute for Genocide Studies and the Association of Genocide Scholars (which holds conventions) attract an interdisciplinary group of scholars, including a small number of philosophers. And the Society for the Philosophic Study of Genocide and the Holocaust sponsors sessions at conventions of the American Philosophical Association.

On the whole, historians, psychologists, sociologists, and political scientists have contributed more than philosophers to genocide scholarship.

Naturally, their contributions as social scientists have been empirically oriented, focused on such matters as origins, contributing causes, effects, monitoring, and prevention. Yet, philosophical issues run throughout the literature. They include foundational matters, such as the meaning of "genocide," which appears to be a highly contested concept, and such issues of ethics and political philosophy as whether perpetrators can be punished in a meaningful way that respects moral standards. If adequate retribution is morally impossible, and if deterrence is unlikely for those who are ideologically motivated, then what is the point in punishing perpetrators? If there is nevertheless some point sufficient to justify doing so, then who should be punished, by whom, and how?

Controversies over the meaning of "genocide" lead naturally to the closely related question of whether genocide is ethically different from nongenocidal mass murder. The practical issue here is whether, and if so why, it is important to add the category of genocide to existing crimes against humanity and war crimes. Crimes against humanity were important additions to war crimes in that, unlike war crimes, they need not be perpetrated during wartime or in connection with a war, and they can be inflicted by a country against its own citizens. But given that murder of civilians by soldiers is already a war crime and a human rights violation, one may wonder whether the crime of genocide captures anything they omit.

If the social death of individual victims is central to genocide, then, arguably, genocide does capture something more. What distinguishes genocide is not that it has a different kind of victim, namely, groups (although it is a convenient shorthand to speak of targeting groups). Rather, the kind of harm suffered by individual victims of genocide, in virtue of their group membership, is not captured by other crimes. To get a sense of what is at stake in the hypothesis that social death is central, let us turn briefly to controversies over the meaning of "genocide."

The definition of "genocide" is currently in such flux that the International Association of Genocide Scholars asks members on its information page (printed in a members' directory) to specify which definition of "genocide" they use in their work. A widely cited definition (Robinson 1960, 147) is that of the 1948 U. N. Convention on the Prevention and Punishment of the Crime of Genocide:

> Genocide means any of the following acts committed with the intent to destroy, in whole or in part, a nation, ethnical, racial or religious group, as such: (a) killing members of the group; (b) causing serious bodily or mental harm to members of the group; (c) deliberately inflicting on the group conditions of life calculated to bring about its physical destruction in whole or in part; (d) imposing measures intended to prevent births within the group; (e) forcibly transferring children of the group to another group.

Every clause of this definition is controversial.

Israel Charny (1997) and others criticize the U. N. definition for not recognizing political groups, such as the Communist Party, as possible targets of genocide. In fact, political groups had been recognized in an earlier draft of the genocide convention, and Chalk and Jonassohn (1990) do recognize political groups as targets of genocide in their historical survey. Some scholars, however, prefer the term "politicide" for these cases and reserve the term "genocide" for the annihilation of groups into which one is (ordinarily) born—racial, ethnic, national, or religious groups. Yet, one is not necessarily, of course, born into one's current national or religious group, and either one's current or one's former membership can prove fatal. Further, some people's political identity may be as important to their lives as religious identity is to the lives of others. And so, the distinction between "genocide" and "politicide" has seemed arbitrary to many critics. A difficulty is, of course, where to draw the line if political groups are recognized as possible victims. But line drawing is not a difficulty peculiar to political groups.

The last three clauses of the U. N. definition—conditions of life intended to destroy the group "in whole or in part," preventing births, and transferring children—count as genocidal many acts that are aimed at cultural destruction, even though they are not homidical. "Preventing births" is not restricted to sterilization but has been interpreted to include segregation of the sexes and bans on marriage. Social vitality is destroyed when the social relations—organizations, practices, institutions—of the members of a group are irreparably damaged or demolished. Such destruction is a commonly intended consequence of war rape, which has aimed at family breakdown. Although Lemkin regarded such deeds as both ethnocidal and genocidal, some scholars prefer simply to call them ethnocides (or "cultural genocides") and reserve the term "genocide" (unqualified) for events that include mass death. The idea is, apparently, that physical death is more extreme and therefore, presumably, worse than social death. That physical death is worse, or even more extreme, is not obvious, however, but deserves scrutiny, and I will return to it.

Even the clauses of the U. N. definition that specify killing group members or causing them serious bodily or mental harm are vague and can cover a wide range of possible harms. How many people must be killed in order for a deed to be genocidal? What sort of bodily harm counts? (Must there be lasting disablement?) What counts as "mental harm"? (Is posttraumatic stress sufficient?) If the definition is to have practical consequences in the responses of nations to perpetrators, these questions can become important. They become important with respect to questions of intervention and reparations, for example.

Although most scholars agree on including intention in the definition of genocide, there is no consensus regarding the content of the required intention. Must the relevant intention include destruction of all members of a group as an aim or purpose? Would it be enough that the group was knowingly destroyed, as a foreseeable consequence of the pursuit of some other aim? Must the full extent of the destruction even be foreseeable, if the policy of which it is a consequence is already clearly immoral? Bedau (1974) makes much of the content of the relevant intention in his argument that whatever war crimes the United States committed in Vietnam, they were not genocidal, because the intent was not to destroy the people of Vietnam as such, even if that destruction was both likely and foreseeable.

Charny (1994), however, objects to an analogous claim made by some critics who, he reports, held that because Stalin's intent was to obtain enough grain to trade for industrial materials for the Soviet Union, rather than to kill the millions who died from this policy, Stalin's famine was not a genocide. Charny argues that because Stalin foresaw the fatal consequences of his grain policies, those policies should count as genocidal. As in common philosophical criticisms of the "doctrine of the double effect," Charny appears to reject as ethically insignificant a distinction between intending and "merely foreseeing," at least in this kind of case.

The doctrine of double effect has been relied on by the Catholic Church to resolve certain ethical questions regarding issues of life and death (Solomon 1992, 1:268–69). The doctrine maintains that under certain conditions it is not wrong to do something that has a foreseeable effect (not an aim) which is such that an act *aiming* at that effect would have been wrong. The first condition of its not being wrong is that the act one performs is not wrong in itself, and the second condition is that the effect at which it would be wrong to aim is not instrumental toward the end at which the act does aim. Thus, the Church has found it wrong to perform an abortion that would kill a fetus in order to save the mother but, at the same time, not wrong to remove a cancerous uterus when doing so would also result in the death of a fetus. The reasoning is that in the case of the cancerous uterus, the fetus's death is not an aim; nor is it a means to removing the uterus; it is only a consequence of doing so. Many find this distinction troubling and far from obvious. Why is the death of a fetus from abortion not also only a consequence? The aim could be redescribed as "to remove the fetus from the uterus in order to save the mother," rather than "to kill the fetus to save the mother," and at least when the fetus need not be destroyed in the very process of removal, one might argue that death due to extrauterine nonviability is not a means to the fetus's removal, either.

The position of the critics who do not want to count Stalin's starvation of the peasants as a genocide would appear to imply that if the peasants' deaths were not instrumental toward Stalin's goal but only an unfortunate consequence, the foreseeability of those deaths does not make Stalin's policy genocidal, any more than the foreseeability of the death of the fetus in the case of a hysterectomy performed to remove a cancerous uterus makes that surgery murderous. Charny's position appears to imply, on the contrary, that the foreseeability of the peasants' mass death is enough to constitute genocidal intent, even if it was not intended instrumentally toward Stalin's aims.

Some controversies focus on whether the intent was "to destroy a group as such." One might argue with Bedau, drawing on Lang's discussion of the intent issues (Lang 1990, 3–29), that the intent is "to destroy a group as such" when it is not just accidental that the group is destroyed in the process of pursuing a further end. Thus, if it was not just accidental that the peasant class was destroyed in the process of Stalin's pursuit of grain to trade for industrial materials, Stalin could be said to have destroyed the peasants "as such," even if peasant starvation played no more causal role in making grain available than killing the fetus plays in removing a cancerous uterus. Alternatively, some argue that the words "as such" do not belong in the definition because, ethically, it does not matter whether a group is deliberately destroyed "as such" or simply deliberately destroyed. Chalk and Jonassohn (1990) appear to take this view.

Further, one might pursue the question of whether it is really necessary even to be able to foresee the full extent of the consequences in order to be accurately described as having a genocidal intent. Historian Steven Katz argues in *The Holocaust in Historical Context* (1994) that the mass deaths of Native Americans and Native Australians were not genocides because they resulted from epidemics, not from murder. The suggestion is that the consequences here were not reasonably foreseeable. David Stannard, an American Studies scholar at the University of Hawaii, however, finds the case less simple, for it can be argued that the epidemics were not just accidental (Stannard 1992 and 1996). Part of the controversy regards the facts: to what extent were victims deliberately infected, as when the British, and later Americans, distributed blankets infected with the smallpox virus?[5] And to what extent did victims succumb to unintended infection stemming from ordinary exposure to Europeans with the virus? But, also, part of the controversy is philosophical. If mass deaths from disease result from wrongdoing, and if perpetrators could know that the intolerably destructive consequences had an uncontrollable (and therefore somewhat unpredictable) extent, then does it matter, ethically, whether the wrongdoers could foresee the full extent of the consequences? One might argue that it does not, on the ground that they already knew enough to appreciate that what they were doing was evil.

What is the importance of success in achieving a genocidal aim? Must genocide succeed in eliminating an entire group? An assault, to be homicide, must succeed in killing. Otherwise, it is a mere attempt, and an unlawful attempted homicide generally carries a less severe penalty than a successful one. Bedau and Lang point out, however, that "genocide" does not appear to be analogous to "homicide" in that

---

[5] See Stiffarm with Lane (1992, 32–33).

way. There may still be room for some distinction between genocide and attempted genocide (although Lang appears not to recognize any such distinction) if we distinguish between partially formed and fully formed intentions, or if we distinguish among stages in carrying out a complex intention. But in paradigmatic instances of genocide, such as the Holocaust, there are always some survivors, even when there is clear evidence that the intention was to eliminate everyone in the group. There is general agreement that at least some mass killing with that wrongful intention is genocidal. The existence of survivors is not sufficient to negate fully formed genocidal intent. There may be survivors even after all stages of a complex genocidal intention have been implemented. Bedau observes, however, that there is a certain analogy between "genocide" and "murder" that enables us to contrast both with homicide. Both genocide and murder include wrongfulness in the very concept, whereas a homicide can be justifiable. Homicide is not necessarily unlawful or even immoral. In contrast, genocide and murder are, in principle, incapable of justification.

On my understanding of what constitutes an evil, there are two basic elements: (1) culpable wrongdoing by one or more perpetrators and (2) reasonably foreseeable intolerable harm to victims, resulting from that wrongdoing.[6] Most often the second element, intolerable harm, is what distinguishes evils from ordinary wrongs. Intentions may be necessary to defining genocide. But they are not always necessary for culpable wrongdoing, as omissions—negligence, recklessness, or carelessness—can be sufficient. When culpable wrongdoing *is* intentional, however, its aim need not be to cause intolerable harm. A seriously culpable deed is evil when the doer is willing to inflict intolerable harm on others even in the course of aiming at some other goal. If what is at stake in controversies regarding the meaning of "genocide" is whether a mass killing is sufficiently evil to merit the opprobrium attaching to the term "genocide," a good case can be made for including assaults on many kinds of groups inflicted through many kinds of culpable wrongdoing. Yet that leaves the question of whether the genocidal nature of a killing has special ethical import, and if so, what that import is and how, if at all, it may restrict the scope of "genocide." I turn to these and related questions next.

4. The Specific Evils of Genocide

Genocide is not simply unjust (although it certainly is unjust); it is also evil. It characteristically includes the one-sided killing of defenseless civilians—babies, children, the elderly, the sick, the disabled, and the injured of both genders along with their usually female caretakers— simply on the basis of their national, religious, ethnic, or other political identity. It targets people on the basis of who they are rather than on the

---

[6] See Card (2002, chap. 2) for development of this conception of an evil.

basis of what they have done, what they might do, even what they are capable of doing. (One commentator says genocide kills people on the basis of *what* they are, not even *who* they are.)

Genocide is a paradigm of what Israeli philosopher Avishai Margalit calls "indecent," in that it not only destroys victims but also first humiliates them by deliberately inflicting an "utter loss of freedom and control over one's vital interests" (1996, 115). Vital interests can be transgenerational and thus survive one's death. Before death, genocide victims are ordinarily deprived of control over vital transgenerational interests and more immediate vital interests. They may be literally stripped naked, robbed of their last possessions, lied to about the most vital matters, witness to the murder of family, friends, and neighbors, and made to participate in their own murder; if female, they are also likely to be violated sexually.[7] Victims of genocide are commonly killed with no regard for lingering suffering or exposure. They, and their corpses, are routinely treated with utter disrespect. These historical facts, not simply mass murder, account for much of the moral opprobrium attaching to the concept of genocide.

Yet such atrocities, it may be argued, are already war crimes, if conducted during wartime, and they can otherwise or also be prosecuted as crimes against humanity. Why, then, add the specific crime of genocide? What, if anything, is not already captured by laws that prohibit such things as the rape, enslavement, torture, forced deportation, and degradation of individuals? Is any ethically distinct harm done to members of the targeted group that would not have been done had they been targeted simply as individuals rather than because of their group membership? This is the question that I find central in arguing that genocide is not simply reducible to mass death, to any of the other war crimes, or to the crimes against humanity just enumerated. I believe the answer is affirmative: the harm is ethically distinct, although on the question of whether it is worse, I wish only to question the assumption that it is not.

Specific to genocide is the harm inflicted on its victims' social vitality. It is not just that one's group membership is the occasion for harms that are definable independently of one's identity as a member of the group. When a group with its own cultural identity is destroyed, its survivors lose their cultural heritage and may even lose their intergenerational connections. To use Orlando Patterson's terminology, in that event, they may become "socially dead" and their descendants *"natally alienated,"* no longer able to pass along and build upon the traditions, cultural developments (including languages), and projects of earlier generations (1982, 5–9). The harm of social death is not necessarily less extreme than that of

---

[7] Men are sometimes also violated sexually (usually by other men), although the overwhelming majority of sex crimes in war are perpetrated by men against female victims of all ages and conditions.

physical death. Social death can even aggravate physical death by making it indecent, removing all respectful and caring ritual, social connections, and social contexts that are capable of making dying bearable and even of making one's death meaningful. In my view, the special evil of genocide lies in its infliction of not just physical death (when it does that) but also social death, producing a consequent meaninglessness of one's life and even of its termination. This view, however, is controversial.

African American and Jewish philosopher Lawrence Mordekhai Thomas argues that although American slavery natally alienated slaves—that slaves were born severed from most normal social and cultural ties that connect one with both earlier and later generations—the Holocaust did not natally alienate Jews (1993, 150–57). He does not explicitly generalize about genocide and natal alienation but makes this judgment in regard to the particular genocide of the Holocaust. Yet, the apparent implication is that a genocide no more successful than the Holocaust (an accepted paradigm of genocide) is not natally alienating, because enough victims survive and enough potential targets escape that they are able to preserve the group's cultural traditions. Thomas's analyses of patterns of evil in American slavery and the Holocaust are philosophically ground breaking and have been very helpful to me in thinking about these topics. Yet I want to question this conclusion that he draws. I want to consider the Nazi genocide in light of the more fundamental idea of social death, of which natal alienation is one special case, not the only case.

Thomas's conception of natal alienation is more specific and more restricted than Patterson's conception of social death. Thomas seems to be thinking not of lost family connections and lost community connections, the particular connections of individuals to one another, but rather of the connections of each individual with a culture in general, with its traditions and practices. He finds members of an ethnic group natally alienated when the cultural practices into which they are born "forcibly prevent most of them from fully participating in, and thus having a secure knowledge of, their historical-cultural traditions" (1993, 150). He notes that after seven generations of slavery, the memories of one's culture of origin are totally lost, which is certainly plausible. Patterson used the term "natal alienation" for the extreme case of being *born* to *social death*, with individual social connections, past and future, cut off from all but one's oppressors at the very outset of one's life. Hereditary slavery yields a paradigm of natal alienation in this sense. Slaves who are treated as nonpersons have (practically) no socially supported ties, not only to a cultural heritage but even to immediate kin (parents, children, siblings) and peers. As a consequence of being cut off from kin and community, they also lose their cultural heritage. But the first step is to destroy existing social ties with family and community, to excommunicate them from society, as Patterson puts it (1982, 5). In Rawlsian terms, they are first excluded from the benefits and protections of the basic structure of

the society into which they were born and in which they must live out
their lives. Loss of cultural heritage follows.

Those who are *natally* alienated are *born* already socially dead. Natal
alienation might be a clue to descent from genocide survivors (although not
proof, insofar as genocide depends also on intent). Thus, the natal
alienation of slaves and their descendants, when slavery is hereditary, is
one clue to a possible history of genocide committed against their ancestors.

Thomas recognizes that alienation is not "all or nothing." A lost
cultural heritage can be rediscovered, or partially recovered, later or in
other places. Those who were alienated from some cultures may become
somewhat integrated into others. Still, he denies that the Holocaust
natally alienated Jews from Judaism, "because the central tenets of
Judaism—the defining traditions of Judaism—endured in spite of
Hitler's every intention to the contrary" (1993, 153).

The question, however, should not be simply whether the traditions
survived but whether individual Jewish victims were able to sustain their
connections to those traditions. Sustaining the connections meaningfully
requires a family or community setting for observance. Many Jews, of
course, escaped being victimized, because of where they lived (in the United
States, for example) and because the Axis powers were contained and
defeated. They were able to maintain Jewish traditions with which survivors
might conceivably connect or reconnect. But many survivors were unable
to do so. Some found family members after the war or created new families.
Many did not. Many lost entire families, their entire villages, and the way of
life embodied in the *shtetl* (eastern European village). Some could not
produce more children because of medical experiments performed on them
in the camps. Many survivors lost access to social memories embodied in
such cultural institutions as libraries and synagogues.

Responding to the observation that entire communities of Jews were
destroyed and that the Yiddish language is on the way out, Thomas
argues that members of those communities were destroyed not "as such"
(as shtetl Jews, for example) but more simply "as Jews," and that the
entire community of Jews was not destroyed.[8] He concludes that "the
question must be whether the Holocaust was natally alienating of Jews as
such, without regard to any specific community of Jews" (1993, 153). In
answering negatively, he is apparently thinking of survivors who reestab-
lished a Jewish life after the war, rather than of non-European Jews who
were potential victims and whose positions might be regarded as somewhat analogous to those of unhunted and unenslaved Africans at the time
of the African slave trade.

---

[8] It is commonly estimated that two-thirds of European Jews died. That leaves not only
one-third of European Jews but also Jewish communities in other parts of the world, such as
Israel (to which some European Jews fled), the Far East, Australia, and the Americas.

Some European Jews survived, however, only by passing as Christians. Some hidden children who were raised by strangers to be Christians only discovered their Jewish heritage later, if at all. If they were full members of the societies in which they survived, Thomas does not consider them natally alienated. Those who pass as members of another religion need not be socially dead, even if they are alienated from their religion of origin. Still, if they were originally connected in a vital way with their inherited religion and if they then experienced no vital connection to the new one, arguably they do suffer a degree of social death. More clearly, those who were made stateless before being murdered were certainly treated, socially, as nonpersons. National Socialist decrees robbed them of social support for ties to family, peers, and community, stripped them of their rights to earn a living, own property, attend public schools, and even ride public transportation, and on arrival at the camps they were torn from family members. Although they were not *born* to social death, they were nevertheless intentionally deprived of all social vitality before their physical murder.

For those who survive physically, mere knowledge and memory are insufficient to create social vitality, even if they are necessary. Those who cannot participate in the social forms they remember do not have real social vitality; they have only the memory of it. Further, from 1933 to 1945 many children were born to a condition that became progressively more *natally* alienating. Contrary to the apparent implication of Thomas's hypothesis regarding the differences between American slavery and the Holocaust, social death seems to me to be a concept central to the harm of genocide, at least as important to what is evil about the Holocaust as the mass physical murder.

Although social vitality is essential to a decent life for both women and men, the sexes have often played different roles in its creation and maintenance. If men are often cast in the role of the creators of (high?) culture, women have played very central roles in preserving and passing on the traditions, language, and (daily) practices from one generation to the next and in maintaining family and community relationships. Where such generalizations hold, the blocking of opportunities for creativity (being excluded from the professions, for example) would fall very heavily on men. But disruptions of family and community, such as being alienated from one's family by rape or being suddenly deported without adequate provisions (or any means of obtaining them) to a strange environment where one does not even know the language, would also fall very heavily, perhaps especially so, on women.

Most immediate victims of genocide are not born socially dead. But genocides that intentionally strip victims, prior to their murders, of the ability to participate in social activity do aim at their social death, not just their physical death. In some cases it may appear that social death is not an end in itself but simply a consequence of means taken to make mass murder easier (concentrating victims in ghettos and camps, for example). When assailants are moved by hatred, however, social death may become an end in itself. Humiliation before death appears often to have been an end in itself, not just a means. The very idea of selecting victims by social group identity suggests that it is not just the physical life of victims that is targeted but the social vitality behind that identity as well.

If the aim, or intention, of social death is not accidental to genocide, the survival of Jewish culture does not show that social death was not central to the evil of the Holocaust, any more than the fact of survivors shows that a mass murder was not genocidal. A genocide as successful as the Holocaust achieves the aim of social death both for victims who do not survive and, to a degree and for a time, for many survivors as well. Thomas's point may still hold that descendants of survivors of the African diaspora produced by the slave trade are in general more alienated from their African cultures of origin than Holocaust survivors are from Judaism today. Yet it is true in both cases that survivors make substantial connection with other cultures. If African Americans are totally alienated from their African cultures of origin, it is also true that many Holocaust survivors and their descendants have found it impossible to embrace Judaism or even a Jewish culture after Auschwitz. The survival of a culture does not by itself tell us about the degree of alienation that is experienced by individual survivors. Knowledge of a heritage is not by itself sufficient to produce vital connections to it.

The harm of social death is not, so far as I can see, adequately captured by war crimes and other crimes against humanity. Many of those crimes are defined by what can be done to individuals considered independently of their social connections: rape (when defined simply as a form of physical assault), torture, starvation. Some crimes, such as deportation and enslavement, do begin to get at issues of disrupting social existence. But they lack the comprehensiveness of social death, at least when the enslavement in question is not hereditary and is not necessarily for the rest of a person's life.

Still, it is true that not all victims of the Holocaust underwent social death to the same extent as prisoners in the camps and ghettos. Entire villages on the Eastern front were slaughtered by the *Einsatzgruppen* (mobile killing units) without warning or prior captivity. Yet these villagers were given indecent deaths. They were robbed of control of their vital interests and of opportunities to mourn. Although most did not experience those deprivations for very long, inflicted en masse these murders do appear to have produced sudden social death prior to physical extermination. The murders were also part of a larger plan that included the death of Judaism, not just the deaths of Jews. Implementing that plan included gradually stripping vast numbers of Jews of social vitality, in some places over a period of years, and it entailed that survivors, if there were any, should not survive as Jews. The fact that the plan only partly succeeded does not negate the central role of social death within it or the importance of that concept to genocide.

If social death is central to the harm of genocide, then it really is right not to count as a genocide the annihilation, however heinous, of just any political group. Not every political group contributes significantly to its members' cultural identity. Many groups are fairly specific and short lived, formed to support particular issues. But then, equally, the annihilation of not just any cultural group should count. Cultural groups can also be temporary and specialized, lacking in the continuity and comprehensiveness that are presupposed by the possibility of social death. Some mass murders—perhaps the bombings of September 11, 2001—do not appear to have had as part of their aim, intention, or effect the prior soul murder or social death of those targeted for physical extermination. If so, they are mass murders that are not also genocides. But mass murders and other measures that have as part of their reasonably foreseeable consequence, or as part of their aim, the annihilation of a group that contributes significantly to the social identity of its members are genocidal.

References

Bedau, Hugo Adam. 1974. "Genocide in Vietnam?" In *Philosophy, Morality, and International Affairs*, edited by Virginia Held, Sidney Morgenbesser, and Thomas Nagel, 5–46. New York: Oxford University Press.

Card, Claudia. 1996. "Rape as a Weapon of War." *Hypatia* 11, no. 4: 5–18.

———. 1997. "Addendum to 'Rape as a Weapon of War.'" *Hypatia* 12, no. 2:216–18.

———. 2002. *The Atrocity Paradigm: A Theory of Evil*. New York: Oxford University Press.

Chalk, Frank, and Kurt Jonassohn, eds. 1990. *The History and Sociology of Genocide: Analyses and Case Studies*. New Haven: Yale University Press.

Charny, Israel. 1997. "Toward a Generic Definition of Genocide." In *Genocide: Conceptual and Historical Dimensions*, edited by George Andreopoulos, 64–94. Philadelphia: University of Pennsylvania Press.

Dawidowicz, Lucy W. 1975. *The War against the Jews, 1933–1945*. New York: Holt, Rinehart, and Winston.

Glover, Jonathan. 2000. *Humanity: A Moral History of the Twentieth Century*. New Haven: Yale University Press.

Katz, Steven. 1994. *The Holocaust in Historical Context*, vol. 1, *Mass Death before the Modern Age*. New York: Oxford University Press.

Lang, Berel. 1984/85. "The Concept of Genocide." *Philosophical Forum* 16, nos. 1–2:1–18.

————. 1990. *Act and Idea in the Nazi Genocide*. Chicago: University of Chicago Press.

————. 1992. "Genocide." In *Encyclopedia of Ethics*, vol. 1, edited by Lawrence C Becker with Charlotte B. Becker, 399–401. New York: Garland.

Lemkin, Raphael. 1944. *Axis Rule in Occupied Europe: Laws of Occupation, Analysis of Government, Proposals for Redress*. Washington, D.C.: Carnegie Endowment for International Peace, Division of International Law.

Margalit, Avishai. 1996. *The Decent Society*. Translated by Naomi Goldblum. Cambridge, Mass.: Harvard University Press.

Minow, Martha. 1998. *Between Vengeance and Forgiveness: Facing History after Genocide and Mass Violence*. Boston: Beacon.

Novick, Peter. 1999. *The Holocaust in American Life*. Boston: Houghton Mifflin.

Orentlicher, Diane F. 1999. "Genocide." In *Crimes of War: What the Public Should Know*, edited by Roy Gutman and David Rieff, 153–57. New York: Norton.

Patterson, Orlando. 1982. *Slavery and Social Death*. Cambridge, Mass.: Harvard University Press.

Rawls, John. 1999. *A Theory of Justice*. Rev. ed. Cambridge, Mass.: Harvard University Press.

Robinson, Nehemiah. 1960. *The Genocide Convention: A Commentary*. New York: Institute of Jewish Affairs, World Jewish Congress.

Rosenbaum, Alan S., ed. 1996. *Is the Holocaust Unique? Perspectives on Comparative Genocide*. Boulder: Westview.

Sartre, Jean-Paul. 1968. *On Genocide*. Boston: Beacon.

Schott, Robin. 1999. "Philosophical Reflections on War Rape." In *On Feminist Ethics and Politics*, edited by Claudia Card, 173–99. Lawrence: University Press of Kansas.

Solomon, William David. 1992. "Double Effect." In *Encyclopedia of Ethics*, vol. 1, edited by Lawrence C. Becker with Charlotte B. Becker, 268–69. New York: Garland.

Stannard, David E. 1992. *American Holocaust: The Conquest of the New World*. New York: Oxford University Press.

————. 1996. "Uniqueness as Denial: The Politics of Genocide Scholarship." In *Is the Holocaust Unique?*, edited by Alan S. Rosenbaum, 163–208. Boulder: Westview.

Stein, Edith. 1964. *On the Problem of Empathy*. Translated by Waltraut Stein. The Hague: Nijhoff.

Stiffarm, Lenore, with Phil Lane Jr. 1992. "The Demography of Native North America." In *The State of Native America*, edited by Annette Jaimes, 23–53. Boston: South End.

Thomas, Lawrence Mordekhai. 1993. *Vessels of Evil: American Slavery and the Holocaust*. Philadelphia: Temple University Press.

3

CLARIFYING THE CONCEPT OF GENOCIDE

MOHAMMED ABED

1. Introduction: The Nature of Genocide vs. Instances of Genocide

In his *Axis Rule in Occupied Europe*, the Polish American jurist Raphael Lemkin coined the term "genocide" and characterized it in the following way:

> Genocide has two phases: one, destruction of the national pattern of the oppressed group; the other, the imposition of the national pattern of the oppressor. This imposition, in turn, may be made upon the oppressed population which is allowed to remain, or upon the territory alone, after removal of the population and colonization of the area by the oppressor's own nationals. (Lemkin 1944, 79)

Several important philosophical questions can be derived from Lemkin's definition.[1] If there is a justification for thinking that genocide is a distinct category of political violence, then there must be something ethically unique about genocide. Such atrocities as rape, ethnic cleansing, torture, and other forms of degrading violence are currently punishable as war crimes or crimes against humanity. Is genocide reducible to any of these categories? Are the harms inflicted by genocide qualitatively distinct from the harms imposed by other forms of political violence?

Lemkin rejected the idea that the "destruction of the national pattern of the oppressed group" necessarily involves the mass physical death of group members. He argued that destroying the social relations on which a group's identity and communal life is based can be genocidal. Implied in this is the counterintuitive idea that social and cultural death is not necessarily less extreme than physical death. Can this thought be philosophically substantiated? Another important question concerns the

[1] I would like to extend my thanks to the following people for their invaluable engagement and commentary on both the content of this essay and the broader issues it raises: Emily McRae, Eugene Marshall, Hallie Liberto, Harry Brighouse, Karima Berkani, Lilian Friedberg, Mavis Biss, and especially Claudia Card.

character of the groups Lemkin refers to. What is a "national pattern," and can groups other than nations have this feature?

Clearly formulated, the main questions are:

Q1: Can we identify an ethically relevant property of genocide that serves to distinguish it from other forms of political violence?

Q2: What kind of group is vulnerable to the harms peculiar to genocide?

Providing a rigorous definition of genocide is not a mere exercise in conceptual analysis. It has important ramifications for international public policy. Once we understand the special nature of the harms that accompany genocide, we can justify prioritizing its treatment in positive international law. The institutions charged with implementing international public policy can then realize mechanisms to ensure effective deterrence and punishment of perpetrators, prompt intervention, and adequate reparations for survivors and their descendants.[2]

Policy makers currently rely on the definition given in the 1948 U.N. Convention on the Prevention and Punishment of the Crime of Genocide.[3] Article 2 of this document states that "in the present convention, genocide means any of the following acts committed with intent to destroy, in whole or in part, a national, ethnical, racial or religious group, as such." The acts referred to include (a) killing members of the group; (b) causing serious bodily or mental harm to members of the group; (c) deliberately inflicting on the group conditions of life calculated to bring about its physical destruction in whole or in part; (d) imposing measures intended to prevent births within the group; and (e) forcibly transferring children of the group to another group.

---

[2] The importance of implementing mechanisms to ensure prompt and effective intervention cannot be overstated. The consequences of not doing so were clearly illustrated in 1994 when Hutu extremists engaged in state-sponsored massacre of 800,000 ethnic Tutsis in Rwanda. The international community was fully aware of what was happening from the first days but failed to intervene militarily, even though this option was recommended in the strongest terms by Romeo Dallaire, the U.N. commander in Rwanda. In fact, two weeks into the massacre, Dallaire's troops were withdrawn. The failure to act decisively was a result of political apathy, on the one hand, and structural impediments in the U.N. organizational framework that included unnecessary bureaucratic complexity and inflexible decision making and interpretation, on the other. In particular, some of the most powerful states in the world failed to create the conditions that would have empowered the United Nations to implement its mandate by acting forcefully against the slaughter. For political reasons, the U.S. government withdrew its own forces and nationals from Rwanda and then actively lobbied for the withdrawal of Dallaire's troops. For a detailed discussion of these issues, see Power 2002.

[3] The full text of the convention is available at http://www.unhchr.ch/html/menu3/b/p_genoci.htm

The U.N. definition is beset with conceptual shortcomings. It fails to provide an adequate answer to either of the central questions inspired by Lemkin's work. Insofar as they have neglected to identify features the possession of which makes a group vulnerable to the harms peculiar to genocide, the authors of the convention have failed to articulate satisfactory reasons for thinking that "national, ethnical, racial or religious groups" can be the victims of a genocide whereas gay men, lesbians, political parties, and the class of people who enjoy karaoke cannot (Q2 above). We also have no basis for explaining why, to take one example, some religious groups can potentially be victims, while others cannot. In the absence of the necessary identity conditions, the choice of groups listed in the convention seems arbitrary. It's also important to note that no available definition of *any* of these groups is unproblematic, and for the overall definition to be adequate, each of its constituent parts must also be clearly defined.

This arbitrariness is also mirrored in the choice of acts (a)–(e) to be included in the definition. The physical elimination of a group "in whole or in part" may be sufficient for some act or series of acts to be considered genocidal, but questions remain as to whether it is necessary. Since the language of the definition seems to imply that (a)–(e) are individually sufficient ("*any* of the following acts"), the same issue surfaces once again. The U.N. definition does not provide us with the conceptual tools to answer these questions, nor does it provide a nonarbitrary way of determining whether some subset of (a)–(e) is individually necessary and jointly sufficient. Furthermore, what qualifies as "part" of a national, ethnic, or religious group? If individuals intend on physically eliminating the con-gregation of their local mosque ("part" of the worldwide Muslim commu-nity), are they guilty of genocide if they succeed in doing so? The important point to note is that even if we could make these distinctions and clean up the existing language of the definition, Q1 above would still remain unanswered; an enumeration of genocidal acts tells us very little about the specific quality of the harms that underlie them. If $\psi, \varphi, \chi \ldots$ are all F, then we want to know what specific property γ makes them all F. In the absence of this information, the job of marking out a conceptual distinction between genocide and other forms of political violence becomes problematic.

Other issues arise when we come to consider the convention's emphasis on intent. When we contemplate harms of the magnitude and quality of those that accompany genocide, why should we stress intent rather than foreseeability? If a definition refers solely to the former, it will likely succeed in capturing paradigm cases but may be unsuccessful at drawing attention to cases that are not widely recognized as such.[4] If we rely too

---

[4] Examples include Stalin's policies of rapid industrialization and forced collectivization of agriculture in the late 1920s and 1930s, Mao's "great leap forward" policy in the 1950s, and the "cultural revolution" of the 1960s and 1970s. A more recent example is the sanctions imposed on Iraq after the first Gulf War.

heavily on the latter, we may give a definition that's too broad and admits cases we would intuitively exclude. Even if there is wide disagreement among fully informed rational thinkers as to whether some case is an instance of genocide rather than of mass death, the U.N. definition would still have failed to provide us with the concepts essential to making decisions about borderline or controversial cases.

In this essay, I move beyond the shortcomings of the U.N. definition by developing an account of the features that make a social group susceptible to the harm of genocide. The account is therefore a response to the second of the two questions motivated by Lemkin's work. I argue that three features are individually necessary and jontly sufficient to distinguish between groups structured around what Lemkin called a "national pattern" and those that are not.

Although there are important philosophical questions about genocide, there is very little in the way of answers to those questions in the philosophical literature. Claudia Card is one philosopher who has noted this absence: "The literature of comparative genocide that historian Peter Novick . . . calls 'comparative atrocitology' so far includes relatively little published work by philosophers . . . historians, psychologists, sociologists, and political scientists have contributed more than philosophers to genocide scholarship . . . yet philosophical issues run throughout the literature" (Card 2003, 67). In addition, most of this philosophical work has tended to focus on giving an account of the features that distinguish genocide from other forms of political violence (Q1 above) rather than the issue central to the present discussion (Q2). As a consequence, the account I give is exploratory and is conceived of as a stimulus to further discussion and debate. After presenting the account, I consider two objections and reply to them. The first objection disputes my reliance on the notion of culture by constructing a thought experiment that tests our intuitions about what kind of groups can suffer the harms that make genocide an ethically distinct species of political violence. The second objection points to a difficulty in individuating the groups we are interested in.

In the later sections of this essay, I defend and attempt to develop further Card's (2003) hypothesis of "genocide as social death." Card's account is the only conceptually adequate response to the central dilemma posed by Lemkin's original definition. It tells us what is uniquely harmful about destroying the "national pattern" of the oppressed group and replacing it with the national pattern of the oppressor: "When a group with its own cultural identity is destroyed, its survivors lose their cultural heritage and may even lose their intergenerational connections" (2003, 73). I provide further support for Card's view by showing that although ethnic cleansing may not involve mass murder, it often even- tuates in the ethically unique harms that result from physically eliminat- ing members of a group *as such*. If ethnic cleansing results in harms that are qualitatively indistinguishable from those that accompany physical elimination, then we have further support for the thesis that social death is what makes some act or series of acts genocidal.

Card's account does face one substantial worry. The objection is that even the Holocaust was not "natally alienating"; a sufficient number of actual victims survive and enough potential targets escape and are able to practice, develop, and preserve the group's cultural heritage and traditions.[5] I argue that this objection is difficult to sustain if the genocidal deed involves—as it did in the Holocaust—massive displacement of populations, the destruction and expropriation of private and collectively held property, and the elimination of a variety of institutions that supported the common life of a group. The birth and growth of cultural traditions and practices do not occur in a vacuum; in almost all cases, a particular landscape and social setting are the context for their development and for the influence they exert on the identity of the individual. Without these foundations, survivors and their descendants will become "socially dead" even if *most if not all* the members of a group escape. Reestablishing cultural bonds is made more difficult for survivors if social capital (rather than economic relations) was the basis of a group's association and unity before its displacement. In the developing world, societies are often organized on the basis of social relations and forms that are highly dependent on the specific territories they inhabit. If this is the case, then their expulsion from their lands is a genocidal measure, as Lemkin implied in his seminal work.

2. Individual Interest and the Ethically Relevant Aspects of Belonging

Suppose we give a conceptually adequate response to Q1, a response that identifies ethically relevant properties that distinguish genocide from other forms of political violence. Does this response—whatever it turns out to be—imply an answer to Q2? If we know what genocide *means*, do we thereby know something about why it is that Armenians can be the victims of genocide whereas the class of people who enjoy karaoke cannot? If we know that social death is what makes genocide distinct from mass murder, do we thereby know the identity conditions for vulnerable groups? Card seems to answer in the negative:

> If social death is central to the harm of genocide, then it really is right not to count as a genocide the annihilation of just any political group, however heinous. Not every political group contributes significantly to its member's cultural identity. Many are fairly specific and short-lived, formed to support particular issues. But then, equally, the annihilation of not just any cultural group should count, either. Cultural groups can also be temporary and specialized, lacking in the continuity and comprehensiveness that are presupposed by the possibility of social death. (2003, 77)

[5] See Card's discussion of this issue in her 2003, 74–78.

This implies that short-lived political groups and some cultural groups are impervious to social death. Although this is consistent with our basic intuitions (these groups have no intergenerational connections to disrupt), it does little to substantiate them theoretically. We still don't have an adequate response to Q2.

It may be of theoretical relevance that some groups have a significant influence over the well-being of their members, while others do not. For example, I belong to the class of people who do analytic philosophy. Although it would be a heinous thing if someone attempted systematically to annihilate this group, it would not have a significant and long-standing impact on my well-being and personal flourishing. In contrast, an attempt to eliminate the Palestinian Arab people would likely eventuate in my cultural alienation and the loss of personally and socially significant connections to past generations and to the historical narratives they embodied. However, facts about the interrelationship of group membership and individual flourishing will not by themselves suffice to conceptualize adequately the distinction we need. Membership in a swingers' club will make significant contributions to your well-being and flourishing. These benefits are a direct consequence of your attachment to the group and are very difficult to come by elsewhere. If a disgruntled ex-member decided to eliminate physically the group, we would be right to call the act an atrocious crime. However, in the absence of the "continuity and comprehensiveness presupposed by the idea of social death," there would be no justification for thinking this instance of mass killing is genocidal, irrespective of whether individuals derived unique benefits from membership in the targeted group. To give an adequate answer to Q2, the concept of culture needs further clarification. Some group cultures mark individuals in more profound ways than do others. The source of this influence must be understood if we are to substantiate the distinction we need.

The perspective from which we define culture matters: "culture" is not to be understood as an objectively specifiable phenomenon. After all, the actual practices of a group are constantly changing and marked by contingency. Identity is fluid and adaptable partly as a result of the political and social upheavals that affect a group. To arrive at a conceptually adequate account of culture, theoretical emphasis must be placed on the individual member's consciousness and understanding of tradition. Members will imagine their community through its particular historical trajectory and cultural achievements. This implies that as a basic prerequisite, individual members must be both willing and sufficiently knowledgeable to be able to imagine their group in this way. When this condition is satisfied, it becomes possible to believe that the group's practices represent a historical continuity that distinguishes members from nonmembers. If a historical continuity is imagined, then some of its narratives will be more mythology than objective truth, and some of its traditions will be instrumental in the sense developed by Eric Hobsbawm, that is, "a set of practices, normally governed by overtly or tacitly accepted rules and of a ritual or symbolic nature, which seek to inculcate certain values and norms of behavior by repetition, which automatically implies continuity with the past. In fact, where possible, they normally attempt to establish continuity with a suitable historic past" (Hobsbawm 1983, 1). If members must be both willing and able to imagine their group's history and cultural achievements, then this suggests the following feature as the first component of our definition:

C1: Consent

Consent plays an important role in individuation of groups.[6] The historian Ernest Renan made the point about the importance of consent in the most eloquent way: "One [feature of a nation] is the possession in common of a rich legacy of remembrances; the other is the actual consent, the desire to live together, the will to continue to value the heritage which all hold in common. . . . The existence of a nation (pardon this metaphor!) is an everyday plebiscite" (quoted in Synder 1964, 9–10).

The role that consent plays can be illustrated through the following example. Suppose Lebanese people are either Syriophobes or Syriophiles. It is in virtue of their territorial proximity to Syria that the Lebanese Syriophiles like the Syrians (let's suppose that territorial proximity fosters understanding and dialogue). Moreover, the Lebanese Syriophiles are legitimate residents of the territory they inhabit, and despite their like of the Syrians, they resist assimilation by actively working to maintain their own cultural heritage and traditions. Finally, on the basis of their friendly relations with the Syrians, the Lebanese Syriophiles consent to a political union with the Syrian body politic (or maybe just the body politic of the class of Syrians who in virtue of living near the Lebanese tend to like them). Suppose further that the union of the Lebanese Syriophiles and Lebanese-loving Syrians is a long-standing and peaceful political union based on shared ethical and political principles. If we define culture without making reference to the consent that individuals either explicitly or implicitly give to be members of a group, then physically eliminating the Lebanese Syriophiles and Lebanese-loving Syrians would not be considered an act of genocide. After all, the Lebanese Syriophiles have purposefully maintained their cultural identity and national uniqueness. Without consent being a component of our definition, political attachments based on shared principles, mutual accommodation, and recognition have no role to play in making the distinction between groups that can be genocide victims and those that cannot. Pretheoretically, it seems

---

[6] Thanks to Harry Brighouse for his input into the development of the argument presented in this section.

uncontroversial that the mass murder of Belgians would be an instance of genocide, even though the country is comprised of two culturally distinct ethnic groups. This very same intuition extends to the union of Lebanese Syriophiles and Lebanese-loving Syrians.

In light of these considerations, we can see that consent is a *necessary* condition for being the kind of group that's susceptible to the harm of genocide. However, consent by itself is not a *sufficient* condition. If it were, then swingers, trade unions, the Rotary Club, and the Michigan militia would qualify as members of the category we are interested in. Our intuitions tell us that this is not the case, and there are also good reasons that lead us to the same conclusion.

C2: Comprehensiveness[7]

Card has suggested a direction for our inquiry to follow. If culture is to be a condition of individual well-being, then it must determine individual identity in a strict way. For this to be the case, culture must be comprehensive; a group must possess traditions, practices, and rituals that influence more than a single area or a few areas of the life of an individual. Many of these areas should be of great importance to the flourishing and well-being of individuals.

Several examples of what comprehensiveness consists in come to mind. Culture is often accompanied by well-worn narratives that trace a group's trajectory through history. Often these narratives ignore some facts and emphasize others. The elimination of troubling facts from the collective consciousness of a group fosters the well-being of its members; after all, recognizing that the group to which you belong was responsible for massive atrocities is a cause of psychic distress and guilt. It may force you to reassess your status as a member or to question the implications of being who you are. On the other hand, as Renan has pointed out, cultural narratives often emphasize shared experiences of suffering and oppression. "In fact, national sorrows are more significant than triumphs because they impose obligations and demand a common effort" (quoted in Synder 1964, 9).

The mechanisms through which a comprehensive culture conditions and shapes the contours of memory are varied. When the state creates the nation as it did in the case of the United States and many other immigrant societies, there is usually an institutionally driven effort to make an appropriate selection of facts for use in the dominant account of the origins and development of the nation. With the passage of time, this narrative embeds itself more deeply in the nation's collective consciousness and as a result becomes self-perpetuating. It passes from generation

---

[7] An account of comprehensiveness has already been given by Margalit and Raz (1990). In the following section, I draw on their work and try to develop their ideas in more detail.

to generation without systematic intervention from state institutions. In indigenous societies, among ethnic groups, and where a self-conscious nation with long-standing traditions and cultural practices founds a state, the standardized narrative is more often propagated from the bottom up, without methodical institutional intervention. In time, an editorialized version of this narrative will be adopted and disseminated by state institutions. Whatever the mechanism, every nation's reconstruction of the past is selective. The same can be said of the major world religions. Nations with a higher degree of ethnic homogeneity are more likely to have a mythic component to their reconstruction of the past. At the end of the continuum are some indigenous peoples who explain their origins largely in mythical terms.

The important point to note is that at least some of the social groupings we have already mentioned fail to shape the memory and consciousness of their members in any of these ways. However, some social groupings that we would intuitively exclude from our category of interest indulge in a selective reconstruction of the past and are made up of individuals who freely consent to being active members. For example, Heaven's Gate and other millennial cults satisfy these conditions.

And yet comprehensive cultures make their mark on many other areas of life. They affect behavioral routines in the home, in the public domain, and at work. They structure and regulate a whole range of different relationships both within and beyond the immediate family. They determine holidays and set constraints on the educational system. A comprehensive culture will ritualize people's birth, important events in their life, and their death in idiosyncratic ways. Finally, it will set an order of priorities for members of the group and will provide them with several models of the "good life" to emulate. Notice that the conceptual relationship between comprehensiveness and continuity is asymmetric; continuity does not imply comprehensiveness (although continuity of method is a feature of analytic philosophy, a philosophical method is not by itself a set of practices and rituals that condition conduct in many areas of social exchange). However, if Hobsbawm is right that values and norms of behavior are inculcated by repetition over time, then a comprehensive culture is one that implies continuity of practice.

One indicator of a comprehensive culture is that its members usually recognize one another. Orthodox Jews and Muslims can distinguish between members and nonmembers in most circumstances whereas short-lived cults and political groups can only do so in very few areas of social intercourse. Groups that satisfy this condition are usually anonymous; mutual recognition is not secured by intimate knowledge of the type that characterizes family relations or a small circle of friends, or cults and political parties formed around specific issues (Margalit and Raz 1990, 447). Members are known to one another via the presence of general characteristics and identifying behaviors that usually do not include insignias, uniforms, or other explicit identity markers. Since membership in anonymous cults and large political parties does not usually regulate a wide range of behaviors, it is difficult to give an account of how individuals in these groups pick one another out in more than a few areas of life. The general nature and pervasiveness of these behaviors contribute to the prominent social profile of group membership (Margalit and Raz 1990, 446). Group membership is also one of the principal ways through which individuals are identified by outsiders. If the group is culturally solidified and historically well founded, its collective identity generates heuristics or general rules of thumb about what individual members are like and how they are likely to behave. Margalit and Raz (1990, 446) observe that because our perceptions of ourselves incorporate expectations about how others see us, being a member of such a group is an important (often the most important) identifying and performative feature for all the individuals in the group. This is why people are more likely to self-identify as members of a national, ethnic, or religious group than to cite their shared love of karaoke.

When a culture imprints itself on almost every area of an individual's life, the individual is influenced in profound and far-reaching ways. Developing as a person in the midst of or in close proximity to such a group means internalizing its narratives, rituals, practices, and norms. This experience does much more than shape the inner life of an individual. Belonging gives a person a sense of security and orientation in an otherwise confusing world; it sustains the unity and coherence of the self rather than being a mere aspect of it. This observation explains why the flourishing of the group has such a serious impact on the well-being of its individual members. If the ability of a group to engage in cultural reproduction is impeded, the individual suffers serious deprivations, even if members of the group to which they belong survive and make a serious effort to piece together their culture and identity.

If this is an adequate account of the concept of comprehensiveness, then we have succeeded in theoretically substantiating the intuition that most if not all political groups and cults cannot be the victims of genocide. Similarly, analytic philosophers, the class of people who love karaoke, swingers, and the class of people murdered on 9/11 will also be excluded from our categories of interest. In line with the U.N. definition, most national, ethnical, and long-standing religious groups will be included. The features we have discussed so far provide us with the conceptual basis for recognizing that the U.N. definition excludes groups with cultures that have an enormous impact on the lives of their individual members. For example, lesbian and gay communities may qualify as belonging to the relevant category. At the very least, we can now coherently argue about these and similar cases. We already know that the first condition above (C1) is necessary but not sufficient. As we have seen, there are also good reasons to think that condition 2 is necessary. Without it, we lack the conceptual tools to explain how the full or partial elimination of a group can have such profound effects on surviving members and subsequent generations.

C3: Arduous Exit

Renouncing one's membership in the groups we are interested in is usually a difficult thing to do. We may be tempted to think that this is a consequence of membership being determined by nonvoluntary criteria. If group membership is a matter of *who you are* rather than *what you do or what you agree to*, if all that determines membership is the projection of the contingencies of birth into the future rather than voluntary and conscious engagement with social and cultural norms, then how can consent play a necessary role in the production of culture as I claimed above? In response to this, it's important to note that although membership may be a matter of "belonging" to a group in most cases, this does not imply that belonging—rather than active and consenting engagement with culture—is the factor that determines whether the destruction of a group's social fabric will have profound and far-reaching effects on the well-being of its members. What we are interested in are the features that explain why the "destruction of the national pattern" of an oppressed group has such a serious impact on the psychological (and perhaps physical) profile of its individual members. It's possible that a person born into an ethnic or religious group comes to be estranged from her community to such an extent that an attack on the culture and identity of the group will fail to affect her in a meaningful way. However, the same cannot be said of the person who actively engages with the culture of her chosen community.

The idea that one "belongs" to an ethnic or national group implies that group identity and group culture are reducible to essential characteristics. This view does not stand up to critical scrutiny, for the simple reason that one can in principle choose to belong to an ethnic group and in time become, in many ways, indistinguishable from members born with the identity in question. This may happen in mixed marriages and partnerships when the nonmember freely decides to adopt the norms, rituals, and practices of the spouse's culture. When the process of enculturation is complete, the nonmember's well-being may come to depend on the group's continued flourishing in much the same way as the partner's. However, this is not an easy process, and its arduousness explains why group membership is socially significant. The important point to note is that the groups we are interested in are very difficult to leave once a person consents to membership. A clue to this is that even public disavowal of your connection to the group will not prevent both insiders and outsiders from continuing to perceive you as a member of the community.

We can, however, be sure that at least some people will disagree that a person can "become" a member of an ethnic group regardless of the fact that he was not born into it. A German American could not become an African American no matter what cultural practices he adopted. Further, if someone is raised Catholic and upon further reflection decides to become an atheist, why would her departure from the group be difficult? It is true that if someone has certain outward appearances that most people associate with a specific ethnic group (skin color, and the like), then it would be hard for that person to be perceived as having left the group. Renouncing being Chinese is not like renouncing being a Catholic theist, or so the objection goes.[8]

Although this is a forceful objection, there is a reasonable response. We can agree that no matter how hard a German American tried, she would never be perceived as African American by African Americans, or anyone else for that matter. This, however, is not the central point of the original argument I gave. What I have attempted to show is that a person's well-being can come to depend on the flourishing of the group he "adopts" in the right kind of way, that is, in a way that explains why the destruction of the group would have such a profound impact on him as an individual. In some cultures, a person may actually come to be perceived as a member by individuals who were born into the group. But this is not necessary to the distinction I make. Rather, what matters is that an individual can in principle become affiliated with her chosen group to the extent that significant disruption of the group's means of cultural reproduction will have a negative impact on her flourishing as an individual. Furthermore, leaving the Catholic Church is perhaps not as easy as the objection assumes. Renouncing Catholicism has a status closer to abandoning your ethnic identity than to disavowal of your membership in the Labor Party. Once again, you would still be perceived as Catholic—albeit nonpracticing—by people who have a basic level of familiarity with you. We have to keep in mind that the theoretical focus is on the cultural practices of the group rather than belief in its doctrines. The fact that we can have the category "nonpracticing Catholic" shows that the culture of the group marks people in a way that belief in its theology does not.

Although actual examples are few and far between, we can imagine groups that satisfy our condition on consent (C1) and our condition on comprehensiveness (C2) but not our intuitions about what kind of group can be the victim of genocide. Analytic philosophers could conceivably articulate a comprehensive set of cultural norms and practices. As a result, members may become mutually recognizable in many areas of social exchange despite the anonymity of the group. Though this may satisfy C1 and C2, it is not sufficient for being the kind of group that

---

[8] Many thanks to Gene Marshall for bringing this objection to my attention.

interests us. The development of cultural norms and rituals seems ad hoc and an aberrant extension of a philosophical method common to an otherwise unrelated set of individuals. What we are looking for is *coherent* development of culture and continuity of practice. Our intuitions are confirmed when we notice that a group of this nature is very easy to leave. Unlike membership in an ethnic, religious, or national group (our paradigms), exiting the discipline of analytic philosophy is easy, and once you leave, no one will continue to perceive you as a member of the group. C3 is therefore necessary, and C1 to C3 are jointly sufficient for being the kind of group that can suffer the harms peculiar to genocide.

If this definition holds water, then we do not need to provide an adequate characterization of ethnical, racial, national, and religious groups *and then* show why it is that these particular groups—and not some political or gay communities—can be the victims of genocide. This arbitrariness is removed when an overarching set of identity criteria are specified. Some religious groups will qualify, others will not. Muslims, Christians, Jews, and Buddhists can suffer social death. Fine-grained confessional divisions may not be important enough to the identity of individual members. These distinctions, however, exist along a contin-uum, and as they become more fundamental and historically entrenched, the relevant identity conditions may be satisfied; the doctrinal schism between Shia and Sunni Muslims is are difference that matters to individual well-being, as are the divisions between Catholic and Protes-tant Christianity, and among Orthodox, Conservative, Reform, and other major branches of Judaism.

Some groups that were not included in the U.N. list will also qualify. Lesbian and gay identities satisfy the conditions I have articulated. There are many indicators of the important role these group cultures play in the lives of their members. For example, just as minorities and indigenous peoples do, lesbian and gay activists make identity an important feature of their political outlook and work to mobilize broad public support for their communal and individual rights as lesbians and gays, not as U.S. citizens, whites, or blacks. Like minority ethnic groups, lesbians and gay men often tend to live and congregate in specific areas of cities where their culture and norms have a high political profile. Some political groups with deeper historical roots and more well-developed and comprehensive worldviews will also qualify (for example, some communist and socialist parties). Finally, rather than viewing cultural communities as static and immovable, this theory of group identity allows for the cultural transi-tions that accompany social and political upheaval.

3. Objection 1: The Dull Liberal-Democratic Society

Can consent by itself be sufficient for some group to be a member of the category we are interested in? In the previous section, I mentioned that if consent were sufficient, then swingers, the Rotary Club, and other specialized social groupings would qualify. Although our intuitions seem opposed to this at first, they can be tested further with a thought experiment.

The Dull Liberal-Democratic Society (henceforth DLDS) is not the kind of place people want to visit. The history of its founding and development makes for tedious reading. The ancestors of its members moved to an uninhabited territory from neighboring countries in the hope that they could live uninteresting lives free from the yoke of cultural practice and national sentiment. In time their numbers grew, and they contracted to found a state based on liberal-democratic principles. The current citizens have an accurate factual understanding of their past, and neither they nor the state attempt to embellish this narrative in any way. Although freedom of expression is guaranteed by the constitution, there is an implicit understanding that DLDS ought to remain a country without a culture or national identity. There are no public monuments or holidays that celebrate important events in the nation's past. No communal values and norms regulate relationships, delineate appropriate behavior in the home or in public spaces, set constraints on the educational system, or issue in a standardized model of the "good life." In the end, the only thing that holds this society together is consent and an understanding that each citizen has basic rights and the obligation not to interfere in the lives of others in such a way as to frustrate the universal realization of these rights.

DLDS seems to belong to the category of groups that can be the victims of genocide. One way to account for this intuition is to say that despite appearances, a "people" organized in this way differs from specialized social groups in the same way that groups satisfying C1 to C3 do. Swingers and analytic philosophers lack comprehensive cultures, whereas the people of our dull liberal-democratic society have a set of implicitly held commitments that influence their conduct in many areas of life. It's important to the well-being of people from DLDS that they *not* behave in certain ways and that their fellow citizens do the same. Arguably, practicing culture in DLDS has the same effects as systematically impeding the practice of culture in other societies.

Attractive as this response seems, it trades on a misunderstanding. All we have shown is that consent implies having shared commitments that influence conduct in many areas of life. We have not thereby established that consent is *not* a sufficient condition for some group to be prone to genocide. A further argument is needed to show this. In fact, if consent does imply shared commitments and if shared commitments imply a comprehensive influence on behavior, then we may have shown that C2 (and perhaps C3) are conceptually redundant. This position is consistent with our intuition that both DLDS and the political union of Lebanese Syriophiles and Lebanese-loving Syrians qualify as members of the categories under investigation. It also uncovers what on closer inspection may be an unwarranted assumption. Underlying the emphasis on particularity is a judgment to the effect that the value of membership in cultural groups is not only ethically significant but also *more fundamental* than the value of membership in the global human community. Once again we need a further argument to establish this.

Such an argument would be difficult to make. Most territories around the globe are culturally heterogeneous, and the world is becoming more economically, socially, and politically interdependent than it ever was before. The nation-state is slowly being superseded by diverse multi-national states that cooperate with each other in many spheres of common interest and enter into arrangements for regional governance (such as the European Union). Under these conditions, identifying oneself as a member of the global community of human beings ought to be a higher priority than expressing affiliation with an ethnic or national group. Greater interdependence and the global influence exerted by developed nations should also lead us to question the extent of our obligations to peoples beyond our own borders.

4. Response to Objection 1

1. Consent does imply having shared commitments. Both swingers and the citizens of DLDS consent because they want to be members of a group that shares their commitment to swinging or to expunging culture from public life.
2. However, shared commitments do not necessarily imply comprehensiveness. It depends on the nature of the commitment.
3. In the case of swingers and analytic philosophers, the commitment involved is not one that has an influence over many areas of a member's life. Swingers swing once in a while, and analytic philosophers apply the method of conceptual analysis to philosophical questions and not much else.
4. However, in the case of DLDS, the consent to be a member of the society implies commitments that *are* comprehensive, although they may not be cultural commitments in the standard sense. At most, this objection shows that we ought to expand our conception of what counts as a cultural practice, ritual, or behavior. The nature of the practice matters less than the scope of its influence on the individual.

5. Objection 2: Individuation

So far, the conditions of consent, comprehensiveness, and arduous exit appear to be sufficient to distinguish genocide-prone groups from other social groupings. We may, however, run into problems individuating these groups. More specifically, the problem is that any subset of a group that satisfies C1 to C3 can itself satisfy the very same conditions, and so on, until we get to the smallest group that can sustain the kind of relational properties that the satisfaction of C1 to C3 depends on.

Consider an example. Suppose that the members of some nation—call it X—habitually tell derogatory jokes about members of the nation that come from a specific region—call it Y. For the most part, these jokes focus on an alleged lack of common sense and intelligence on the part of the inhabitants of Y. After putting up with this ridicule for a long time, the people of Y decide they've had enough, and the overwhelming majority expresses the wish to secede from the rest of the nation. On the face of it, the people of Y satisfy C1 to C3. Most of them have consented to live together, the Y culture is comprehensive, and being a Y-er is very difficult to disavow. If the nation of which Y-ers were formerly part decided physically to eliminate the inhabitants of the Y region "as such," it would count as genocide. In time, the inhabitants of Y might start victimizing people from a specific quarter of a certain city, who in turn might victimize the inhabitants of a specific street, who then oppress a particular family. Pretheoretically these groups do not belong in our categories of interest. On the face of it, however, they do satisfy C1 to C3.

6. Response to Objection 2: Relational vs. Intrinsic Comprehensiveness

It's not a sufficient response to say that the population of Y has an unjustifiably "parochial mentality," whereas our paradigm groups do not. It also does nothing to shore up the conceptual adequacy of our account to point to the esoteric nature of the conditions under which groups fracture in the way I have described. What this objection shows is that further distinctions are needed if our characterization of culture is to be conceptually adequate.

The cut-and-dried version of the response to this objection is that in order to be considered genocide prone, the people of Y would have to satisfy C2 in virtue of being Y-ers rather than in virtue of being members of the more inclusive national culture. It's at best unclear whether the inhabitants of Y satisfy C2 in this way.

The identity and social practices of some groups reflect the cultures that encompass them. Rather than being absolute, these associations are a matter of degree. Dearborn in Michigan has one of the largest Arab populations outside the Middle East. The sights and sounds of Dearborn are not radically different from what you would experience when walking the streets of a city or town in the Arab world. However, Dearborn is distinguished by being a town in the United States; both its inhabitants and its sites are Arab in an American way. To take another example, many towns in Vermont are fiercely independent. Their inhabitants will identify themselves as being from their town and state before they identify themselves as members of the American nation. Other towns and cities are influenced by the American national identity to a greater degree. Places like Cuba City in Wisconsin (the "City of Presidents") are fiercely nationalist; their inhabitants would identify themselves as Americans before anything else.

This points us in the direction of the relevant distinction. If our "parochially minded" inhabitants of Y have a comprehensive culture in virtue of their (former) membership in X, then C2 is conditionally satisfied, and conditional satisfaction is not sufficient to account for the interrelationship of individual well-being and group flourishing. Suppose someone intends on physically eliminating the inhabitants of Cuba City simply because they inhabit Cuba City. However heinous, this would not result in the kind of harms that distinguish genocide from mass death, whereas killing them qua their membership in the American nation would. If we could show that the members of Y have a comprehensive culture in virtue of being Y-ers (that is, if their identity and social practices were sufficiently distinct from any of the cultures that encompass them), then we have good reasons for thinking that an attack on Y-ers "as such" would be genocidal.

However, there are reasonable questions one could ask about this distinction. *How much* difference is required to show that comprehensiveness is an *intrinsic* rather than a *relational* property of a group? Absent the right kind of empirical investigation, there can be no adequate answer to this question. Since the judgments involved are comparative, we need to observe different groups individually and in relation to others in a variety of contexts. We will look both to the subjective attitudes of group members and to facts about their social practices. With this data in hand, we would have a basis for making the relevant judgments.[9]

7. Social Death, Ethnic Cleansing, and Genocide

Claudia Card argues that "specific to genocide is the harm inflicted on its victims social vitality ... when a group with its own cultural identity is destroyed, its survivors lose their cultural heritage and may even lose their intergenerational connections ... they may become 'socially dead' and their descendents 'natally alienated,' no longer able to pass along and build upon the traditions, cultural developments (including languages), and projects of earlier generations ... the special evil of genocide lies in its infliction of not just physical death (when it

---

[9] Many thanks to Emily McRae for our extensive discussions about the arguments presented in the previous two sections.

does that) but social death, producing a consequent meaninglessness of one's life and even of its termination" (2003, 73). One implication of Card's view is that physical elimination is not necessary for some act or series of acts to be considered a genocide rather than mass death. The account follows Lemkin in his resistance to the idea that distinctions between "cultural genocide," "ethnocide," and "genocide" are either theoretically useful or sustainable. In addition to encompassing the "paradigm" cases, Card's account provides us with the conceptual machinery to deliberate over those cases that are controversial or border-line and to identify instances of genocide that are not commonly recognized as such.[10]

The main objection to Card's account is that even paradigm cases of genocide—the European Holocaust included—did not lead to survivors becoming "socially dead" or their descendents "natally alienated." In almost all cases, a sufficient number of people survive to keep on living and to preserve the group's culture and traditions, and this is no less true of European Jews who survived the atrocities of the Nazi regime than it is of Armenians or American Indians.

In responding to this objection, Card points out that what matters is not simply the survival of tradition and culture but the ability of individual victims to sustain a socially meaningful connection to those traditions (2003, 75). It is this that in the worst-case scenario becomes impossible in the aftermath of genocide. Jewish families were torn apart by the Holocaust, and the family context is perhaps the most important medium for cultural production and transmission. The family is the social space where individuals learn how to relate to their traditions, and it is also where they become imbued with the values of their community. The loss of family connections is therefore a serious impediment to social vitality. Furthermore, entire villages and communities were destroyed, and survivors lost the material and institutional foundations of their common life. Without this institutional basis, the social memories of a group begin to fade, and it becomes increasingly difficult to regain any sense of identity and security.

I want to extend this response further by arguing that when a group satisfies C1 to C3 and exemplifies what I call a "territorially bounded culture," the forced removal of its population from their traditional lands eventuates in social death. If the argument is successful, it lends support to the idea that killing members of a group is sufficient but not necessary for some act or series of acts to be considered genocidal. Although the

---

[10] Card (forthcoming) explains that by "paradigm" she means "an instance that appears, to relevantly informed and clear-headed thinkers, indisputably an instance, a non-controversial case. In this sense of 'paradigm,' there need be no consensus on what *makes* a deed terrorist [or genocidal], only on whether it is an instance. Such judgments are firm but not unrevisable. Our paradigms are cases about which we are most confident now, based on what we think we know now."

methods of forced expulsion often include massacres, a group can become socially dead even if nonlethal coercive means are used to expel its members. Many if not all cases of genocide involve forced displacement of populations, and many of these populations have cultures that are, in varying degrees, "territorially bounded." Where they lie on this continuum determines how difficult it will be for survivors and their descendants to reconstruct the social bonds of the group and to reconnect with their traditions. Although Jewish culture(s) in Europe may have survived the Nazi onslaught, the loss of their material and institutional foundations severely disrupted the ability of individuals to connect to those cultures and once again have a sense of belonging and rootedness.

At the end of the continuum are groups that treat land as a historical endowment rather than as a commodity. The social structure of such a group is in many cases derived from its system of communal ownership, and the landscape itself embodies the historical narrative and cultural achievements of the community. The displacement of a group with this kind of relationship to the physical space it inhabits will cause serious and lasting harm that may be irreparable unless its members are returned to the lands they were forcibly removed from. This observation has consequences for the way we think about reparations for groups whose culture is territorially bounded to this extent. If the argument of this section stands up to scrutiny, the burden of proof shifts to those who claim that insofar as survival can check social death, social death cannot be the harm central to genocide. The burden of proof also shifts to those genocide theorists who claim there are theoretically sustainable distinctions among "ethnocide," "cultural genocide," and "genocide." I shall present the argument and then go on to defend what I take to be its most controversial premise.

1. If a group satisfies consent, comprehensiveness, and arduous exit, then the well-being of its members depends on whether the group can give full expression to its culture in the public domain (def.).
2. The culture of a group is "territorially bounded" if the practices, rituals, and traditions of the group are articulated relative to a specific landscape (def.).
3. A group is "socially dead" if its cultural inheritance cannot be passed on to subsequent generations in any meaningful way (def.).
4. If some group G that satisfies 1 and 2 is forcibly removed from its traditional territory, then the group will no longer be able to practice, develop, and preserve its cultural heritage and traditions.
5. G will therefore be unable to pass these traditions on to subsequent generations (from 4).
6. Therefore, G is socially dead.

Defense of 2

Loss of land and property is not the only deprivation suffered by an exiled people. Exile denies individuals their past and condemns them to a future of diminished agency. Whatever friendships they worked hard to cultivate are lost, families are torn apart, and feelings of belonging and security are replaced by a sense of instability and alienation. If the cultural inheritance that members of each generation are supposed to pass on to their successors is inseparably bound up with the possession of a particular territory, then exile can also deprive individuals of the collective identity that makes them who they are.

The people of a nation learn to arrange their lives around the activities their land can accommodate and sustain. Over the years, they alter their landscape in such a way as to extend the range of possibilities open to them. They construct dwellings, institutions, and monuments that modify the physical and social forms of their environment. Landscape can become an important element of myths and a central feature of the traditions and spiritual life of a nation.[11] The stories and legends that add substance to cultural practices often dramatize specific aspects of a group's territory. Prominent landmarks become the narrators of a nation's historical trajectory, and different features of the landscape come to be permeated with meanings. The dead are buried in its soil, and something as simple as an olive tree can come to be imbued with memories of the loving hands that cared for it over the years. A cactus or orange can come to symbolize a people's steadfastness or their struggle to continue their traditional life in the face of existential threats.[12] Descendants of members of a nation acquire the skills appropriate to making a living from their land, and they are taught to revere customs associated with a particular place. In the course of discussing the effects of Zionist colonization on the rural Palestinian Arab community prior to the founding of the state of Israel, Palestinian novelist and Marxist political analyst Ghassan Kanafani argues, in a similar vein, that agricultural practice in underdeveloped societies is more than a means of subsistence: "[T]he expropriation of nearly one million dunams—almost

---

[11] Perhaps the most vivid example of how features of a landscape can be part of the spiritual life of a nation concerns the Black Hills of South Dakota and the Lakota Sioux. The Lakota Sioux consider this site to be their most sacred place of worship, comparable to a cathedral, a synagogue, or a mosque for the monotheistic faiths. The images of several former U.S. presidents now adorn the rock face, men who were not known for their tolerant attitudes toward the native peoples of North America. Lilian Friedberg points out how deeply offensive this must be to new generations of Native Americans, particularly since "synagogues and churches can be rebuilt, but Mount Rushmore is not likely to be restored to its original glory by geological cosmetic surgery" (2000, 20).

[12] Nasser Abufarha (2006) offers an excellent discussion of the precise sense in which symbolism is the main driving force for self-expression and is the manifestation of culture in Palestinian Arab society.

one-third of the agricultural land—led to a severe impoverishment of Arab peasants and Bedouins. By 1931, 20,000 peasant families had been evicted by the Zionists. Furthermore, agricultural life in the under-developed world, and the Arab world in particular, *is not merely a mode of production* [emphasis added], but equally a way of social, religious and ritual life. Thus, in addition to the loss of land, the Palestinian Arab rural society was being destroyed by the process of colonization" (1972, 8).

With these considerations in mind, it becomes clear that the transgenerational projects and activities associated with the collective life of a nation often depend on the continued possession of a particular territory. It can therefore be argued that if a nation is forcibly uprooted and exiled, great harm is done to both its existing members *and* their successors. Subsequent generations are robbed of the cultural, social, and economic inheritance to which they are entitled, and the nation may no longer be able to carry on its common life. In short, under the conditions I have specified, ethnic cleansing will lead to social death, and social death is the harm that makes genocide an ethically unique form of political violence.

8. Conclusion: Intention and Genocide

How much weight should we place on intention when we define genocide? Too little emphasis opens up the social-death thesis to a serious objection. Modernization of a traditional society at the hands of a more developed nation or transnational institution (such as the United Nations) would then be tantamount to the cultural death of a group. For example, imagine that provision of aid by a powerful nation-state is made contingent on the elimination of certain cultural practices deemed physically and psychologically harmful to the people of a traditional society. Further, let's suppose that the inhabitants of this state are given the option of learning other languages and adopting the norms of other cultures, including the culture of the nation providing aid. Now, let's say that the next generation of children in this society prefer the new languages and cultural norms to their traditional language and norms. This example involves the breakdown of cultural and social institutions, loss of language ability, and, in the longer term, intergenerational social death. Perhaps the powerful nation-state would be guilty of economic exploitation and cultural imperialism, but we have no good reason to think it is guilty of genocide.

This is a serious objection. At the beginning of this essay, I questioned whether intent is required for a perpetrator to be held culpable of genocide. The concern was to account for borderline cases like Stalin's elimination of twenty to thirty million people in the course of industrialization and forced collectivization. In the absence of uniform intuitions regarding such cases (and there are none), a conceptually adequate definition of genocide will have to place some emphasis on intent if it is to avoid the conclusion that any form of modernization or cultural exchange and transformation is a form of genocide. If it were carried out systematically and with the intent of destroying culture, modernization would count as genocide. In the absence of this intention, it would be something else.

In this essay, I have attempted to develop an account of the features that make a group susceptible to the harms of genocide. If the members of a group consent to a life in common, if the culture of the group is comprehensive, and if the social structure of the group makes leaving it arduous, then its social vitality (or lack thereof) will have profound and far-reaching effects on the well-being of its individual members. If individuals are unable to connect to the culture and social ethos of their community, they will suffer the harms and deprivations peculiar to the crime of genocide. The later sections of the essay illustrated and defended the thesis that social death is the harm that distinguishes genocide from other forms of political violence. When a group has a territorially bounded culture, forced deportation of its members—insofar as it inhibits social vitality—will count as a form of genocide.

References

Abufarha, Nasser. 2006. "The Making of a Human Bomb: State Expansion and Modes of Resistance in Palestine." Doctoral dissertation, Department of Anthropology, University of Wisconsin—Madison.

Card, Claudia. 2003. "Genocide and Social Death." *Hypatia* 18, no. 1: 63–79. Included in this collection.

———. Forthcoming. "Recognizing Terrorism." *Journal of Ethics.*

Friedberg, Lilian. 2000. "Dare to Compare: Americanizing the Holocaust." *American Indian Quarterly* 24, no. 3:353–80.

Hobsbawm, Eric. 1983. "Introduction: Inventing Traditions." In *The Invention of Tradition*, edited by Eric Hobsbawm and Terence Ranger, 1–14. Cambridge: Cambridge University Press.

Kanafani, Ghassan. 1972. *The 1936–39 Revolt in Palestine.* New York: Committee for a Democratic Palestine.

Lemkin, Raphael. 1944. *Axis Rule in Occupied Europe: Laws of Occupation, Analysis of Government, Proposals for Redress.* Washington, D.C.: Carnegie Endowment for International Peace, Division of International Law.

Margalit, Avishai, and Joseph Raz. 1990. "National Self-Determination." *Journal of Philosophy* 87, no. 9:439–61.

Power, Samantha. 2002. *A Problem from Hell: America and the Age of Genocide*. New York: Basic Books.

Synder, Louis Leo. 1964. *The Dynamics of Nationalism: Readings in Its Meaning and Development*. Princeton: Van Nostrand Press.

4

GENOCIDE AND THE MORAL AGENCY OF ETHNIC GROUPS

KAREN KOVACH

Genocide is a crime committed against a collectivity. It is the deliberate destruction, in whole or in part, of a *people*. Genocide is also a crime that is committed *by* collectivities. The contributions of many individuals, working cooperatively, are necessary for the destruction, in whole or in part, of a people. If we are to speak sensibly about morality and genocide, we must be able to speak sensibly about wrongs committed by and against collectivities, and about the relationship between the moral properties of social groups and the moral lives of individuals.

Most modern genocides have been inspired, facilitated, or ordered by governments. To secure the willing participation of large numbers of people in acts of unbelievably hideous cruelty and injustice, governments regularly play upon the sentiments and beliefs of groups about themselves and about those who are to be humiliated and destroyed. It is typically individual members of particular ethnic groups who carry out genocidal plans. Ethnic Turks, for example, executed the Armenian genocide. In Rwanda, Hutus carried out the Tutsi genocide. Ethnic Serbs were called on to cleanse Bosnia of Croats and Muslims. Genocide typically involves the collective violence of one ethnic group against another ethnic group. I wish to propose an analysis of the concept of what I call an *ethnic identity group* and suggest that questions about the moral wrong of genocide, and a number of questions about moral responsibility for its commission, are best understood as questions about such groups and their agency. The analysis makes use of Max Weber's idea that the concept of a social group is analyzable in terms of a possibility that certain kinds of social action will be performed.[1] A Weberian analysis of a *kind* of social group involves a characterization of the types of social action that are possible in relation to groups of that kind. Weber defines a *nation* as a social group whose existence is based on the possibility that

---

[1] For Weber's discussions of social groups and the social phenomena in terms of which they are analyzed, see Weber 1947 or "Basic Sociological Terms" in Weber 1978, 1:3–62; "Ethnic Groups" in Weber 1978, 1:385–98; and "The Nation" in Weber 1978, 2:921–26.

social actions oriented in a special way to the idea that a particular group of individuals share an ancestry may be performed by the individuals who are supposed to be so related. It is this conception of the nation that I wish to develop.[2]

I will be suggesting that one very important social concept is that of a social group defined in terms of the availability to members of standing in a particular relation to an idea of the group, where that idea is, more specifically, the idea of a collective agent—the idea of a particular entity with beliefs, goals, and values; with a history of successes and failures; and subject to the "social" experiences of being appreciated or resented, elevated or humiliated, trusted or suspected, attended to or snubbed. A collective agent of this kind is just an idea, but potentially one with tremendous significance—as such ideas have today—because individuals orient their actions to it. Insofar as it is only an idea, the collective agent cannot, properly speaking, act. But we have an idea, and again an important idea, of the acts and psychological states of groups—an idea which is, I will argue, built on an understanding that group members may stand in a significant relation to the group and act out of this under-standing of themselves. The account of an ethnic identity group that I wish to recommend essentially involves an account of collective agency.

I wish to suggest that what distinguishes members of an ethnic identity group from individuals who are not members of that group is the availability to the former of standing in this relation to the group—a relation I call "moral alignment." Roughly, an individual aligns herself with a group to the extent that she sees the group's agency as an extension of her own. A group member is socially placed so as to have access to the idea that other members may act for her and she for them. The concept of a social group that is based on the availability to members of aligning themselves with the group is the concept of an *identity group*. When the idea of the group also involves a belief in the shared ancestry of its members, it is the concept of an *ethnic identity group*.[3] An ethnic identity

[2] I do not follow Weber's use of "nation" to refer to this concept, because this term has come to be defined by many as an ethnic group that is to some extent self-governing, or that aims at some form of political self-determination. I will argue that Weber distinguishes the concept of a group based on the shared belief in a common ancestry *as such* and that of a group based on the shared belief in a common ancestry, insofar as that belief is experienced, in part, as the recognition of a shared relation to an idea of the group, where that idea is the idea of a collective agent. The latter is the concept of a nation. It is possible for such a group neither to possess nor to seek political power. It may turn out that every such group has a *right* to some form of autonomy, but this claim must be argued for, and the argument would seem to require some nonnormative definition of the group.

[3] Ethnic identity is often blended with religious or race identity. The census of the former Yugoslavia listed "Muslim" along with "Serb" and "Croat" as an "ethnicity." In the United States, we are asked to report our "race or ethnicity." I take it that such groups as *the Muslims of the former Yugoslavia* and *African Americans* fall within the extension of the concept of an ethnic identity group. The analysis I propose allows for this, because it takes

group is *a collection of individuals, each of whom may align himself with an idea of the group—where that idea is an idea of a particular collective agent, whose collectivity rests on the shared ancestry of the collected individuals—and each of whom may, therefore, act and respond emotionally as a member of the group.*

In the first section of this essay, I argue for a particular interpretation of Weber's analysis of the nation. The nation, according to Weber, is a social group that is defined not only in terms of an idea of shared ancestry but also in terms of the nature of the relation of individual members to the group that forms on the basis of that idea. The concept of the nation involves not only a relation of individuals to each other but also a particular relation of individual members to the group as a whole. In the second section, I introduce the idea of moral alignment and argue that the possibilities for thought and action that inhere in ethnic-identity-group membership involve the possibility of aligning oneself with the group, understood as a collective agent. I explore some implications of this analysis for the assessment of individual moral responsibility for acts of ethnic groups and, in particular, for genocide. In the third and final section, I compare with culturalist accounts of group rights the account that might be developed from the concept of an ethnic identity group and suggest that the latter is better suited to explain the specific moral offense of genocide. In that section, I also address individualist concerns about the idea that groups act and are acted upon and suggest that we have moral as well as theoretical reasons to accept this idea. Cycles of violence will be broken and injustices adequately addressed only if group members make the right use of the power they have to steer the moral histories of the groups to which they belong.

1

According to Weber, a nation is a kind of *social group*, and a social group is a kind of *social relationship*. We cannot understand Weber's definition of a nation without looking at his definition of a social group, nor can we understand the latter without considering his definition of a social relationship. A plurality of agents forms a social relationship, according to Weber, if and only if (1) the action of each is oriented to the action of the others, and (2) this mutual orientation of action has a stable source.

> The term "social relationship" will be used to denote the behaviour of a plurality of actors in so far as, in its meaningful content, the action of each

an ethnic identity group to be, in Karl Barth's words, "an organizational vessel that may be given varying amounts and forms of content in different socio-cultural systems" (Barth 1969, 14). If a particular religion or race is seen by group members as characteristic of those who share an ancestry, it will be part of the defining idea of that ethnic group. I will not be addressing the distinct questions of religious and race identity.

takes account of that of the others and is oriented in these terms. The social relationship thus *consists* entirely and exclusively in the existence of a *probability* that there will be, in some meaningful sense, a course of social action. For purposes of definition there is no attempt to specify the basis of this probability. (Weber 1947, 118)

Weber gives here what appear to be two distinct conditions, and he clearly believes that they are closely and obviously linked.

1. The action of each of a plurality of actors is oriented to the action of the others.
2. There is a likelihood (or reasonably high probability) of a course of social action.[4]

Action is oriented to the behavior of another person, according to Weber, if the agent's idea of what he is doing includes reference to the behavior, broadly construed, of that person. Any action oriented to the behavior of another person is a *social action*. The action need not, in any other sense, be *directed at* the other person. Its *subjective meaning*, which is the agent's understanding of what he does in performing the action, must simply involve the other person's behavior—past, present, or future—in some way. Weber does not say that *all* of the actions of each individual in a social relationship must be oriented to the actions of the others. There must only be some amount of mutual orientation of action. It is also not necessary that the subjective meaning of the other-oriented action be of any particular kind. No specific intentional content is necessary for there to be a social relationship of some kind, nor is any particular *kind* of intentional content necessary for a plurality to form a social relationship. The orientation need not be one of fellow feeling, say, or concern. What is necessary is that the mutual orientation of action *have a stable source*.[5] We are told that "for purposes of definition there is no attempt to specify the basis of this probability." It is not, I think, that there is a specifiable general basis of the probability that there will be a course of social action, which Weber simply doesn't specify. There is no single basis underlying the great variety of social relationships.

According to Weber, a *social group* is "a certain kind of development of actual or possible social actions of individual persons" (1947, 102). Since all actual social actions are possible social actions, we can say that a

---

[4] The idea of a probability, likelihood, or chance is used repeatedly in Weber's definitions. Consider, for instance, his definition of power. "'Power' (*Macht*) is the probability that one actor within a social relationship will be in a position to carry out his own will despite resistance, regardless of the basis on which this probability rests" (Weber 1947, 152). This seems a matter of method that warrants further study. For a discussion that is both insightful and brief, see Dahrendorf 1979, 62–74.

[5] Cf. Dahrendorf 1979, 65: "For Weber the probability of sequences of action postulated in the concept of chance is not merely an observed and thus calculable probability, but it is a probability which is invariably anchored in given structural conditions."

social group is a certain kind of development of possible social actions. For the case of social groups, at least, the difficult idea of there being a *likelihood* that certain kinds of social action will be performed is explicated in terms of a definitional *possibility* that certain kinds of social action will be performed, given the existence of a particular social group. This is where Weber's analysis ends, but we can say more. The kind of possibility at issue is, presumably, *social* possibility. As we have seen, a social action, according to Weber, is an action the subjective meaning of which is oriented to the behavior of another. Intuitively, to say that a particular kind of social action is possible is to say that an action of that kind—behavior fitting a particular act description—may be performed by some agent. We can divide the details of the description of a kind of social action into two parts: (1) a particular "other" is picked out, and (2) a certain kind of orientation is described.[6] If there is an individual person for whom a social action of a particular kind is possible, I will say that a social action of that kind is *available* to him. Whenever there is a person to whom a social action of a particular kind is available, a social action of that kind is a possible social action.

Using this rough understanding of a possible social action, a Weberian account of social groups may be said to combine two claims: (1) the existence of a particular social group requires the possibility of certain kinds of social action, and (2) central among the possible action types associated with a particular group are kinds of action that are available only to group members. Analyzing a *kind of social group* would seem, then, to involve specifying the types of social action that are possible in relation to groups of that kind and, in particular, the types that are available only to members.

The availability of particular kinds of social action to individuals is what separates members of any social group from nonmembers. Weber's analysis of the concept of a social group is general and provides a framework for the development of analyses of individual kinds of social group. The question to be asked is: What possibilities for social action correspond to a particular kind of social group? Group members may perform actions that are oriented to the group *in a particular way*; nongroup members are not free to orient their actions to the group *in this way*. The question concerns the availability to group members of forms of practical thinking that are not available to outsiders. Nongroup members can certainly act with the group in mind. Those who despise the group may do so much of the time.

---

[6] For some purposes, we would want to define "a kind of social action" differently. In order to capture the phenomenon of patriotic feeling, for example, we would want to describe the nature of the orientation and require that it have as its object the agent's own state, whatever that might be. For the purpose of analyzing social groups, however, and so of being able to distinguish one from another, it is essential that we distinguish kinds of social action in terms of their objects as well as their non-object-specific content.

But the practical thinking of group members may engage the group in a special way.

I wish to explore the idea that the possibility of particular kinds of social action, in terms of which an ethnic identity group may be analyzed, is, more precisely, a possibility of certain kinds of *group*-oriented action—action the orientation of which is to shared ideas about the group and about the standing of individuals within it. It will therefore be necessary to explain the way such ideas may function in the practical thinking of group members. I will argue that only group members can *align* themselves with the group, in the technical sense I will describe. Social actions that depend on the agent's standing in this relation to the group are available only to group members.

The idea that there are social groups that are based on the availability to members of standing in a special relation to an idea of the group is an aspect of Weber's analysis of the nation. It is, according to Weber, what distinguishes *ethnic groups* and *nations*. Weber defines an ethnic group as a "group" whose existence is based on the shared belief of its members that they belong together in virtue of their shared ancestry, but he also claims that an ethnic group is not a *social group* in the technical sense he has described. There are no implications from the existence of an ethnic group for the possibility of related kinds of social action. A nation is distinguished from an ethnic group in terms of this idea of a social group. A nation is a social group. Weberian ethnic groups are not the groups that motivate questions about group rights and the ethical significance of group membership in attributions of moral responsibility. Ethnic groups that are also *social groups* Weber calls "nations."

According to Weber, all nations are ethnic groups, but not all ethnic groups are nations. What makes an ethnic group a nation has to do with the way in which individuals believe themselves to belong together.

> We shall call "ethnic groups" those human groups that entertain a subjective belief in their common descent because of similarities of physical type or of customs or both, or because of memories of colonization and migration; this belief must be important for the propagation of group formation; conversely, it does not matter whether or not an objective blood relation exists. (Weber 1978, 1:389)

Weber goes on to say that "ethnic membership," or membership in an "ethnic group," "does not constitute a group; it only facilitates group formation in the political sphere" (1978: 1, 389). If we look at the definition of "ethnic group" in the light of Weber's definition of "social group," we see that if an ethnic group were a social group, then the basis of the likelihood of other-member-oriented social action for members would be the possibility of certain kinds of social action arising from this subjective belief in their common ancestry. What Weber is denying is that this subjective belief alone makes possible the performance of distinctive other-member-oriented social actions. Weber does not say that ethnic groups may not *also* be social groups, in his sense. He says that "ethnic membership does not *constitute* a group; it only *facilitates* group formation [my emphases]."

Consider Weber's discussion of the nation:

> The idea of the nation is apt to include the notions of common descent and of an essential though frequently indefinite homogeneity. The "nation" has these notions in common with the sentiment of solidarity of ethnic communities, which is also nourished from various sources, as we have seen before [chap. 5:4]. *But the sentiment of ethnic solidarity does not by itself make a "nation."* Undoubtedly, even the White Russians in the face of the Great Russians had always had a sentiment of ethnic solidarity, yet even at the present time they would hardly claim to qualify as a separate "nation." The Poles of Upper Silesia, until recently, had hardly any feeling of solidarity with the "Polish nation." They felt themselves to be a separate ethnic group in the face of the Germans, but for the rest they were Prussian subjects and nothing else. (1978, 2:922)

In these examples, a plurality of individuals share a belief in their common ancestry—a belief that comes to the fore when they are confronted with a group of which they are not members. *Acknowledging* a shared descent with, presumably, all other Poles, wherever they might be, the Poles of Upper Silesia "had hardly any feeling of solidarity with the 'Polish nation.'" Their ethnic identity was not defined in terms of a relation to the collective agency of the Polish nation. How does *identifying with a nation* differ from sharing the feeling that the members belong together on the basis of a shared belief in common descent? This is, I believe, the same question as that concerning the difference, in my terms, between an ethnic group and an ethnic identity group. The difference is between a group whose every member stands in a certain relation to the other members *as individuals*—that of a feeling that he belongs with them—and a group based on a relation of each individual to *the group as a whole*, by way of an idea of the group as an agent.

I wish to suggest that ethnic-identity-group members may stand in a specific moral relationship with the group that I call *moral alignment*. Roughly, *an individual aligns herself with the group to the extent that she sees the group as an extension of her own agency*. Quite a bit more must be said before this definition can be made precise. It should become clear why no one outside the group can align herself with the group. Appreciation of the group, sympathy with it, even love for it are available stances for the nonmember to take toward the group; but the nonmember cannot (reasonably) see the group as an extension of her own agency. Moral alignment is the basis of the possibility of certain kinds of social action.

2

I suggest that individual group members can take a particular ethically significant stance toward the group; the individual can align herself with the group. What distinguishes group members from nonmembers is the availability of doing so. It is not only that she has access to the language of value articulation used by this group; outsiders *might* get access to that. It is that the member is socially placed so as to have access to the understanding that certain others may act for her and she for them. It is not that a group member must or even ought to see the group to which she belongs as extending her own agency; it is simply that she may.[7]

To the extent that an individual aligns herself with a group, she sees the acts and emotional responses of the group as her will being done on a stage larger than that on which she acts alone; the group functions, to that extent, as an extension of the individual's agency.[8] As the group's goals are met, so are the goals of the individual who aligns herself with the group; when its values are respected, so too are hers. When individuals think practically, they often invoke ideas of social groups, understood as collective agents. The collective agent is just an idea, but individuals frequently orient their actions to ideas of collective agency. It is sometimes part of the aim of individuals to have this shared idea altered in some way. They may wish to alter its fate or they may wish to get it to change its ways. An individual may want the group to perform certain actions, resist others, perhaps become less stubborn or more patient. The acts and emotional states of the group are themselves formed and shaped by members who, to some significant extent, align themselves with the group. While an outsider may also have ambitions for the group, he can only alter the course of this collective agent by persuading or manipulating group members to act, think, or feel differently. An individual group member who does not align herself with the group may yet have an interest in what the group does—perhaps because acting through this group will be one of her few options for participating in social life on a large scale, and certainly when the acts of the group may have consequences for all of its members.

---

[7] I am not here considering the question of whether individuals *should* align themselves with the ethnic identity groups to which they belong. I would reject the claim that ethnic-identity-group members in general ought to align themselves with their groups. It might well be argued, however, that members of a particular group ought to align themselves with that group, but such an argument would depend on the details of the circumstances of the group—of how the group has been treated or of what the group has done, for instance, and of what might help it to do well. The present point is simply that it is only group members who *may* align themselves with the group.

[8] Real individuals will align themselves to a greater or lesser degree with the group. I will often speak of "aligning oneself with the group" and mean *aligning oneself to a significant extent*, leaving this idea somewhat vague and intuitive.

Since it is only an idea, the collective agent cannot, properly speaking, act; yet we routinely speak of the acts as well as the beliefs, hopes, fears, trust, and distrust of ethnic groups. The idea of a group act or psychological state is built on an understanding that group members may align themselves with the group and act out of this view of themselves. A group member may *react emotionally* to some event in a way that he understands to be *reacting as a member of the group*. Similarly, a group member may *act* out of an interpretation of the history, goals, and values of the group—out of a perception of its needs and rightful claims. When individuals experience events in this way and act out of an ethnically interpreted experience, they contribute to the moral personality and history of the group. An ethnic identity group is said to have performed a particular act when "our" idea of the history of the group agent has assimilated that act.

Of course, there may be—and often is—disagreement over which act description fits best. There is typically disagreement about the character and history of an ethnic identity group. The important point is that the appropriateness of any particular act description will depend in part on the subjective meanings of the social acts of individual group members and in part on conventions of social narrative—conventions governing the translation of talk about the actions and psychological states of individuals into talk about the actions and psychological states of social groups. Insofar as it depends on the subjective meanings of the actions of members, the act of a group depends on those actions of group members that arise from their moral alignment with the group. When an individual acts or responds emotionally as a member of an identity group, he contributes to the social construction of a group act. Since it is only group members who can align themselves with the group, only they can contribute directly to the construction of a group act. Nonmembers may influence group members, of course, and even influence the way we translate their acts into the language of group agency, but nonmembers cannot act *as members.*[9]

The ideology of Rwanda's "Hutu Power" was that Hutus should rule Rwanda—the rationale for Hutu violence that it was necessary for the secure establishment of Hutu leadership. The leaders of Hutu Power claimed to align themselves with the group and to be acting for its sake. Many individual Hutus who rejected mass violence as the group's response to a perceived threat were coerced into participating. We say, all the same, that the Rwandan Hutus committed genocide against the Rwandan Tutsis, because the little-challenged interpretation of Hutu

---

[9] Essential to this account of group acts is the idea that we cannot analyze the acts of social groups solely in terms of the acts of individuals. If the group agent is an *idea*, then a complete theory of group acts must include an account of social narrative. One important topic much in need of study is the nature of our conventions of social narrative.

violence appealed to the history, values, goals, and needs of the group. There was no significant Hutu resistance proposing an alternative self-understanding and plan of action. Still, individual Hutus who did challenge the choice of violence thereby altered somewhat the nature of the group act. This kind of internal conflict and the differences in motive behind the individual acts of individual agents (self-defense, for example, versus ideology) are what make it controversial to say that it is *the group* that has acted. No plausible account of group acts can ignore the potential disparity between what an individual member of a group does and what is done by the group to which he belongs. Every theory of collective acts owes an account of how collective responsibility is related to individual responsibility.

While individuals are morally responsible only for their own actions and omissions, morally adequate descriptions of the actions and omissions of individuals often make reference to the acts and attitudes of the groups to which those individuals belong—to the acts of states, the attitudes of societies, or the acts and attitudes of ethnic identity groups. Attribution of moral responsibility to an agent is always attribution of responsibility for an act under a particular description. Describing what an individual has done or failed to do requires information about the circumstances of her choice. It requires a grasp of the range of considerations that should have entered into her practical thinking in the period of time at issue. We need to know not only what the agent could have done but also what she should have been mindful of or attentive to. Group membership will be relevant for the attribution of moral responsibility to individual members, if members have reason to be mindful of the acts and intentions of the groups to which they belong.

Membership in an ethnic identity group may, of course, be *situationally* relevant for a group member's practical thinking. If a Hutu in 1994's Rwanda believed that only a Hutu might be able to perform some particular act that he thought ought to be performed—perhaps because it involved travel and a Hutu would more likely be able to move about without being harmed—he would have had reason to acknowledge his membership in the group, simply because of the possibilities it opened up for him. Aligning oneself with a group gives one a standing reason to consider the acts and attitudes of the group when planning one's own course. To the extent that individuals align themselves with a group, they see themselves as participating in a communal project of continuing the development of the character and history of the group, through shared conversation and thought and through an understanding that each of those who align themselves with the group may act for the others. The group functions for each individual as an extension of her agency, to that extent, because each may see the acts of the group as, to that extent, expressions of her own will. By aligning herself with the group, she transforms the reach of her own agency. But just as when I pick up and use a walking stick—Aristotle's example of an extension of agency—I have reason to be mindful of where exactly that stick will land and with what it will come into contact, when I align myself with a group, I have reason to be mindful of what it does, what it has done, and what it is preparing to do. If an ethnic identity group performs a morally repugnant act, ethically adequate descriptions of what aligning individuals do or have done may well make reference to that act. If such an individual has not tried to keep the act from being performed, omissions of failing to do what she might have done to steer the group away from the act would legitimately be attributed to her.

Of course, a member may have no interest in availing herself of the option of seeing the group as an extension of her own agency. It is not simply having access to some particular walking stick that gives an individual reason to be mindful of where that stick ends up; it is picking the stick up and using it, making of it an extension of her own agency, that gives her reason to be attentive to its location and responsive when it creates dangers. It is not the *availability* of aligning oneself with a group that gives one reason to be mindful of the group's acts and plans, it is *actually* aligning oneself with the group. The Serb who never aligned himself with the Serbs is not responsible for failing to try to prevent Serbian aggression *in virtue of his ethnicity*. If he is responsible for this kind of omission, it will be because he was in a position to prevent harm and did not, but many non-Serbs bear this sort of responsibility, as any serious evaluation of the reaction of the international community reveals.

One of the profound tragedies of the fact that our social world is largely structured in terms of ethnicity is that while only aligning members of ethnic identity groups shape the acts of these groups and bear moral responsibility for individual acts and omissions in virtue of their alignment, all members are targeted by hostile groups when group acts form part of a narrative of ethnic conflict. Further, being forced to share a common interest in survival with others, with whom one may otherwise share very little, may create alignment where there would have been none. Another tragedy of ethnic identity reflects the difficulties common to doing anything as a group; our lives are enhanced and our powers broadened when we live and work with others, but our personal control is lessened when we allow that others may act for us. An individual Serb may have aligned himself with the group without having adopted the goal of achieving a "Greater Serbia" or accepting ethnic cleansing as a means to any end. He might have been proud of his heritage, sympathetic to many of the group's thoughts and attitudes, and prone to react to ethnic slights as a member of the group, while believing that the best next step for his nation would be an acceptance of the inevitability and suitability of a pluralist society. When the idea takes hold that one person may extend the agency of another even when the ethical differences between them are profound, the simplicity of the idea of acting together for a shared end is lost to the complexity of internal disagreements among aligning individuals with competing views of what a group should do, many of which are in fact resolved by the coercion or manipulation of group members.

3

An ethnic identity group is a collection of individuals, each of whom may align himself with an idea of the group—where that idea is, more precisely, the idea of a particular collective agent, whose collectivity rests on the shared ancestry of the individuals—and each of whom may, therefore, act and respond emotionally as a member of the group. This analysis does not fall neatly into either category of the traditional distinction between "objective" and "subjective." On the one hand, ethnicity is not simply a matter of biological descent. It has to do with the ideas members have about shared ancestry. We don't disprove the existence of Serbs and Croats by pointing out that, if we go back far enough, the two groups share an ancestry. It is a mistake to save preconceived ideas of what ethnicity is all about by attributing mass ignorance and dull-mindedness to individuals who identify ethnically with groups in spite of the fact that the groups with which they identify cannot claim to be biologically self-perpetuating entities that can trace their beginnings far into the past. No other objective criterion has been mentioned. In particular, no overt sharing of culture is required. For that matter, no shared beliefs or values are required.[10]

On this view, it is not guaranteed that we will find a one-one correspondence of ethnic groups and cultures.[11] This is consistent with the assumption that ethnic identity groups retain their identity despite cultural change; changed cultures do not imply distinct groups. Ethnic identity groups exist over time because there is a continuity in their way of maintaining boundaries—in the availability to some individuals of aligning themselves with the group and the unavailability to others of standing in this relation to the idea of the group. Shared culture may be a contributing factor in the formation of an ethnic group, or it may result from ethnic thinking, but it is not essential to the concept of an ethnic identity group.[12] The Weberian approach to ethnicity focuses on what is, in Karl Barth's words, "socially effective," whatever that might be.

---

[10] It might be said that the existence of an ethnic identity group requires a shared belief in the shared ancestry of the group members, but this belief need not be shared by all members. It need only be widely enough believed to generate a widely acknowledged idea of collective agency.

[11] See Barth 1969, especially 11–15. For a philosopher's defense of the view that a nation is a culture, see Tamir 1993.

[12] Many groups form in response to social changes arising from the activity of other groups and develop distinct cultures later (Horowitz 1985). Kukathas (1992, 233) points to the creation of a Malay people in Indonesia as a response to both colonialist line drawing

[A]lthough ethnic categories take cultural differences into account, we can assume no simple one-to-one relationship between ethnic units and cultural similarities and differences. The features that are taken into account are not the sum of "objective" differences, but only those which the actors themselves regard as significant. Not only do ecologic variations mark and exaggerate differences; some cultural features are used by the actors as signals and emblems of differences, others are ignored, and in some relationships radical differences are played down and denied. (Barth 1969, 14)

But if ethnic identity is not essentially a matter of sharing a culture with others, then the ethical significance of ethnic identity does not arise from the sharing of a culture.[13] If it can be shown that ethnicity is relevant for attributions of moral responsibility to individuals, the argument will not involve the claim that a shared culture embroils individual group members in each other's acts. If it can be shown that ethnic identity groups have rights, the argument will not simultaneously show that *cultural* groups have rights. On the other hand, while an argument that defends a right to culture might support the claim that a *cultural* group has a right to political power, it could have no direct implications for the claim that a *nation* has a right to political power. And if it can be shown that membership in an ethnic identity group entails special obligations, provides reasons for acting or, at least, excuses partiality, it will not follow that membership gives members reason to preserve or defend a particular culture or provide an excuse for any missteps taken in an effort to do so.

The failure to recognize the ethical significance of *ethnic* groups as such is especially pronounced in the literature on group rights. The social groups that are argued to have rights to a portion of political power, to some form of regional autonomy, to secession, to the continued use of a particular language or territory, or to reparations for past wrongs are typically cultural groups, even when the discussion is nominally about "nations." Of course, traditional defenses of nationalism appeal to a connection between nations and cultures; they find in the value of culture the legitimacy of nationalist claims. There is already in Herder (1969) the idea that individuals cannot develop without a culture in which to do so.[14] This same idea is the basis of Isaiah Berlin's defense of nationalism (Berlin 1992a and 1992b). For Herder and Berlin, nations are the subjects of cultural development and maintenance. Nations *possess* cultures. Will Kymlicka (1995b, 1994, and 1989), Charles Taylor (1997), and Yael

and Chinese immigration. The colonialist influence is widespread. When individuals are treated as belonging together in a certain way, they may respond as group members.

[13] Sharing a culture may turn out to be ethically significant as well, but a separate argument would be needed to show this.

[14] For discussion of Herder's view, see Hampshire 1991.

Tamir (1993), among others, appeal to considerations of this kind in their defense of "cultural nationalism."[15]

According to Kymlicka, cultural nationalism "defines the nation in terms of a common culture, and the aim of the nationalist movement is to protect the survival of the culture" (1995a, 132–3). This approach is in some ways like Herder's and Berlin's, but it is in one important respect very much out of step with its tradition. According to the traditional view, a nation is not a group that is *defined* in terms of its culture. It is essentially an ethnic group with political standing or aspirations, and it typically possesses a distinct culture. The point, however, of contemporary "culturalist" approaches is to elevate the cultural and dismiss the ethnic element of nationality.[16] Cultural nationalism is typically seen as at least *less* suspect than ethnic nationalism. It appeals not to categories of arbitrary exclusivity but to categories of the fundamental "ways of life," out of which may be developed the coherent individual life plans that it is liberalism's business to protect. I would suggest that there may be national rights *and* cultural rights but that these must be kept distinct. Collapsing the distinction tends to lead us away from the problem of nationalism altogether.

The problem with a culturalist approach to nationalism is that significant *cultural* differences seem to be neither necessary nor sufficient for *national* difference. The culturalist must require that there be significant cultural differences between distinct nations if cultural differences are to justify protective group rights. In their influential discussion of the right of self-determination, Avishai Margalit and Joseph Raz introduce the concept of an encompassing group (Margalit and Raz 1990). Encompassing groups are the bearers of the right to self-determination. The essential characteristics of an encompassing group are (1) a pervasive common culture and (2) the importance of membership for individual self-identity. As Margalit and Raz acknowledge, their characterization of encompassing groups is designed to highlight those aspects of such groups that would form part of the moral argument for group rights. With this kind of group in mind, it is easy to see questions of group rights as questions of the stakes for individuals of group harms. A plausible argument for group rights would then involve discussion of the nature of an individual group member's *dependence on* the group of which he is a member—an explanation of how the well-being of the individual depends on the well-being of the group and how the self-respect of the individual depends on the self-respect of the group. If

---

[15] Tamir is perhaps the most consistent in her claim that a nation is a culture; as such, it is open to all who wish to belong. It is all the harder to see how the right of a group to a culture that she describes as following from the right of individuals to a culture could *ever* result in the right of a cultural group to a state of its own. See Kymlicka's criticisms in 1995a.

[16] "Culturalist" is Brian Walker's term. See Walker 1999.

either the well-being or the self-respect of individuals can be shown to rest
on the flourishing of the groups to which they belong, then special protections for such groups would seem to be in order.[17] The problem is
that this analysis of the groups that would be the bearers of moral
rights excludes outright particular groups that are intuitively at least
legitimate candidates for autonomy rights and includes groups that
intuitively are not.

Michael Ignatieff recounts a conversation he had with a Serbian
soldier in Croatia in March 1993.

> I'm trying to figure out why neighbors should start killing each other. So I say
> I can't tell Serbs and Croats apart. "What makes you think you're so different?"
>   The man I'm talking to takes a cigarette pack out of his khaki jacket. "See
> this. These are Serbian cigarettes. Over there they smoke Croatian cigarettes."
>   "But they're both cigarettes, right?"
>   "You foreigners don't understand anything." He shrugs and begins cleaning
> his Zastoro machine pistol. (Ignatieff 1995, 91)

Ignatieff's point is that nationalism is nonsense. "It is as if the nationalist
myth—that Serbs and Croats are radically distinct people who each
deserve a separate homeland—is struggling with this man's lived experience that, really, not much distinguishes him from his Croat neighbors"
(92). But why should we expect the peoples of distinct nations to be
"radically distinct" from each other? When Ignatieff asks for the
"difference" between Serbs and Croats, what kind of difference is he
looking for? Undoubtedly, virulent nationalist rhetoric often takes the
form of claiming that the people of another nation are essentially *bad* in
one way or another. This may be what *ethnic hatred* is all about. But it is
not obvious that this fact about rhetoric and its emotional impact has any
implications for what we are to say about distinguishing nations and
assessing their claims. What is behind Ignatieff's question, I suspect, is an
acceptance of a culturalist conception of nationalism.

Even when an ethnic or national group might be said to have a distinct
culture, the group's rights do not necessarily follow from that fact about
culture. If the indigenous peoples of North America have a right to
noninterference, that is largely the result of treaties accepted by a state
and *by the groups themselves*, and of the reasonable expectations *of those
groups*. These claims are based on a recognition that the group is to be
treated as a moral agent. Shared culture is not essential to such
arguments; the existence of a collective agent is essential. What we
must understand if we are to understand national rights is not how
sharing a pervasive culture influences individuals but what it is for a
group to live among other groups—what it is for a group to act and be

---

[17] For other arguments of this kind, see Taylor 1993, Tamir 1993, Nickel 1994b and
1994a.

acted upon, to have successes and failures, and to make unreasonable or legitimate claims—and what it is for an individual to be a member of a group so understood.

Finally, a shared culture, however pervasive, does not seem to distinguish *national* groups from other kinds. The culture of small-farm life in the United States has, as Brian Walker (1999) has pointed out, been destroyed with the passing away of small farms and the rise of "agribusiness." Surely this culture was as pervasive and as identity involving as French Canadian culture is for many Québecois, but it is not clear that the small farmer may be said to have distinctive cultural rights and is clear enough that if he has, these rights are not *national* rights.[18]

Ethnic identity groups are plausible candidates for autonomy rights. It is not simply that the analysis of an ethnic identity group involves an idea of collective agency. Members of an ethnic identity group are distinguished from nonmembers by the possibilities for action that are available to them. It might be argued that we respect individuals *qua group members* by respecting the rights of groups to determine their own course. The choices of individuals are not necessarily enhanced by the availability of particular cultural forms, which may indeed be oppressive or confining, but *the character of the choices that individuals have insofar as they may align themselves with a group is necessarily altered by the way the group is treated by outsiders.* This is also what makes genocide morally different from nongenocidal mass killing. Genocidal acts aim at the destruction (and typically also the deep humiliation) of a group. Such acts take as their intentional objects *all* members of the group—past, present, and future. Mass violence is, of course, always depraved, but instances of mass violence may differ in their moral nature and may do so, I think, without necessarily also differing in moral magnitude. King Leopold's killing of millions of people in the Congo, for example, was not the result of an intention to destroy a people; it was a different kind of evil, despite the fact that it was not an evil of lesser magnitude than genocide.

The Weberian analysis is also not *simply* a subjectivist analysis. For while at its center is an *idea* of group agency based on shared ancestry, this idea is shared and is contentful; the idea has implications for ethnic ascription. I cannot claim to be Hungarian, for example, or Korean if I have no reason to believe that somewhere in my ancestry is an individual who shares an ancestry with other Hungarians or Koreans. Each idea has been shaped by the history of the people whose idea it is. It is important to remember that it is *the idea shared by members* that determines the criteria of group membership. Weberian views are not simple subjectivist views because it is not an individual idea of each member that makes each a

---

[18] It may be that the Québecois have national rights to make cultural choices, but an argument for this claim would have to involve a concept of the rights of nations as well as that of the rights of individuals to a culture.

member; it is the idea of membership shared by members that determines the criteria of membership. This means, however, that if, generally speaking, individuals did not identify themselves ethnically, there would be no ethnic identity groups.

The suggestion that the definition of an ethnic identity group must involve an *idea* of the group, viewed as a collective agent, is loosely related to Benedict Anderson's suggestion that a nation may be defined as an "imagined political community" (Anderson 1991). According to Anderson, we must say that the nation is an *imagined* community, because "the members of even the smallest nation will never know most of their fellow members, meet them, or even hear of them, yet in the minds of each lives the image of their communion" (1991, 6). This passage has been very influential but not, I think, always well understood. It is often cited in support of the claim that ethnic groups are not what they seem.[19] Anderson explicitly rejects the association of "imagined" with "false" or "fabricated" (6). Nations are imagined communities, according to Anderson, not because they are *unlike* but because they are *like* other communities. The importance of Anderson's work lies not in an unmasking of the nationalist lie but in his appreciation of an essential but underappreciated aspect of nations—or of ethnic identity groups—that "in the minds of each [member] lives the *image* of their communion" (my emphasis). It is, more precisely, an *idea* of their communion. We understand the nature of the group by understanding what this idea is an idea of and by understanding more fully how the idea might "live" in the minds of members.

Weberian theories allow for all variety of strengths of ethnic identification. At a given time and place, ethnicity may have a strong or a scarcely detectable influence on behavior. There are ethnic groups in a particular place at a particular time if the organization for ethnically motivated action is in place. While individuals living through periods of ethnic conflict can often look back to times when, far from extensively determining their lives, their ethnicity had very little influence, it would be a mistake to ignore the existence of ethnic identity groups before the onset of group-based intimidation or violence.

It should also be noted that while the proposed analysis is "individualist" according to some understandings of what individualism amounts to, it is not individualist according to others. It is individualist in the

[19] Consider Russell Hardin's reference to Anderson's idea: "Further evidence that the ethnic purists [in the Balkans] stand on air is that two-thirds of the half million people of Montenegro believe that Montenegrins are indistinct from Serbs, while the other third claim there are irreconcilable differences. Whichever definition a Montenegrin accepts, the implicit nation–greater Serbia or Montenegro–is surely an instance of what Benedict Anderson calls imagined communities" (Hardin 1995, 157). What Hardin wishes to show here, I think, is that the claims of the nationalists are false, but this is not what being an instance of Anderson's imagined communities would imply.

important sense that every nonindividual entity is analyzed in terms of individuals; we might call this "explanatory individualism." It is not individualist if individualism is understood to imply that every claim about a nonindividual can be *reduced to* some set of claims about individuals; this is perhaps what we have come to mean by "methodological individualism." We might say that two sorts of entity are involved in the theory: individual agents and shared ideas. An ethnic identity group is a social entity made up of individuals, a shared idea, and the social possibilities this idea opens up for those individuals—that is, for group members. The claims we make about the acts of a group are claims about this idea; they cannot be reduced to claims about the acts of individuals. This is important, because philosophical discussion of the ethical significance of ethnic groups has foundered on the issues of individualism—explanatory, methodological, and moral. The first two are not always distinguished, but some philosophers have avoided the difficulty of saying what a social group is by rejecting explanatory individualism, while others have avoided the difficulty of saying what a social group is by denying that there (really) are any—by claiming that the group is nothing more than its members.

Moral individualism is the position that only individual persons are moral agents and only they can make fundamental moral claims on us. The traditional divide on this issue is between those who defend the ethical significance of social groups by rejecting moral individualism and those who save moral individualism by denying the ethical significance of social groups. The moral individualist is typically dismissive of the idea that ethnicity might be ethically significant, because membership in an ethnic group is nonvoluntary or unchosen. He argues that the concepts of collective responsibility and group rights are conceptually confused and potentially dangerous. The idea of collective moral responsibility is said to be conceptually confused, because the attribution of moral responsibility to an individual not on the basis of what she has done but because of her nonvoluntary association with others, who may well do what she never would, is simply not attribution of *moral* responsibility. It is also, according to the moral individualist, practically unwise to defend the concepts of collective responsibility and group rights, because to do so is to lend support to the ideology that stands behind the massive violence of contemporary ethnic conflict, with its gross violations of the individual rights of so many. The individualist response is, I think, cogent, but it ends too soon—leaving us with the misguided impression that whatever their sociological or political importance, ethnicity has no ethical significance and need interest the moral philosopher only insofar as she wishes to understand the ways in which our efforts to do right go wrong.

I believe that both the moral individualist and the "collectivist" express an important aspect of the truth. Membership in an ethnic identity group may be unchosen, but it involves the availability of choices that are not available to individuals who are not members of the group. Given this analysis of ethnic-identity-group membership, it may be argued that while membership alone has no implications for the attribution of moral responsibility to individuals, aligning oneself with the group, as only members can, does have such implications. It can also be argued that as an important source of the options of individual agency, groups have rights. It is, I think, a mistake to reject either explanatory individualism in the analysis of collectivity concepts or moral individualism in our evaluation of the conduct of individuals. One challenge is to capture the robust reality of social groups without ignoring their dependence on the psychological attitudes of individuals. Another is to respect the integrity of the individual moral agent without ignoring the social context of her agency.

As for the practical wisdom of taking up these issues, the dangers of lending support to the idea that an ethnically defined group might have a right to self-determination at a time when nationalist rhetoric is behind the most appalling ethnic violence are obvious, as are the dangers of discussing collective responsibility when what is needed is an end to ethnic hatred. Less obvious perhaps are the dangers of *not* reaching a better understanding of the moral status of ethnic groups. Philosophers often *seem*, at least, to believe that if there is to be an end to ethnic conflict, it will come from a global embrace of rational universalism. A number of diplomats and theorists involved in conflict resolution foresee a much different course.

> [Essential to the resolution of the most entrenched ethnic conflicts is] a completed mourning process by which a victim or victim group "lets go" of its losses from historic or contemporary violence and reintegrates and adapts to a new, reasonably secure status so that it can get on with the business of life. For the mourning process to occur, however, requires that the victimizers accept responsibility for their acts or those of their predecessor governments and people, recognize the injustice done, and in some way ask forgiveness of the victims. (Montville 1990, 538)

I have not addressed the question of whether it is "natural" for human beings to form ethnic identity groups or whether it is a good thing that they do so. There is, of course, a vast literature on the question of whether identification in terms of ethnicity is the result of a "primordial" impulse in human nature or is instead the (inefficient) result of the efforts of individuals to act in their own self-interest. I suspect it is neither, and the analysis I offer of such groups suggests an alternative explanation.[20] This

---

[20] One problem with rational-choice explanations of group behavior is that they ignore the ideas that group members themselves have about why they do what they do–at least, whenever they would not explain their actions in terms of self-interest. The problem with primordialist views is that they are unable to account for the ease with which many

question must, in any case, be distinguished from questions about the moral significance of group membership. I am not here asking whether there ought to be ethnic identity groups. Our history already contains the morally significant actions and experiences of such groups. To act in this context out of a belief that ethnicity is not morally significant is to give up on the ideas that those who have been wronged are owed something and those who have done wrong have a moral debt to pay.

The competent moral agent does not spend much time trying to wish away the difficult, unpleasant, or inconvenient realities that shape the context in which she must act. She looks them in the face, acknowledging that it is *with them* that she must work. Much of the work involved in the restoration or creation of morally responsible relations between groups after genocide will be carried out by generations of group members who were not yet born when the killing took place, but whose lives will be substantially shaped by it all the same.[21] Social and moral theory should not obfuscate their social powers and moral duties.[22]

References

Anderson, Benedict. 1991. *Imagined Communities*. Rev. ed. New York: Verso.

Barth, Karl. 1969. "Introduction." In *Ethnic Groups and Boundaries: The Social Organization of Cultural Difference*, edited by Karl Barth, 9–38. Boston: Little, Brown.

Beiner, Ronald, ed. 1999. *Theorizing Nationalism*. Albany: State University of New York Press.

Berlin, Isaiah. 1992a. "The Bent Twig." In *The Crooked Timber of Humanity*, edited by Henry Hardy, 238–61. Princeton: Princeton University Press.

———. 1992b. "Two Concepts of Nationalism." *New York Review of Books* (November 21):19–23.

Connor, Walker. 1994. *Ethnonationalism: The Quest for Understanding*. Princeton: Princeton University Press.

Dahrendorf, Ralf. 1979. *Life Chances*. Chicago: University of Chicago Press.

Hampshire, Stuart. 1991. "Nationalism." In *Isaiah Berlin: A Celebration*, edited by Edna and Avishai Margalit, 127–34. London: Hogarth Press.

individuals live without ethnic attachment or for the significant variation in the strength of ethnic ties among individuals and for particular individuals over time. The explanation of ethnic identity that fits best with the analysis I have offered of ethnic groups begins with the fact that historical understandings, systems of value, and shared goals are, as it happens, often developed within groups that see themselves as sharing an ancestry.

[21] On the potential role of subsequent generations of group members in breaking cycles of violence, see Hoffman 2003. For one account of the ways in which Hindu/Muslim violence in India shapes the lives of subsequent generations, see Kakar 1996.

[22] I am grateful to Virginia Held and William Fisk for helpful comments on earlier drafts of this essay.

Hardin, Russell. 1995. *One for All: The Logic of Group Conflict*. Princeton: Princeton University Press.

Herder, J. G. 1969. *J. G. Herder on Social and Political Culture*. Edited by F. M. Barnard. Cambridge: Cambridge University Press.

Hoffman, Eva. 2003. "The Balm of Recognition: Rectifying Wrongs through the Generations." In *Human Rights, Human Wrongs*, edited by Nicholas Owen, 278–303. New York: Oxford University Press.

Horowitz, Donald L. 1985. *Ethnic Groups in Conflict*. Berkeley: University of California Press.

Ignatieff, Michael. 1995. "Nationalism and the Narcissism of Minor Differences." *Queen's Quarterly* 102, no. 1:13–25. Reprinted in Beiner 1999, 91–102.

Kakar, Sudhir. 1996. *The Colors of Violence: Cultural Identities, Religion, and Conflict*. Chicago: University of Chicago Press.

Kukathas, Chandran. 1992. "Are There Any Cultural Rights?" *Political Theory* 20:105–39.

Kymlicka, Will. 1989. *Liberalism, Community and Culture*. Oxford: Clarendon Press.

———. 1994. "Individual and Community Rights." In *Group Rights*, edited by Judith Baker, 17–33. Toronto: University of Toronto Press.

———. 1995a. "Misunderstanding Nationalism." *Dissent* 42:130–37. Reprinted in Beiner 1999, 131–40.

——— 1995b. *Multicultural Citizenship*. Oxford: Clarendon Press.

———, ed. 1995c. *The Rights of Minority Cultures*. New York: Oxford University Press.

Margalit, Avishai, and Joseph Raz. 1990. "National Self-Determination." *Journal of Philosophy* 87, no. 9:439–61.

Montville, Joseph. 1990. "Epilogue: The Human Factor Revisited." In *Conflict and Peacemaking in Multiethnic Societies*, edited by Joseph Montville, 537–38. Lexington, Mass.: Lexington Books.

Nickel, James. 1994a. "Ethnocide and Indigenous Peoples." *Journal of Social Philosophy* 25 (special issue): 84–98.

———. 1994b. "The Value of Cultural Belonging." *Dialogue* 33, no. 4:635–42.

Tamir, Yael. 1993. *Liberal Nationalism*. Princeton: Princeton University Press.

Taylor, Charles. 1993. "The Politics of Recognition." In *Multiculturalism: Examining the "Politics of Recognition,"* edited by Amy Gutmann, 25–73. Princeton: Princeton University Press.

———. 1997. "Nationalism and Modernity." In *The Morality of Nationalism*, edited by Robert McKim and Jeff McMahan, 31–55. New York: Oxford University Press.

Walker, Brian. 1999. "Modernity and Cultural Vulnerability: Should Ethnicity Be Privileged?" In Beiner 1999:141–65.

5

MORAL TAINT

MARINA A. L. OSHANA

1. Introduction

An accepted part of our practice of ascribing responsibility is that we regard people as blameworthy and liable for the wrongful acts they have performed or have directly contributed to bringing about.[1] The corrupt corporate CEO, the hit-and-run driver, the military commander who turns a blind eye to the abuse of detainees by soldiers under her command all are culpable for acts they have committed or have permitted others under their authority to commit. We tend to regard these wrongdoers with a kind of moral loathing, and we may rightly regard them as morally defiled—tainted—as a result of their wrongdoing.

But sometimes we think people are blamable because their character or moral record has been affected in a negative way by the wrongful acts of those with whom they are associated. So we might regard the spouse of the corrupt CEO, or the parent of the hit-and-run driver, or the other members of the renegade military unit as somehow culpable. We even might regard descendants of wrongdoers as morally compromised where the wrongdoing of their ancestors was grave and had intergenerational consequences. My interest is not to defend this tendency as fair or as a reasonable response to wrongdoing. Some have charged that to regard one person as blameworthy for the wrongs of another person (or persons) with whom she is associated is a vestige of a barbaric culture, not suited to modern enlightened times (Lewis 1991). My interest in this essay is merely to explore what generates the phenomenon of having one's moral record sullied by the unjust conduct of those with whom one is associated. I will refer to this as the phenomenon of moral taint.

As an example of this phenomenon, consider the case of David Kaczynski, the brother of "Unabomber" Ted Kaczynski. David

[1] An ancestor of this article was presented at the 32nd Annual Conference on Value Inquiry, Louisiana State University, Baton Rouge, 10 April 2005. I am grateful to members of the audience for their comments. Thanks are also due to David Copp, Matt King, and Jon Tresan for comments and discussion.

Kaczynski led the FBI to his brother; his feelings about the role he played in the apprehension were reported in the *Sacramento Bee*:

"I regret what I did every moment, every time I think about it. I regret Ted's suffering. On the other hand, I don't think there is anything I could have done differently." [David Kaczynski says he] went to authorities because "I could not have lived with myself" if another person were hurt and killed by a bomb that he might have prevented. David's inner torment, he said, has been made worse by the belief that he and his wife may have unwittingly helped fund some of the bombings with loans to Ted. [Over the years, David sometimes bought airline tickets for his brother.] Two of those trips were to cities where the Unabomber struck. "There is no question that my feeling of sorrow has been intensified by the thought that we may have assisted Ted, provided him with the means to do some of these things. That is an awful thought." (Hubert 1997)

If David Kaczynski bears taint, what is it for? How could his relation to Ted, founded on the circumstance of birth, have left him somehow defiled, and positioned—indeed, expected—to make amends for what his brother had done? Certainly David experienced guilt over having inadvertently assisted his brother. He also experienced guilt over what he had done to his brother, but we would think it odd if he did not: " 'I deeply love Ted, and that love has been made more poignant, more real in some ways by the tragedy of this whole situation,' David Kaczynski told *The Bee*. 'It's agony when you love someone, when you want what's best for them, you want to protect them, and yet you are afraid that they may be hurting other people' " (Hubert 1997).

The case of David Kaczynski is one to which I will return in this discussion. Although my suspicion is that the concept of moral taint is for all practical purposes unnecessary and, moreover, metaphysically suspect, I believe the concept is helpful as a heuristic device in assisting our comprehension of more vexing cases of responsibility and blame. The concepts of responsibility and blame are well developed in philosophical scholarship; the concept of taint does not replace them, and we could get along without the idea by making fuller use of responsibility and blame. But the concept of taint is a way of making vivid the combined presence of responsibility and blame in cases where shame and atonement would be appropriate. Hence, we can get some philosophical mileage out of the idea of moral taint, even if the idea is ultimately expendable.

2. What Is Taint?

Let us begin with a working definition of the idea of taint. Something tainted is contaminated, stained, fouled, polluted—ruined with respect to some essential attribute. The alteration wrought by taint is not merely superficial. A tainted substance is altered in ways sufficient to cause it to lose the properties that make it valuable to us, and sometimes in ways sufficient to require reclassification. Consider the familiar phenomenon of food spoilage, or taint. Food is deemed tainted when it suffers an unfavorable alteration in color, flavor, odor, or texture and this alteration renders the food unfit for consumption. For example, milk that is tainted no longer satisfies a property essential to it qua foodstuff, namely, the property of being fit for human consumption. Rather than having certain nutritive properties, as food must, the tainted milk has acquired properties of the opposite sort, namely, those of depriving the body of nutrients or of compromising the health of the imbiber. Similarly, water is tainted when certain bacterial organisms are introduced. The tainted water loses the quality of being potable; it no longer counts as a substance essential to our survival but takes on the contrary property of threatening survival. The onset of food spoilage is generally a gradual process arising from a number of environmental factors, including inadequate sanitation, enzymatic or chemical reactions, improper temperature controls, microbial growth, or physical neglect (Schuler et al. 1984).

Similar examples can be drawn from the cases of bodily integrity, psychological or emotional health, and interpersonal relations. A tainted flesh wound eats away at the healthy organism. The wound calls for medical intervention to repair and to cure it; when the taint is severe, the flesh ceases to function properly; gangrene sets in, and the ruined flesh must be removed. An intimate relationship (personal or professional) that is tainted by infidelity or a breach of trust no longer counts as a union or a partnership. There is a departure from what is plausibly expected of the relationship in light of what is characteristic of healthy relations of the type. The tainted relationship sustains a change in normative quality and thus in value to those who are party to it. If the alteration is extensive, the relationship might no longer resemble what we think of as a "relationship." Even when the taint is alleviated, some vestige lingers. Its presence continues to be felt.

3. What Is Moral Taint?

One is said to be morally tainted when one's moral personality has been compromised by the introduction of something that produces disfigurement of the moral psyche. Less metaphorically, taint significantly diminishes the degree to which one's moral personality qualifies as virtuous and one's moral record as unblemished. As with tainted food and tainted relationships, moral taint may be introduced by a variety of factors. The primary sources of moral taint are personal relations marked by a major injustice—associations that are immediate and direct in some cases, remote and unrecognized in others.

These relations set the stage for taint, but they need not complete it. David Kaczynski's taint owes its genesis to the connection he bears with his brother Ted. But where it persists and flourishes, taint is due to a defect of character, such as the absence of a desire or a disposition to do the right thing for the right, noninstrumental reasons.[2] The morally tainted person may exhibit an inadequate level of concern for or a persistent indifference to considerations of moral import that bear on her relations with others. Sometimes moral taint is due just to a privation of this sort—to an absence or insufficient level of good will, as it were. As a result taint leaves (to borrow from Eleonore Stump) an unsavory "moral residue" upon one's relations with others and upon one's moral identity or, if you will, upon one's soul (Stump 2004).

This is, of course, too rough. The concept of moral identity and the specifics of the defect of character at stake need to be fleshed out. As stated, these intuitions could be employed to describe any of a variety of moral shortcomings other than taint. But let us keep them in mind as possible indicators of taint. If literature and social commentary are any indication, moral taint is a character flaw ubiquitous in the human animal. Although not a subject of study for medical science, psychology, or sociology (unless we wish to claim psychopathologies as subspecies of taint, and I do not), the character flaw suffers no shortage of examples. Many of the examples of moral taint that spring to mind are literary—Adam and Eve's colossal fall from grace, the mark of Cain, Lady Macbeth's famously bloodied hands. Examples of moral taint that loom large in recent popular memory are the alleged taint of German citizens for the actions of the Nazi regime during the Second World War, the taint of segregationists and slave owners in the United States, and the taint of white South Africans for actions during the apartheid regime. The nineteenth-century industrialists and financiers are derogatively referred to as "robber barons," tainted for their staggering accumulation of capital and extravagant displays of material greatness at the expense the public welfare and of labor.[3] (The same might be said of the corporate chiefs of Tyco, Enron, and the like recently in the news.) Is there reason to attribute taint, and not just straightforward responsibility and blameworthiness, to these persons?

I believe these examples do provide an introduction to the idea of taint. In the cases mentioned above, three things are true. First, each of the parties bears *liability*, of either a direct or a vicarious variety, for contributing to the occurrence of an ethically questionable state of affairs and for their response to this state of affairs. The liability borne is of a moral sort, augmented in some cases by political and criminal liability. Second, each of the parties has done something (or deliberately refrained

---

[2] This characterization of taint has been influenced by Nomy Arpaly's discussion of the hallmarks of moral worth.

[3] These include the industrialist Andrew Carnegie of Carnegie Steel, John D. Rockefeller of Standard Oil, Cornelius and William Vanderbilt of the railroad empire, J. Pierpont Morgan of banking and U.S. Steel, and Eleuthère Irénée Du Pont, whose invention of nitroglycerine explosives changed the course of modern warfare.

from attempting to prevent the occurrence of something) for which they ought to feel *shame* (and perhaps ought to *be shamed*).[4] The liability is thus one for which the party is culpable or deserving of censure. Third, the incident or state of affairs is one for which *atonement* of some variety—reparation, public philanthropy, or a public apology, for example—is fitting. A moral burden to make restitution to others is produced. Together these components generate an idea of taint. Let us examine each in turn.

4. Liability

Traditionally, when we ascribe liability for harm we assume the harm resulted from faulty behavior (active or omitted) on the actor's part and that the actor is open to judgment and response on our part for this reason. That is, we assume what might be called contributory fault on the part of the actor. In cases of the sort described above—tacit or active acceptance of the genocidal racism of the Nazis, the evil of slavery, the greed and hubris of the early industrialists—we have the familiar tests for responsibility and liability at our disposal. What we observe and object to in such cases as these is not, first and foremost, taint; we do not zero in on the contamination or moral defilement that malfeasance produces in the actor. Rather, we note immediate cause for answerability and blame in the malfeasance; we note that the standard criteria for responsibility have been met. Among these are the satisfaction of certain epistemic conditions of moral agency—self-awareness, attunement to moral norms, and sensitivity to one's environment—coupled with a sufficient level of control and an absence of excusing or exonerating factors, such as ignorance, duress, or coercion, and interpersonal competencies.

In each of these cases we look to the action performed, to the quality of will displayed by the actor, and to the level of attention given to morally salient considerations or to the level of care given to obligations to others—duties of care, perhaps—and in each of these cases we have evidence of failure in at least one of these respects. It is on the basis of such failure that we decide the propriety of demanding an account of the agent and apportioning fault. These are failures that, in paradigm cases, can unambiguously be attributed to the actor, failures for which an account of the actor's intentions and beliefs about the behavior in question can be expected; others may rightly regard the actor with approbation and treat her accordingly. In such cases, taint is not the basis of liability and is not needed to illuminate liability, though it may be a mark of liability and a result of liability. What we call moral taint in these cases is the product of moral failure, at minimum the failure to

---

[4] The idea that shame is at the heart of moral taint was suggested to me by Eleonore Stump in correspondence.

exhibit an adequate measure of concern for relevant moral considerations in one's interactions with others.

But if common practice is a reliable indicator, contributory fault is not needed for liability. We believe it is reasonable for parents to assume vicarious or indirect liability of a financial, legal, or moral nature for the activities of their minor children, for employers to be held liable for the professional reputation of their employees, and so forth. The law recognizes that liability may be apportioned vicariously and states as much in treating strict liability as a legitimate basis for fault.[5] Perhaps moral taint can arise when we are vicariously liable for some wrong. The idea is not that taint of a counterfeit or diluted sort may be produced but that garden-variety taint may be produced by a vicarious route, along with liability for this garden-variety taint. Each of these ideas—the first addressing the manner of acquisition and the second addressing liability—are contentious: Can we acquire taint "by proxy" or by association, as it were? And can we be liable for what we acquire vicariously, whether or not we are responsible for this acquisition? Let us survey some extant views and then turn to the position I recommend.

5. Vicarious Liability and Collective Responsibility

Some philosophers—Anthony Appiah most notably—argue that moral taint implies neither guilt nor liability but affects only the moral integrity of individuals, or how one's moral reputation appears to others in society (Appiah 1987). I will return to Appiah's view shortly. But many philosophers treat moral taint as an effect of vicarious liability and treat liability as a product of collective responsibility. Joel Feinberg, for example, contends that taint is an acceptable byproduct of collective responsibility when "parties who are largely of one mind to begin with are led (or forced) by circumstances to act in concert and share the risk of common failure or the fruits of an indivisible success" (Feinberg 1991, 62). Feinberg allows that responsibility for wrong can be generated by fault on the part of others within a collective to which a person belongs. This liability can encompass something like a debt that must be paid. But he denies that vicarious liability generates guilt. Feinberg states:

> [E]ven when it is reasonable to separate liability from fault, it is only the liability that can be passed from one party to another. In particular, *there can be no such thing as vicarious guilt*. Guilt consists in the intentional transgression of a prohibition. . . . In addition, the notion of guilt has always been essentially connected with the idea of "owing payment." The guilty party must "pay" for his sins, just as a debtor is one who must correct his moral imbalance by

---

[5] See the dissenting opinion of Justice Andrews in *Palsgraf v. Long Island Railroad Co.*, New York Court of Appeals, 248 N.Y. 339 (1928); *Farwell v. Keaton*, 240 N.W. 2d 217 (Michigan, 1976) on a strict duty to rescue; *Tison v. Arizona*, 481 U.S. 137 (1986) on strict liability where murderous intent and direct involvement in murder are absent.

repayment. To be guilty is to be out of balance, or unredeemed, stained or impure. The root idea in guilt, then, is to be an appropriate person to make atonement, penance, or self-reproach, in virtue of having intentionally violated a commandment or prohibition. (1991, 60)

Feinberg describes guilt in terms I have been employing for taint. To be tainted is to be out of balance, unredeemed, stained, or impure. If what Feinberg is describing as guilt is what I have called taint, and if his analysis is correct, a person cannot be tainted absent the intentional transgression of a prohibition or violation of a duty. That is, taint cannot be due to vicarious liability for harm. Feinberg appears to be saying that only taint grounds a legitimate demand that moral justice be restored; vicarious liability does not generate taint, and so vicarious liability does not generate a legitimate demand for moral restitution. Supposing Feinberg is correct, then if the associates of slave owners, of the Nazis, of the nineteenth-century industrialists, of white South Africans in the apartheid years, and so forth are merely vicariously liable, they are not "out of balance" and owe nothing in the form of atonement, restoration to others, and repair of their own moral personality or moral record. Moreover, if Feinberg is correct, the degree of liability is irrelevant to the degree of guilt or taint. One can be vicariously responsible for grave wrongdoing, including wrongdoing that does not transpire at a temporal distance, and yet on Feinberg's account be sheltered from guilt.

Larry May similarly locates the basis for taint in collective liability. But in contrast to Feinberg, May believes room for guilt (of a variety that implies impurity) and penitence does exist beyond the deliberate violation of a prohibition. Following Karl Jaspers, May characterizes moral taint as a form of *metaphysical guilt* or shame. Unlike *moral guilt*, which pertains to persons acting as individuals, arises out of the violation of some duty (or more generally out of what an agent has done), and entails blameworthiness, metaphysical guilt "arises out of each person's shared membership in groups that shape their identity, such that each member is implicated in the activities of any other member of the group" (May 1991, 240). May states:

The solidarity of a community often creates a shared feeling of responsibility for what occurs within the group. This feeling of responsibility is linked to that part of one's identity which is based on the groups of which one is a member. It is not merely that one is a member of a group within which harmful attitudes, for instance, have become dominant. Sometimes responsibility is based on the feeling that there was something wrong done by one's group members which one could easily have also done. Sometimes there is the feeling that one should have done something to break the chain which links one, as a nonoffending party, to the rest of the group. (1991, 247)

Any view of vicarious liability rests on the crucial assumption that bearing moral responsibility for the actions of other agents is a coherent concept. This assumption needs to be addressed, but before we turn to it, let us consider the three factors on which vicarious liability, as May presents the idea, depends. The core factor consists of a sense of solidarity integral to the identity of the tainted party. The second factor is the existence of a collective to which certain responsibilities or allegiances are owed. The third factor consists of a feeling or awareness that one's identity is compromised by the wrongdoing of members of one's identity group. With respect to this third point, it seems plausible that the feeling or awareness that one's identity is compromised by the activities of persons in one's identity group would generate shame, the feeling that there is something wrong with oneself. Perhaps it can also generate guilt, the feeling that one has done (albeit vicariously) something wrong. But how can the feeling or awareness that one's identity is compromised by the activities of persons in one's identity group generate actual responsibility or liability for wrong? And does taint rest on such feelings of compromised identity?

We can begin to answer these questions by taking up the first element of May's view, the idea that vicarious liability rests on group solidarity. The groups to which a person belongs that are implicated in the person's identity are various, but each captures distinctive attitudinal and dispositional traits; membership imparts a distinctive configuration to a person's life and generates a level of emotional involvement sufficient to color a person's view of herself. Membership in the female sex and membership in the African American ethnic group are examples; being a resident of one's community and a good neighbor may count as membership in a group for this purpose as well, as might belonging to the class of animal lovers or the class of academic philosophers. A person who is a member of such a group is expected to recognize her membership and acknowledge, if not wholeheartedly embrace, the burdens membership thrusts upon her. Solidarity may rest on the acceptance of a shared history (parental or geopolitical or ethnic or sexual, for example) or on giving credence to whatever way of thinking or behaving might plausibly be associated with the group. In David Kaczynski's case, for instance, whatever measure of taint he bears originates in a shared familial history. Had David Kaczynski never known his brother, never known he had a brother (suppose the two had been fostered or adopted by different families at infancy), he would not have formed any bond with his sibling, no occasions for fond memories and tearful recollections would have taken place, no links other than biology would exist between them. David Kaczynski's taint exists because his relation with Ted is personalized.

If taint is impossible absent the experience of solidarity, then (contra Jaspers) May asserts it cannot be "appropriate that *all* Germans [even those who repudiated Nazism and worked to resist its force] feel tainted by what fellow Germans did and [that] such a feeling should persist even in those cases where there is nothing that many of these people could have done differently, in terms of individual or collective behavior, that would have prevented Hitler's reign of terror" (May 1991, 244).[6] If solidarity is fostered only where there are attitudes in common that have been intentionally endorsed, then it is only appropriate that those Germans who consciously did nothing to dissociate themselves from the wrongful acts of their countrymen can be tainted—only they should suffer shame and be shamed.

What constitutes the parameters of the relevant identity group remains open to debate. It is also unsettled which of the many aspects of a person's identity are at stake. Depending on the circumstances, different aspects of one's identity will be implicated in the taint. But it makes sense to treat the applicable identity traits as those without which a person would fail to recognize or understand herself. These characteristics personalize the agent and consist of beliefs and desires, values, articles of faith, and commitments that the agent acknowledges as important to her—to who she is and to the kind of person she wants to be. They constitute the agent's self-conception. Such characteristics are self-reflexive in this fashion, and they can be fairly specific. In the case of David Kaczynski, for example, the compromised elements of his identity might be those of being a loving brother; being a compassionate person; being a law-abiding citizen of the United States; being a faithful Buddhist; and so forth.

Jaspers takes a more comprehensive view than I do of both the parameters of the relevant identity group and the relevant aspects of personal identity. Of metaphysical guilt he says: "There exists a solidarity among men as human beings that makes each co-responsible for every wrong and every injustice in the world, especially for crimes committed in his presence or with his knowledge. If I fail to do whatever I can to prevent them, I too am guilty" (Jaspers 1947, 32). Few persons can escape the charge of metaphysical guilt. So construed, moral taint, like sin, is a universal and even inevitable feature of human life.[7] In this vein Jaspers speaks of "the inevitable guilt of human existence" wrought by the fact that "every human being is fated to be enmeshed in the power relations he lives by" (34). But if all are metaphysically guilty and taint rests on metaphysical guilt, then taint is rather vacuous—no one is responsible in any deep sense. Given the breadth of membership in the human race the scope of liability will be quite wide, a point that invites specific concerns. The guilt of being human and thus as likely as anyone to transgress would erase the moral fence that separates the wrongdoers from the righteous. If

---

[6] Compare Jaspers (1947, 103) on the purification of opponents of National Socialism.

[7] Moral taint, however, is not sin and must not be confused with sin. Sin is essentially a religious notion. It is behavior contrary to that which God intends for his creation, behavior in opposition to God's laws and God's will. Of course, while moral taint is not synonymous with sin, and taint need not stem from a transgression of one's relationship with God, some cases of taint might originate in sin.

all are metaphysically guilty, persons who actually engaged in moral transgressions could be exculpated as readily as those who committed no offense.[8] None of this seems tenable, a point that perhaps accounts for Appiah's insistence that taint only concerns the moral integrity or reputation of individuals—their moral record, if you like. Perhaps Appiah realizes the difficulty of establishing suitable parameters for liability where taint is of a sort premised on the idea of metaphysical guilt.

The most plausible element of May's account of vicarious liability is the idea that, given the fact of membership, taint or its absence depends on a person's chosen response to the harms perpetrated by communities to which the person belongs—specifically, on "how one positions oneself in terms of one's membership in a biologically or geographically defined group" (May 1991, 245) in light of which one has been socialized to form certain dominant attitudes. The choice of who to be—of how to regard oneself and how respond to who one is—is under one's control, even if the mere fact of membership in a group is not.

So described, moral taint is still traced to activity for which one can rightly be held liable—namely, the refusal to assess oneself and one's attitude toward one's community, and to choose one's identity on the basis of this assessment. This strikes me as a straightforward and rather modest assertion. The idea is not that responsibility for wrong can be communicated by relations of kinship and community. Rather, the idea is that, just as the appearance of moral taint can be traced to human action (or culpable inaction) that affects the moral status of the tainted party, the removal of taint—the ability to purify oneself and restore one's moral personality or moral record to its proper form—is within the power of the individual. Of course, self-assessment and assessment of one's attitude toward one's community must transpire within a climate that does not constrain the ability of individuals to reflect upon the moral status of their community and upon the identity they wish to craft for themselves. Even with this proviso some contend such assessment is impossible and perhaps even undesirable given the dissociation it can involve from groups central to one's identity (MacIntyre 1981; Taylor 1989). What dissociation calls for is not a question I am prepared to resolve. (Is it sufficient that one refuse to accept the evil activities of one's group, or must one actively and publicly renounce those evils? It seems to me that the latter is the case.) For the purpose of this discussion, let us agree that persons can dissociate (to the required minimum) from the community in which some attitudinal and dispositional aspects of their identity are founded.

When all is said and done, however, I suspect taint is a more complicated matter, and certainly a more comprehensive phenomenon, than an analysis of vicarious liability premised on collective guilt suggests.

---

[8] Jaspers notes the difference: "The question of original sin must not become a way to dodge German guilt" (1947, 100).

At the same time, I worry about the broad inclusiveness, the sweeping universal reach, conveyed by the idea of metaphysical taint. Let us put these concerns on hold for the moment and turn our attention to the second component of taint, the phenomenon of shame.

6. Shame

The *Oxford English Dictionary* (2nd ed., 1988) defines shame as "the painful emotion arising from the consciousness of something dishonouring, ridiculous, or indecorous in one's own conduct or circumstances (or in those of others whose honour or disgrace one regards as one's own), or of being in a situation which offends one's sense of modesty or decency." Since the 1960s, shame has fallen into disfavor, regarded as a constraint on self-esteem. Shame has been denounced as an unhealthy vestige of an uptight social psychology in which the pressure to conform and acquiesce to authority infects—sullies, contaminates, taints—the way people ought to feel about themselves. Dr. Joyce Brothers of pop-psychology fame attempts to sum up the problem with shame. She writes:

> While guilt is the feeling that you have done something wrong, shame is the feeling that there's something wrong *about* you. Nothing could be more all-encompassing. When we've had too much exposure to shame, our joy in life is severely diminished. . . . Carrying around the "baggage" of shame, inflicted in childhood, people could only feel bad about themselves. . . . To feel good, one had to forget the nagging voice of conformity, set one's own standards of right and wrong and send shame, with all its toxicity, packing. (Brothers 2005, 5)

Dr. Brothers concedes that "bad shame," shame that "attacks you as a person," that "gets passed along to your children," and "that humiliates just for the sake of humiliation . . . is shame we can do without" (5). But she argues that to divest ourselves of shame *simpliciter* is to deprive ourselves of its positive characteristics. She advises us to accept "good shame" of the sort that is deserved and that "is instructive." Among the beneficial properties of shame in its positive guise are that it "gives you new insight about yourself," "makes you more sensitive to others," and "makes you want to elevate the culture around you"(5).

Is moral taint a fanciful synonym for shame of either the good or the bad variety? The analogy is inexact, as there need not be a phenomenological experience of taint that mimics that of either good or bad shame. Clearly taint need not generate guilt—the feeling that one has done something wrong—and taint is not always a vestige of the feeling that one is flawed is some way. Taint does not appear diminished if the requisite self-reflexive attitude of shame (or guilt) is absent. But even if the phenomenological experience of shame is absent, taint might be characterized counterfactually. A person who confronts her tainted character recognizes something is wrong with her and feels shame. More precisely, the tainted person would feel shame if she felt as she ought to feel.

My belief is that taint can share some of the characteristics of "bad" shame. One such characteristic is that taint can attach to someone whether or not the person has done something wrong or blameworthy, something for which it seems taint is deserved. In this respect moral taint is not just a byproduct of straightforward contributory or vicarious liability. Taint might even be, as with bad shame, transitive—it "gets passed along" and censures us and our descendants as persons. (This is one of the odder features of moral taint, as we shall see.) As with good shame, taint can be put to positive effect when recognition of it motivates a person to become more sensitive to others and (it is hoped) to take steps to repair the group, or group culture (if not wrongs done by the culture), in which one is steeped.

Shame, as with pride, is an emotion to which we are susceptible on the basis of our relations with others. As with pride, an index of shame is the degree of closeness or solidarity marking the relationship. Clearly we tend to take vicarious pride in the good deeds and noble accomplishments of those with whom we feel kinship. Consider the depth of pride we take in the accomplishments of our children, our spouses, and our parents, or in the pride we feel when the "home team" wins the championship or "brings home the gold." We feel pride or a similar positive affect in the face of these accomplishments because we believe they are in some way our own. They reflect who we are, and how we see ourselves. Similarly, we tend to feel shame when our loved ones or those with whom we identify behave in ways that reflect badly on their character and, by extension, reflect badly on ourselves.

This would explain why, perhaps more than guilt, David Kaczynski felt shame pressing upon him—"bad" shame of the sort that makes you feel awful about what kind of person you are, and "good" shame of the sort that calls upon you to define your moral identity through action. Perhaps David Kaczynski experienced shame of the sort we suspect one ought to feel given the behavior of those with whom one is connected by birth, by shared history, by friendship, and by pride. If so, the shame David Kaczynski felt was due to more than the fact that he believed himself guilty of abetting (albeit unwittingly) his brother's heinous activities. David's shame rests in the intimate connection he shares with his brother, a connection wrought of a common history, parentage, and culture.

Shame need not be the product of so emotionally devastating a situation as this. Suppose you discovered that your daughter was plagiarizing her term papers, or that your brother was a serial philanderer. If you had previously experienced pride in the laudable achievements of these persons would you not feel shame in the face of their dishonorable behavior—shame because this is not the kind of person *you* would want to be and not the kind of character you believe your nearest and dearest should have? One who takes pride but refuses to accept shame is disingenuous or hypocritical. Perhaps good shame, shame of the sort that supplies fresh insight into oneself and into the salient groups of which one is a member, is the cousin of good pride, as the error of "self-abasing lamentation in confessions of guilt" is the cousin of the error of "defiantly self-isolating pride" (Jaspers 1947, 108). (It is also interesting to consider whether there can be vicarious laudability for good actions. Can a person be vicariously praiseworthy?)

7. The Oddity of Moral Taint

The discussion thus far has assumed that taint can only be acquired in one of two ways: either by active participation or collusion on one's part or vicariously, by solidarity and collective-liability arrangements. But there is a third possible source of moral taint. Moral taint might attach to people in light of the connections they share with other persons even where these connections are not deliberately forged. Earlier I stated that there may be cases of taint forged by relations that are remote and perhaps even unrecognized. This is odd, since it suggests that we might acquire taint and liability for taint in some way that is utterly involuntary. It is plausible that moral taint can attach to individuals in virtue of voluntary shared membership in collectives for whom group liability is an accepted feature of membership. Collectives of this sort include teams or collaborative enterprises—sales teams, athletic teams, manufacturing teams, hospital emergency-room teams, military units, joint artistic and scholarly efforts, and so forth. But the children and the descendants of Germans who complied with the Nazi regime, like the descendants of segregationists and slave owners and the current generation of white South Africans (and perhaps all white Americans who have benefited from a legacy of systemic discrimination), were part of no collaborative team. Nonetheless, it may be argued that these persons are morally compromised by their heritage. If there is reason to believe they are tainted, the stain they bear is the legacy of their patrimony or matrimony, or of their citizenship. What residue of liability can persist over generations or be transitive—not just associative—in quality? Is "tainted" the right way to characterize the moral status of these individuals?

We may be inclined to dismiss moral taint in such cases because it would be inescapable. How far removed from shameful behavior or how closely implicated in shameful behavior must a person be in order to be within taint's reach? For instance, can we plausibly regard as tainted the moral personality of American citizens (or some subset of American citizens) in light of the political activities of the U.S. government in, say, southeast Asia or in parts of the Middle East? Can we regard American citizens as morally tainted in light of the failure of the U.S. government—a representative democracy, after all, one that claims to speak for the people in its actions—to intervene in genocide abroad, as in Rwanda

in 1994 or more recently in Darfur in the Sudan? At the very least our
government is to be faulted for its failure to display a strong negative
affect in reaction to the genocide, a step that would cost very little and
could nevertheless have substantial positive effect. Perhaps all adult
citizens of the United States are liable for results of actions taken by
their state. Jaspers alleges that political taint describes just such a burden,
one borne by all members of a nation, and one that yields a kind of
collective moral guilt. An alternative is to follow Appiah and deny taint as
a form of liability or a source of shame. Perhaps as citizens it is merely our
reputation that is affected by the actions of our nation.

I do not recommend either alternative. Certainly our reputation is
compromised by the actions of those with whom we associate, but it
seems to me that something greater than this is at stake. I concede that
straightforward cases of liability and of deserved shame become problematic cases of moral taint when liability and shame are acquired not by
deliberate action but by circumstantial luck. In such cases, moral taint is
of an entirely accidental and involuntary quality. Bad luck, it seems,
ought not to lead to deserved shame. But I think deserved moral taint,
and with it genuine liability and the justified expectation of a level of
shame, can be inherited, like a flawed gene. Familial luck connected
David Kaczynski to his brother Ted, and it seems David has some reason
to feel shame. All residents of Jasper, Texas, share the unfortunate
circumstance of being indelibly linked in the public mind with the brutal
murder of James Byrd by white supremacists on June 7, 1998. All
residents of Laramie, Wyoming, and of Casper, Wyoming, are connected
by geographic circumstance with the vicious homophobic murder of
Matthew Shepard in October 1998. All adult citizens of the United States
are politically connected with the actions (or culpable omissions) of the
U.S. government in, say, Iraq or in Rwanda or in Darfur. Perhaps one
can even be tainted upon birth, given the facts about one's heredity. If so,
this would explain why some people regard white Americans (perhaps all
of them, or some subset) as morally burdened by the privileged status they
enjoy owing to generations of systemic racial discrimination.

An odd thing about moral taint in such cases is that it demarcates a
sphere of responsibility over which none of the standard criteria for
responsibility need obtain. Most notably, the burden of responsibility
found in cases of inherited taint is not the result of direct and immediate
transgression, wrongdoing, or harboring of evil on the part of the tainted
party. Unlike cases in which strict liability or vicarious liability are
assigned, persons can be tainted for transgressions they could not
reasonably be expected to anticipate, and for reasons that are independent of any act of intentional wrongdoing that can retrospectively be
assigned to them. David Kaczynski feels shame. The residents of towns in
which heinous racist and homophobic violence occurred, shocking the
sensibilities of an entire world, feel shame. These activities happened in

their midst, after all, in places they call home, places where they had established partnerships through neighborliness, education, and employment, faith and civic spirit. The problem is that if these people were never in a position to control the evil behavior that produced the taint in the first place, whatever taint they bear is not due to a deficient level of care or to an unsavory quality of will on their part.

If taint can be acquired in this fashion, then taint is not something for which epistemic foresight is necessarily available. One cannot be excused from taint in the way one can be excused from standard cases of culpability or blame for reasons of innocence or ignorance. One cannot manage for inherited or associational taint as one might for risk. No degree of vigilance can preempt taint that is acquired by circumstantial misfortune. So what, exactly, are people who are tainted by circumstance responsible for? And can blame for wrongdoing be assigned and apportioned in these cases?

8. Responsibility and Authenticity

In the case of David Kaczynski, as in the cases of the descendants of segregationists and slave owners, the children of Nazis and Nazi sympathizers, white South Africans, the residents of Jasper and of Laramie, and so on, we have persons who are morally defiled by circumstantial ill luck. Their moral taint is acquired as the result of connections of blood, of geography, of culture, and, perhaps, of principle. But their taint is deserved, and shame is appropriate, because key aspects of their identity are bound up with the lives of particular other beings, and as a result of the wrongdoing of those persons with whom their identity is bound, their moral personalities are tarnished and compromised. The extent to which each of these persons remains tainted and their moral record darkened is a function of the person's refusal to repudiate the wrong that has been done and to repair the circumstances within the community or family or relevant group that might have sustained the wrong.

Inherited taint of the sort we are considering imposes a burden of responsibility in at least one of the four standard senses of responsibility. The first sense of responsibility is that of credit for wrongdoing. Clearly the child of Nazis, the descendants of wealthy slave owners, and the average person in the United States cannot be credited in the manner of attribution for bringing about, initially at any rate, the morally problematic states of affair that continue to afflict us today. David Kaczynski can only be indirectly credited for helping his brother, since he was ignorant of the manner in which Ted would use the financial support he provided; David had no reason to suspect his brother of anything untoward.

The second sense of responsibility addresses duty. In none of these cases did the parties have clear duties or obligations to the victims of the wrong that they failed to uphold. Nor, as a third sense of responsibility claims, is it plain that the parties are rightly subject to attitudes and practices on the part of others in reaction to the quality of will they exhibit unless the quality of their will reflects the unsavory wills of their ancestors, relatives, neighbors, or government. Each party may be humane and motivated to do the right thing for the right reasons. The remaining possibility is that these persons are responsible in the sense that they ought to account for their behavior, where doing so involves giving some statement of their beliefs or intentions. In cases of inherited taint, however, what behavior is there to account for?

What there is to account for as well as to attribute to the agent, and to praise or blame her for, is (to borrow from Jaspers and May) *authenticity with respect to one's self-conception*. What does this mean? Here is the idea. Authenticity consists in truthfulness toward oneself and about oneself in word and in deed. One who is authentic "meets head on his or her faults, or those of one's fellow community members, and regards oneself as at least partially responsible for them" (May 1991, 243). By contrast, one is inauthentic with respect to one's self-conception when one deceives oneself about one's position in the world and about one's ability to transform or adjust or take a stance with respect to that position. Similarly, one is inauthentic when one refuses to take a stance about one's position in the world in circumstances that pressure one to do so. Inauthenticity marks a kind of dishonesty with respect to one's self-conception. But how does the concept of authenticity help clarify the notion of a legacy of liability for harm wrought by inherited moral taint?

9. Atonement and Blame

Moral taint implies a proper susceptibility to shame when the stance of the individual confronted with a legacy of wrongdoing and harm is inauthentic. One need not be morally responsible in the sense of bearing contributory liability (or even accepted vicarious liability) for the wrong. Nonetheless, one is liable, and directly so, for how one answers—addresses—the wrongdoing in question. One is liable because of the nature of the association and the degree of solidarity one shares with the wrongdoer, both of which figure in one's authentic self-conception. One is directly liable provided that the ability to restore the moral order disturbed by the wrong is within one's reach. The person who does not attempt to erase the residue imprinted upon his moral personality or moral record where this is possible simply because he is indisposed to do so ought to feel shame and, perhaps, ought to be shamed. The person who does attempt to erase the residue imprinted upon his moral personality or moral record by his relations with others does so by attempting gestures or actions of atonement.

Repairing taint may mirror the process of repairing sin. Just as sin signals a fissure in one's relationship with God, moral taint signals distance from what is right and proper in human relations. Just as a person's relationship to God is not repaired immediately upon cessation of sin, taint is not erased with mere acknowledgment, repentance, and contrition.[9] The process of erasing taint, like that of erasing sin, calls for atonement—a willed, purposeful effort to travel the distance between the wrong committed and the parties, both perpetrator and victim, who have been affected, morally diminished, by it.

Dr. Yael Danieli, a psychologist renowned for her study of trauma in survivors of the Holocaust and, more recently, for her work with groups forging a path of reconciliation, notes that the remedy for taint is complex, multilayered, and long term—what she describes as a process rather than a fact or an event. At a minimum this process calls for acknowledgment of the wrong and, if relevant, of the "intergenerational transmission of trauma" wrought by the wrong (Danieli 1998). In most cases this involves turning a critical lens upon oneself, one's culture, and one's intimate associations. Frequently the process is psychically painful.[10] But it is necessary: There is a redemptive quality in confronting and acknowledging moral taint. In cases where taint is brought about by direct wrongdoing or by a defect of moral character, atonement restores one's moral worth.

The restoration is of something different from goodness, as it seems plausible that a morally tainted person can be good. David Kaczynski is good—indeed, it is his goodness that compels him to seek atonement. In cases such as Kaczynski's, where taint is the result of emotional or social connection, atonement affirms and settles one's identity as a morally just person. One's moral integrity or worth is not so much restored as it is brought to light.

Note that atonement is not, first and foremost, a matter of the restoration of one's reputation or appearance to others, although an improved reputation may be an unintended and secondary result of atonement. Moral taint does not only emerge where the opinion of others matters. It is not a phenomenon that grows only in the face of damage to

[9] I am indebted here to Eleonore Stump's exploration of the phenomena of moral taint and sin.
[10] At any rate, this has been the reported experience of German citizens in the postwar era and of white South Africans who took an active part in the process of reconciliation following the dissolution of apartheid. See the archived reports of South Africa's Truth and Reconciliation Commission, as well as The Institute for Justice and Reconciliation at http://www.ijr.org.za/about.html. The intensity of effort as it plays out in a case of psycho-physical taint illuminates the difficulty. An addict in the process of recovering his identity as a healthy, substance-free person (particularly in the initial stages of recovery) must turn a critical lens upon himself and upon the elements of his environment (this includes intimate associations) that sustain his addiction. What the lens reveals is often shameful and unpleasant to behold.

one's moral reputation. One who is tainted need not suffer any deprecia-
tion of her moral reputation if the taint goes unnoticed and no one is the
wiser. The question of moral taint is one we put to ourselves, even if
others never do so and even though it can be put to us by others.[11]

So here are my suggestions. First, we should stipulate that taint of a
sort associated with shame and liability calls for acknowledgment of
wrong on the part of the tainted party. Second, the tainted party must
have a genuine emotional connection with the perpetrator of the harm (as
with Kaczynski) or with the social-political context that gave birth to the
harm (as with the citizens of Jasper, Texas); the connection must be clear
cut (it cannot be merely tenuous); and the tainted party must be in a
position to know of this connection. Third, the charge of taint must stem
from an actual moral failing or injustice. Fourth, as an index of solidarity
we look for evidence of vicarious shame (or pride) taken by the tainted
party in the broader practices of the person, group, or community with
whom the party is connected. The experiences of shame (or of pride)
might reflect self-centered attitudes of embarrassment (or of honor) or
"mortification at being associated by others with actions of which one
disapproves and of which one is totally innocent" (Feinberg 1991, 64). We
expect one who perceives his soul as tainted, who notes defects in the
quality of his own personality, to suffer as a result and we look askance at
the person who does not acknowledge his taint, usually by sincerity of
word or by self-reproach. But we do not usually call this person "tainted"
just because of this failure any more than we call a person "tainted" just
because he is vulnerable to psychic suffering or just because he is the
recipient of reprobation, perhaps uncharitably, from others.

There is, however, a lingering worry. Even if the idea of taint is
coherent, acts of atonement seem fitting only where there is blameworthiness. It is plain that an experience of shame does not suffice for
blameworthiness and a need to make atonement, for one might feel shame
inappropriately, having committed no wrong. But is it not equally plain
that circumstantial, inherited taint cannot suffice for blameworthiness?
Does it make sense to blame a person for being tainted in these cases,
especially when taint already involves moral self-assessment?

Some philosophers argue that a person is blameworthy (or praiseworthy) if the person believed she was doing the wrong (or right) thing for
the wrong (or right) reasons (Zimmerman 1997). On this view, a person is
blameworthy if the person believes she has deliberately and intentionally
committed a wrong or contributed to the perpetration of a wrong, or
believes she has cultivated an objectionable disposition, whether or not
she is correct in this belief. The person is blameworthy because the person

---

[11] It is in this vein that Jaspers, speaking of political guilt, notes "that victors condemn us
is a political fact which has the greatest consequences for our life, but it does not help us in
the decisive point, in our inner regeneration" (1947, 28).

has displayed ill will and is positioned to account for her behavior. One who is innocently ignorant of the quality of her will or of what is perceived as a fault of character is not blameworthy.

Such accounts are controversial. In general, our judgment that people are praiseworthy or blameworthy rests on the quality of will we in fairness believe they exhibit in acting. We regard a person as praiseworthy or blameworthy if the person did the right or wrong thing for the right or wrong reasons, whether or not she regarded herself as doing right or wrong. Indeed, we often do not blame people for doing the right thing despite their sincere belief that they are doing wrong: Consider a case beloved of philosophers, that of Huck Finn, who gives up hope of being a morally upright person and allows his love of Jim, and his recognition of Jim's humanity, to steer him away from doing what he believes is the morally "proper" course of restoring Miss Watson's property to her. Huck was not morally tainted and was not blameworthy despite his belief that he was a bad person who did the wrong thing for the wrong reasons.

In any case it is doubtful that an analysis of blame in terms of the subjective, first-person beliefs of the actor alone or in terms of an objective, third-person assessment of the quality of the actor's will alone can explain the connection between blameworthiness and taint, especially taint of an inherited variety. Taint seems to elude this neat conceptual arrangement. Consider again the case of children whose parents or grandparents or great-grandparents were Nazi sympathizers, or were residents of eighteenth- and nineteenth-century America whose quality of life was dependent on a slave- and plantation-based economy. Assume the descendants are tainted in light of the harms perpetrated by their (perhaps distant) relatives. Note that their primary relation is to the harmers rather than to the harm done. The question of whether a relation to the harm itself can be wrought from this primary relation to persons or to a culture is precisely what is at issue. Typically, blame is a response to one's relation to an action, such as a harm, that has been committed.

None of the remote descendants directly contributed to the perpetration of the horrors of slavery or of the Holocaust, just as did very few of the children of slave owners and Nazis. Few believe they have played a role in nurturing the residue of anti-Semitism and racial discrimination set in motion by their ancestors. However, at some point in their lives, assuming they have a capacity for empathic response, the adult descendants become capable of confronting and responding to their ancestral legacy and to the disturbing imprint—what might be called the "intergenerational trauma"—it has left upon their culture and upon their identity as morally sound persons. After David Kaczynski turned in—betrayed—his older brother (and only sibling) to the FBI (Ted in fact denounced him as "Judas"), he took time off from his job "to process his feelings about what had happened," a task he says will continue throughout his life. At the same time, he corresponded with family members of the Unabomber's victims: "I thought about what the victims may have suffered, and it sunk into me. It felt so sad and so tragic that I wanted to reach out to them in some way. I wanted to express sorrow for what had happened" (Hubert 1997). This sounds like atonement to me.

The task of these adults is that of becoming authentic. The task of becoming authentic lends expression to three ways in which those who are tainted by inherited or circumstantial guilt are responsible. First, it is appropriate that others, particularly those who inherited the burden of their victimized ancestors, expect the adult descendants and relatives to acknowledge and to supply an account of their beliefs about the wrong-doing of their ancestors. At the least, the adults can be held to talk about, and so put to rest, the wounds produced by previous generations.[12] Second, the adults have an obligation to restore, to the degree they are able, the self-worth of those who suffered at the hands of their parents and grandparents and great-grandparents or at the hands of members of their community. Depending on the nature of the harm wrought, there may be an obligation to restore at least a modicum of the psychic security and socioeconomic worth of the harmed parties. Third, if they fail to make a good-faith effort to acknowledge the wrong and make redress, they can rightly be subject to attitudes and practices on the part of others in reaction to the quality of will they exhibit. Contra Jaspers, the one accused of moral taint is not just charged "from within, by his own soul" but can also be charged "from without, by the world" (Jaspers 1947, 39), by members of the injured group. A person is blameworthy when the person deliberately or out of indifference or unwarranted ignorance refuses to acknowledge, confront, and take steps to expunge the legacy of ill will he has inherited. In sum, persons can be held responsible in three ways: they have obligations; they ought to account for their behavior; and they are properly vulnerable to reactive attitudes. I do not know if a good-faith effort to meet these responsibilities is adequate for atonement. But I am not sure what more we can reasonably expect.

10. Conclusion

Three things are true of cases where taint exists. First, the tainted parties are liable, either directly or vicariously, for the occurrence in question or for their response to it. Second, the tainted parties have done something or have refused to take a stand in light of which they ought to feel shame. The morally tainted persons may exhibit a deficient level of care for considerations of moral consequence that bear on their relations with

---

[12] Here I borrow from Holocaust survivor Bruno Bettelheim, who said: "What cannot be talked about can also not be put to rest, and if it is not, the wounds continue to fester from generation to generation" (1985, 162).

others. Third, the wrongful state of affairs is one for which atonement of some variety is appropriate. Taint produces a moral burden to make restitution to others and to authenticate one's identity as a moral agent.

Moral taint may become a defect of character when a person responds inappropriately to deserved shame or to guilt. This is what makes moral taint a variety of standard cases of liability. It is appropriate to judge a person to be morally responsible only if we can credit the person with an appreciation of the moral import of his behavior and this appreciation exerts motivational force upon the person. The adult descendants of slave owners, for example, can appreciate the evils of slavery and thus can take steps to dissociate themselves from the evil, even though there was no possibility of doing so at the time the evil was occurring.

Moral taint is especially perplexing when it is the vestige of circumstance, such as a legacy that leaves its beneficiary morally disfigured and expected to atone for the act that resulted in this disfigurement. While moral guilt entails the ability to change oneself or one's situation, moral taint can obtain even at those times when there is nothing one could have done, even with the assistance of others, to obviate the harm and even if the involvement of specific members of the group was not essential to producing the harm. As with certain viruses, moral taint can infect, though the tainted party may have no knowledge of its presence and have played no role in its cultivation.

If we are to believe Jaspers and May, taint is a product of (among other things) metaphysical guilt, and one can escape metaphysical guilt only if one endeavors to improve one's moral fiber on every occasion where the opportunity arises (May 1991, 243). But this is casting too wide a net. Unless we want to charge that taint rests on solidarity of a broader, more general sort—say, on solidarity with the collective that is the human race out of which certain duties to all of humanity emerge—taint must encompass a narrower, more manageable range of cases. In this manner, the concept of taint can be of philosophical use in illuminating perplexing cases of inherited liability and shame.

While first-person attitudes (especially such self-censorious attitudes as shame, guilt, and mortification) might fail to accompany an awareness of one's taint, a good-faith willingness to confront the taint is called for. Beliefs about ancestral wrongdoing and attitudes toward this wrongdoing supplemented by self-reflexive attitudes of shame or embarrassment and injured pride implicate the adult descendant in the wrongdoing and set the stage for atonement and the restoration of moral worth. Moral taint and its antidote, moral atonement, are outgrowths of a person's response to moral, metaphysical, or political guilt. Direct blame for the original wrong may seem beside the point here. But liability obtains where these persons are invited to share certain attitudes in common with the perpetrators of evil or to reaffirm their approval of the perpetrators. They are liable for how they respond to the invitation.

References

Appiah, Anthony. 1987. "Racism and Moral Pollution." *Philosophical Forum* 18:185–202.

Arpaly, Nomy. 2002. *Unprincipled Virtue: An Inquiry into Moral Agency.* New York: Oxford University Press.

Bettelheim, Bruno. 1985. Afterword to *I Didn't Say Goodbye: Interviews with Children of the Holocaust*, edited by Claudine Vegh and translated by R. Schwartz. New York: E. P. Dutton.

Brothers, Joyce. 2005. "Shame May Not Be So Bad After All." *Parade Magazine*, 27 February:4–6.

Danieli, Yael. 1998. *Workshop Transcripts, Reparation and Rehabilitation Committee,* South Africa's Truth and Reconciliation Commission. Johannesburg, 18 February. At http://www.doj.gov.za/trc/ (accessed on 23 March 2005).

Feinberg, Joel. 1991. "Collective Responsibility (A Defense)." In *Collective Responsibility: Five Decades of Debate in Theoretical and Applied Ethics*, edited by Larry May and Stacey Hoffman, 53–76. Savage, Md.: Rowman and Littlefield. Previously published in Joel Feinberg, *Doing and Deserving.* Princeton: Princeton University Press, 1970.

Frankfurt, Harry G. 1999. "On the Necessity of Ideals." In *Necessity, Volition, and Love*, 108–16. Cambridge: Cambridge University Press.

Holliday, Jana. 2001. "Either It's Moral or 'Taint: An Exploration and Application of Moral Taint." Ohio Institute for Applied and Professional Ethics. At http://freud.citl.ohiou.edu/ethics/proceedings/holliday.html (accessed on 6 April 2004).

Hubert, Cynthia. 1997. "Role in capture haunts Kaczynski's brother." *Sacramento Bee* (19 January). At http://www.unabombertrial.com/archive/1997/011997-2.html (accessed on 25 March 2005).

Jaspers, Karl. 1947. *The Question of German Guilt*, translated by E. B. Ashton. New York: Capricorn Books.

Lewis, H. D. 1991. "Collective Responsibility (A Critique)." In May and Hoffman 1991, 17–33. Previously published in *Philosophy: The Journal of the Royal Institute of Philosophy* 24, no. 83 (1948).

May, Larry. 1991. "Metaphysical Guilt and Moral Taint." In May and Hoffman 1991, 239–54.

May, Larry, and Stacey Hoffman, editors. 1991. *Collective Responsibility: Five Decades of Debate in Theoretical and Applied Ethics.* Savage, Md.: Rowman and Littlefield.

MacIntyre, Alisdair. 1981. *After Virtue: A Study in Moral Theory.* London: Duckworth.

Oshana, Marina. 1997. "Ascriptions of Responsibility." *American Philosophical Quarterly* 34, no.1 (January): 71–83.

Schuler, George, and William Hurst, Estes Reynolds, and James Christian, revised by P. T. Tybor. 1984. "Food Spoilage and You."

University of Georgia College of Agricultural and Environmental Sciences, Cooperative Extension Service, Extension Bulletin 906.

Stump, Eleonore. 2003. The Gifford Lectures, University of Aberdeen, Scotland. Forthcoming as *Wandering in Darkness: Narrative and the Problem of Suffering*. Oxford University Press.

———. 2004. "Personal Relations and Moral Residue." In *History of the Human Sciences,* issue entitled *Theorizing from the Holocaust: What Is to Be Learned?"* edited by Mark S. Peacock and Paul A. Roth, 17, no. 3 (August): 33–57.

Taylor, Charles. 1989. *Sources of the Self: The Making of Modern Identity*. Cambridge: Cambridge University Press.

Zimmerman, Michael J. 1997. "A Plea for Accuses." *American Philosophical Quarterly* 34:229–43.

———. 2005. "Deontic Luck." Presented at the Conference on Action and Agency, University of Florida, 18 February.

6

COLLECTIVE ACTION AND THE PECULIAR EVIL OF GENOCIDE

BILL WRINGE

1. Introduction

It is widely believed that there are significant moral differences between mass murder, on the one hand, and genocidal killing, on the other. While both are horrifying, the latter evokes the peculiar revulsion that has resulted in genocidal acts being given a unique moral and legal status as "crimes against humanity." Although very few people would be willing to question that special status, it is not immediately obvious how it is to be explained. Putative explanations that look to the characters of the agents of genocide, to their intentions in committing genocide, or to the scope of the crime all seem to miss the mark.

This might lead one to question the intuition that genocidal killing does indeed have a peculiar moral status. One way of doing so would be to attempt to explain it away. In doing so, one might perhaps appeal to the special salience of morally significant events in relatively recent history, or to the pragmatic, consequentialist benefits of according genocidal crimes a peculiar status. However, whatever their merits, these ways of explaining away the intuition seem unable to do justice either to its force or to its structure.

In this essay I argue that we can explain at least some of our intuitions about the peculiar evil of genocide by paying particular attention to the ways in which genocidal killing involves collective action. It does so in a way that distinguishes genocides from other sorts of mass murder. The explanation I have in mind can be described as a "vindicatory explanation": it is supposed to explain the intuition in a way that enables us to continue to endorse it in a relatively straightforward manner, and not merely as an intuition that we should be glad we have, regardless of its truth, on (for example) indirect utilitarian grounds.

More specifically, I shall be claiming that this intuition represents a rational response to the callous attitudes expressed in the collective willing that is typically to be found in cases of genocidal killing, and in particular to the fact that the collective willing involves a deliberate, explicit and conscious lack of respect for the humanity of its victims. In arguing in this way, I shall be engaging at two points with important recent work by Claudia Card (2001, 2003).

Card has argued that accounts of evil which focus on the qualities of will that are embodied in evil action—as mine in effect does—are inadequate in so far as they lead us to neglect the significance of the suffering of victims of evil (Card 2001, esp. chaps. 1 and 4). Card has also proposed her own account of the peculiar evil of genocide. Central to her account is the idea that genocidal killing inflicts a particular kind of harm on victims, especially on survivors, which she refers to as "social death" (Card 2003).

My disagreements with Card focus on two main points. First, while I agree with her that an adequate analysis of evil needs to make appropriate reference to the suffering of victims of evil, I do not agree that any account of evil which locates evil in qualities of will need neglect such suffering. More narrowly, while I agree that some possible accounts of evil that locate evil in collective willing might be problematic in precisely this way (and I discuss one such account), I shall argue that my account accommodates—as Card says any adequate account should accommodate, and as her account aims to—reference to both the intentions of perpetrators and the suffering of victims.

Secondly, while I take the notion of social death to be an important analytical tool in understanding the evil of genocide, and I draw on it at a key stage of my argument for my own view, I do not think that the genuine dreadfulness of the harm that individuals who suffer social death undergo is sufficient to account for our intuitions about the peculiar status of genocide. Card's account of social death seems to leave open the possibility that in at least two sorts of case individuals might suffer social death without being the victims of genocide. These are cases in which the harm of social death is inflicted in ways that do not involve the destruction of a society or a way of life. While I take it that such cases would involve profound harm to individuals, and that the appropriate response to victims of such harms might have much in common with appropriate responses to victims of genocide, I shall argue that our response to the situations that bring them about is not, and should not be, identical to that evoked by genocidal killing.

2. A Puzzling, but Powerful, Intuition

I have alluded several times to the existence of an intuition to the effect that genocidal killing has a peculiar moral status. It is now time to say something more about its content. The intuition I am discussing is that the fact that a class of killings can be correctly characterised as "genocidal killings" makes them significantly worse, from a moral point of view, than a similar quantity of killings that are non-genocidal but in other respects similar.

A few clarificatory remarks are in order here. I shall take it for granted, for present purposes, that the intuition about the special moral status of genocide that I refer to does exist and is fairly widely shared (though I leave open the question of exactly how widely shared it is). I take the existence of a special legal category of crimes against humanity to provide evidence, but not indefeasible evidence, for this claim. (To be clear: I don't take this as evidence that the intuition is true, only that it is widely shared. But, to forestall misunderstanding, I should probably state explicitly at this point that I don't have any doubt that it *is* true.)

One could take the legal recognition of this category of crime to be capable of explanation in ways that do not presuppose moral beliefs of any sort. Such modes of explanation are characteristic, for example, of doctrines that go by the name of "realism" in the field of international relations. However, although realist views of this sort might be capable of explaining how crimes against humanity have attained the status that they have within international law, it is much harder for them to explain why the recognition of this category of crime strikes so many people as such a significant moral achievement.

I shall also take it for granted that it is appropriate to look for an explanation of this intuition that vindicates it. This is not because I think that the intuition is one that is beyond all possibility of doubt: there could be circumstances in which one might have good epistemic grounds for doubting it (although I do not think that those possible circumstances are at all close to actual circumstances). Nor do I think that our entitlement to be confident in the truth of the intuition depends on our being able to provide a vindicatory explanation of it.[1] Rather, I take it that the intuition is one that has (at least) a prima facie entitlement to be taken at face value, and that the task of explaining why it is true is a legitimate, and significant, philosophical task.

I shall be arguing that the peculiar evil of genocide is best explained by focusing on the idea that genocidal killings involve collective action, and then appealing to the nature of that collective action to explain the sort of evil involved. However, before going any further, it may be worth making a brief observation about the generality and modal status of the claim that I am making about the connection between genocide and collective action. I shall not be claiming that every conceivable instance of genocide involves collective action. We might perhaps be able to imagine possible instances of genocidal killing that do not. The sorts of case I have in mind here are cases that involve small numbers of very destructive agents. For

---

[1] I use the phrase "vindicatory explanation" here in a way slightly different from that pioneered by David Wiggins (Wiggins 1987). For Wiggins, a vindicatory explanation shows that "there is simply nothing else to think" about a certain subject matter. On my usage a vindicatory explanation explains a belief while at the same time showing that we are justified in holding it, but does not necessarily show that "there is nothing else to think."

example, someone might dream up an example of a single individual armed with a nuclear weapon that he or she manages to fire at an island inhabited entirely by the members of a single ethnic or national group.

Fictional examples of this sort should not detain us for very long.[2] When described in any detail, putative examples like this tend to fall into one of two categories: cases where collective action does turn out to be involved after all, and cases that are so far removed from the circumstances of the real world that there seems little reason to give much weight to any moral intuitions they might invoke. Consider the case of the individual with the nuclear weapon in more detail. Such weapons typically require a great deal in the way of maintenance, hardware support and software for guidance and targeting. Once we say something about these sorts of features of the situation it becomes much harder to deny that the firing of the weapon is likely to involve collective action. But if we set aside these features of the situation we find ourselves in the realm of morally irrelevant (and in this case morally offensive) science fiction.[3]

3. Is the Intuition to Be Explained?

At this point, it may be worth trying to pre-empt a significant sceptical response to what I shall be saying. This is to suggest, without denying either the truth or the force of the intuition in question here, that there is no explanation of it to be had. I shall introduce the line of thought I have in mind here in a slightly oblique manner.

It is sometimes suggested that there is something wrong about any attempt to explain the Holocaust. In doing so, it is said, one undermines its status as a uniquely evil event. Whether or not this line of thought is correct, it suggests something that one might take to be at odds with any attempt to give an explanation of what is peculiarly evil about genocide per se. For one might think that although every act of genocide is peculiarly evil, each instance of genocide is evil in its own particular way. In order to understand this evil we need to confront the particular details of particular instances of genocidal killing. We cannot do so by subsuming genocide under a general category and trying to explain what it is that makes events which fall into that category peculiarly evil.[4]

The only response to this line of thought that is likely to carry any weight is to provide a convincing general account of the peculiar evil of

---

[2] It bears emphasis that the objection is not to fictional examples *as such* but to that peculiar fictional genre, the *philosophical example*—typically, highly abstract and presented so briefly as to discourage reflection on the question of whether the examples could be filled out in a plausible and consistent manner without undermining the point that they have been employed to make.

[3] Some people might hold that it is a sign of a certain moral shallowness (perhaps characteristic of some forms of analytic moral philosophy) even to consider such cases. I sympathise with the charge, though I do not entirely endorse it.

[4] For discussion of various generalizing accounts of the Holocaust see Roth 2004.

genocide—as I shall be trying to do. Still, it may be worth speaking to the unease that such an attempt may arouse by pointing out that there is no reason why one should not believe both that there is something distinctively evil about genocidal killing per se and that particular instances of genocide may themselves be peculiarly evil in further, more distinctive ways. Someone who believes this may also believe that these further, more particular evils can only be understood—if they can be understood at all—by confronting the concrete detail of particular cases.

4. Genocide and Collective Action

We are now in a position to consider in more detail the claim that genocidal killings involve a form of action that is distinctively collective. In talking of a form of action's being "distinctively collective," I mean to draw attention to something over and above the number of agents who are involved in it. So the claim that genocidal killing involves distinctively collective action is not simply equivalent to the fact that genocidal killing typically involves a large number of perpetrators, although that fact is, of course, relevant to my discussion.

I shall argue that the perpetrators of genocide act collectively (or act together—I shall use both phrases) in a sense in which organized groups and, possibly, less formally co-ordinated groups such as crowds can act together, but in which a set of randomly selected individuals whose actions do not impinge on one another cannot be said to act together. This sort of collective action has been illuminatingly discussed by a number of contemporary philosophers, including Margaret Gilbert (1989, 2000), Peter French (1984) and Christopher Kutz (2000a and 2000b). It is a sense in which two individuals can take a walk together; a group of friends can plan and undertake an outing; a corporation can make a third of its employees redundant; and so on. These are mundane examples, and I choose them for the sake of emphasizing that the sort of phenomenon that I have in mind is not meant to be something especially mysterious, even though, as I shall argue, its presence in the context I am discussing is not negligible either.

Authors who have discussed collective action have differed on a number of issues. Among these issues is the question of the sorts of metaphysical implications that our talk of collective action might have. For Gilbert and French it commits us to taking seriously the existence of collective subjects or collective agents. For others it does not. On this second sort of approach, talk about collective agency should be understood as being talk about individuals acting collectively, not as talk about the actions of collectives.

I shall be relying on an account of collective action of the second sort—Kutz's recently developed "minimalist" account of collective action (Kutz 2000a and 2000b). On Kutz's account, collective action involves a group of individuals acting with what he calls "participatory intentions." An individual who has participatory intentions does what he or she does while intending his or her action to constitute a contribution to a collective project.

One important corollary of this account is that although an individual who is engaged in collective action needs to have some sort of conception of the joint project that he or she is engaged in, he or she need not be aware of who the other participants in the project are or what their roles might be. For such awareness is not a precondition of forming the relevant sorts of participatory intention. Consequently, the account is well able to accommodate cases of collective action that are not centrally co-ordinated and do not involve a significant degree of mutual self-recognition on the part of participants. (This is not, of course, to deny that central co-ordination can contribute to the success of collective action in many cases.)

As Kutz points out, many criminal conspiracies fit this characterisation: they are set up in such a way as to ensure that, while all the participants have some idea of the nature of the proceedings involved, they are ignorant of the identities or contributions of all the other members of the conspiracy (Kutz 2000a passim). However, it seems plausible that the point has broader application, a matter of some significance for our current purposes. Historically documented instances of genocidal killings typically involve large numbers of perpetrators acting in ways that require the actions of different individuals to interlock in various mutually reinforcing ways. Successful campaigns of genocide require much more than the existence of a large class of individuals who are prepared to kill: killers must have access to weapons and food; victims must find themselves in a situation where possible avenues of escape have been cut off; individuals who might intervene need to be prevented or deterred from doing so. But actions of this sort can occur without requiring detailed central co-ordination. What is required in the absence of such co-ordination is just that individuals understand what they need to do on any given occasion in order to promote a certain overall goal and that they act accordingly.[5] It is difficult to see how this sort of concerted action could be sustained over an extended period, in any realistic situation, without some sort of sense on the part of perpetrators that they are involved in a collective project, and without a desire to play their part in sustaining that collective project. (To this extent, it is perhaps unsurprising that mechanisms of national or tribal self-identification often seem to have played a role in enabling genocidal killing to take place.)

5. Collective Wrongdoing and Collective Evil-doing

If what I have said so far is correct, then actual instances of genocide do seem to fit Kutz's account of collective action. I now need to explain what

[5] The Rwandan genocides of 1994 seem to fit this model well. See Gourevitch 2000.

role this fact might play in providing us with an illuminating and vindicatory explanation of the moral intuition whose existence I drew attention to at the start of the essay. My argument here will run as follows. I shall start by explaining why one might think that an appeal to the idea that genocide involves collective action should be able to explain any aspect of our intuitions about the peculiar evil of genocide. I shall then identify two constraints that explanations of this evil should meet. Finally I turn to the task of finding an account that meets those constraints.

In what follows, I shall use Kutz's views about collective wrongdoing as a useful starting point and object of comparison with the view I shall be developing. My account differs from Kutz's in various ways. The most obvious is that mine is an account with a slightly different target. Kutz is interested in the relatively broad issue of collective wrongdoing. But, as Card and others have argued, wrong and evil are not coextensive categories (Card 2001, Morton 2004). While it is plausible that all evil-doing involves wrongful action, not all wrongful action involves the commission of evils. (One fairly uncontroversial difference between them is that wrongdoing can be trivial, while evil cannot.)

Perhaps unsurprisingly, Kutz's account does not provide us with a satisfactory account of the collective commission of evil. Nevertheless, it does contain one significant insight that will be important for the purposes of this essay. For it suggests an illuminating way of thinking about forms of wrongdoing whose wrongness seems to outrun anything that is easily accounted for by consideration of the wrongness of individual contributions to that wrongdoing. The key thought here is that once we take at all seriously the idea of collective wrongdoing involving distinctively collective action, we can locate some of the wrongness of the action not in the individual contributions to the wrongdoing but in the collective action as a whole.

If this is right, then what we need is an account that incorporates this insight of Kutz's, while being sensitive to the significant conceptual distinction between evil-doing and wrongdoing. Arguing for such an account will require us to say something about what that distinction amounts to; I shall turn to this task in due course. Nevertheless, and anticipating my ensuing discussion somewhat, I am now in a position to say something further about the difference between Kutz's general account of collective wrongdoing and my account of the peculiar evil of genocide. As we shall see in what follows, Kutz focuses his account on formal features of some of the maxims that he takes to be involved in some instances of collective action. By contrast, my account of the peculiar evil of genocide focuses on features of their content. More specifically, it relies on the idea that the collective action involved in genocidal killing involves disregard of and disrespect for the humanity of its victims.

6. Kutz on Collective Wrongdoing

I suggested earlier that Kutz's account of collective wrongdoing incorporated an insight that will play an important role in giving an account of the peculiar evil of genocide. That insight arises out of the idea that what makes some sorts of collective wrongdoing wrong may be features of the collective action that we might be inclined to overlook when focusing on the rightness or wrongness of individual contributions to that collective action.

The move that Kutz makes which is of interest here, and which enables him to go some way towards substantiating this line of thought, is to identify something that we can regard as a maxim of action, and thus something to which we can apply Kantian tests of universalisability and the like, without its being the maxim of any particular individual. We do this by considering the participatory intentions involved in the constitution of the collective action.

As Kutz argues, this suggestion gives an illuminating account of some cases of conspiratorial wrongdoing. Consider someone who is a getaway driver for a gang of armed robbers. Viewing the driver from a narrow perspective, we may find it difficult to explain why we should regard him or her as doing anything wrong. This will certainly be the case on certain sorts of Kantian account. What sorts of maxims might such an individual have that fail of universalisability? If we focus only on the actions involved in driving the getaway vehicle, it is difficult to see how any of them might involve a culpable maxim. But once we see him or her as a willing participant in a project of armed robbery, we can ask whether the maxims implicated in this project are ones that we can universalise. If not, then we can say that we have an instance of collective wrongdoing here. We can then go on to explain the culpability of the driver in terms of his or her willing participation in a collective action that is wrong.

Since Kutz's account deals well with the culpability of conspirators and indirect participants in crimes, one might well think that it is likely to have something to offer in the current context. One aspect of the debate over the responsibility of "ordinary Germans" for the Holocaust has been over whether we can regard those who did not participate directly in the slaughter of Jews as bearing any sort of responsibility for their fate. Kutz's account suggests one way in which they could be.

Nevertheless, Kutz's account is an account of collective wrongdoing, not collective evil. Since, as I have already suggested, not all wrongdoing involves evil, we should expect to find that a plausible account of collective evil-doing, in particular of the kind of evil whose presence in genocidal killing accounts for the intuition that this essay sets out to explain, will be subject to constraints that Kutz's own account does not need to satisfy.

One such constraint is fairly obvious. While it is no objection to an account of collective wrongdoing that it should entail that such wrong-doing might be relatively widespread (particularly in cases where large numbers of people participate in a collective project in ways that are relatively tangential), a view that aims at accounting for collective evil-doing, in particular for some kind of peculiar evil, should not have such consequences.

This claim is not intended as an expression of moral complacency. The point is not that collective evil-doing could not have been widespread or that certain kinds of reflection might not help us to discern it in places where we might not previously have suspected it. It is rather that we are trying to find some sort of explanation for a distinction that we are inclined to make between, on the one hand, the sorts of serious wrongdoing involved in, say, our collective neglect of the environment and, on the other hand, something that is peculiar to genocidal killing. So an account that effaces that distinction is, to that extent, unsuccessful.

A second constraint, which is less obvious but equally important, relates to a point that has been importantly emphasised in recent work by Card (2001). Card convincingly argues that any account of evil needs to do justice to the moral significance of the suffering of the victims of that evil. She goes on to suggest that this rules out certain well-known accounts of wrongdoing, particularly Kantian ones, as plausible accounts of evil. This is because, in focusing on the nature of the will of the perpetrators of evil, they neglect the suffering of victims. While Card says nothing explicit about accounts of evil that locate evil in collective rather than individual willing, the point she makes about the moral significance of the suffering of victims seems applicable here as well, particularly given Kutz's stress on such paradigmatically Kantian considerations as the non-universalisability of maxims involved in collective wrongdoing.

7. Genocidal Killing, Collective Action and Social Death

Despite the ways in which Kutz's account of collective wrongdoing is unsatisfactory as an account of the peculiar evil of genocide, there seems at least some reason to think that a variant account might be more successful. Like Kutz's account, the account I have in mind focuses on features of the participatory intentions that are involved in the sort of collective action I have taken to be present in typical cases of genocidal killing. However, unlike Kutz's account of collective wrongdoing, which focuses on formal features of that collective willing, mine considers its content and the sorts of collective attitudes that we can take to be manifested by it, in particular the fact that this collective willing involves a deliberate, explicit and conscious lack of respect for the humanity of its victims.

For this line of argument to succeed, I need to do two things. The first is to show that the collective willing involved in genocidal killing does indeed have the features that I have attributed to it. The second is to show that the account that I have put forward meets the constraints that I have argued an account of collective evil-doing needs to meet. Once these two tasks have been completed I shall go on to address some objections to my account as a whole.

In arguing that the collective willing involved in genocidal killing does involve deliberate, explicit and conscious lack of respect for the humanity of its victims, I draw heavily on Card's suggestion that the notion of social death plays a central role in understanding the evil of genocide (Card 2003). More precisely, I claim that it is *because* genocidal killing involves participation in a collective project of inflicting social death on individuals that we can see that the collective willing involved in genocidal killing involves a lack of respect for its victims' humanity. Nevertheless, my view differs from Card's in a crucial respect. For Card, it is the nature of the harm that genocidal killing inflicts on its victims that is central to explaining the peculiar status of genocide. On my account, by contrast, what is significant is that the infliction of this harm is—in ways that I raised in section 4—a collective project.

Card introduces the notion of social death in the following terms:

> When a group with its own cultural identity is destroyed, its survivors lose their cultural heritage and may even lose their intergenerational connections . . . in that event they may become "socially dead" . . . no longer able to pass along and build on the traditions, cultural developments and projects of earlier generations. (2003, 73)

As this passage suggests, and as Card emphasises, although social death results from the destruction of communities, it is to be conceived of as a harm inflicted not on communities themselves but on individuals who make up those communities, or who would have done so had those communities survived intact.[6]

I take the notion of social death to be important in this context for the following reason. Earlier I argued that genocidal killing involved collective action. I now want to argue that it involves collective participation in a project of inflicting social death on its victims, and that as such it involves disregard for their humanity.

In order to establish the first of these claims, I need to do more than simply show, as Card aims to, that survivors of genocide typically suffer social death, and that this is inflicted in a culpable manner. These claims could be true if the suffering of cultural death was merely an unintended consequence of such killing. For the claim that I am making to be true,

---

[6] Card's understanding of this notion strikes me as importantly different form that of Orlando Patterson, whom she cites in this context. See, for example, Patterson 1982, 39–45.

the notion of social death needs to figure in the participatory intentions of the individuals involved in genocidal killing.

It is highly plausible that some such notion has played an important role in the planning and execution of many paradigmatic examples of genocidal projects. Such projects have aimed not only at the destruction of a group of individuals falling into a certain class but also at the destruction of the very conditions of the possibility of there being individuals who fall into that class. So, for example, the Nazis' destruction of European Jewry had the goal not simply of exterminating large numbers of Jews but also of wiping the Jewish people from the pages of history (Goldhagen 1996). Something similar seems to be true of the genocidal killing that took place in Rwanda in 1994. Part of the point of this killing was not simply to destroy those Tutsis who were in Rwanda; it was to destroy the possibility of being a Tutsi in Rwanda (Gourevitch 2000). (Card's remark that genocide targets people because of who they are seems apposite in this context; but one might go even further and say that genocide targets not only individuals but also who they are, the very possibility of bearing a particular kind of identity.)

One might wonder, nevertheless, whether what is true of these paradigmatic cases is true in all cases. One particularly problematic case concerns the suffering of Native American peoples in both North and South America at the hands of European invaders. It is plausible to claim that much of the cultural destruction that occurred as Europeans took possession of territory in the Americas occurred as the unforeseen consequence of otherwise culpable actions. For example, it is clear that huge falls in the indigenous populations of Central America during the Spanish conquest were the result of the introduction of microbially transmitted disease, a process of which the invaders had no understanding. It also seems likely that in some cases the destruction of indigenous populations was experienced as a frustrating problem by invaders, especially in so far as it deprived them of a source of easily exploitable slave labour (Stannard 1991).

On Card's account, such facts as these present no obstacle to classifying the actions of early European settlers in America as genocidal. For it is clear that although those individuals had no understanding of the consequences of their actions, they acted culpably in various respects, and in acting culpably they inflicted the intolerable harm of social death on their victims, even if they had no understanding of the nature of the harm they were inflicting or the mechanisms by which that harm was inflicted, and even if, in some cases, this may have run counter to their actual intentions (Card 2003, 73). By contrast, it is less obvious whether on my account these actions did involve the peculiar evil of genocide. For it might be thought that such facts as these show that, although the destruction of indigenous peoples in the Americas may have involved collective projects of various sorts (for a project of invasion must certainly do so), the infliction of social death need not have figured among them.

Nevertheless, I think that matters are not so clear-cut as this suggests. For, as David Stannard documents, and at least some contemporary sources testify, there is a strong case for thinking that the destruction of Central and South American civilisations by European invaders involved not just disease and mistreatment but also the deliberate destruction of the cultural resources on which their way of life depended, all of which was facilitated by a religiously fuelled ideology that regarded the members of those civilizations as less than fully human, and their way of life as being of no value. If this is correct, there is a good case for thinking that the invaders were engaged in a collective project that aimed at the infliction of social death, and that this collective project involved a lack of respect for—underpinned by an ideological lack of belief in—the humanity of its victims.

8. Social Death and Disregard for Humanity

I have now argued that the collective action involved in genocidal killing involves a project of inflicting social, not merely physical, death on its victims. Earlier I claimed that in so far as it does so it involves conscious disrespect of their humanity. This point may seem either otiose or inapposite. One reaction to it might be to say that what is significant about social death in this context is that it is an intolerable harm, suffered by victims. On this view, we need to go no further than pointing to this harm, and the fact that it is intolerable, in explaining the peculiar evil of genocide. A second reaction might be that talking of "respect for humanity" in this context is beside the point. For this phrase, with its Kantian overtones, is apt to suggest that what is involved here is a lack of respect for individuals' rational capacities; and it might well be said that the harms inflicted on individuals who suffer social death go further, and deeper, than their rational nature.

However, while both these reactions are understandable, neither is quite correct. To explain why not, I shall have to say more about what I take the notion of humanity, and respect for it, to entail, and something about the role it plays in my argument. I shall start by saying something about the relationship between rationality and humanity. One point that may be worth making is that even within a Kantian framework there is room for making a distinction between these notions. For Kant, one thing that distinguishes human rationality from rationality as such is that the former is, while the latter need not be, embodied rationality.

Putting the point as abstractly as this leaves indeterminate what might be constitutive of embodied rationality. For Kant, what is significant is that the human will is capable of being determined by what he calls "sensuous impulses"—which he regards both as a limitation on our moral natures and as something that, because it is a precondition of there being any imperatives at all, is a precondition of the possibility of moral imperatives, and hence of our being moral beings at all (Kant 1993, 23–25). But we need not follow Kant at this point. For we might also think that it is characteristic of actual human beings' rational natures, if not of rationality conceived of in the abstract (what we might, perhaps misleadingly, describe as "rationality as such"), that these natures should be embodied in and sustained by traditions, cultural institutions and practices that are sustained across generations.

In talking of such traditions, I am talking less of what one might describe as "high culture" and rather in terms of low-level institutions, such as counting systems, stories told to children, ways of growing and preparing food, moral and social codes expressed in day-to-day behaviour and the like. These are precisely the sorts of things that individuals who suffer from social death, under Card's understanding of it, are deprived of. To that extent, we can talk of the infliction of social death on individuals as involving disregard of and disrespect for their embodied rationality, and hence for their humanity. We can also see one line of thought that might help to account for Card's important, but somewhat under-explained, claim that to suffer social death may be as bad as to suffer physical death (Card 2003, 73).

We are now in a position to see the role that appeal to this notion of humanity as embodied rationality plays in my account of the peculiar evil of genocide. The notion is significant for two reasons. First, it allows us to flesh out the claim that genocide involves evil-doing. As I have already observed, Card characterises evil as "intolerable harm, culpably inflicted" (Card 2001, 3–5; Card 2003, 66; Card 2004, 216). No one would deny, I think, that on this account genocidal killing involves the infliction of evil. Nevertheless, as Adam Morton has suggested, the notion of something's being "intolerable" that Card appeals to here is a normatively loaded one: it refers to what we should not tolerate, rather than what we cannot tolerate (Morton 2004, 199). And in so far as our aim is not to defend the claim that genocidal killing is evil (since that is not in dispute) but rather to have a better understanding of what that claim is, we might be inclined to ask what it is about the kind of harm involved in the infliction of social death that makes it intolerable. Part of the answer to this question is provided by pointing to the ways in which it involves the destruction of humanity, not just of human beings.

Furthermore, and relatedly, appeal to the notion of disrespect for humanity as embodied rationality helps us to address the issue with which this essay is primarily concerned: that of explaining the peculiar evil of genocide. For, while it may be the case that some intolerable harms are intolerable because they involve disrespect for and disregard of the humanity of their victims, it is not clear that all are. There are some harms that we should not tolerate because they involve such disrespect.

There are others that we should not tolerate because of the magnitude of the suffering involved, or its pointlessness, or the cruelty involved in inflicting it.

9. Is the Account Too Complex?

My explanation of our moral intuition of the collective evil of genocide has been that this intuition represents a rational response to the disregard for humanity (or embodied rationality) expressed in the collective willing that is typically to be found in cases of genocidal killing. Thus it appeals to two different aspects of genocidal killing. It is natural to wonder whether a simpler account appealing to only one of these features would be preferable.

I addressed some aspects of this question in section 6. There I argued that an account of the peculiar evil of genocide that appealed only to the fact that genocidal killing involved collective wrongdoing would be unsatisfactory, at least in part because it would not address what was *peculiarly* evil about genocide, or indeed why we should see genocide as evil at all, rather than merely wrong. While arguing for that view, I identified two constraints that an adequate account of this evil needed to meet.

The first constraint was that an account of the peculiar evil of genocide needed to appeal to some feature of the genocidal killing that was not so widespread as to make it the case that the evil of genocidal killing was commonplace. To propose an account that did not meet this constraint would have been to reject the terms in which the guiding question of this essay is posed. Kutz's account of collective wrongdoing, which appealed to the non-universalisability of a maxim present in the collective willing of a group of individuals, did not satisfy this constraint, precisely to the extent that it succeeded as a more general account of collective wrong-doing. However, the account that I developed in the previous two sections does satisfy it. For it is not true that all collective wrongdoing involves disregard for the embodied rationality of its victims. For example, collective wrongdoing that involves destruction of wilderness environments or the infliction of unjust but not intolerable inequalities would not have this feature.

The second constraint was, in effect, that the account needed to do justice to the moral significance of the suffering of victims of genocide. I argued that Kutz's account of collective wrongdoing was unlikely to meet this constraint in view of its strongly Kantian aspects. Nevertheless, one might wonder whether the account I have put forward, which also stresses the nature of the collective willing involved in acts of genocide, is any more successful, particularly given that it has its own Kantian resonances.

Before I address this issue, however, it may be worth saying a bit more about Card's position. She holds that there is something wrong with accounts of evil that do not make reference to the suffering of individuals who are the victims of that evil. However, she does not take it to be a constraint on a plausible account of evil that it should make no reference to the will of the perpetrator. Rather, the suggestion is that an adequate account of evil should make reference to both. (Card's own view accommodates this by defining evil in terms of the culpable infliction of intolerable harm on victims and allowing for will-related conditions to contribute to an account of culpability.)

It is clear that the account I have put forward of the peculiar evil of genocide makes reference to the collective willing of perpetrators. In doing so it also makes reference to their individual willing: this is ensured by Kutz's metaphysically lightweight account of collective action. The only question that remains to be addressed is whether my account grants sufficient moral significance to the suffering of victims. The answer to this is yes. Notice that the feature of the collective willing involved in acts of genocide that explains the peculiar evil of genocide consists in a relationship between the willing of perpetrators and the suffering of victims. This contrasts significantly with Kutz's account of collective wrongdoing: on that account, the suffering of victims seems irrelevant to explaining a collective action's status as a collective wrongdoing.

One might doubt this on the grounds that we can conceive of cases in which there is the sort of collective willing that I take to be constitutive of the peculiar evil of genocide, but without any actual suffering taking place—for example, among a group of ineffectual and witless conspirators. I want to make two points about such cases. First, it is not obvious that it is a disadvantage of my view that it allows for ineffectual evil provided that there are good grounds for taking the possibility to be marginal. Second, we do have such grounds, on my account. Given my stress on the role of participatory intentions and what they must manifest, it is very difficult to flesh out the possibility of collective action of the requisite sort that does not involve inflicting actual evil. It is hard to have participatory intentions that refer to an entirely unrealized project.

This completes the task of showing that an account of the peculiar evil of genocide that incorporates the notion of collective willing embodying disrespect for embodied rationality is superior to one formulated simply in terms of collective wrongdoing. But one might equally wonder whether reference to collective willing is necessary at all. One reason for thinking so, which I alluded to earlier, lies in the idea that the fact that the evil of genocide is located in features of collective rather than individual action could help us to explain why it is so difficult to give an account of that evil. For we are often inclined to forget the collective dimensions of action in giving an account of what is morally significant.

This argument can only be successful, however, if all other candidate views are unsuccessful. To make a plausible case for this, I must at least address Card's view that the peculiar evil of genocide can be accounted for not by reference to the sort of collective action that perpetrators of genocide undertake but simply by reference to the idea that it involves the culpable infliction of social death. My main difference from Card on this point arises from the fact that it is possible for individuals to inflict social death on others in ways that are not genocidal and, atrocious as they are, do not involve the peculiar evil of genocide.

The sorts of case I have in mind here are cases involving extreme and long-term neglect of young children over periods of time that makes it impossible for them to acquire the linguistic abilities of normal human beings. (It is perhaps worth emphasising that we are talking about actual and tragic cases here, and not the sort of morally offensive science fiction whose relevance I dismissed earlier on.) It seems plausible that such individuals are, in Card's words, "no longer able to pass along and build on the traditions, cultural developments and projects of earlier generations." To that extent they seem to fit Card's characterisation of social death. It also seems plausible to think that their treatment involves disregard of and disrespect for their embodied rationality. Furthermore, in many cases the harm that these individuals suffer will have been culpably inflicted.

On Card's account it seems hard to deny that individuals in this situation have suffered the same sort of evil as survivors of genocide. (Notice that this point depends on Card's characterisation of social death as a harm suffered by individuals.) Indeed, in so far as the inability of such individuals to engage in cultural projects of any sort goes deeper, in some ways, than that of genocide survivors (for these individuals have no capacity to engage in any attempt at a project of cultural recovery), their situation seems worse. While this cannot be described as a refutation of Card's view, it strikes me as a significant drawback. For we might well have hoped that an account of the peculiar evil of genocide would isolate something unique to genocidal killing.

One advantage of the account that I have put forward is that it does seem to allow us to draw a distinction here. For it is not obvious that this sort of treatment of children need involve collective action; it may simply involve individuals acting cruelly and negligently. There may also be cases where it does involve collective action: for example, where the neglect is institutionalised, as in some orphanages in some of the formerly communist countries of Eastern Europe. But these sorts of cases seem to shade into ones that Card would want to characterise as analogous to genocide, such as the forcible destruction of the cultural ties of very young children by fostering them in alien cultures.

References

Card, C. 2001. *The Atrocity Paradigm.* Oxford: Oxford University Press.

————. 2003. "Genocide and Social Death." *Hypatia* 18, no. 3 (winter): 63–79. Included in this collection.

————. 2004. "*The Atrocity Paradigm* Revisited." *Hypatia* 19, no. 4 (fall): 210–20.

French, P. 1984. *Collective and Corporate Responsibility*. New York: Columbia University Press.

Gilbert, M. 1989. *On Social Facts*. London: Routledge.

————. 2000. *Sociality and Responsibility: New Essays in Plural Subject Theory*. Lanham, Md.: Rowman and Littlefield.

Goldhagen, D. 1996. *Hitler's Willing Executioners: Ordinary Germans and the Holocaust*. London: Little, Brown.

Gourevitch, P. 2000. *We Wish to Inform You That Tomorrrow We Will Be Killed with Our Families*. London: Picador.

Kant, I. 1993. *Grounding for the Metaphysics of Morals*. Translated by James W. Ellington. Third edition. Indianapolis: Hackett. Originally published in 1785.

Kutz, C. 2000a. *Complicity: Law and Ethics for a Collective Age*. New York: Cambridge University Press.

————. 2000b. "Acting Together." *Philosophy and Phenomenological Research* 61:1–31.

Morton, A. 2003. *On Evil*. London: Routledge.

————. 2004. "Inequity/Iniquity: Card on Balancing Injustice and Evil." *Hypatia* 19, no. 4:197–202.

Roth, P. 2004. "Hearts of Darkness: Perpetrator History, and Why There Is No Why." *History of the Human Sciences* 17, nos. 2–3:211–51.

Stannard, D. 1991. *American Holocaust*. Honolulu: University of Hawaii Press.

Wiggins, D. 1987. "Truth, and Truth as Predicated of Moral Judgments.'" In *Needs, Values, Truth*, 139–85. Oxford: Oxford University Press.

7

ON THE POSSIBILITIES OF GROUP INJURY

STEPHEN WINTER

1

The concept of genocide has political importance, but it rests upon problematic ethical premises.[1] Individuals are the ultimate moral subjects of liberal ethics—at ground, moral justification is in terms of individual persons (Eisenberg 1995). Therefore, insofar as a concept is a moral concept, it can have no rightful ultimate application beyond individuals. While this ethical individualism, or something very close to it, is required in any liberal theory, its implications for the concept of group injury are uncertain. For many authors, genocide is an example of a group injury; an obvious case where people are injured by virtue of group membership. This essay asks whether genocide, as a "group injury," describes a normatively significant, distinctly group-level concept or whether it reduces, without remainder, to an n-series of injuries to individuals.

There are valid uses of the terms "group" and "injury"; the objection considered by this essay concerns their compounding. Is the term "group injury" something like a category mistake, wherein the attribution of injury to a group subject is in error or really means something else? Consider a sentence that on the surface makes such an error: "*The Gulag Archipelago* is an angry book." This sentence does not attribute emotional experiences to the book itself. Books do not exist in a manner permitting the experience of emotions. Similarly, when a statement attributes injury to a group, an objector believes this must be either an error or something else must be meant, as groups do not exist in a manner that allows them to experience injury.

The objection emerges from the definitions of group and injury so that the definition of one will not allow its straightforward conjunction with the other. There is an undemanding definition of a group: groups are

[1] The author expresses a deep appreciation for discussions with Cissie Fu, Omar Khan, Tiago Mendes, James Moruta, Dwight Newman, Shlomi Segall, and Stuart White. More general thanks are due those in attendance at the 2004 Oxford Political Theory Seminar and the 2005 European Conference for Analytic Philosophy.

populations sharing a characteristic. In respect to injury, Joel Feinberg's common formulation defines it as a wrongful interest-setback (Feinberg 1977; Feinberg 1984).[2] If we accept these definitions, a statement pertaining to group injury puts three key terms in play: "group," "wrongful," and "interest-setback," and a skeptic may oppose the attribution of injury by pressing two concerns. The first is whether groups are the sort of entity that can have interests. The second is whether groups are the sort of entity that can be treated wrongfully. These two concerns can be formally stated as:

1A: Injury consists in a wrongful setback to an interest.
1B: Groups cannot have interests.
1C: Because groups cannot have interests, they cannot be injured.

2A: Injury consists in a wrongful setback to an interest.
2B: Groups cannot be treated wrongfully.
2C: Because groups cannot be treated wrongfully, they cannot be injured.

Of course, further objections might be developed. These could challenge the definitions or integrity of the terms. But for the sake of the argument, I assume the definitions are sufficiently correct and further assume that these terms can all be employed meaningfully. The questions addressed here explore whether these terms can be employed meaningfully in concert. Since 1A and 2A are stipulated as true, the essay discusses premises 1B and 2B. First motivating supporting arguments for 1B, the essay then assesses several responses, and finally advances what is termed a "comprehensive account." Subsequently, because it is possible to accept 1B but reject 2B, the essay addresses certain objections to the normative consideration of group interests. Having argued that group interests are plausibly of moral consequence, the essay summarizes the argument in its concluding section and offers a short analysis of its consequences for the concept of genocide.

2

Granting that there are objects in which groups might be interested if they could be so (the objection is not a dearth of candidate objects), support for 1B presses on the character of groups—their ability to be interested. This concern of ethical individualism holds that groups cannot be injured, because they fail to meet plausible criteria for having interests: something in the nature of interests prevents their being held by entities such as groups (or vice versa). Authors like Raz, Feinberg, Dworkin, and Held argue that interests are justified by reference to a theory of the good life

---

[2] While other options exist, I would defend something like Feinberg's interest-based approach. For alternatives and further discussion see Callahan 1987; Raz 1988; Meyer 2003; Perry 1992; Shiffrin 1999.

(such as well-being) wherein an interest is an element in the life of an entity pursuing a theory of the good (Held 1970; Feinberg 1984; Raz 1988; Feinberg 1994; Dworkin 2000). Consequently, with respect to premise 1B, there are two lines of support for the argument that groups suffer a character deficiency preventing them from having interests as described above. One line of support draws attention to the inability of groups to have and pursue a theory of the good life. Another line of support notes that groups are unable to have the right sort of affective experiences—that they are unable to experience significance, to be satisfied, or know gains and losses.

Considering the first line of support for 1B, it may seem that groups qua groups are not capable of having or pursuing the good life because they lack a mind. This argument would be similar to those of authors who, like Manuel Velasquez, deny group moral agency by virtue of a group's inability in respect to intention or other mental attributes (cf. Velasquez 2003). The objection does not deny that groups are efficacious, the problem lies in a further step—that having interests requires some form of agent-object directedness. A Velasquez-type objector runs a 1B-supporting argument as: Having interests requires mental object directedness. No group has this character. No group has interests. A Velasquez-type objector concludes that any group interest reduces to an n-series of member's individual interests.

Instead of attacking a group's inability to act, the second line of support attacks a group's inability to experience. Philosophers tend to agree that part of having an interest depends on the object of interest being significant to the subject (cf. Callahan 1987; May 1987; Dworkin 1993) or the subject experiencing a level of well-being dependent on that object (Posner and Vermeule 2003). The implication is that if an entity is incapable of experiencing variable states of welfare, it cannot have interests.[3] Though it is unlikely to be a sufficient condition, affect is a necessary condition of having interests. To refer to an example, for an agent to have an interest in her car entails that she could have affective car-regarding experiences. If this is the case, an objection to group injury finds firm ground in the claim that a group qua group cannot experience the affective sensations that ground the possibility of interests.

This brief discussion offers an overview of some potential avenues for supporting an objection to group injury by virtue of support for 1B. The essay accepts the constraints posed by these supports. Something like what is argued above will indeed prevent the straightforward attribution of interests to a group qua group, and thus support for ethical individu-

---

[3] This line of argument is similar to that of Stephen Kershnar's. Kershnar rejects the possibility that "blacks *qua* group have a legitimate claim to compensation," because an entity can have a legitimate claim to justice only if it has the capacity to enjoy different levels of well-being" (2002, 256).

alism seems to require agreement with the support for 1B (when groups are understood qua group). However, we must be careful how this agreement is formulated. References to group interests are ubiquitous. Although popularity is not necessarily evidence of verity, given their conventionality the attributions of group interest ought not to be discarded too quickly. The demands of ethical individualism need not abolish talk about group interests; rather, they require a way of talking about group interests that predicates neither affection nor object direct-edness to supra-individual agents. However, if talk about group interests as objects is to remain normatively meaningful, it cannot be superfluous, reducing "simply" to an elliptical means of referring to an n-series of individual interests. The remainder of the essay argues that although groups cannot be the ultimate subjects of interests, this eliminates neither group interests nor group injury.

3

The commitment to ethical individualism provides the basic structure for the account of group interest, committing us to a derivative approach following the work done on group membership, group agency, and group intentions from a formally individualistic methodological stance.[4] This third section explores several such possible accounts. The first of these is called the "account from public goods," the second the "account from group agency," and the third is Larry May's "account from interconnectedness." On their own, the surveyed accounts produce either counterintuitive or insufficient results. However, they provide a founda-tion upon which the fourth section builds a more successful position.

The Account from Public Goods

Writers on the subject of group rights have been particularly interested in the concept of public goods. Public goods are often described as those goods that are either contingently or intrinsically non-excludible. A good is contingently non-excludible if it is conceptually possible to exclude individuals from its enjoyment. A frequent example is a town's water supply, which is contingently public insofar as no technology exists to restrict individual access. An intrinsically non-excludible public good is a good that cannot be denied to an individual. Following Joseph Raz's influential discussion, a commonly used example is life in a cultured society (Raz 1988).[5] There is a potential to collapse the distinction. Denise

---

[4] This work includes that of Michael Bratman, Margaret Gilbert, and Raimo Tuomela.

[5] Joseph Raz (1988) uses the term "collective good" to describe intrinsically public goods. Although there is potential for some confusion, Raz seems to treat collective goods as a sub-variety of public goods.

Reaume notes that it is always possible (at least theoretically) to deny an individual access to a public good, if only by killing him (Reaume 1988).

The literature on public goods is large, and reviewing its byways will not advance our analysis.[6] Instead, I will concentrate on Michael Hartney's description of collective interests that are non-individualizable (Hartney 1991). By avoiding Reaume's point, this concept seems more promising than non-excludability. A non-individualizable public good exists when its enjoyment requires the participation of a plural set of individuals—the concept of the good has an essential group character. A non-individualizable public good, such as living in a cultured society or enjoying a public festival, requires that others participate as an important or essential aspect of enjoying and/or producing the good. Though we might agree that, in the final analysis, these goods are only good for individuals, there is a groupness to the good that is essential to satisfying the individual's interest.

The account of group interests as non-individualizable public goods is intuitively plausible. But the account looks both overinclusive and underinclusive. It looks overinclusive if an individual who was part of a group producing a non-individualizable public good is *necessarily* a member of the injured group if and when the public good is wrongfully set back. If the good in question is living in a cultured society and the member of that society has a reason to wish that this culture is set back (we might think about fifth columnists), then it seems odd to include her in the group of those injured by the setback.

Further, the criterion of non-individualizablity seems underinclusive, as many examples of interests (setbacks to which we would normally talk about as group injuries) will not be encompassed by this definition. A rural bridge serving a small island community will assist as an example. Although we might commonly say that the community has an interest in the bridge, we might "individualize" this interest into the interests of each member of the community in the use of the bridge. The bridge is a contingent (usually non-rival) public good, but it is not a conceptual necessity to describe it as a group attribute. There is no innate groupness to a bridge, as, unlike a public festival, a bridge might satisfy only a single individual (or none) and yet remain a perfectly adequate bridge. If group interests were predicated only on non-individualizable public goods, we would need to discard as meaningful any non-elliptical group attributions arising from the concatenation of individual interests. Suppose all members of the community have an interest in using the bridge to get to their separate workplaces. It would be odd to define this interest in commuting as a public good, yet we might wish to talk about the members of the community's interest in using the bridge so that they can get to work. Authors are right to attend to non-individualizable

---

[6] For an overview, see Sunstein and Ullmann-Margalit 2001.

goods, but in many cases these goods will not capture all the salient interests.

The Account from Group Agency

The account from public goods primarily depends upon the nature of the good itself. However, we might think that an account of group interest ought to connect with the nature of the interested group. As the support for 1B indicates, interests and agency are connected; therefore, resources for defining group interests could emerge from accounts of group agency. Although I call this the "account from group agency," the label only reflects its literary origins; the emphasis is on group attitudes.

The first condition of an account that begins by describing the group itself is the existence of a set of individuals (group members) to whom moral agency is rightly attributed.[7] The second condition argues that a group interest obtains when a sufficient number of group members have "we-interests," where a we-interest is (or is the potential ground for) a type of "we-attitude" among a sufficient number of group members. Therefore, a we-interest is a particular mode or content of thought, a thought taking the form "We (the group) have attitude x." The conclusion holds that a group interest exists when sufficient members of the group have a we-interest. For an example described in the terms of this account, British motorists would have a group interest in commuting when there is a set of members (British motorists) of whom a sufficient number have an interest in commuting, and this interest is the ground of a we-attitude among them.

Where the emphasis lies, so does the grounds for contention, and readers will probably pause at the complex second condition—that a group interest is the product of a we-attitude among a sufficient number of group members. In accounts of group intentions the conditions of having a we-attitude are a matter of ongoing discussion, but something along the lines of Raimo Tuomela's position seems roughly correct.[8] Tuomela argues that a person has we-attitude if she has the attitude, believes that the others in her group have the attitude, and believes in addition that there is a mutual belief in the group that the members have the attitude (Tuomela 2002, chap. 1). In short, having a we-attitude involves the presence of the attitude in the individual and the belief that this attitude is common to other members of the group.[9] The truth of the statement "We British car-owners love driving to work"

---

[7] I put aside the possibility of nonmoral agents.

[8] Some of the discussion involves the conditions of mutual belief and whether we-mode thinking is a content or form of thought (see Kutz 2001, chap. 3).

[9] Different authors offer different mutual-belief accounts. Tuomela (1995) offers a regressive account that amounts to this: X and Y believe that p, and X believes that Y believes that p (and similarly for Y), with the necessary iteration being set contextually.

requires that the individual making the statement rightly believes that some sufficient number of other car owners like driving to work and that some threshold number of other car owners believe that other car owners like driving to work.

If the essay were to continue to press this account from group agency, it would need to stipulate how we-interests are included as a particular sort of we-attitude, but perhaps this attempt would only clarify obvious problems. The identity of attitudes and interests seems unlikely, although it may be acceptable that an agent having attitudinal stances is a characteristic by virtue of which interests might be ascribed. Even if this assimilation could be made palatable, we might think that group interests could exist regardless of group attitudes. The above sketch implies that a we-interest must be present to the awareness of group members, that the we-attitude pertaining to the interest must be actual for at least some number of group members. This differs substantially from the predication of an interest to an individual. It is not normally held to be necessary for an individual to be aware of his interest for him to have an interest in respect to it. If Henry Ford slanders William Morris within the hearing of a potential car buyer, Morris's lack of awareness regarding his interest in selling a car to the potential buyer will not prevent Ford from acting injuriously in respect to Morris's interest. This would seem to be true in regard to group interests, as it would only seem necessary to the having of interests that the group's set of interests included the relevant interest, not that the group members were aware of the interest. Strong conditions of mutual belief prevent the assimilation of group interests to we-attitudes. While individualist theories of group agency require this condition to manage the need for intragroup responsiveness in joint action, the premise is too strong for a plausible account of group interest. A credible account of group injury requires conditions wherein group interests may obtain regardless of the member's actual attitudes.

The Account from Interconnectedness

A third account emphasizes object-group relationships. Both Joel Feinberg and Larry May argue that group injury obtains when a wrongful act negatively affects all members of the group (May 2005; May 1987; Feinberg 1977). "Harms," says May, "are group-based when there is something about the structure, or perceived structure, of a given group that makes all of the members of the group at least indirectly or vicariously harmed whenever one of the members is directly harmed" (1987, 116). If this is to be our account, the definition of "group" will require strengthening, as it will have to include information about the relationships among group members. This is not a criticism of the account. Indeed, it may be advantageous to limit the type of groups to which interests are attributable, since intuitively it seems unlikely that *any* population sharing a characteristic can suffer group injury. But an account of the interconnections enabling the indirect harm will have to be procurable. One possible approach emphasizes a group's decision-making infrastructure. The essay does not pursue this line, as I think more inclusive yet credible conditions are possible.

If understood as a necessary condition, the account from interconnectedness excludes the possibility of predicating group interests to members without the necessary interconnections between individual interests. For example, transportation infrastructures are commonly said to be examples of group interests, where the group is said to be the regional population the infrastructure serves. A setback to this infrastructure (such as a bridge's destruction), if wrongful, would seem a good candidate for a group injury. Yet, it might be the case that small-scale setbacks to the infrastructure (such as the destruction of an out-of-the-way rural bridge) will not set back interests attributable to many people in the region. If members of the larger society do not have interlocking interests with respect to the destroyed bridge, its state cannot be a setback to members of the larger group. On May's account, the group that has the interest is delimited to those affected by changes to the interest.

If groups can be injured, only those experiencing interest-setback will be part of the injured group. This result will be plausible for those who argue that just being a member of a group is insufficient to ground injury when other members are injured (cf. Thompson 2002, 98–107). But this move may encourage those skeptical of normatively significant group interests by indicating that this account reduces to individual interests. Our aim is an account of how these interlocking individual interests are comprehensible as a group interest where talking about group interests is not elliptical for an n-series of simple individual interests. However, Velasquez-type supporters of 1B will conclude that because May is discussing a series of interlocking or interdependent individual interests, to refer to such interests as "group interests" does not posit something different from individual interests. Instead, the term "group interest" merely summarizes the interests of individuals.

There are resources within May's account to resist this line of criticism. At several points May discusses the need for an account of a group injury (he discusses South African apartheid) to refer to the social group in an accurate account of the injury. This need becomes apparent when group-oriented aspects are necessary to an adequate account (cf. Postema 1987). A reading of May could then discuss group interests as those interests the picking out of which requires reference to the group. In May's example, an account of apartheid is incomplete without reference to its group-level aspect. Not only is it incomplete, the description is normatively unsatisfying. In another example, on the morning of November 10, 1938, a German Jew filing a civil complaint for his broken shop window has not articulated an adequate description of his injury.

4

The Comprehensive Account

The essay is now in a position to outline a defensible account of group interests. The previous accounts provide some of the criteria this account must meet. We will need the account to include most interests normally attributed to groups, exclude most interests not so attributed, and do both in a manner that does not reduce simply to an *n*-series of individual interests. We will want to include non-individualizable public goods but not make group interests identical with these. Moreover, the idea that changes to a group interest will affect the whole group seems attractive, for there is resistance to saying that unaffected individuals are interested. At the same time, the account must make the groupness of the interest an essential aspect. Arguing that group interests have certain characteristic properties, the essay terms this final account of group injury the "comprehensive account." Constructed out of conditions discussed in section 3, the argument provided is an outline of necessary and sufficient conditions and a defense against several objections.

The first condition is the existence of a group. The existence of a group requires the existence of group members (as a population sharing a characteristic). On the comprehensive account, the nature of membership in the group is taken over wholesale from the account from group agency. Membership assumes a set of individuals to whom moral agency is rightly attributed and who can be taken as members of the group.

The second condition elaborates upon the properties of the group. In the previous paragraph, the account stipulates the moral agency of its members. Further, these members must have personal interests. For an example, we might think of a group of scholars who individually have an interest in accessing a particular book. Not that each scholar is interested in a single book; rather, each scholar is interested in access to particular books $x_1 \ldots x_n$ (perhaps copies of John Rawls's *Theory of Justice*). These kinds of simple individual interests are subsequently termed x_1 interests.

Furthermore, it is plausible to think that a group interest obtains in the conditions that fulfill x_1 interests. Usually, having an x_1 interest entails having an interest in conditions of fulfillment; the point of emphasizing the restriction of group interests to fulfillment conditions is apparent in the oddity, to use our example, of saying that the scholars could have a reparatively relevant group interest in each and every scholar's x_1 interest. Instead, in a manner similar to that of public goods, a group is not interested in the actions or interests of single individuals but instead has an interest in the possibility of members realizing their x_1 interests. To use another example, commuters from Oxford to Banbury may not be interested in whether my wife's car starts, but they are quite likely to have an interest in whether the conditions are such that it is possible to drive between the towns. This third condition concerns the content of a group interest as fulfilling x_I interests by enabling the possibility of their realization. In the case of the scholars, the group's interest might be described (among other possibilities) as being in a distributive system of book access ensuring that all members can fulfill their x_I interests. However, as having an interest entails an interest in the conditions for fulfillment, the fulfillment condition can be thought of as a subset or an elaboration of the second condition.

On the comprehensive account, the fourth condition will be the existence of what was termed "interlocking personal interests" (such as May describes) where a direct effect upon an object affects a plural set of individuals.[10] The term "interlocking" should not be taken to imply that the interests of all agents in the group will be equally set back by setbacks to all others. It is possible that interlocking interests enabling indirect harm have differing effects on different members. Further, the interlocking requirement places conditions on the sorts of groups that can suffer injury, as only groups with such structures can be described as having group interests. Not just any interest can be a group interest, and not just any group can have a group interest. In the example of our scholars, they could only have a group interest in that which impinges on each of their x_I interests. One possibility would be a distributive system of book access. Moreover, the interlocking requirement indicates that group interests are coextensive with those members having x_I interests. This limitation forces those that argue for a group injury to describe how the injury imposes interest-setbacks upon individuals, but it accords with the intuition that only interested individuals would be party to the group interest.

So far, the comprehensive account has offered four conditions necessary to a group interest. These are the "rightfulness of holding," the idea of "fulfillment," the "nature of membership," and the "interlocking" aspect of the interests. In one sense these conditions provide the conditions of a group interest. They describe interests of individuals as members and by virtue of the fulfillment and interlocking requirements delimit an appropriate scope to group interests. However, the account is yet lacking. First, it is in need of an essential groupness to the group interests as described. So far, an interest described as a group interest loses nothing in being described as an n-series of simple individual interests. This first lack implies a second. No normatively significant consequences flow from the account as it is. Nothing has yet been added to our understanding of interests as simple individual interests.

We return to May's account for the final condition. Above we observed May's position that those interests, an accurate description of which requires reference to the group, provide material for resisting the criticism that a discussion of group interests adds nothing to our under-

---

[10] Cf. Leslie Green: "[I]t is not the individual interest that grounds these rights, but rather the set of linked collective interests that does so" (1991, 323).

standing. Our account would be improved by a condition motivating this property. But what is it to say that an accurate description requires reference to the group? Possibly, it could mean that a group entity stands as the object of an individual interest. Put another way, practically stating the relevant interest of an individual could not be accomplished without making either explicit or implicit reference to a group. But this would be misleading. Such interests might well be interests of individuals *in* group properties, not the interests of individuals *as* groups. I think a better construal describes the fifth condition in perspectival terms. The content of the interest refers to a group when the interest is perceived from the perspective of the group. The group interest is an object of an individual's interest in being a property attributable to the group as a whole (of which she is a member). The import of the group's existence and its effect upon the individual is captured by the idea of either a member or another adopting the perspective of the group.

Our language contains both plural and singular subjects. Adopting the perspective of the group in perceiving a group interest requires that the interest be viewed from the position of a plural subject. This plural subject is hypostatized without being reified. It is a *comprehending* by the individual.[11] Something similar to "adopting the perspective of the group" emerges in accounts of group agency. In formally individualistic accounts of group agency it is argued that membership in groups trans-forms how individuals view themselves and their actions. Bernard Williams tells us that "What should we do?" is a practical question with implications different from its singular version (Williams 1995, 125). Understanding what that question asks requires not only understanding who it is that is asking the question but also what his relationship is with some set of other individuals. In some sense we must view the "we" as a group composed of, or defined by, those relations, and this understanding of those relationships is basic or non-reducible. In a like-minded approach, the content of a group interest is captured by viewing particular individuals as a group and asking, "What is our/your/their interest?" (cf. Hollis 1998, 138–42). The plural possessive transforms the content of the interest so ascribed.

With the addition of the comprehending condition, the comprehensive account has five conditions. These are: "rightfulness of holding," the idea of "fulfillment," the "nature of membership," the "interlocking" aspect of the interests, and the content of the interest comprehending the group as a whole. The formulation describing what it is to have a group interest X is:

[11] Albeit in a slightly different context, Allen Buchanan offers a formulation capturing this approach: "If I am a member of a community I share goals and values with other members. I and they conceive of these as *our* goals, not just as goals which we each have as individuals and that happen to be the same for all of us" (author's italics) (1989, 857). Unfortunately, the remainder of Buchanan's well-known essay does not follow up this line of thinking.

A group has an interest X when members have interlocking personal interest(s) x_1, X fulfills x_1, and X is perceived as an object of the group as a whole.

Returning to our example of the scholars, they have a group interest X in that which fulfills their interlocking x_1 interests and this interest is viewed from the perspective of the group as a whole. This is an interest that members have as members and might include a distributive system for book access. Each member has an interest in ensuring access to particular books $x_1 \ldots x_n$. Individually, each has an interest in a distributive system. Comprehended as a group, they have a group interest in the maintenance and observance of this system understood as the conditions of fulfilling their individual x_1 interests.

Group interests are held by members as comprehended from a plural perspective. This is similar, but not identical, to what Joseph Raz (1988) calls "interests of individuals as members."[12] Rather than being opposed, the account can be seen as deepening Raz's account, expanding group interests beyond public goods. For example, without meeting the non-excludability or non-individualizablity criteria for public goods, our comprehensive account can accommodate the rural-bridge example as a group interest while retaining plausible limiting conditions. Not only does the comprehensive account provide criteria for determining the nature of a group interest (in the form of the "interlocking," "content as a whole," and "fulfillment" conditions), it also involves the identity of the group whose interest it is. The interest is a group interest as understood from the perspective of a particular group.

Similar to Raz's account, the comprehensive account is reductive in the sense that the only evident interests are those of individuals, but it is not "simply" reductive, as the interests of those individuals are interests pertaining to a group. Group interests emerge from x_1 interests, insofar as x_1 meet the specified conditions. The justifiability of group interests "runs up" from the justifiability of individual x_1 interests. Thus not only are the sets of individuals with x_1 and X interests identical, the interests of individuals are divisible into x_1 and X interests. The comprehensive account is therefore only moderately non-individual, to adapt Keith Graham's phrase (Graham 2000). It does not pose a new subject for morality; rather, it adopts an inclusive understanding of how people are. Group interests are interests that are potentially comprehended by the

---

[12] Raz offers this account of a collective right: "First, it exists because an aspect of the interest of human beings justifies holding some person(s) to be subject to a duty. Second, the interests in question are the interests of individuals as members of a group in a public good and the right is a right to that public good because it serves their interest as members of the group. Thirdly, the interest of no single member of that group in that public good is sufficient by itself to justify holding another person to be subject to a duty" (1988, 194–95).

individual as attributable to the group. The thesis stipulates inference from *certain* interests of individual members to group interests.

5

If the comprehensive account is acceptable, it goes some way toward answering ethical individualism's first concern with group injury: that group interests are inconsistent with the reasons we have to support 1B. However, this discussion has left the second concern of the ethical individualist untouched, as the possibility of group interests is not obviously sufficient to the possibility of group injury. A skeptic might accept the possibility of group interests and yet attack the other necessary aspect of injury: the requirement of wrongful behavior. This second development could grant that members of the group have comprehensive-account group interests but in accordance with 2B hold that an agent cannot behave wrongfully toward a group. Joseph Wagner construes this concern as: "Our concepts of right, wrong and justice apply to individuals, not to groups. Therefore, ideas of group rights, group injury and group compensation have no place in accepted interpretations of justice" (1990, 79).[13]

After outlining the central thesis supporting the possibility of wrongful treatment, this fifth section reviews several possible supporting arguments for 2B. These include the straightforward concern that group interests (on the comprehensive account) are not the sort of interests that garner wrongful treatment. Moreover, since group interests are held to emerge from x_1 interests, further questions arise in respect to "double counting." Finally, as she is primarily interested in individuals, the ethical individualist may deem any questions regarding groups as necessarily of secondary concern.

As before, our analysis could proceed by defining "wrongfulness" and then seeing if some aspect of it precluded application to group interests. However, an analysis of wrongfulness would take us far away from our topic. Instead, the argument relies upon what I take to be part of this full account: that the possibility of acting wrongfully in respect to an interest emerges from the reasonable potential of that interest's significance to the individual.[14]

Earlier, the essay suggested that for an interest to instantiate the relevant concept it must be predicated to a subjectivity capable of finding

---

[13] Wagner's article does not, in the end, support this statement. He argues that it accurately reflects a characterization of our regulative structure concerning the morality of injury, but that this can be validly criticized from a constitutive perspective (Wagner 1990).

[14] Without pressing the point, "the reasonable possibility of significance" is a condition for wrongfulness on at least three influential moral theories. First, in Scanlonian contractualism the condition is such that reasonable parties would accept it as a *pro tanto* reason for prohibiting detrimental action. Rule utilitarianism would similarly accept a prima facie prohibition of such actions. Finally, what we might call "conventional intuitionism" contains a simple prejudice against actions likely to cause others to complain.

it significant. A complement to this condition is that we will be likely to find the relevant concept among the class of things found significant. Similarly, we might think that the moral salience of an interest depends upon whether it could reasonably be expected to be of significance. This thought has counterfactual support in that if some object could not be expected to be of significance then it cannot be an object of wrongdoing. No wrong is done by my reshuffling the pens on the public reading desk. Further, it always seems to be a defense against the accusation of wrongdoing that it was not reasonable to expect that anyone would be adversely affected by an action (even if this defense might sometimes fail). Finally, the claim of significance is characteristic of arguments seeking to extend morality into new areas. However, wrongfulness does not directly arise from the fact of significance. When individuals unexpectedly or irrationally invest objects with significance, setbacks to such "interests" might not engender wrongfulness. Further, if individuals find to be significant (in the relevant fashion) objects that are harmful to others, interference with these objects may not be wrongful. As a necessary but insufficient condition, wrongfulness depends *in part* upon the likelihood that an agent will suffer as a result of an action. Once it is expected that an act will adversely affect agents, the possibility of it being wrong emerges. This is, in essence, a version of Mill's harm principle.

Following upon this, the moral relevance of group characteristics (such as interests) depends (in part) on the significance that such groups have in the life of human individuals. The crucial step in the argument is therefore: Group characteristics (such as group interests) may be morally relevant when it is reasonable to hold that they are significant to persons. If group characteristics are reasonably held to be morally significant, it will be possible to act wrongfully with respect to them. We must carefully distinguish between "an object of significance" and "a significant mode of human life." When discussing group injuries, the key point is the latter. Human individuals experience life as group members, and this "we-experience" will demand moral consideration if it is a significant, stable, and deeply rooted aspect of human life.[15] That certain types of groups may have significant import for the lives of individuals is reasonably well established. The past few centuries have seen substantial scholarship on the significance of certain groups, often outlining the powerful roles that identity groups play in human lives. Much of this discussion has attempted to delineate the political and moral relevance of such groups as the family and the neighborhood and civic, ethnocultural, and national identities.[16] If group membership is (or ought to be) important to individuals and those individuals pick out or might be reasonably expected

[15] I take this to be an argument of Harold Laski's (1996, 256).

[16] Those familiar with this literature may see some similarity between my account of group injury and Will Kymlicka's account of group-differentiated rights.

to pick out group interests when perceiving matters from the perspective of the group, the group interest obtains *pro tanto* moral importance (Gutmann and Thompson 1996). This imposes limits on the account, as only those groups by virtue of which persons experience a reasonably expectable level of significance will engender group interests of moral concern.

Some readers may reject the possibility that a subjectivity's perspective can affect what is and what is not properly the subject of morality. In support they will point out that other facts about the world do not change depending upon the perspective from which they are viewed. There are two possible answers. The first is that the change in perspective only reveals what is already there. A second answer comes from Hume, who tells us that significance depends on human life. The sole point here (through perhaps not for Hume) is that how human life is lived is an important aspect in determining what is morally significant. If we accept that deeply important aspects of human life are lived as a we-experience, then we cannot dismiss the possibility of group interests being on a par with individual interests.

Of course, the lived significance of group membership is an insufficient condition for ensuring moral consideration; there may be other reasons why an object should not engender this kind of moral consideration. That Nazis hold it important (have a group interest) in continuing to be a group that engages in genocide does not mean their interest exerts this kind of moral significance. In the case of the Nazis there are reasons to act otherwise. This will be the case in less extreme situations, where group interests are ignored or superseded during reflection or deliberation. Simply declaring one's group to be interested will often be insufficient, but having import is a critical initial property of moral significance, potentially requiring the moral consideration of the object.

Given the above, it seems untenable that if group interests are reasonably expected to be important to individuals, they could simply be held morally inadmissible just because they are group interests. However, a related argument holds that group characteristics are not to be given moral consideration because to do so violates plausible premises concerning the distribution of benefits and burdens. Many antidiscrimination arguments posit that it is wrong to distribute on the basis of some forms of group membership (such as the ethnocultural group relevant to genocide). Many people believe that it is an error, or even an injustice, to provide members of one ethnocultural group with benefits or burdens because they are members of such a group. In an analogous manner it may seem unjust to consider burdens to group interests when those interests obtain on the condition of membership. If there is merely a "correlation" between the set of those individuals suffering injury and those with the group characteristic (which ought to be considered morally irrelevant), then if group members obtain moral consideration of interests by virtue of their membership this is a consideration unjustly denied to non-group members (Edwards 1994, 61).

I think this argument fails to get off the ground. Some kinds of discrimination are acceptable, and an argument that distinguishes acceptable from unacceptable discrimination will usually begin by discussing relevance. Acceptable discrimination is done for relevant reasons. The restaurant does not discriminate wrongfully when it hires a skillful cook as chef and denies the benefit of this particular employment to those without the required skills or talents. Discrimination is not wrongful; rather, discrimination for irrelevant reasons is wrongful. It does not seem that in the context of group interests these could be irrelevant simply because they are those of a group.[17] Edwards's point of correlation is a red herring. A group interest does not rest upon a correlation between the set of interested individuals and the group membership; instead, it emerges from the x_1 interests of those members comprehended from the perspective of the group. Group membership is an internal condition of a group interest and not a mere correlation.

This last point might seem to indicate that group injury entails double counting. A skeptic could hold that setbacks to rightfully held x_1 interests ought to be remedied, but it is superfluous to address group interests in addition (cf. Cowan 2002, 7–8). This is plausible if an adequate remedy for all x_1 setbacks would eliminate any group interest-setback. For example, suppose our group of scholars was prevented from accessing copies of *A Theory of Justice*. On our account, if wrongful this could constitute both a personal and a group injury. Suppose access were restored to each scholar without this being known to all the other members. This would, it seems, repair the personal injury and repair the group injury (since it would be true that both interests were no longer set back). Since group interests emerge from x_1 interests, changes to x_1 interests influence group interests. Since knowledge of the state of an interest is not morally relevant to injury, imagining that group members are unaware of the repair is only a heuristic device, and the example demonstrates that the group interest is morally extraneous. A defender of the comprehensive account must deny this, but the denial may indicate that the ultimate reducibility of group interests to individual interests entails the failure of the account to offer any distinct normatively significant group characteristic.[18] Recall the example of the German Jew the morning after *Kristallnacht*.[19] If the next morning some appropriate entity had repaired his window, would not the repetition of this throughout the community also repair the group injury and indicate that group membership is ultimately morally irrelevant?[20]

[17] For discussion on the difficult question of a good reason, see Scanlon 1998.

[18] Daniel McDermott pressed me to consider this point.

[19] I am aware that the term *Kristallnacht* is not universally accepted, but it is perhaps the most commonly used label for the events of that period.

[20] This assumes that the only relevant wrongful actions consisted in breaking glass. This is, of course, historically inaccurate.

The right way to respond to this line of thinking is to juxtapose our understanding of reparation with the comprehensive account. Reparation is that which responds appropriately to the injury. The double-counting concern is probably best put as saying that our account of responding to group injury does not square with our intuitions about appropriate and proportional response in other cases of reparation. To push the *Kristallnacht* case even further, suppose that the window of the German Jew's non-Jewish neighbor was also broken during the night. If the same act can repair each person's interests in his windows, then it seems nothing significant has emerged from our group-interest account. If something significant had obtained, then greater repair would be required for the Jewish man.

One way of dealing with this point is to affirm that the German Jew has an injured interest that is not duplicated by his neighbor; this is a group interest X, but then point out that the relevant concept of interest is not necessarily aggregative. A thoroughgoing discussion of this point would require more space than we have here, but quickly we might say that we cannot suppose simply because the one agent suffers setbacks to x and another suffers setbacks to $x+X$ that the appropriate reparation will be remuneratively greater in the latter scenario. Because interests are not necessary aggregating components of a person's welfare, repair of X can occur via repair of x_1.

As an example, imagine that N is a mail-order vendor of bicycles and O is the purchaser, and that N sells a misrepresented and non-functioning bicycle to O. Suppose further that in repair N owes O a replacement bicycle and an apology. Now, let's change the scenario so that before the sale O1 appropriately considered N1 to be a friend. This change adds another affected interest to the situation, as it seems that O1 has suffered setback to an interest that O has not. But would this change the required reparation? Plausibly, we still think a replacement bicycle and an apology continue to be an appropriate response. Because interests are not necessarily aggregating components of a person's welfare, it is possible that reparation to interest y proceeds via repairing interest x. In the same fashion, repair of X can occur via repair of x_1. But this does not make y or X morally insignificant. Clearly N1 suffers a worse injury than N. In a similar fashion, the German Jew suffers a worse injury than his non-Jewish neighbor, but that these injuries could be repaired by similar acts does not indicate a failure of the comprehensive account to accommodate the significance of a group's injury.

The above response seems correct, but we could say a bit more. We could hold that the German Jew is not owed more but perhaps his group is. Because a group-level act like a memorial or a public apology looks fitting, we might hold that he, as member of the group, is owed "more" than whatever he is owed for his individual injury. We might then think that the German Jew could not claim an individual share of this "more," but that his group and its members (the two being normatively identical) could.

The double-counting objection captures the spirit of the account by emphasizing the relationship between individual and group interests but is attractive only insofar as it neglects the emergent group character of interests on the comprehensive account. Group interests are derivative of—without being objects of—individual interests. Normatively, the critical point is that the difference expresses a significant aspect of human existence—our existence in groups. The perspective of the group, from which we comprehend its interests, is a perspective of lived human existence on a par with other morally significant perspectives. The defender of group interests takes the position that any perspective (either singular or plural) admitting to human significance may reveal interests of moral significance, and that it is for the skeptic to provide reasons why the interests so revealed ought not to be considered morally relevant. Where the skeptic points out that repairing the individual interests also repairs the group interest, the defender of parity between the perspectives might equally point out that repairing the group interest repairs the individual interests.

Practical deliberation is radically first person (Williams 1995). The mental characteristics commonly associated with moral action are all possible only in individual agents, and practical normative questions must ultimately address individuals. But this does not imply a prima facie subordinate status for group interests. Just as many important practical questions of morality are posed from a we-perspective, there is little reason to think that interests comprehended by a we-perspective will be of a secondary nature. Instead, the question of preeminence is more likely to depend on the importance of the interest to the individual or upon other considerations of justice, not the internal structure of the interest.

Considering this discussion, premise 2B seems implausible. Acceptance of group injury requires that our understanding of injury comprehend objects apparent from the perspective of the group. Because these objects are reasonably expected to be important, an accurate description of individuals, exerting moral significance, may include group interests. It does not seem tenable that group injuries are prima facie secondary or amoral.

6

To conclude, this essay supports talk about group injuries that neither predicates interests to entities other than individuals nor asks that liberal ethics include non-human entities. It seems possible to give an account of group injury that is both grounded in ethical individualism and not "simply" reducible to individual interests. The comprehensive account provides criteria for predicating group interests. The interests must be interlocking, derived from the rightfully held personal interests of members, and described in terms of fulfilling those interests. Furthermore, it argues that for an action to be wrong it must be reasonably expected to set back objects of significance. Therefore, the description of group injury provided here depends on the significance of individuals adopting the perspective of a group.

For discussions of genocide, this description has both advantages and disadvantages. It is an advantage, theoretically and perhaps practically, that the description accords with conventional premises of ethical individualism and resists appeal to objectionable theses pertaining to group minds or ghostly collectives—appeals that are perhaps particularly objectionable to the liberal-individualist cast of international discussions on genocide. But the description imposes burdens as well. The description of group interests as derivative from the interests of group members requires that setbacks to group interests be explicable in terms of interest-setbacks to members. Simply being a member will not be sufficient; the description must appeal both to individuals as members and to members as individuals.

References

Buchanan, A. 1989. "Assessing the Communitarian Critique of Liberalism." *Ethics* 99, no. 4:852–82.

Callahan, J. C. 1987. "On Harming the Dead." *Ethics* 97, no. 2:341–52.

Cowan, J. L. 2002. "Inverse Discrimination." In *The Affirmative Action Debate*, second edition, edited by Steven Cahn, 5–8. New York: Routledge.

Dworkin, R. 2000. *Sovereign Virtue: The Theory and Practice of Equality*. Cambridge, Mass.: Harvard University Press.

———. 1993. *Life's Dominion*. London: HarperCollins.

Edwards, J. 1994. "Group Rights v. Individual Rights: The Case of Race-Conscious Policies." *Journal of Social Policy* 23:55–70.

Eisenberg, A. 1995. *Reconstructing Political Pluralism*. Albany: State University of New York Press.

Feinberg, J. 1977. "Harm and Self-Interest." In *Law, Morality, and Society: Essays in Honour of H. L. A. Hart*, edited by P. M. S. Hacker and J. Raz, 285–308. Oxford: Clarendon Press.

———. 1984. *Harm to Others*. Oxford: Oxford University Press.

———. 1994. "Wrongful Life and the Counterfactual Element in Harming." In *Freedom and Fulfillment: Philosophical Essays*, edited by J. Feinberg, 3–36. Princeton: Princeton University Press.

Graham, K. 2000. "Collective Responsibility." In *Moral Responsibility and Ontology*, edited by T. van den Beld, 49–61. Dordrecht: Kluwer Academic Publishers.

Green, L. 1991. "Two Views of Collective Rights." *Canadian Journal of Law and Jurisprudence* 4, no. 2:315–27.

Gutmann, A., and D. Thompson. 1996. *Democracy and Disagreement.* Cambridge, Mass.: Belknap Press of Harvard University Press.

Hartney, M. 1991. "Some Confusions Concerning Collective Rights." *Canadian Journal of Law and Jurisprudence* 4, no. 2:293–314.

Held, V. 1970. *The Public Interest and Individual Interests.* New York: Basic Books.

Hollis, M. 1998. *Trust: Within Reason.* Cambridge: Cambridge University Press.

Kershnar, S. 2002. "The Inheritance-Based Claim to Reparations." *Legal Theory* 8, no. 2:143–267.

Kutz, C. 2001. *Complicity.* Cambridge: Cambridge University Press.

Laski, H. 1996. *A Grammar of Politics.* Vol. 6 of *Democratic Socialism in Britain: Classic Texts in Economic and Political Thought, 1825–1952*, edited by D. Reisman, 10 vols. London: Pickering and Chatto. First published in 1925.

May, L. 1987. *The Morality of Groups: Collective Responsibility, Group-Based Harm, and Corporate Rights.* Notre Dame: Notre Dame University Press.

———. 2005. *Crimes against Humanity.* Cambridge: Cambridge University Press.

Meyer, L. 2003. "Past and Future: The Case for a Threshold Notion of Harm." In *Rights, Culture, and the Law: Themes from the Legal and Political Philosophy of Joseph Raz*, edited by Stanley Paulson, Thomas Pogge, and Lukas Meyer, 143–59. Oxford: Oxford University Press.

Perry, S. 1992. "The Moral Foundations of Tort Law." *Iowa Law Review* 77, no. 2:449–514.

Posner, E. A., and A. Vermeule. 2003. "Reparations for Slavery and Other Historical Injustices." *Columbia Law Review* 103, no. 3:689–747.

Postema, G. 1987. "Collective Evils, Harms, and the Law." *Ethics* 97:414–40.

Raz, J. 1988. *The Morality of Freedom.* Oxford: Clarendon Press.

Reaume, D. 1988. "Individuals, Groups, and Rights to Public Goods." *University of Toronto Law Journal* 38, no. 1:1–27.

Scanlon, T. M. 1998. *What We Owe to Each Other.* Cambridge, Mass.: Belknap Press of Harvard University Press.

Shiffrin, S. 1999. "Wrongful Life, Procreative Responsibility, and the Significance of Harm." *Legal Theory* 5, no. 2:117–48.

Sunstein, C., and E. Ullmann-Margalit. 2001. "Solidarity Goods." *Journal of Political Philosophy* 9, no. 2:129–49.

Thompson, J. 2002. *Taking Responsibility for the Past: Reparation and Historical Injustice.* Cambridge: Polity Press.

Tuomela, R. 1995. *The Importance of Us: A Philosophical Study of Basic Social Notions.* Stanford: Stanford University Press.

———. 2002. *The Philosophy of Social Practices*. Cambridge: Cambridge University Press.

Velasquez, M. 2003. "Debunking Corporate Moral Responsibility." *Business Ethics Quarterly* 13, no. 4:531–62.

Wagner, J. 1990. "Groups, Individuals and Constitutive Rules: The Conceptual Dilemma in Justifying Affirmative-Action." *Polity* 23, no. 1:77–103.

Williams, B. 1995. "Formal and Substantial Individualism." In *Making Sense of Humanity*, edited by Bernard Williams, 123–34. Cambridge: Cambridge University Press.

8

THE COUNTERFACTUAL CONCEPTION OF COMPENSATION

RODNEY C. ROBERTS

There are only two species of justice: distributive justice and rectificatory justice. Distributive justice is primarily concerned with the distribution of rights and duties to members of society by way of society's institutions. Included in this concern for a just distribution of rights and duties is a concern for those members of society who are disadvantaged with respect to their opportunity to participate in the benefits of social cooperation. When such disadvantages arise, distributive compensation is owed to these members of society as a means of removing the disadvantage. To compensate for something is to counterbalance it, to give something equivalent in value to the thing. "The root of 'compensate' is 'to weigh,' that is to weigh different things together in order to establish a balance between them ... 'compensation' carries the connotation of providing something *equivalent* in value to that which has been lost" (Lomasky 1987, 142). In the case of distributive compensation, this rendering of an equivalent in value is done in order to alleviate some disadvantage or natural loss that is thought to pose an undue hindrance on members of society.

Rectificatory justice, on the other hand, is the species of justice employed as a means of addressing those situations that arise when the requirements of a just system of distributive justice have broken down. Although the aim of rectificatory justice is clearly remedial, since it purports to remedy these situations, its specific aim is to take an unjust situation and set it right. Part of what is typically required to right an injustice is to provide compensation. Indeed, it is perhaps more common that when we think of compensation as a matter of justice, what comes to mind is making up for losses resulting from some injustice rather than the alleviation of some disadvantage that is not the result of any injustice. When an injustice occurs, those upon whom the injustice has been perpetrated oftentimes suffer a loss for which compensation is thought to be due.[1] It is this sort of compensation, namely, rectificatory compensation, that I shall be concerned with in this essay.

---

[1] For a fuller account of my taxonomy of justice, see my 2002.

My aim is to "remov[e] some of the rubbish that lies in the way" (Locke 1975, 10) of an appropriate understanding of rectificatory compensation, by arguing for the rejection of the counterfactual conception of compensation.[2] Identifying the problems with this idea is of particular importance because of the significant extent to which contemporary theorists have relied upon it (e.g., Arnold 1980, Kershnar 1999, Morris 1984, Paul 1991, and Schedler 1998). But the counterfactual conception of compensation is merely a popular assumption, having no positive argument in support of it. Moreover, it can make rendering compensation impossible, and absurd notions of compensation can result from its use, results that may themselves constitute injustices. This latter difficulty is most troubling when the counterfactual conception is employed in large compensatory cases like the case of rectificatory compensation for the descendants of American slaves. I want to suggest that, taken together, the difficulties with the counterfactual conception of compensation yield sufficient reason for rejecting it as an acceptable rectificatory notion.

1

The popularity of the counterfactual conception of compensation (CCC) seems to have begun with the work of Robert Nozick. According to George Sher, Nozick's idea is both the *official view* (1997, 29) and the standard interpretation (18) of compensation. On Nozick's view, "Something fully compensates a person for a loss if and only if it makes him no worse off than he otherwise would have been; it compensates person X for person Y's action A if X is no worse off receiving it, Y having done A, than X would have been without receiving it if Y had not done A" (Nozick 1974, 57). So, according to the CCC, it is both a sufficient condition and a necessary condition that individuals who have been wrongfully harmed be placed in the position they would have been in had the injustice never occurred.

A

The popularity of the CCC is perhaps due in large part to its initial appeal. There is a sense in which it paints a utopian picture of rectificatory compensation. On this view, we seek to alter history in response to injustice by erasing the unjust event(s). This fantastic aim might explain why James Nickel thinks that the CCC seems to be the ideal. However, Nickel recognizes that there are often practical reasons why it is unwise or impossible to follow the CCC (1976, 380). Indeed, even theorists like Robert Goodin, who ultimately employ the notion, acknowledge con-

---

[2] This argument expands upon my analysis of the counterfactual conception of compensation in my 2003, 134–36.

cerns about the impossibility of achieving its aim (1989, 74).[3] This is the first problem with the CCC.

Of course, some might object to this first difficulty. An objector might say: "So what if it is sometimes impossible to figure out what would have been the case had some injustice not occurred? This hardly gives us reason to think that the CCC ought to be rejected." The ground for this objection is simply that the problem of impossibility does not weigh very heavily against the CCC. What this objection ignores, however, is the tension between the CCC and the requirements of justice that arise from this first difficulty. If there are any axioms in moral theory, "ought implies can" is certainly one of them. Most find this implication entirely reasonable precisely because it makes little (if any) sense for a normative view of justice to require us to do that which cannot be done. But this is exactly what we end up with when we include the CCC in our view of rectificatory justice. In those cases where it is impossible to say what would have happened had some injustice not occurred, we are unable to compensate for those wrongful losses and therefore unable to fulfill the requirements of justice. Put another way, any theory of rectificatory justice that includes the CCC will at some point require us to do the impossible. Consequently, "ought implies can" is reduced to "ought *may* imply can." Hence, contrary to the objection, this first problem weighs significantly against the CCC. Indeed, it seems to fail as a legitimate rectificatory concept on this ground alone.

B

The second problem with the CCC is that (as near as I can tell) no positive argument has been advanced in support of it. Consequently, we have no good reason for thinking that this is how we ought to conceive of rectificatory compensation. This being the case, the CCC amounts to nothing more than a very popular *assumption*.

Some might claim support for the CCC by way of an unspoken connection between it and a legal conception of compensation. On this view, since the law is regularly concerned with compensating for unjust losses, it is understood that an analogous relationship exists between a legal conception of compensation and a moral conception of compensation; moreover, this moral conception of compensation is a counterfactual one. Given this argument from analogy, the concern that there is no positive argument in favor of the CCC can easily be laid to rest, since conceiving of compensation counterfactually is a generally accepted legal notion. This argument, however, does not go through. Indeed, the argument is itself based on a mistaken assumption, namely, that the

---

[3] Recognizing this difficulty, Jeremy Waldron suggests that the CCC aim at bringing the present "as close as possible" to a history without the injustice (1992, 13).

standard legal notion of compensation is a counterfactual one. In relevant part, compensation in the law is "[p]ayment of damages, or any other act that a court orders to be done by a person who has caused injury to another and must therefore make the other whole" (*Black's* 1999, 277). There is nothing in this legal definition which suggests, much less entails, that individuals be "made whole" *as if* the injury had never occurred. Alternatively, adequate, due, or just compensation is, "[u]nder the Fifth Amendment, a fair payment by the government for property it has taken under eminent domain—usually the property's fair market value, so that the owner is no worse off after the taking" (*Black's* 1999, 277). But this definition is more troublesome for the argument from analogy than the first. Employing the CCC in cases of eminent domain would nullify the state's aim. On the definition from the Fifth Amendment, the aim of compensation is to counterbalance the loss arising from the state's taking (albeit a taking that we might have to assume is both lawful and just). To aim at making the owner as if the taking had never occurred, flies in the face of the state's objective. The state's objective in such cases is to acquire *a particular* piece of property. If the property owner is made as if the taking had never occurred, that is, if the property owner is made as if the state had never acquired the property it sought to acquire by invoking its legal right of eminent domain, then it will always be impossible for the state to fulfill its objective in such cases. Consequently, a legal conception of compensation does not carry over to a moral conception of compensation that entails the CCC, so the argument from analogy fails.

C

The third problem with the CCC is that it can result in absurd notions of compensation, the employment of which may itself constitute injustice. Suppose the following scenario by Jules Coleman: "I am scheduled to take a plane from New Haven to Washington. Five blocks from the airport, the taxi hits another car. My leg is broken; I'm taken to the hospital; I miss my flight. The plane I would have taken crashes. There are no survivors. Had I caught the plane, I would have died. Only the taxi driver's recklessness keeps me alive" (1992, 323). Now suppose the taxi driver provides me with some compensation for my broken leg—say, one dollar. According to the CCC, the dollar compensates me for the taxi driver's reckless driving if I am no worse off receiving the dollar, the taxi driver having driven recklessly, than I would have been without receiving the dollar if the taxi driver had not driven recklessly. Since I am clearly no worse off (in fact, much better off) than I would have been without the dollar if the cabby had not driven recklessly (I am alive instead of dead), the dollar fully compensates me for my loss!

Moreover, on this view, making me no worse off than I otherwise would have been had the taxi driver not driven recklessly and caused me a broken leg is both a sufficient condition and a necessary condition for having been fully compensated. Since I am clearly better off with the broken leg than I would have been had I died in the plane crash, we wind up with the absurd idea that the taxi driver has already fully compensated me for my broken leg by making me miss my flight! The CCC may also raise a more general moral concern in such cases. One consequence is that we might end up giving the taxi driver a moral status similar to that of someone who (for example) has rescued me from a burning building. While I am clearly better off with the broken leg than I would have been had I died in the plane crash, there is also a sense in which the taxi driver saved my life. Granted, this was purely accidental, and it is far from how we think of supererogatory acts like rescuing someone from a burning building. Still, but for the driver's actions I would be dead. So, in addition to the absurd idea that the taxi driver has already fully compensated me for my broken leg by making me miss my flight, on this account I could end up with a moral debt of something like gratitude to the driver.

Some might object to this analysis of the reckless cabbie on the grounds that it is an anomaly. According to this objection, the fact that absurd notions of compensation result when the CCC is employed in this atypical scenario ought not to weigh against this generally accepted idea. However, this objection ignores the second difficulty with the CCC. Even if the reckless cabbie example is atypical, without a positive argument in favor of the CCC we have no good reason for thinking that we ought to conceive of compensation counterfactually in the first place. Hence, *any* coherent counterexample weighs in favor of our rejection of the CCC.

As the absurdities arising from the reckless-cabbie example show, the CCC leads us afoul of how we ought to think about compensation. Since we can end up grossly undercompensating those who have suffered unjust losses, or providing them with no compensation at all, employing the CCC can itself result in an injustice. The aim of rectificatory compensation is *not* that I be made no worse off than I would have been without receiving the compensation had the injustice not occurred. In the reckless-cabbie example the taxi driver is obliged to give all passengers some reasonable standard of safety as a means to maintaining their bodily integrity. Hence, the broken leg I suffered is a wrongful loss that resulted from the violation of my right to that standard (through the reckless driving). When we take rectificatory justice seriously, we see that the cabby has wronged me and that I have suffered an unjust loss. The aim of compensation is to counterbalance that loss. One way this can be accomplished is by rendering a package or combination of goods that is structured in such a way as to provide an equivalent in value for the losses to my interests that occurred as a result of the adverse effect upon those interests that were caused by the injustice. A Package Conception of Compensation calls for equivalent means to pursue the same interest as the one affected by injustice, and currency or some other good(s) to facilitate the pursuit of some interest(s) other than the particular one(s) affected by the injustice that is equivalent to the remaining value (if any) of the adversely affected interest(s), and/or of any further loss that may have been incurred as a result of the adverse effect to that interest.[4]

The present argument is strengthened when we consider that the third problem with the CCC is exacerbated in cases where far greater losses than a broken leg are at stake. Were we to err by employing the idea in large compensatory programs, we may, just as in the reckless-cabbie example, end up grossly undercompensating those deserving of rectificatory compensation, or providing them with no compensation at all. Thus, we would end up with a public policy the employment of which may itself constitute an injustice.

D

An example of just such an error would be to employ the CCC in the case of the descendants of American slaves. First, notice what happens when the CCC is embraced by the descendants themselves. At first blush, some may find this idea troublesome, because it "doesn't seem to make sense for a person to claim that she has been wronged by a historical injustice if she would not have existed at all if the injustice had not been done" (Thompson 2002, 104). But this view just assumes that it is impossible for one to be wronged by a historical injustice *and* have that injustice be a necessary condition for one's own existence. The real trouble here is that subscribing to the CCC entails the absurd idea that if the descendents of slaves desire compensation for slavery, they also desire never to have existed!

Second, consider an argument grounded in the CCC that has recently been advanced by Stephen Kershnar. He claims that, since the descendants of slaves were not harmed by slavery, they are not due rectificatory compensation for the injustice of slavery. Kershnar supports his premise by arguing that "the descendants of slaves were not harmed by slavery since they owe their existence to slavery" (2002, 243). For ease of reference, let us call this the Existence Argument. This argument includes the claim that the descendants of slaves owe their existence to slavery, with the inference that, because of this, these descendants have not been harmed by slavery. Put another way, according to the Existence Argument, owing one's existence to the circumstances created by an injustice, in this case a particularly egregious and long-standing one, is sufficient to support the idea that the descendants of those who were the particular victims of that injustice are not harmed by it. Of course, we need not venture into the metaphysics of personal identity to see that the claim

---

[4] For my argument in favor of the Package Conception of Compensation, see my 2002, 11–14.

regarding the existence of descendants vis-à-vis American slavery is probably true. I probably would not be "me," that is, I probably would not be the particular person that I am, had there been no transatlantic slave trade, and had my maternal and paternal ancestors not been enslaved at the Somerset Place plantation in Creswell, North Carolina. No doubt this is also probably true of all the other descendants of the African peoples who were enslaved in the Americas. So the question becomes whether or not the premise upon which the Existence Argument is based, is sufficient to sustain a reasonable inference for the conclusion that the descendants of slaves are not harmed by slavery. I do not think that it is.

To begin, it may be helpful if we "look to the bottom" by trying as best we can "to relate theory to the concrete experience of oppression" in the case of the slave descendants (Matsuda 1987, 325).[5] After all, it is not unreasonable to think that many of those who have embraced the CCC have (perhaps unwittingly) assumed a dominant perspective in their view of compensation. Consider an injustice that was clearly a part of the slave experience—the injustice of rape. While few, if any, would deny that rape itself constitutes an injustice from which the victim sustains an unjust loss, and is therefore due rectificatory compensation, advocates of the CCC might object to compensating any offspring that may have come to be as a result of the injustice. The reason for this is the same as in the case of the slave descendants: the child of the rape victim owes her existence to the injustice of rape. Were it not for the rape, this child would not exist. So, just as in the case of the slave descendants, we are left with the intuition that this person has indeed been harmed. However, the likelihood that this intuition is the appropriate one is strengthened when we consider the existence premise from the dominant perspective. From the perpetrator's perspective, it is difficult to see that any offspring resulting from his rape of the victim has suffered any unjust harm. The perspective here is this: "Were it not for my 'sexual encounter' with your mother, you wouldn't even be here!" Hence, as we saw in the reckless-cabbie example, there seems to be a sense that something like a debt of gratitude is owed.

In this case we would end up thinking that children conceived as a result of rape owe a debt of gratitude to the rapists who violated their mothers. Surely this must be mistaken. Likewise, in the case of the descendants of American slavery, the perspective is this: "If your ancestors had not been brought here from Africa and enslaved, you wouldn't even be here!" So again, there seems to be a sense that something like a debt of gratitude is owed by the slave descendants to those who brought about and helped to perpetuate slavery in North America. But surely this too must be mistaken.

---

[5] Cf. Julie McDonald's argument for a perspectival approach to moral theory (McDonald 1998, ix–xi, 634–40).

Since one is only grateful when one has been done some good, and since these examples suggest that it is a mistake to be grateful for the injustice that facilitated one's own existence, it appears that the injustice in these cases is not a good. This makes sense because injustices are, by definition, *not* goods. Second, the notion entailed in the existence premise that "being brought into existence (with decent life prospects) is a benefit" is, like the CCC itself, "assumed without argument" (Benatar 1997, 345). Consequently, it makes sense to think that the existence premise is *not* sufficient to sustain the conclusion that the descendants of slaves were not harmed by slavery, and that the Existence Argument fails.

2

Of course, even those who are persuaded by my argument will rightly remain concerned because, even after jettisoning the CCC and the Existence Argument, we still need to make sense of the idea that the descendants of American slaves were wrongfully harmed by slavery. One way to make sense of this wrongful harm is by way of an argument from analogy. Even though the unjust conditions of what would come to be known as the Jewish Holocaust led to the conceiving of the descendants of those who suffered that horrible event, many of us still think that these descendants were due rectificatory compensation. Both American slavery and the Jewish Holocaust were clearly atrocities (see Card 2002). Indeed, many hold that because American slavery lasted for 246 years, during which time "hundreds of millions of black people endured unimaginable cruelties," including "deaths in the millions during [the] terror-filled sea voyages" of the Middle Passage (Robinson 2000, 208), it was an even greater injustice than the Jewish Holocaust. Since it made sense to render compensation for "the interests of the Jewish people as a whole who were entitled to indemnification for property that had been left by those who had died without known heirs" (Robinson 2000, 223), and since "[n]ot only have the actual victims of the Nazi regime received compensation, but their children have as well" (Ozer 1998, 481), it makes sense to think that the descendants of the actual victims of the Jewish Holocaust were harmed by that injustice. Hence, it likewise makes sense to think that the descendants of American slaves were harmed by slavery.

Another approach is by way of a group conception. Since black folk "have been discriminated against, not as individuals, but rather solely because of the color of their skins" for hundreds of years (*Bakke* 1978, 400), we have good reason for thinking that such a conception is appropriate in this case. We could therefore argue thus. There is clear evidence of direct harms to those individuals who were enslaved in North America, and rectificatory compensation is due as a result of these harms. There are interdependencies and interrelationships among those who were enslaved and their descendents such that additional harms, consequent upon the direct harms to those who were enslaved, were transmitted to the descendents, and these additional harms represent indirect harms to the descendants of American slaves. Finally, there exists a negative stereotype of the members of the group that is culturally pervasive, a stereotype squarely grounded in the institution of slavery.[6] Consequently, the descendants of American slavery have been harmed by slavery.

We might also establish the moral legitimacy of rectificatory compensation for the descendants of American slaves by rejecting the need for discrete wrongs and identifiable wronging and wronged parties. I suspect that hardly anyone would deny that the "kidnapping, sale as livestock, . . . backbreaking toil, beatings, rapes, castrations, maimings, [and] murders" (Robinson 2000, 208) that chattel slavery in North America entailed are injustices for which rectificatory compensation is due. However, as Andrew Askland has pointed out, "despite the social utility of making such connections between injuries sustained and discrete wrongful acts, it is not clear that such a relationship is a necessary precondition to awarding compensation for an injury" (1998, 364). Indeed, in spite of those who might think that clearly identified discrete wrongful acts and specific wrongful actors in the case of American slavery are required, the case is one in which "an overall pattern of abuse will suffice as the wrong with which to justify the award of compensation" (365). The overall pattern of abuse perpetrated by the institution of slavery suffices because, as Derrick Bell reminds us, "the fact of slavery refuses to fade, along with the deeply embedded personal attitudes and public policy assumptions that supported it for so long" (1992, 3). So, "the persisting subnormal condition" that is the fact of slavery "creates a presumption that the impact of the original wrong has not been superseded by intervening causes" (Askland 1998, 368). Thus, in the case of American slavery "the wrongful act[s] w[ere] endorsed by law and morality at the time [these acts] occurred[d] and [the] profoundly detrimental impacts have not been overcome by succeeding generations" (368). Hence, "society is justified in providing compensation to the descendants," and that justification "prevails despite the otherwise governing concerns that disfavor such delayed compensation strategies" (368).

A fourth approach has recently been advanced by Bernard Boxill. On Boxill's view,

> The present black population is not entitled to reparation for the harms that slavery caused it because slavery, that is the slave holders and their helpers, did not cause it any harms. The succeeding white generations caused the harms that entitles blacks to reparation. They did so by preventing the slaves and their descendants from recovering from the harms that slavery caused them. It is this injustice, the injustice of preventing the slaves and their descendants

---

[6] This line of reasoning is adapted from Friedman and May 1985, 220–21.

from recovering from the harms that slavery caused the slaves, not the injustice of slavery, that is the cause of the harms that entitles the present black population to reparation. (2003, 87)

Hence, on Boxill's account, when we consider the question of rectificatory compensation for any particular descendant of American slavery, we would hold that the unjust harm "was the U.S. Government's failure to compensate her parents after her conception, as well as the unjust policies it enacted and enforced to prevent them from recovering from the effects of slavery" (89).[7] Boxill's account is of particular interest because it suggests a move away from the idea that the injustices perpetrated against the slave ancestors during slavery were also perpetrated against the present-day descendants of slaves. I think this may be a move in the right direction. However, I want to suggest a somewhat different approach.

A dominant perspective suggests the deviation from the status quo that is typically found in conceptions of rectificatory compensation. However, this notion is absent in the case of the children of slaves and their progeny.[8] It is only from the dominant perspective that we begin with the assumption of a status quo, a norm possessed by all. Hence, from the dominant perspective, we conclude that any unjust loss must have dropped below the norm those who have suffered the loss. The problem with this assumption was brought out in some of the criticism raised against the decision in *Brown v. Board of Education*. The decision "was criticized for not being 'neutral' because the existing distribution of power and resources between Blacks and whites was taken by the courts as simply 'there'—the base line from which all actions should be measured. All subsequent departures from the status quo were the 'preferences,' or violations of neutrality" (Harris 1993, 1768 n. 264). So instead of supposing that the descendants of American slaves begin life at the status quo, we ought to suppose that they begin life at some position *below* that which is the norm for the dominant group. As Robert Goodin points out with respect to compensation for the congenitally handicapped, we are not

restoring them to some status quo ante in which they were able to walk: if their handicaps are congenital, their impaired mobility has been lifelong. That

---

[7] Although Boxill advances this account of harm in defense of a counterfactual argument for black reparations that he claims avoids any difficulty with the aforementioned concerns regarding the existence of slave descendants: (1) he is not arguing for the CCC itself, that is, he is not advancing a positive argument which claims that the CCC ought to be employed in all (or even most) cases of rectificatory compensation; rather, he is trying to show how it can be successfully employed in this particular case, and (2) there seems to be nothing in Boxill's account of harm to the descendants of slaves that renders it incompatible with noncounterfactual conceptions of compensation.

[8] This is an acceptable characterization since, contrary to popular belief, some children of slaves still remain (see Robertson 2003).

makes this case very unlike the ordinary practice of compensation. What we are doing here is not restoring the congenitally handicapped to some status quo ante. Rather we are bringing them up to a standard that, while normal for the species, is one that those particular individuals never actually enjoyed. (1991, 163)

Likewise, the slave descendants are not due compensation so that they can be restored to some status quo ante. Rather, they are due compensation because of the diminished status they are born into. They are also due compensation for the plethora of racial injustices perpetrated against blacks in America which perpetuate that status. Theirs is not the harm of slavery itself. It is not a status that entails a life of bondage. As children they are not likely to be systematically disciplined even before they have learned to walk. They probably will not be "whipped for crying" in order "to make them subdue" (Jefferson 1977, 217). Nor does their status entail the possibility that while pregnant and having failed to do what was demanded of them at work, they would be flogged while being held down at their hands and feet by four others (Jefferson 1977, 220). And if they should one day decide to leave their current places of residence, they are unlikely to be followed by an overseer "and a pack of bloodhounds" into a swamp, torn up by the dogs, shot "in the hip with 14 buck-shot," burned on their "back[s] with a red hot iron, and [on their] legs with strong turpentine," then be forced to wear "an iron collar" around their necks and "irons, one on each leg," for a period of eight months (Wilson 1977, 339). Rather, their status, along with their perpetual harm, is the result of racial injustice. What is often overlooked, however, is that "[r]acism and racial caste ... issue from racial slavery" (Huggins 1995, 255). This is so because "racial slavery required a sophisticated racist rationale to justify and sustain it. That rationale was not created by slavery, but a slave society drew upon already existing assumptions and attitudes to produce it" (271 n. 47). "[T]he establishment of racial slavery gave a meaning and authority to racial and color prejudice that would dominate race relations in the new society" (272). As former slave Frederick Douglass observed in the second decade following emancipation,

> Slavery had the power at one time to make and unmake Presidents, to construe the law, dictate the policy, set the fashion in national manners and customs, interpret the Bible, and control the church; and, naturally enough, the old masters set themselves up as much too high as they set the manhood of the Negro too low. Out of the depths of slavery has come this prejudice and this color line. It is broad enough and black enough to explain all the malign influences which assail the newly emancipated millions to-day. In reply to this argument it will perhaps be said that the Negro has no slavery now to contend with, and that having been free during the last sixteen years, he ought by this time to have contradicted the degrading qualities which slavery formerly ascribed to him. All very true as to the letter, but utterly false as to the spirit.

Slavery is indeed gone, but its shadow still lingers over the country and poisons more or less the moral atmosphere of all sections of the republic. The money motive for assailing the negro which slavery represented is indeed absent, but love of power and dominion, strengthened by two centuries of irresponsible power, still remains. (1999, 653)[9]

Hence, slavery itself is often cited as the source of harm to the slave descendants, not because we were victims of this invidious institution but because there is a clear sense in which slavery is the *genesis* of racial injustice.[10] It is in this sense that the descendants of American slaves are harmed by slavery. While the view from the top ignores the adverse impact of slavery on the slave descendants, those who look to the bottom "have no trouble linking the wrongs against ancestors to the condition of living descendants" (Verdun 1993, 632). The dominant historical narrative "has continued to amplify the myths of automatic progress, universal freedom, and the American Dream without the ugly reality of racism seriously challenging the faith" (Huggins 1995, 255). As Justice Thurgood Marshall reminds us: "The dream of America as the great melting pot has not been realized for the Negro; because of his skin color he never even made it into the pot" (*Bakke*, 400–401).

If any of these accounts of harm goes through, we can make sense of the idea that the descendants of American slaves have indeed been wrongfully harmed by slavery.

3

I have tried to show that the CCC, while standardly employed in analyses of rectificatory compensation, is nevertheless highly problematic. It is merely a popular assumption, having no positive argument in support of it. It can make rendering compensation impossible, and absurd notions of compensation can result from its use, results that may themselves constitute injustices. Taken together, these difficulties show that the CCC is an unacceptable rectificatory notion, and therefore ought to be rejected.[11]

[9] Cf. Randall Robinson's more recent claim that slavery seems to "produc[e] its victims *ad infinitum*, long after the active stage of the crime has ended" (Robinson 2000, 216). Also, there may be a new "money motive for assailing the negro"; see my 2005, 159.

[10] Much of the global community, sans the United States of America, recognized this when it acknowledged "that slavery and the slave trade are a crime against humanity and should always have been so, especially the transatlantic slave trade, and are among the major sources and manifestations of racism, racial discrimination, xenophobia, and related intolerance, and that Africans and people of African descent [among others] were victims of these acts and continue to be victims of their consequences" (United Nations 2002, 11–12).

[11] My thanks to Claudia Card and Falguni Sheth for their comments on earlier versions of this essay.

References

Arnold, Christopher. 1980. "Corrective Justice." *Ethics* 90:180–90.

Askland, Andrew. 1998. "A Justification of Compensation to the Descendants of Wronged Parties: An Intended Analogy." *Public Affairs Quarterly* 12:363–68.

Bakke, Regents of the University of California v. 1978. 438 U.S. 265.

Bell, Derrick. 1992. *Faces at the Bottom of the Well: The Permanence of Racism*. New York: Basic Books.

Benatar, David. 1997. "Why It Is Better Never to Come into Existence." *American Philosophical Quarterly* 34:345–55.

Black's Law Dictionary. 1999. 7th ed. St. Paul: West Group.

Boxill, Bernard R. 2003. "A Lockean Argument for Black Reparations." *Journal of Ethics* 7:63–91.

Brown v. Board of Education. 1954. 347 U.S. 483.

Card, Claudia. 2002. *The Atrocity Paradigm: A Theory of Evil*. New York: Oxford University Press.

Coleman, Jules. 1992. *Risks and Wrongs*. Cambridge: Cambridge University Press.

Douglass, Frederick. 1999. "The Color Line." In *Frederick Douglass: Select Speeches and Writings*, edited by Philip S. Foner, 648–56. Chicago: Lawrence Hill Books.

Friedman, Marilyn A., and Larry May. 1985. "Harming Women as a Group." *Social Theory and Practice* 11:207–34.

Goodin, Robert E. 1989. "Theories of Compensation." *Oxford Journal of Legal Studies* 9:56–75.

———. 1991. "Compensation and Redistribution." In *NOMOS XXXIII: Compensatory Justice*, edited by John W. Chapman, 143–77. New York: New York University Press.

Harris, Cheryl I. 1993. "Whiteness as Property." *Harvard Law Review* 106:1707–69.

Huggins, Nathan Irvin. 1995. *Revelations: American History, American Myths*. Edited by Brenda Smith Huggins. New York: Oxford University Press.

Jefferson, Madison. 1977. Interview. (Jefferson was an enslaved Virginia house servant, field hand, and herder; he was interviewed in England in 1841.) In *Slave Testimony: Two Centuries of Letters, Speeches, Interviews, and Autobiographies*, edited by John W. Blassingame, 217–25. Baton Rouge: Louisiana State University Press.

Kershnar, Stephen. 1999. "Are the Descendants of Slaves Owed Compensation for Slavery?" *Journal of Applied Philosophy* 16:95–101.

———. 2002. "The Inheritance-Based Claim to Reparations." *Legal Theory* 8:243–67.

Locke, John. 1975. *An Essay Concerning Human Understanding*. Edited by Peter H. Nidditch. Oxford: Clarendon Press.

Lomasky, Loren E. 1987. *Persons, Rights, and the Moral Community.* New York: Oxford University Press.

Matsuda, Mari J. 1987. "Looking to the Bottom: Critical Legal Studies and Reparations." *Harvard Civil Rights–Civil Liberties Law Review* 22:323–99.

McDonald, Julie. 1998. *Contemporary Moral Issues in a Diverse Society.* Belmont: Wadsworth.

Morris, Christopher W. 1984. "Existential Limits to the Rectification of Past Wrongs." *American Philosophical Quarterly* 21:175–82.

Nickel, James W. 1976. "Justice in Compensation." *William and Mary Law Review* 18:379–88.

Nozick, Robert. 1974. *Anarchy, State, and Utopia.* New York: Basic Books.

Ozer, Irma Jacqueline. 1998. "Reparations for African Americans." *Howard Law Journal* 41:479–99.

Paul, Ellen Frankel. 1991. "Set-Asides, Reparations, and Compensatory Justice." In *NOMOS XXXIII: Compensatory Justice*, edited by John W. Chapman, 97–139. New York: New York University Press.

Roberts, Rodney C. 2002. "Justice and Rectification: A Taxonomy of Justice." In *Injustice and Rectification*, edited by Rodney C. Roberts, 7–28. New York: Peter Lang.

———. 2003. "The Morality of a Moral Statute of Limitations on Injustice." *Journal of Ethics* 7:115–38.

———. 2005. "Criminalization and Compensation." *Legal Theory* 11:143–62.

Robertson, Tatsha. 2003. "Alive and Well: Children of Slaves Are Still Living and Calling for Reparations." *The Crisis* (May/June):24–29.

Robinson, Randall. 2000. *The Debt: What America Owes to Blacks.* New York: Plume.

Schedler, George. 1998. *Racist Symbols and Reparations: Philosophical Reflections on Vestiges of the American Civil War.* Lanham: Rowman and Littlefield.

Sher, George. 1997. *Approximate Justice: Studies in Non-Ideal Theory.* Lanham: Rowman and Littlefield.

Thompson, Janna. 2002. *Taking Responsibility for the Past: Reparation and Historical Injustice.* Cambridge: Polity.

United Nations. 2002. *Report of the World Conference Against Racism, Racial Discrimination, Xenophobia and Related Intolerance, Durban, South Africa, August 31–September 8, 2001*, U.N. Doc. A/CONF. 189/12. http://daccessdds.un.org/doc/UNDOC/GEN/N02/215/43/PDF/N0221543.pdf?OpenElement (accessed on July 20, 2006).

Verdun, Vincene. 1993. "If the Shoe Fits, Wear It: An Analysis of Reparations to African Americans." *Tulane Law Review* 67:597–668.

Waldron, Jeremy. 1992. "Superseding Historic Injustice." *Ethics* 103: 4–28.

Wilson, Tom. 1977. Interview. (Wilson was an enslaved Mississippi and Louisiana cotton presser and fireman; he was interviewed in England in 1858.) In *Slave Testimony: Two Centuries of Letters, Speeches, Interviews, and Autobiographies*, edited by John W. Blassingame, 338–40. Baton Rouge: Louisiana State University Press.

9

COMPENSATION AND REPARATION AS FORMS OF COMPENSATORY JUSTICE

HAIG KHATCHADOURIAN

This essay aims (a) to distinguish and define compensation and reparation as two forms or parts of compensatory or corrective justice, as against distributive and penal justice; (b) to provide a moral justification of a social practice of reparation and of compensation; (c) to illustrate by means of a main historical example the peculiar difficulties in realizing reparative justice when wrongful injury is perpetrated by a sovereign state; and (d) to emphasize the paramount importance, in such cases, of the acknowledgment of wrong by the perpetrator.

1. Compensatory Justice

In book 5 of the *Nicomachean Ethics* Aristotle distinguishes two main categories of justice: distributive justice and corrective justice. Distributive justice, in William Blackstone's words, "involves criteria for the distributions of goods, offices, and honors among the citizens of the state"; corrective justice, by contrast, "corresponds closest to what we call compensatory justice" (1975, 254). Blackstone elaborates:

> Corrective justice ... involves a rectifying or reparatory transaction between one person or party and another. Here there is an attempt to restore the equality which existed prior to the injury of one party by the other. The penalty imposed on the party who inflicted the injury and the corresponding benefit bestowed on the injured party should be proportional to the difference created by the injury. This proposition is no easy matter to ascertain even when it is restricted, as Aristotle seems to do, to individuals. (254)

Applying these categories to the modern institutions of compensation, Blackstone observes:

> Current demands for compensation include Aristotle's sense of corrective justice, but go well beyond the rectification of an injury wrongfully committed by one person on another.... Thus the current sense of compensatory justice differs from corrective justice in Aristotle in two important respects: (1) It

involves compensation between rather indeterminate classes of persons as opposed to compensatory actions between individuals. (2) It does *not* require that wrongful injury be committed by the party obligated to pay the compensation. (255; italics in original)

Thus, the traditional Aristotelian analysis of corrective justice captures only part of corrective justice as we understand it today, and as it is embodied in our social practices and legal institutions. In recognition of this fact, Bernard R. Boxill distinguishes two forms of corrective justice: *compensation* and *reparation* (1979, 256). He notes that although both are part of justice, "they have different aims, and hence compensation cannot replace reparation" (256). The crucial difference between the two is that "whereas the latter is due only after injustice the former may be due when no one has acted unjustly to anyone else" (257–58). Reparation "aims precisely at correcting a prior injustice" and is due when "someone has infringed unjustly on another's right to pursue what he values." This may be done by dispossession, or by "thwarting unfairly another's legitimate attempt to do or possess something . . . [or when] someone makes it impossible for others to pursue a legitimate goal" (259).

In expressing the distinction in terms of wrongs committed by "some-one" rather than "some agent," Boxill's formulation may suggest that reparative justice is limited to cases of wrongs committed by individuals against individuals. However, the term has important application to cases of wrongful injuries by corporations, or even by nations, against individuals or against groups of individuals. In some cases, determinate classes of individuals are involved (such as the class identified in a class action). But we must also recognize Blackstone's important point that corrective justice—including reparative justice—can confer rights and impose duties of repair on "indeterminate classes of persons," such as nations or groups identified by, for example, race or gender. The institution of American slavery and the age-old injustices inflicted on women by male-dominated societies are examples of cases in which corrective justice requires reparation, though women and the descendents of slaves constitute groups whose membership is constantly changing as members are born and die. The death and destruction wreaked on a nation by another nation's military aggression against it is another paradigm instance in which compensation may be required between indeterminate groups.

Boxill emphasizes a point that will be crucial for what follows: reparation is not just a matter of *transferring resources* from the injurer to the victim. For reparation to be complete, the injurer must also *acknowledge* the wrongfulness of his act:

Part of what is involved in rectifying an injustice is an acknowledgment on the part of the transgressor that what he is doing is required of him because of his prior error. This concession of error seems required by the premise that every person is equal in worth and dignity. Without the acknowledgment of error, the injurer implies that the injured has been treated in a manner that befits him; hence, he cannot feel that the injured party is his equal. In such a case, even if the unjust party repairs the damage he has caused, justice does not yet obtain between himself and the victim. (1979, 259)

Acknowledgment of wrong in such cases is required out of respect for the humanity of victims as persons "born free and equal in dignity and rights," in the words of the United Nations' Universal Declaration of Human Rights (United Nations 1961, 492). Denial of a wrongful injury by the perpetrator is a continuing affront to the dignity and humanity of victims.

By contrast with reparation, compensation can be required in cases where no wrong has been done. Boxill describes several types of cases in which, he believes, justice requires compensation. Society must ensure that none of its participants "suffers from a removable handicap" or from unfair competition, and justice also requires "compensating victims of 'acts of God' such as floods, hurricanes, and earthquakes" (1979, 256). These examples hew closely to the existing U.S. federal system of compensation, which provides disability compensation for individuals with congenital or acquired physical or mental handicaps or disabilities; workers' unemployment compensation; and federal aid by the Federal Emergency Management Agency (FEMA) to help compensate property owners for the loss of, or damage to, private property affected by disasters.

As we saw above, Boxill holds that reparation and compensation have "different aims." Compensatory programs are "essentially 'forward looking'" (1979, 258), while the "justification of reparation is essentially 'backward looking'"; reparation is due only *after* a breach of justice has occurred (259). This characterization could be misleading, and it might be better expressed in terms of the *moral conditions or grounds* for reparation and compensation than in terms of their *aims*. The grounds of reparation are indeed in the past, while those of compensation may be in the past as well as in the present. As for their *aims*, however, both are forward looking (as the very term "aims" could suggest). Both aim at the just rectification, correction, or amelioration of the condition of those who have suffered certain kinds of injury or loss.

Although the distinction between reparation and compensation is clear, moral philosophers have not always made this distinction or made it in those terms. Some speak of "compensation" in describing, for example, deliberate preferential treatment of blacks and other minorities in U.S. university admission policies. A good instance is provided by Carl Cohen in "Race and the Constitution," where he continually speaks of compensation rather than of reparation in discussing preferential treatment of minorities:

There is . . . [an] interest that the advocates of racially preferential policies aim to advance: *compensation*. That wrongful injuries earlier done be compensated for now, to the extent possible, is part of the demands of justice. (1979, 224; italics in original)

What Cohen here characterizes as *compensation* is not compensation in the sense in which I am using the term—rather, it is *reparation*. Further examples of this use of "compensation" can be found in James W. Nickel's "Preferential Policies in Hiring and Admissions":

Considerations of *compensatory* justice can justify a person's getting more in the present than would be fair if his past losses were not considered. For a person who has been unable to get any decent job because of discrimination, it may be feasible to make up for his past losses by using preferential policies to provide special employment opportunities. (1979, 233)

Nickel adds, in a footnote: "A distinction should be drawn between compensation for services and compensation for injuries, for the concept of compensatory justice is concerned only with the latter" (233, n. 7). In this essay I refer to the latter as *reparation*.[1]

Although my focus is on the distinction between compensation and reparation as forms of corrective justice, it is also important to distinguish a third part of corrective justice: penal justice. In some cases where past or present injustices are perpetrated, particularly by private individuals, and involve serious violations of law, corrective justice may require *punishment*. Penal justice can also include *restitution*—for example, in the form of the return of stolen goods or payment of their monetary value. Though the distinction between restitution and reparation is important, it will not be necessary to discuss it further in this essay.

---

[1]   Further examples of the use of "compensation" in lieu of "reparation" can be found in D. W. Greig, *International Law*, second edition (London: Butterworth, 1976); p. 596: "In the *Naulilaa* and *Maziua* claims, Portugal sought compensation from Germany in respect of a series of reprisal raids undertaken by German forces against Portuguese forts and other installations in Portugal's African territories"; p. 598: "The Canadian claim [in the "*I'm Alone*" case] was in respect of the sinking of a British ship, registered in Canada, by a U.S. coastguard cutter. . . . The Commissioners held that . . . no compensation ought to be paid in respect of the loss of the ship or the cargo"; and p. 599: "In the Union Bridge Company Case, . . . broad and well-recognized principle of international law . . . gives what, in all circumstances, is fair compensation for the wrong suffered." (See also pp. 600–01.) On the other hand, the following passage (p. 599) illustrates the use of "reparation": "International Tribunals have found no difficulty in reconciling the theory of responsibility with the actuality of damage. Thus the Permanent Court was able [in the *Chorzow Factory* case] to analyze the position as follows: 'The reparation due by one State to another does not . . . change its character by reason of the fact that it takes the form of an indemnity for the calculation of which the damage suffered by a private person is taken as the measure.'"

2. Justification of a System or Practice of Compensatory Justice

What is the moral ground or justification for instituting a system or practice of compensatory and reparative justice? In this section I consider a number of accounts, beginning with that of Boxill. I discuss in turn his account of reparation and his account of compensation. Boxill argues that the need for reparation is occasioned by the fact that "necessarily, someone has infringed unjustly on another's right to pursue what he values." The infringement of this right can take various forms, "dispossession being perhaps the most obvious." However, I also infringe another's "equal right to pursue what he values ... if I thwart, unfairly, another's legitimate attempt to do or possess something" he values, or if "someone makes it impossible for others to pursue a legitimate goal, even if those others never actually attempt to achieve" it (1979, 258).

To support his account of reparation, Boxill appeals to Locke's conception of the state of nature, in which "every man has the right to claim reparation from his injurer because of his right of self-preservation; if each man has a duty not to interfere in the rights of others, he has a duty to repair the results of his interference." Importantly, Boxill maintains that "no social contract is required to legitimate compelling him to do so" (258). Thus, Boxill supposes along with Locke that each person has a natural right, or a prepolitical human right, to pursue what he values without interference. Boxill offers no defense of this supposition (whether here or in relation to compensation), nor does he explain the source of these rights (but see my 1999, chaps. 6 and 7). However, many will regard his supposition as plausible, and it can be interpreted as a way of formulating the internationally recognized human right to "life, liberty and security of the person" (United Nations 1961, 492; cf. also Articles 1 and 3, including the declaration "All human beings are born free").

No similarly straightforward argument is available to Boxill in defense of a system of compensation. Unlike reparation, compensation requires blameless persons who are better off to assist others who are worse off because of misfortune. Thus, instituting a system of compensation entails the coercion of blameless parties (normally through taxation) in order to support it. The coercion of blameless individuals would seem to infringe on what Boxill must regard as their natural rights, or their prepolitical human rights, to pursue what they value without interference. Thus, he needs an argument that can justify such coercion. He writes,

> Justification of compensation rests on two premises: first, *each* individual is equal in dignity and worth to every other individual, and hence has a right, equal to that of any other, to arrange his life as he sees fit, and to pursue and acquire what he considers valuable, and second, the individuals involved must be members of a community. (1979, 257)

From these basic premises, Boxill aims to defend the conclusion that justice requires that compensatory programs be implemented in order to ensure that none of the participants [in a community] suffer[s] from a removable handicap. The same reasoning supports the contention that the losers in the competition be given, if necessary, sufficient compensation on equal terms with others. In other words, the losers can demand equal opportunity as well as can the beginners. (256)

An initial (incomplete) formulation of Boxill's argument is as follows:

(1) (a) Each individual is equal in dignity and worth to every other individual, hence
(b) each individual has an equal right to pursue what he considers valuable.
(2) The individuals involved are members of a community.
(3) Therefore justice demands that compensatory programs be implemented to secure for each individual the equal right to pursue what he or she considers valuable.

Premises (1) (a) and (b) are, I believe, unobjectionable. As I have already noted, we can interpret these claims as alternative formulations of internationally recognized human rights. Premise (2) is simply a stipulation (Boxill is not here defending a claim about individuals in the state of nature).[2] What is needed is a further premise that connects (1) and (2) to the conclusion and licenses the inference. Boxill makes a number of comments that seem pertinent to this connection. Commenting on his second premise, he writes: "The case for rights of compensation depends . . . on the fact that the individuals involved are members of a single community, the very existence of which should imply *a tacit agreement on the part of the whole to bear the costs of compensation*" (1979, 257; my italics). The tacit agreement is necessary because "the . . . innocence of all the parties concerned . . . makes it illegitimate, in the absence of prior commitments, to compel anyone to bear the cost of compensation" (258).

The Lockean notion of tacit agreement thus seems to be the key premise in the account Boxill offers. On his view, only actual (though not necessarily express) consent can justify the use of force to compel blameless parties to support a system of compensation. His completed argument thus seems to be as follows:

(1) (a) Each individual is equal in dignity and worth to every other individual, hence
(b) each individual has an equal right to pursue what he considers valuable.

---

[2] It is of course a substantive assumption of Boxill's that membership in a community is a necessary condition for claims of compensation. However, given that assumption, Boxill's argument can only be interpreted as applying to members of a (presumably the same) community.

(2) (a) The individuals involved are members of a community.
(b) The existence of a community implies a tacit agreement by each member to bear a share of the costs of compensation.
(c) The right to compensation depends in part on the fact that each individual has an equal right to pursue what she considers valuable.
(3) Therefore justice demands that compensatory programs be implemented to secure for each member of the community the equal right to pursue what he or she considers valuable.[3]

Besides the fact that in his preceding argument in support of reparation Boxill offers no evidence in support of premise (2), his assumption of tacit agreement is unrealistic, as it entails that those who are able to take care of themselves *actually consent* to take care of others *in the specific ways* that he asserts are required by compensatory justice. Since costs under a system of compensation are born by society collectively, each individual is not only protected by that system but also liable for a portion of the cost. Though all are vulnerable to blameless misfortune—whether by accidental injury, act of God, or large-scale political and economic instability—some are more vulnerable than others. Those whose economic position is most precarious are likely to benefit more than those who are more economically secure. Yet the latter would have to pay the lion's share of the financial support for such a system. It could be to their advantage to pool their risks with other well-off individuals through a system of private insurance. It is therefore not obvious in this case that we can assume the *actual tacit consent* of each member of the community.

We *could* assume it if we were to interpret the term "community," as it figures in Boxill's argument, in the special, normativized sense employed by some communitarians—or if we were speaking of the "good and moral community" that I have described in *Community and Communitarianism*. This is an ideal of a community and contains mutual concern and caring among its fundamental attributes (see my 1999, chap. 1). Alas, no

---

[3] It is interesting to compare Boxill's argument in support of a system of compensation and a system of reparation to Blackstone's argument in their support. For example, Blackstone writes: "Compensatory programs which confront both types of inequalities ["those due to the unfortunate circumstances of one's birth, economic and otherwise (which are unearned in any sense), and those due to past social injustice or invidious discrimination"] are required for equality of treatment and social justice" (1975, 265). More fully: "The democratic ethic, the egalitarian ethic as it has evolved through legislation and social practice, has included this emphasis on compensation (in both senses of compensation) as an essential part of a theory of distributive justice. Emphasis upon [1] equality of opportunity and [2] equal access to public resources, [3] a fair chance to play the game and to compete within the same rules, is the core of that ethic....Without equality of opportunity, competition is unfair ... competition among those who do not have an equal chance of meeting the criteria of merit on the basis of which competition is conducted, is unjust" (265).

existing country or society currently satisfies the conditions for a community in this strong moral sense.[4] Thus, Boxill has provided a plausible account of the justification of a system of *reparation*, but his argument for *compensation* is questionable. It suffers from the weaknesses of all actual-consent theories of legal obligation. I shall consider now the more promising approaches of two hypothetical-consent theories—those of John Rawls and James Sterba.

A. Hypothetical-Contract Theory and the Justification of Reparation and Compensation

John Rawls's hypothetical-contract theory proceeds from a highly sophisticated and refined decision procedure, which he calls "the original position." Parties to the original position are assumed to be rational, mutually disinterested (most important, not motivated by envy), and behind a veil of ignorance that deprives each of knowledge about such matters as her "class position or social status," or "fortune in the distribution of natural assets and abilities" (1991, 44). The principles that Rawls says would be chosen are two. The following formulations are taken from Rawls's definitive *Justice as Fairness: A Restatement*, published toward the end of his life:

(a) Each person has the same indefeasible claim to a fully adequate scheme of equal basic liberties, which scheme is compatible with the same scheme of liberties for all.
(b) Social and economic inequalities are to satisfy two conditions: first, they are to be attached to offices and positions open to all under conditions of fair equality of opportunity; and second, they are to be to the greatest benefit of the least-advantaged members of society (the difference principle). (2001, 42–43)

The difference principle reflects Rawls's contention that each of the parties, lacking not only specific knowledge but also probabilistic knowledge of her own social circumstances, will rationally adopt a "risk-averse" stance, or in other words, will select principles that optimize the worst-case scenario in terms of the life prospects that she may face. This is the basis of the difference principle, from which a system of compensation could seem to follow directly. Although Rawls's derivation of the difference principle is controversial, there is a much clearer and stronger case to be made that parties to the original position, choosing principles to regulate their society, would *at least* choose a system of compensation for misfortune, disability, and the like—even if they would

---

[4] In any case, no tacit agreement would be needed to justify a system of compensation in such a community, since contributions to it would be made freely and voluntarily by each according to her ability, out of concern and caring, love or friendship, and so on.

not choose to restrict inequalities to the extent required by the difference principle.

The argument that the parties would choose a system of *reparation* is less direct but also strong. On the face of it, Rawls's principles are consistent with a no-fault system of allocating the costs of wrongful civil injuries—with society bearing those costs. This would not, strictly speaking, be a system of reparation. However, it is important to note that among the most important of the "primary goods" that are regulated by the difference principle are *the bases of self-esteem*. As we saw above in the discussion of Boxill, a system of reparation is not merely a way of allocating costs; it is also a way of vindicating the dignity of those who are wrongfully injured. A system of reparation publicly identifies wrongs as such and so far as possible forces injurers to recognize, acknowledge, and honor their victim's rights. Such a system seems well recommended to rational, disinterested parties seeking to secure their best advantage, including the good of self-esteem.

One objection to this method of justifying a system of fair compensation and reparation is that hypothetical contracts are not contracts at all and hence cannot bind.[5] As Ronald Dworkin expresses it, "Hypothetical contracts do not supply an independent argument for the fairness of enforcing their terms. A hypothetical contract is not simply a pale form of an actual contract; it is no contract at all" (1977, 151).[6] Dworkin recognizes that Rawls would never have denied this—indeed, he quotes Rawls himself on the very issue: "It is natural," says Rawls, "to ask why, if this agreement is never actually entered into, we should take any interest in these principles, moral or otherwise" (1971, 21). Rawls's response to his own question is "that the conditions embodied in the description of the original position are ones that we do in fact accept" (21). Rawls clarifies this response in the *Restatement*:

> The significance of the original position lies in the fact that it is a device of representation. . . . We are to think of it as modeling two things: First, it models what we regard—here and now—as fair conditions under which the representatives of citizens . . . are to agree to the fair terms of cooperation. Second, it models what we regard—here and now—as acceptable restrictions on the reasons on the basis of which the parties, situated in fair conditions, may properly put forward certain principles of political justice and reject others. (2001, 17)

[5] That problem would not affect Locke's nonhypothetical social contract; but the very fact that he conceives of the state of nature as an actual historical state of affairs is equally damaging to it, if not to Boxill's appeal to Locke to "clarify" his argument in support of just compensation.

[6] Dworkin goes on to argue that the significance of the original position lies in the fact that it "is well designed to enforce the abstract right to equal concern and respect, which must be understood to be the fundamental concept of Rawls' deep theory" (1975, 51).

Rawls's argument is not vulnerable to the objection that hypothetical contracts do not bind. It is, of course, vulnerable to the claim that the original position does not adequately represent what Rawls claims it represents—namely, fair terms under which to reach agreement, and acceptable restrictions on relevant reasons. It is also potentially vulnerable to the charge that the two principles of justice do not follow deductively from the decision procedure. However, as we have seen, it is easier to derive a system of compensation and reparation from the original position than it is to derive the difference principle, and the former may succeed even if the latter fails.

B. A Modified Rawlsian Decision Procedure and Compensation/Reparation

Although Rawls does not directly address the issues of compensation and reparation, James Sterba has applied a modified Rawlsian decision procedure to precisely these issues, and his conclusions tend to confirm those of the previous section (though I shall offer some criticism of Sterba's position in a moment). Like Rawls, Sterba (1991) designs a hypothetical-decision situation; however, the parties to it are not to be understood as being behind a veil of ignorance. Each knows, for example, which particular interests happen to be hers. Nevertheless, according to Sterba the "requirements of fair treatment" of all persons in society are accommodated insofar as the parties discount "knowledge of which particular interests happen to be . . . [their] own." Instead, the parties would reason impartially, and with "knowledge of all the particular interests of everyone who would be affected by . . . [their] decision." Sterba likens them to "judges who discount prejudicial information in order to reach fair decisions" and "give a fair hearing to everyone's particular interests" (1991, 109).

As with Rawls's original position, Sterba's hypothetical-decision procedure can provide no *independent* reason to enforce the principles that issue from it. In Sterba's case, the justificatory force of the decision situation depends on his substantive assumptions about "the requirements of fair treatment"—modeled, in this case, on the fact that the parties "discount" their knowledge of their own particular interests and adopt a fully impartial stance. Applying the procedure to reparation and compensation, Sterba concludes that "we would neither exclusively favor . . . the interests of [those who are fortunate enough not to be victims of injustice or of circumstances] . . . or exclusively favor the interests of [the most unfortunate victims of injustice or of circumstances]" (1991, 109). Rather, "we" would compromise by endorsing a system of fair reparation and of compensation in which victims of injustice would receive reparation proportional to the injury, and/or compensation proportional to their financial or other material loss.

But why should it be supposed that "we" would compromise? Whether or not this would be true in relation to Sterba's own use of the decision procedure in his article, in relation to the welfare rights of distant peoples and future generations, the question is whether this procedure would ensure a social system of fair reparation and compensation. That is, would the fact that "we" are assumed to be both disinterested (self-interested) and rational, in the narrow, economic sense in which Rawls, and presumably Sterba as well, thinks of rationality—that is, as consisting in the pursuit of the most efficient means for maximizing one's interests—lead "us" to put aside "our" prejudicial knowledge, "our" partiality toward "our" own interests? So far as a system of *fair reparation* is concerned, the answer would seem to be an emphatic yes. For "we" would surely know that none of "us," whatever "her" fortunes or position in society, and so on, is immune to injustice in this life; that some time in "our" life each of "us" may become an innocent victim of injustice at the hands of others. Consequently, "we" would all choose a system of fair reparation for "our" protection.

In contrast to reparation, the situation with respect to a system of (fair) compensation would not be as simple or as straightforward. Granted, those among "us" who are economically deprived or constantly face the possibility or likelihood of economic loss or deprivation due to some physical or mental handicap, and/or to our country's economic or political instability, would almost certainly want to choose a system of fair compensation. But given their precarious or uncertain financial condition and the uncertainty of their future economic well-being, they would naturally be concerned about the sacrifice the government may require of them, through taxation, to help cover the costs of the compensatory system.

The well-off and seemingly economically secure among "us" may also be reluctant to choose a compensatory system, but for the very opposite reason: (a) given their desire, as rational persons, to pursue the most efficient means for maximizing their interests, together with their knowledge that it is they who would have to pay the lion's share for such a system's financial support; and (b) given their economic rationality and their disinterestedness in relation to others. Consequently (leaving aside the possible philanthropists among them) they would be reluctant to choose a compensatory system out of a sense of public spiritedness. Matters could be helped, however, if they happen to live in a country where philanthropy redounds to the benefactor's benefit through tax deductions or write-offs.

From the preceding it is seen that Boxill's view that a compensatory system presupposes the community's tacit agreement to bear the responsibility for it is unrealistic—except if we have in mind a community in, for example, the contemporary communitarians' special, normative sense, or in my understanding of a "good and moral community" in *Community and Communitarianism*, which includes mutual concern and caring among its fundamental attributes. Still, no tacit agreement would be needed in such a community, since everyone would willingly contribute to the community according to her ability, out of concern and caring, love or friendship, and so on.

C. Justification of a System of Reparation and Compensation, Continued

Both Rawls's original position and Sterba's modification of it provide justificatory support for a system of fair reparation and compensation. Such a system can also be justified on broadly utilitarian grounds. Here it might be thought that the inherently forward-looking nature of utilitarian justification is ill suited to a system of compensation and reparation. In allocating the costs of wrongful injury and misfortune, such a system does not aim in each case to maximize sum or average welfare. Rather, it provides compensation or repair in proportion to losses and it allocates costs to wrongful injurers or, in the case of blameless losses, to society as a whole.

The uncompromising nature of utilitarian justification thus seems to raise problems similar to those sometimes raised against utilitarian theories of penal justice. If the purpose of punishment is to maximize aggregate social welfare, then there is no reason in principle why we should not sometimes punish the innocent, or punish the guilty to an extent that is not proportional to their crimes. In some cases, doing so will produce the best consequences. Similarly, if the purpose of reparation and compensation is to maximize aggregate social welfare, then there seems to be no reason in principle why we should not sometimes permit those who are wrongfully injured or disadvantaged by blameless misfortune to bear their own costs. In the case of very wealthy individuals, for example, doing so could produce the best outcome in utilitarian terms. Nor is there any reason in principle—on a utilitarian justification—why compensation and reparation should be proportional to loss and injury.

This difficulty can be avoided, however, in much the same way as Rawls handles the case of a utilitarian justification of punishment (Rawls 1970). There, Rawls distinguishes between (1) punishment *as a social practice* and (2) the punishment of *particular cases* falling under that practice. The justification of having a (backward-looking and proportional) system of punishment may lie in the fact that "as a part of a system of law impartially applied from case to case arising under it, it will have the consequence, in the long run, of furthering the interests of society" (1970, 226). Similarly, the justification for having a system of compensation and reparation may be that it furthers the interests of society as a whole, even though the application of the system in particular cases takes no account of the consequences for aggregate social welfare.

Such long-run benefits to society would arise in at least two ways: directly, by contributing to the welfare of those individuals who become victims of injustice or of misfortune, and indirectly, by deterring wrongful injury and by giving individuals the security and peace of mind that comes from knowing that, if they become victims of wrong or misfortune, society will see to it that they receive reparation or compensation in proportion to their needs or deserts. As with the case of criminal punishment, an ad hoc and unpredictable system that applied a utilitarian calculus in each case would probably be inconsistent with the aim of maximizing social welfare in the long run.

With respect to (2) above, it should be noted that the compensation/ reparation in the particular cases falling under the practice should be proportional to the injury inflicted, or, in the case of compensation, proportional to the loss innocently suffered due to one or more of the untoward circumstances I described earlier in the essay—that is, fairly or justly.

3. Compensatory Justice and the Armenian Genocide

The requirements of corrective justice are realized only very imperfectly in the actual world. In this section, I wish to focus on a specific large-scale failure of compensatory justice as reparation. Specifically, I shall focus on the Turkish genocide of Armenians in 1915 and after—a case that illustrates well the peculiar difficulties in realizing reparative justice when the wrongful injurer is a sovereign state. Unlike individuals, each of whom is (normally) subject to the jurisdiction of the law of the country in which she resides, societies themselves are subject only to a relatively weak system of international customary and positive law. In the absence of a coercive system that can impose duties of repair, the voluntary acknowledgment of past wrongs by those who have committed them becomes especially important. Remorseless individuals are routinely compelled by law to repair their wrongful injuries; sovereign societies seldom are. In many cases, repair can never come unless and until the wrong is acknowledged.

I have already emphasized the intrinsic significance of the injurer's acknowledgment of her injury. Such acknowledgment is required not only because it may lead to the repair of wrongful losses but also because it constitutes recognition of the equal rights of the injured party. Denial of a wrong is a continuing affront to the dignity of the victim. In this lies the peculiar vileness of, for example, burning crosses in public view (the emblem of unrepentant American racism) or staging defiant neo-Nazi marches through Jewish communities. When a sovereign society denies its wrong, the injured parties are not only forced to continue to bear the *costs* of their injury but are also *denied recognition* as human beings equal in dignity and worth.

The acknowledgment of wrong by a society is a more complicated thing than such acknowledgment by an individual. Individuals, by and large, either acknowledge or deny their wrongs. Societies tend to do so by degrees. An official apology by a head of state can ring hollow if it is belied by widespread denial in the press, by leaders of civil society, in the educational system, and by public opinion. Where denial of egregious wrong is pervasive across all spheres of public life, as in the case at hand, the failure of reparative justice is all but complete.

The Turkish genocide from 1915 to 1923, in which more than one and a half million Armenians were massacred and more than half a million survivors were expelled from their historic homeland, has been called the twentieth century's "forgotten genocide." In all the years since, no Turkish government has acknowledged the genocide and the "ethnic cleansing" or declared that the Turkish government of the day had moral responsibility for them. This governmental position enjoys wide support in Turkish society.

Two fundamental issues have divided the Turkish authorities and the Armenians, as well as the historians and scholars who support the respective sides—first, the application of the term "genocide" to describe the killing and deportation of Armenians residing in Turkey, and second, the very definition of the term "genocide." The Turkish side and its apologists maintain that the "massacre" and deportation of the victims did not involve "the deliberate and systematic extermination of a national or racial group" (a typical dictionary definition, reflecting the way the expression is used in everyday contexts).[7] Nor, the Turkish side maintains, were the killings and deportations "committed with intent to destroy, in whole or in part, a national, ethnical, racial or religious group," as genocide is defined in the 1948 International Convention on the Prevention and Punishment of the Crime of Genocide (the U.N. Genocide Convention). Rather, the Turkish authorities assert that the "tragedy" in question did not result from any plan by the Turkish government at the time to exterminate the Armenians. The Armenian victims were casualties of the First World War between the Allies and Turkey; or the Armenians had allied themselves with the enemy Russians. And so on.[8]

Justin McCarthy, a well-known American scholar of Turkish history, is a prime example of a writer who denies the Armenian genocide. In his chapter on the First World War in *The Ottoman Peoples and the End of*

[7] *The Random House Dictionary of the English Language,* College Edition (NewYork: Random House, 1969).

[8] See also Yair Auron, *The Banality of Denial: Israel and the Armenian Genocide* (New Brunswick, N.J.: Transaction, 2003); Vahakn Dadrian, *Warrant for Genocide: Key Elements of Turko-Armenian Conflict,* fourth edition (New Brunswick, N.J.: Transaction, 2004); *The Armenian Massacres, 1894–1896,* edited and with an introduction by Armen J. Kirakosian (Detroit: Wayne State University, 2004); Peter Balakian, *The Burning Tigris: The Armenian Genocide and America's Response* (New York: HarperCollins, 2003); Norman M. Naimark, *Fires of Hatred: Ethnic Cleansing in Twentieth-Century Europe* (Cambridge, Mass.: Harvard University Press, 2001).

Empire, one looks in vain for the phrase "Armenian genocide" or the word "genocide." Nor is there any mention of any atrocities committed by Ottomans against Armenians. On the contrary, in the section entitled "Armenian Revolution"—to quote just a few passages—we read about what McCarthy claims was "the internal threat [to Ottomans, during their war with Russia, which started on 2 November 1914]," by "a massive Armenian revolt in eastern Anatolia." On his account, Armenian revolutionaries allied themselves with the Russians, and the "[Armenian] guerrilla and partisan bands ... revolted all across the Ottoman east, acting as agents of the Russians" (2001, 106). At one point in the fighting between the Ottomans and Russians and their Armenian allies, in "Bitlis, ... as in Van, the Muslems in the city were killed in the streets" (107). "Armenian bands targeted all that was necessary to the Ottoman war effort. Local officials, especially army recruits, were assassinated, government buildings burned, gendarmerie stations reduced, isolated defense posts attacked, etc. The east dissolved into near anarchy as Armenian bands attacked Kurdish villages, and Kurds, ... in turn, attacked Armenian villages" (107–08).

In short, asserts McCarthy, "The result of the war, the Russian invasion, and the Armenian revolt was an intercommunal war, a war of extermination, in the Ottoman east" (109).

Concerning the "Ottoman government's deportation of the Armenians who remained in Ottoman controlled areas," McCarthy writes (inter alia):

> On May 26, 1915, the government gave orders to relocate Armenians from potential war zones and the proximity of important installations. The Armenian population in each province was to be diluted so that no more than 10 per cent of the population would be Armenian. The intent, a common one in governments fighting guerrilla war, was to deprive the rebels of the support they needed to carry on their battles. Armenians were to be settled in Greater Syria, far away from the Armenian rebellion and from regions where they might aid invaders. (110)

> The Ottoman intentions in ordering the resettlement of the Armenians have been debated with ferocity ever since 1915. The only actual Ottoman documents on the deportation show a soliticiousness for the welfare of the deportees—instructions on properly selling property, defending columns of Armenians from marauders, caring for health and sanitation, and other measures for their welfare. In reality, such good intentions were seldom carried out. The welfare of the Armenians was left in the hands of local officials whose troops were occupied in fighting Russians and Armenian bands.... Some officials exacted revenge on Armenians. Kurdish tribes attacked Armenian columns for both revenge and plunder.... As with the Muslems attacked by Armenians, the innocent suffered: Armenian rebels were in the field, fighting the Ottomans and killing innocent Muslems. Muslems, especially tribesmen, killed innocent Armenians on the march to Syria. (111)

In the end, approximately 225,000 Armenians survived to arrive in the Ottoman Arab provinces and Egypt. Most of these had been deported; some had fled in advance of armies. (By 1920, 400,000 others were refugees in the USSR, 50,000 in Iran, and the remainder mainly in North America and Europe, making a total of 811,000 surviving Armenian refugees.) In military terms, the deportation was a success. Deprived of the support of local Armenians, the Armenian rebellion died out in the east, but the cost was great. (111)

Vahakn N. Dadrian, in the epilogue to the sixth, revised edition of his *History of the Armenian Genocide*, considers (inter alia) "Armenian acts of vendetta that resulted in atrocities claiming some 4,000 to 5,000 Turks and Kurds in the January to March 1918 period" (2004, 424). Dadrian states that

> in providing some details about this episode, it is hoped that the factors that configure in the World War I Armenian Genocide will have been presented more fully. But, as veteran Austro-Hungarian ambassador Johann Margrave von Pallavicini, the Dean of European diplomats accredited to the Ottoman Empire during the war, and an ally of that Empire, understood, there could be no comparison between the Turkish genocidal initiative and the incident of Armenian response to it. As he and several other high ranking officials pointed out, the Ottoman Turkish initiative involved a centrally planned and organized wholesale extermination, whereas the Armenian acts of atrocities were isolated, individual acts of retaliation, a haphazard, delayed response to organized mass murder. Indeed, no Armenian government did plan and order the wholesale deportation and destruction of the Turkish people. (424)

Dadrian adds that "Armenian atrocities against resident Turkish populations were committed also, albeit on a much smaller scale, prior to the 1918 period described above. The same passions of hatred and savagery had animated the perpetrators, and exactly for the same reasons that had prevailed in 1918" (426). He also discusses the

> exploiting [of] the incidence of Armenian acts of vindictive retaliation . . . [in] the attempt to correlate these acts with an overall Turkish denial syndrome. . . . Turkish wartime losses in their totality had very little to do with Armenian atrocities but involved mainly a mix of battle fatalities and a cluster of warfare-related casualties among the Turkish combatants and the Turkish civilian population. Involved here is an attempt to collapse into a single unitary index two utterly disparate categories. (427–28)

The Turkish side has repeatedly tried to raise questions about the legal definition of "genocide." In Article I of the U.N. Genocide Convention, which came into force in 1951, the parties to the treaty "confirm that genocide 'in time of peace or in time of war, is a crime under international law'" (United Nations 1948). In Article II, genocide is defined as any of a specified list of acts, including (but not limited to) killing, "committed with the intent to destroy, in whole or in part, a national, ethnical, racial or religious group, as such" (United Nations 1948). Article III makes punishable "conspiracy, public incitement or attempts to commit genocide as well as complicity in it" (United Nations 1948). Although the Convention neither mandates nor excludes its retroactive application *as criminal law*, it is perfectly clear that for purposes of *description*, the Convention's definition of "genocide" can be applied to atrocities that occurred before the treaty came into force. Indeed, in the preamble to the Convention, the parties "[recognize] that *at all periods of history* genocide has inflicted great losses on humanity" (United Nations 1948; my italics). There should be no question that the word "genocide," as defined in the Convention, can correctly be applied to events that occurred in the early twentieth century.

After its formation in 2001, the Turkish Armenian Reconciliation Commission (TARC) asked the International Center for Transitional Justice (ICTJ) to facilitate an independent legal study on the applicability of the 1948 Genocide Convention to events that occurred "during the early twentieth century." In its analysis, the independent legal counsel relied on the following statement of the elements of the crime of genocide:

    (i)   the perpetrator killed one or more persons;
    (ii) such person or persons belonged to a particular national, ethnical, racial or religious group;
    (iii) the perpetrator intended to destroy, in whole or in part, that group, as such; and
    (iv) the conduct took place in the context of a manifest pattern of similar conduct directed against that group or was conduct that could itself effect such destruction. (ICTJ 2003)

This language is drawn from *The International Criminal Court Elements of Crimes*, which lays out nonbinding guidelines whose purpose is "to assist [the ICC] in the interpretation and application of articles 6, 7 and 8" (United Nations 2000) of the *Rome Statute of the International Criminal Court*. The Statute, which came into force on July 1, 2002, creates the ICC and gives it jurisdiction in cases of genocide. Article 6 of the Statute defines "genocide" in the language of the U.N. Convention—that is, as a specified list of acts "committed with the intent to destroy, in whole or in part, a national, ethnical, racial or religious group, as such" (United Nations 1999–2003). Thus, in its report to the ICTJ the independent legal counsel was applying language that had been authorized as nonbinding guidelines pursuant to the Rome Statute and the U.N. Genocide Convention.[9]

[9] See also Richard G. Hovannisian, ed., *Remembrance and Denial: The Case of the Armenian Genocide* (Detroit: Wayne State University Press, 1998). In his introduction (pp. 14–15), Hovannisian writes: "According to the United Nations Genocide Convention, genocide means to destroy with intent, in whole or in part, a national, ethnic, racial, or religious group in any one of the following ways:

(a) Killing members of the group;
(b) Causing serious bodily or mental harm to members of the group;

The independent counsel concluded in its report that while the Convention did not apply as criminal law to events before 1951, its *definition* of genocide could apply to events occurring before then, and moreover *did* apply to the disputed events of 1915.

The U.N. Genocide Convention makes no mention of reparation for survivors of genocide (criminal statutes seldom address the matter of repair). However, the legal case for reparations to Armenian survivors and to the Armenian people is not the point at issue here. I am speaking of the moral case for reparation, which is compelling. When the perpetrator is a sovereign state, reparation cannot occur without acknowledgment—in this case, the acknowledgment by Turkish authorities that the genocide of Armenians in 1915 and after did occur. Continuing denial in such a case not only bars the way to appropriate reparation; it is also a moral failure to recognize the dignity and humanity of the victims.[10]

References

Blackstone, William. 1975. "Reverse Discrimination and Compensatory Justice." *Social Theory and Practice* 3:253–88.

Boxill, Bernard R. 1979. "The Morality of Reparation." In *Today's Moral Problems*, second edition, edited by Richard A. Wasserstrom, 255–62. New York: Macmillan.

Cohen, Carl. 1979. "Race and the Constitution." In *Today's Moral Problems*, second edition, edited by Richard A. Wasserstrom, 208–29. New York: Macmillan.

Dadrian, Vahakn N. 2004. *History of the Armenian Genocide: Ethnic Conflict from the Balkans to Anatolia to the Caucasus.* Sixth, revised edition. New York: Berghahn.

Dworkin, Ronald 1977. *Taking Rights Seriously.* Cambridge, Mass.: Harvard University Press.

International Center for Transitional Justice (ICTJ). 2003. *The Applicability of the United Nations Convention on the Prevention and Punish-*

(c) Deliberately inflicting on the group conditions of life calculated to bring about its physical destruction in whole or in part;

(d) Imposing measures intended to prevent births within the group;

(e) Forcibly transferring children of the group to another group.

What is compelling in the Armenian case is that the victims were subjected to each and every one of the five categories. Such drastic and absolute methods not only underscore the premeditated nature of the violence but the single-minded determination of the perpetrator regime to expunge the Armenians from the new society it was determined to create."

[10] A shorter form of this essay appeared in *Proceedings of the 21st IVR World Congress*, Lund (Sweden), 12–17 August 2003, Part 1: Justice, edited by Aleksander Peczenik (Stuttgart: Franz Steiner, 2004), pp. 106–15. Special thanks go to Eric Cavallero for his contribution to the expanded version of the essay published here, including his addition of a section on John Rawls's *Justice as Fairness: A Restatement* and his additions to the section on the Armenian genocide.

ment of the Crime of Genocide to Events Which Occurred during the Early Twentieth Century: Legal Analysis Prepared for the International Center for Transitional Justice. Report by independent legal counsel. Available at http://www.armenian-genocide.org/Affirmation.244/cur rent_category.5/affirmation_detail.html

Khatchadourian, Haig. 1999. *Community and Communitarianism*. New York: Peter Lang.

McCarthy, Justin. 2001. *The Ottoman Peoples and the End of Empire*. London: Hodder Arnold.

Nickel, James W. 1979. "Preferential Policies in Hiring and Admissions: A Jurisprudential Approach." In *Today's Moral Problems*, second edition, edited by Richard A. Wasserstrom, 230–55. New York: Macmillan.

Rawls, John. 1970. "Two Concepts of Rules." In *Readings in Contemporary Ethical Theory*, edited by Kenneth Pahel and Marvin Schiller, 225–49. Englewood Cliffs, N.J.: Prentice Hall.

———. 1971. *A Theory of Justice*. First edition. Cambridge, Mass.: Harvard University Press.

———. 1991. "A Social Contract Perspective." Abridged from *A Theory of Justice*. In *Morality in Practice*, third edition, edited by James P. Sterba, 43–56. Belmont, Calif.: Wadsworth.

———. 2001. *Justice as Fairness: A Restatement*. Cambridge, Mass.: Harvard University Press.

Sterba, James P. "The Welfare Rights of Distant Peoples and Future Generations." In *Morality in Practice*, third edition, edited by James P. Sterba, 106–18. Belmont, Calif.: Wadsworth.

United Nations. 1948. International Convention on the Prevention and Punishment of the Crime of Genocide. 78 U.N.T.S.277. Available at http://www.unhchr.ch/html/menu3/b/p_genoci.htm

———. 1961. "Universal Declaration of Human Rights." In *Value and Obligation*, edited by Richard R. Brandt, 491–96. New York: Harcourt, Brace and World. Also available at http://www.un.org/overview/rights/html

———. 1999–2003. *The Rome Statute of the International Criminal Court*. U.N. Doc. A/CONF. 183/9. Available at http://www.un.org/law/icc/statute/romefra.htm

———. 2000 *The International Criminal Court Elements of Crimes*. U.N. Doc. PCNICC/2000/1/add.2 (2000). Available at http://www.un.org/law/icc/asp/1stsession/report/english/part_ii_b_e.pdf; full report available at http://www.un.org/law/icc/statute/elements/elemfra.htm

10

A NORMATIVE THEORY OF REPARATIONS IN TRANSITIONAL DEMOCRACIES

ERNESTO VERDEJA

Nations emerging from a recent history of mass atrocity or violent authoritarian rule are faced with a number of ethical and practical challenges.[1] They must deal with how to achieve some degree of social and political stability and must establish a functioning government, legal order, and economy. Furthermore, they must confront what is often a sizable number of victims and perpetrators and thus must decide to what extent accountability can be sought without undermining peace. The literature on these issues, known collectively as transitional justice, is vast. Much of it has focused on prosecutions, lustration, truth commissions, the development of the rule of law, and broader debates about what constitutes reconciliation. Less attention has been given to addressing the needs of victims and what an acceptable normative model of reparations would require (though see Barkan 2000; Biggar 2001; Brooks 1999; Cuneen 2001; Zimmerman 1994, 29–48). This essay outlines a normative model of reparations in transitional societies, alternately referred to as reparatory justice. I understand transitional democracies as those emerging from a recent history of violence or repressive authoritarian rule, moving in a broadly positive, liberal-democratic normative direction. A model of reparations consists of those strategies and policies that seek to restore victims' sense of dignity and moral worth, remove the burden of disparagement often tied to victimhood, and return their political status as citizens.

This article has several parts. Part 1 gives a normative framework for understanding the goals of reparatory justice. I begin with current critical-theory debates over recognition and redistribution. I argue that any theory of reparations must include both material and symbolic components and work toward achieving what Nancy Fraser calls "status parity" among victims and the rest of the population. Part 2 outlines a theory

[1] An earlier version of this essay was presented in October 2004 at the Latin American Studies Association Conference in Las Vegas, Nevada. Special thanks to Bettina Spencer and W. Raly.

consisting of four ideal-typical dimensions: "symbolic" and "material" along one axis (a typology of acknowledgment), and "collective" and "individual" along the other (a typology of recipients). Such a model, I claim, gives greater conceptual clarity to the possibilities and limits of reparations and helps us assess how successful actual programs are. I turn to several Latin American examples to illustrate these dimensions: cases in Guatemala, El Salvador, Peru, Argentina, Chile, and Brazil. While different in many respects, all these cases share certain similarities that are relevant to this discussion: the violations occurred in a domestic setting, not among nations; all of these countries have emerged from a recent history of violations, rather than abuses committed several generations ago (McCarthy 2002, 623–48); and for the most part the nations are moving, fitfully, toward a consolidated democratic status (though in some cases success is uncertain). Other cases could be included in this essay, such as Rwanda and South Africa, but because of considerations of space I have chosen to focus on Latin America. In the final section, part 3, I discuss five contributions that reparatory justice can make to transitional societies. While reparatory justice alone cannot bring about reconciliation, I argue that properly framed, it can (a) return to victims some sense of moral worth and dignity; (b) force a society to reconceptualize its sense of identity; (c) foster public trust in state institutions; (d) help undermine perpetrator narratives that justified past atrocities; and (e) promote a critical reinterpretation of a nation's history.

Part 1: The Importance of Status Parity

Victims of mass violence differ significantly on how to face the past.[2] Some emphasize the importance of trials, while others focus on satisfying their need to overcome devastating harm. Others, of course, prefer to avoid any engagement with the past. This multiplicity of responses complicates efforts to fashion a coherent yet nuanced theory of reparations. Nevertheless, the theory should aim to restore the victims' dignity and so far as possible provide them with the necessary means to exercise real autonomy, and do so in a manner that is not patronizing or condescending. The goal should be to provide symbolic and material reparations to victims without simultaneously degrading them as impotent, lacking in agency, and incapable of achieving self-respect and self-worth.[3]

---

[2] In interviews conducted in Santiago, Chile (July and August 2000), with survivors of political violence, I found (unsurprisingly) that they took numerous positions on the past, indicating that there was no one "survivor" position as such.

[3] Some commentators prefer "survivor" to "victim," for it connotes greater agency. Nevertheless, I use "victim" and "survivor" interchangeably, with the understanding that the former should include an equally strong sense of agency.

Some theorists have approached this from the standpoint of a theory of recognition, particularly the Hegelian position of identity construction based on dialogical interaction. For such thinkers, recognition is a reciprocal relation where subjects see each other as equals with legitimate claims to respect. Recognition is thus a principal aspect of subject formation. Beings become full individuals through reciprocal recognition, underscoring the fundamentally intersubjective—that is, social—nature of identity formation. This idea that recognition through social praxis is crucial to stable and healthy identities has been developed by a number of authors (Benjamin 1988; Honneth 1996; Taylor 1989 and 1994, 252–74). For Axel Honneth, a healthy notion of the self is a fundamental element of the good for individuals, and he elaborates the requirements for undistorted identity as consisting of three core components: *self-confidence*, developed through affective relations between intimates and others who are emotionally proximate; *self-respect*, accorded through the legal discourse of rights and implying the individual's capacity for autonomous moral action; and *self-esteem*, developed through participation in communal activities and contributions to a meaningful, ethically substantive social life (Honneth 1996, 88–91, 146–51, 160–79). These components are all developed through the dialogical interactions with other, equal subjects. Moreover, they are crucial for a healthy subject; without them, the individual risks degenerating into pathologies of self-hatred and denigration.[4]

Some thinkers take these insights significantly further, arguing that the dynamics of individual recognition are mirrored at the macro level. Charles Taylor has discussed how patterns of individual misrecognition parallel those of groups; if the self can suffer mistreatment through devaluation, the same holds for entire groups that are consistently oppressed or suffer discrimination. They are unable to actualize themselves satisfactorily, and natural cultural maturation is truncated or, even worse, fatally arrested. Consequently, certain groups require recognition of their uniqueness in some institutionalized manner, a claim that goes beyond the kind of recognition predicated on social equality—beyond the kind, in other words, that is difference blind (Taylor 1994, 25–74).

The criticisms of such strong theories of recognition are well known. Seyla Benhabib (2002) has persuasively argued that Taylor and others, such as Will Kymlicka, fall into traps of cultural essentialism, reifying group identities and privileging authenticity claims above basic equality

---

[4] Honneth identifies three forms of disrespect that endanger healthy identities: (a) at a very basic level, the injury to self-confidence caused by loss over one's physical integrity (through torture, rape, and so forth) and the consequent devastating destabilization of personal identity and predictability in the world; (b) the type of disrespect following the denial of rights enjoyed by other citizens; and (c) the damage done to self-esteem through the pronounced and repeated denigration of one's way of life (ethically understood). See Honneth 1995, 249–54.

concerns. Nancy Fraser has criticized these unduly psychologized multicultural approaches for a variety of reasons, including their inability to define satisfactory criteria for distinguishing between just and unjust authenticity claims (and the implicit essentialism on which such claims rest), their reductive assumptions about the primacy of symbolic recognition over injustices rooted in political-economic relations, and their inability to theorize from a more objective, sociologically informed position that can distinguish between institutionalized or systematized patterns of subordination, which require justice, versus culturally salient differences, which do not (Fraser 1997; 2000, 107–20; 2001, 21–42; 2003, 7–109).

The observations by Benhabib and Fraser are especially helpful in studying post-atrocity societies. Victims' groups frequently make authenticity claims and special recognition demands in transitional settings. On the face of it, these claims appear quite legitimate, and indeed they often are; the individuals in question experienced devastating violations, offenses that may have been facilitated by historical patterns of categorical subordination and discrimination, but whose overwhelming and immediate barbarity demand that we acknowledge the victims' experiences in some nontrivial fashion. The problem consists in how to do so, and what criteria to use. Should we recognize victims as a way of enabling their ethical self-realization, as Honneth argues? While this seems compelling, a theory of victim recognition based wholly on ethical self-realization runs into conceptual challenges, because it is incapable of drawing the line between what constitutes satisfactory recognition and what exceeds it.

Claims of self-realization, as Fraser points out, are significantly more restricted than justice claims precisely because they are based on more "historically specific horizons of value" (Fraser 2003, 28). The difficulty here arises with the potential development of so-called cultures of victimhood, where similar experiences become a shared horizon of authenticity that demands categorical respect based not on the content of any particular claim but rather on the status of the speakers. In other words, in some scenarios victim group elites may transform their status as victims into moral capital to make morally suspect claims (such as a right to oppress internal members), or point to their status as a way to dismiss otherwise valid criticisms or challenges. What if the elites of a particular group that suffered massive human-rights violations, say an indigenous group, argue that proper recognition of their identity requires that the state not interfere with the internal subordination of a particular subgroup, such as women (Okin 1999)? Should the state accede, on the principle that this particular group was victimized and now requires ethical recognition?

Of course, victim demands are not always morally dubious. In fact they are often legitimate, but the principle of ethical self-realization does not give us the conceptual tools necessary to decide which claims are legitimate and which are not. For Taylor and Honneth, intersubjective recognition is a condition for achieving undistorted, healthy identity. Honneth argues that such a theory of ethical self-realization must serve as the grounds for assessing acceptable and unacceptable forms of social organization. Indeed, the "conception of ethical life" can articulate "the entirety of intersubjective conditions that can be shown to serve as necessary preconditions for individual self-realization" (Honneth 1996, 173). The concern here is not with the general conception of intersubjective identity formation, which seems plausible and whose importance is particularly relevant where victims have historically been misrecognized and maltreated by the state, and thus have suffered from a damaged sense of self. Rather, the concern is with privileging a thick theory of ethical life that does not speak to broader claims binding on all persons—in other words, to concerns of justice. To base a theory solely on claims of ethical self-realization leaves us incapable of discriminating between what can be called justice claims—attempts to address systematic forms of economic oppression or marginalization, as well as symbolic misrecognition, which are a product of political violence—and (nonuniversalizable) authenticity claims.

Furthermore, a theory of recognition, preoccupied as it is with concerns about symbolic acknowledgment, risks ignoring forms of material inequality. Honneth, for example, focuses on forms of symbolic misrecognition while subsuming economic marginalization under the former—"the conception of recognition, when properly understood, can accommodate, indeed even entails, a modified version of the Marxian paradigm of economic distribution" (Honneth 2003, 3). Nevertheless, after mass atrocity many survivors find themselves economically destitute, particularly in cases where an entire ethnic or indigenous group was targeted, and material forms of inequality require theorization on a par with symbolic forms.

A primary concern should be to ensure that any model of victim reparation includes both material and symbolic components, and that it be wary of claims premised wholly on ethical self-realization. But this certainly does not entail privileging only liberal individualist rights at the expense of collective claims. Doing so would miss the systematic and large-scale nature of the violations we are concerned with here. But it does mean that we should differentiate between policies that seek to protect culturally essentialist authenticity claims, on the one hand, and those that aim to create status parity among citizens, on the other. Because both misrecognition and economic maldistribution may prevent citizens from participating as equals, both will need to be addressed in any satisfactory theory of reparations. In terms of recognition, the goal should be to remove cultural impediments that prevent individuals from recognizing each other as fellow citizens, or to achieve what Fraser refers to as the "intersubjective condition" of parity of participation (Fraser 2003, 36). At its most general, recognition would involve the positive revaluation of "disrespected identities" and diversity in general, as well as the deconstruction of value patterns that justified violence and continued misrecognition (13, 47, 73). Regarding material redistribution, the goal is to address economic marginalization that prevents individuals from participating as equal citizens, and so achieve the "objective condition" of parity of participation (36). This could include such forms of economic redistribution as compensation and restitution, as well as increased investment initiatives by the state in areas greatly affected by the violence.

Recognition of victims is crucial in transitional societies, but the aim should be to restore victims' dignity and self-worth in such a way that allows them to be full participants in social, economic, and political life. This does not mean that all recognition claims are illegitimate. Rather, it means that these claims should be honored to the extent that they promote reciprocal recognition and status equality, a goal that is unachievable if victims continue to find themselves marginalized, devalued, and forgotten. The aim, then, should be to recognize their experiences as a step toward overturning systemic patterns of discrimination and violence. With these points in mind, we can turn to the theory itself.

Part 2: A Theory of Reparations

As I understand it, a theory of reparations consists of four ideal-typical dimensions: "symbolic" and "material" along one axis (a typology of acknowledgment), and "collective" and "individual" along another (a typology of recipients). These dimensions trace the scope and type of reparation that should be accorded, and though different mechanisms are appropriate within each created space, each dimension is crucial for a normative theory of reparations.

In most cases of large-scale atrocity, crimes are directed at groups of some type, such as cultural, ethnic, religious, national, ideological, racial, or economic groups. Frequently, targeted groups span different categories. Furthermore, the victim group may contain other transversal categories—such as gender—whose members were the targets of specific types of violations (Jones 2004). Because of this broadly collective dimension, reparation requires theorization of a *collective* symbolic element of acknowledgment. Recognizing targeted groups means bringing public attention to the fact that violations were not simply discrete "excesses" but the result of planned strategies of repression (and occasionally extermination) against designated "enemies." To the extent that victims were part of a (perpetrator-defined) group of "objective enemies" (Arendt 1973, 423) the crimes contained a distinctly systematic element. Symbolic recognition of groups, then, means recognizing (a) the way strategies of repression targeted them *as* groups and (b) society and the state's obligation to meet the demands of groups to recognize their experiences and treat them as equal citizens. Commitment to the latter means fighting discourses arguing that groups somehow "deserved" what befell them because of their group identity. Symbolic benefits can be accorded in a number of different ways, including public acts of atonement and official apologies, creating public spaces to pay homage to victims, and establishing museums, monuments, and days of remembrance to preserve collective memory.

After the civil war in Guatemala between U.S.-backed governments and leftist insurgents that left 200,000 dead, the U.N. Commission for Historical Clarification, or CEH, and the church-backed REMHI truth commission called for extensive collective symbolic reparations to the Mayan population, who bore the brunt of the atrocities and violations. Finding that "acts of genocide" had been committed against the Maya, the CEH called for official recognition of the victims, the creation of monuments, parks, and other historical-memory sites, the naming of public buildings after victims, the development and protection of Mayan cultural sites, and the creation of a national day of remembrance (Guatemala 1999; Office of Human Rights of the Archbishop of Guatemala 1998). In El Salvador the U.N. truth commission also called for a national day of remembrance and monuments to ensure that victims would not be forgotten (United Nations 1993). In Chile in 1991, the first democratically elected president after Pinochet, Patricio Aylwin, offered an apology in the name of the state for the crimes of the predecessor regime (*El Mercurio* 1991). Thirteen years later, Aylwin's Argentine counterpart, Néstor Kirchner, also apologized for the state's violations against its own citizens (*Esmas* 2004). Such an apology aimed to recognize, publicly and officially, the state's role in persecuting its citizens in the past and its commitment to treat them all as full members of society in the future. The collective element of recognition addresses the broad dimensions of misrecognition that members of groups may continue to face by virtue of simply belonging to targeted and devalued collectives.

It is important to emphasize, however, that crimes are not merely collective. *Individual symbolic* acknowledgment consists of the need to recognize victims as individuals and not simply to place them in a residual category, reducing them to an amorphous group of passive, voiceless survivors. This type of acknowledgment includes developing ways of underscoring how oppression and terror affected individuals *as such*; how the term *victims' experiences* is not simply the aggregate of mostly similar stories but reflects actual, distinct individuals whose lives were changed in personal and profound ways. It must include, in other words, sensitivity to the multiplicity of distinct experiences that victims recount. While in practice it is of course impossible to recognize *all* victims as individuals in any meaningful sense—we are speaking of crimes committed on a massive scale, after all, and not everyone can be given a public platform to speak about his or her experiences—individual symbolic recognition emphasizes the importance of remembering that victims are not merely a statistic but actual people who often suffered intolerable cruelties. The suffering of an individual—whoever it may be—will always be more than a symbol of systematic crimes; suffering is always deeply personal (Herman 1997; Scarry 1987), and proper recognition requires attention to this fact. Sensitivity to victims as individuals is an important step to reaffirming their status as citizens, for it reflects a respect toward fellow humans that is a necessary element of any political order based on democratic principles of equality. While individual symbolic recognition is not the same as providing individuals with the full panoply of liberal democratic rights that accompany citizenship (negative and positive rights, access to the political process, and so on), it is an important prerequisite, for without recognition of victims as individuals *and* as equals deserving respect it is unlikely that they will secure their status as citizens.

Symbolic recognition—both individual and collective—is fundamental for helping victims recapture their sense of dignity and self-worth. Nevertheless, the symbolic aspects are not enough. In many cases, the devastation wrought by systematic violence and oppression also leaves victims in a position of economic vulnerability, something that cannot be remedied only through symbolic means. Thus, victim recognition also requires a concern with distributive justice.

The *collective material* element of reparatory justice focuses on distributive-justice issues. It seeks to provide resources to victimized groups with the aim of creating the material basis and security necessary for them to become full participants in social, political, and economic life. This provision of resources can take several forms, such as developing programs for housing and employment for groups whose economic condition was directly affected by the violence, as well as health initiatives (psychological and physical) to address the traumas that victims experience. Where victims belong to historically devalued communities whose position worsened during political violence (indigenous groups in Peru and Guatemala, for example), provision of resources may require broader infrastructural investments, including better roads, rural education programs, and credit initiatives for economic development. While the specifics of such programs must be tailored to particular contexts, the programs are collective in that they help groups that were targets of violence, and all entail the redistribution of economic resources with the goal of enhancing the livelihood of victims so that they may realistically pursue their life plans. Truth commissions in Peru, Guatemala, and El Salvador called for significant investments in public education, housing, employment, and economic development in indigenous areas most affected by the violence.

Nevertheless, there are several challenges that such collective material initiatives face. The first concerns how to connect, conceptually, reparatory justice initiatives with general development and distributive programs. Naomi Roht-Arriaza has summarized one position succinctly: "If reparations are integrated into a larger reconstruction and development agenda, the two sets of needs converge" (Roht-Arriaza 2004, 189; she later goes on to criticize this argument). While most of society would benefit from an increase in development, there is a question of whether the specifically normative dimension of reparations risks subsumption under general development and distributive programs, clouding the normative distinction between reparative justice aimed at victims per se and more general state policies to combat poverty. For many victims, reparations are not simply about financial compensation but *also* about the moral force of state acknowledgment, and therefore collapsing reparations into development is normatively problematic. Indeed, what the state may call reparations for victims may be viewed as part of the state's duties to all citizens, allowing the government to build moral and political capital while actually satisfying (or claiming to satisfy) basic obligations.[5] In addition, these programs can hide state-building efforts behind a discourse of human rights and reparations that effectively enhance the bureaucratic reach of the state while not necessarily guaranteeing that the needs of victims are adequately met. The state can use such discourse to promote policies that provide little benefit to survivors yet satisfy government objectives. The possibility that the state can use this type of discourse for its own aims is a particular concern that has received remarkably little attention, both among theorists and among practitioners dealing with victim-reparation schemes, but remains a challenge nonetheless (but see Wilson 2001, 1–32).

Finally, there is an *individual material* component to theories of reparatory justice. This too is a form of distributive justice, insofar as it addresses the importance of redistributing resources to victims, but it places greater emphasis on the autonomy of individuals than the collective dimension discussed above. Certainly, no compensation can substitute for death or torture, and in this sense money—or any reparatory measure—is always insufficient. But compensation can have an impact for economically destitute victims and shows that the state's

---

[5] Consider the following example: the state may argue that collective material reparations include building roads and sanitation infrastructure in historically impoverished rural areas that were the sites of massive violence. For a peasant survivor, this will certainly be a significant benefit. But an urban, middle-class victim will already enjoy access to roads, sanitation, education, and a number of other "benefits" seen as part and parcel of citizenship. Indeed, for such a victim material aid should focus more on psychological and medical support. Thus the question: Is the state's promise to rebuild roads and a sewage system in the countryside really a form of reparation or merely part of its obligations to all citizens relabeled through the moral discourse of reparations?

recognition of victims is not merely an empty symbolic gesture but also a commitment backed by material support. Individualized reparation schemes are varied, but they normally include familial rehabilitation through access to medical, psychological, and legal services, compensation for financially assessable losses, economic redress for harms that are not easily quantifiable, and restitution of lost, stolen, or destroyed property (Goodin 1989, 56–79; Lomasky 1991, 13–44; Van Boven 1993). Guatemala's CEH commission strongly recommended that the state create a National Reparations Program to include compensation for serious injuries and losses, psychological-rehabilitation initiatives, the restitution of or compensation for stolen or destroyed property, and other measures to be developed in tandem with affected communities. In particular, the commission emphasized the importance of individual reparations, with consideration given to the type of violation, the economic and social status of the victim, and special attention to certain categories of people, such minors, widows, and the elderly.

Similarly, in El Salvador the U.N. truth commission recommended the creation of a reparations fund for victims (financed by the state and international actors), and it signaled the importance of creating a state reparations institution that would carry out individual material reparations assessments and disbursals, as well as monitor compliance with the commission's recommendations. The Peruvian Truth and Reconciliation Commission called for a broad array of collective and individual material reparatory programs, many specifically for affected indigenous communities. These programs include cash payments, medical, psychological, and educational support, and employment training, among others (Peru 2003). But most of these programs have not been carried out. It is only in Brazil, Chile, and Argentina that some reparatory measures have been instituted.

Brazil, for example, created a small reparations program through a 1995 law compensating the families of more than 130 people who had "disappeared" during military rule (Brazil 1995; Roht-Arriaza 2004, 170–71). In Chile, where Pinochet's military regime killed approximately three thousand people and tortured thousands more, the successor government instituted one of the broadest reparations programs in Latin America (Chile 1992; Chile National Corporation of Reparation and Reconciliation 1996). Families of the "disappeared" or those killed by state action receive a monthly check of about $480 for life, and such payments cover a total of nearly five thousand people (the family members of the 2,723 disappeared or those killed by the regime as determined by the National Commission on Truth and Reconciliation [Chile 1991] and later the implementation agency, the National Corporation of Reparation and Reconciliation). In addition, families receive a state medical allowance, counseling, and access to a medical program. Benefits also include educational support for the children of the disappeared and killed in the form of full tuition and expenses for university study, as well as a number of smaller addenda, such as military-service waivers for children of victims (military service is mandatory in Chile), reinstated pension plans for persons who lost their state jobs for political reasons with lost years included, and a special automobile reentry tax waiver for political exiles. Crucially, survivors of torture or illegal detention receive no pension, educational benefits, or health support, except for access to state medical services (but no allowance for medication) and some counseling service, though there are ongoing efforts to correct this.

In Argentina, reparatory justice has been more extensive, both in terms of the number of persons covered and the general outlay and aims of the reparations legislation. For families of the disappeared and killed, monetary reparations consisted of a one-time payment of $220,000 paid in state bonds (Argentina 1994b). To qualify, the victims had to be listed in the final report of the National Commission on the Disappearance of Persons (Conadep) (Argentina 1984), or had to have been reported to the state's Human Rights Office and confirmed as disappeared or killed. The potential beneficiaries include family members of approximately fifteen thousand people.[6] Argentina also provides reparations for (a) those illegally imprisoned without trial; (b) those who had temporarily disappeared (that is, where authorities denied their detention) and whose cases were reported in the press, to the truth commission or to a human-rights organization at the time; and (c) those who were forced into exile for political reasons. Moreover, Congress created a new legal category of "forcibly disappeared," which grants the disappeared the status of death for the purposes of law, such as processing wills, permitting spouses to remarry, and closing estates, while allowing for the possibility of the person's reappearance (Argentina 1994a). Before the passage of this law, it was virtually impossible for spouses or family members to maintain control over the property of their disappeared loved ones. The legislature also waived mandatory military service for children of the disappeared (Argentina 1990) (military service is no longer mandatory, however), enacted housing credits for children, and in 2004 passed legislation providing reparations to children of the disappeared who were adopted (that is, kidnapped) by military families.

Individualized payment has the benefit of maximizing individual autonomy by allowing victims to use funds as they see fit, satisfying the needs and preferences identified *by victims*. In this way, it avoids the paternalism inherent in collective material reparations, thus respecting personal autonomy.

Such a fourfold normative model of reparations includes a number of challenges, some of which have been discussed above. Nevertheless, we

---

[6] The commission documented 8,960 disappeared, though subsequent investigations have expanded the number of victims.

must ask whether reparations offer some sense of moral redress. Some victim groups have argued that symbolic reparations always fall short of addressing the injuries caused by violations, and that no form of acknowledgment can suture the wounds of the past. Furthermore, they argue that material reparations can easily become a form of blood money, allowing the state effectively to release itself from any responsibility or future obligation to victims through the disbursal of payments, and in the process silence any legitimate victim complaints that may arise in the future.[7] All of these arguments point to a deeper skepticism about reparations—that their value, for the state, is not moral but largely utilitarian; in other words, that they serve only political ends. Such concern is warranted, particularly in cases where victims have been marginalized for a long time and there is little reason to believe that the state and society have changed their attitudes following the violence.

Nevertheless, such criticisms are fatal only if we think of reparations as free standing, separated from other reconciliatory mechanisms. If presented as the sole method of dealing with the past, then certainly there is good reason to be skeptical. Adequate engagement with the past must include more than symbolic and material reparations, important though these are. For reparatory justice by itself does nothing to end a culture of impunity or to foster accountability, or to promote the rule of law and reformation of corrupt and violent state institutions. It can only assist, not generate or sustain, a critical reappraisal of the past—or at any rate it cannot do so in the way the report of a truth commission can, catalyzing public deliberation. These other strategies point to several normative goals that transitional societies may have: accountability; establishment of the rule of law; truth telling; and the promotion of norms of tolerance and respect, in addition to victim acknowledgment. And while the relationships among these goals can be complex, we should place any theory of reparations within a broader theory of reconciliation that must theorize such connections, rather than expect reparations to achieve normative objectives that fall outside its domain.

What such a theory of reconciliation would look like is beyond the scope of this essay, though at the very least it must show sensitivity to how these normative goals interact at different social registers—among the political elite, state institutions, civil society, and individuals (Crocker 2000). The more modest point here is that if these other goals are pursued sincerely, and if society seeks to give victims status parity and thus invite them to be full citizens, then reparations can be seen as moral, not just instrumental, responses to a legacy of violations. But clearly to expect

---

[7] Indeed, the Argentine *Madres de la Plaza de Mayo*, an important victims' rights group, split precisely over this issue.

reconciliation and justice to emerge from a reparations program is to overburden it normatively. Keeping these points in mind, we can outline five benefits that reparations can contribute to victims and societal reconciliation more generally.

Part 3: Contributions of Reparatory Justice

At their most basic, reparations seek to return to victims some sense of *moral worth and dignity*. This is premised on a particular conception of the individual that sees identity as developing from the intersubjective recognition among equals, which includes recognition of their moral claims to dignity. Dignity is a fundamental property of what it means to be a person. It points to the value of autonomy and respect that is at the core of a healthy sense of self. In the second formulation of the categorical imperative, Kant (1996, 80) argues that to treat another as merely a means, with no dignity, is a moral wrong. While Kant does not espouse a theory of intersubjective morality, the notion that dignity is a fundamental value is at the basis of both deontological and intersubjective theories of morality, and its importance for victims of mass atrocity is clear.[8] Reparations indicate that the state and society consider victims to be bearers of moral worth and dignity, and such a consideration is publicly recognized through these reparatory means (as well as others, including prosecutions and truth-telling initiatives).

Reparations are indicative of this appreciation insofar as they symbol- ize society's recognition of victims as equals deserving respect. Respect here means a relationship premised on the reciprocal recognition of the inherent, and thus not instrumental, value of individuals. This is a public attitude or—as Arendt puts it—of "the domain of human affairs" (1989, 243). To respect another means to accept that the other has some inherent value, and such respect is expressed by behaving in ways that acknowl- edge that value. We do not, for example, measure another's worth through a consideration of our own interests or desires and call this respect—such an attitude (and behavior) merely relegates the other's value to a measure of utility according to our own calculus. Respect requires an acknowledgment of the other's claim *on us* to his or her moral worth and dignity, and we consequently have an obligation to treat him or her in a certain way that expresses this acknowledgment (see, for example, Korsgaard 1993, 24–51, and 1996).

Such respect, grounded on the normative goal of status parity, does not entail the deep reconciliation favored by some theological advocates,

---

[8] Though for Kant autonomy does not mean absolute separation from others. He describes people as "rational beings with needs, united by nature in one dwelling place so that they can help one another." Quoted in Baron, Pettit, and Slote 1997, 67. The authors attribute the quotation to Kant in the *Metaphysics of Morals*.

such as Desmond Tutu (1999) and Miroslav Volf (2001), for whom a reconciled society is one where estrangement is overcome through a process of fundamental ontological transformation on the part of perpetrators and victims.[9] Respect falls short of this and instead requires that social patterns of valuation and economic standing become roughly equal across the board, for without some degree of equality some citizens—primarily victims, in the cases we are discussing here—remain marginalized politically, socially, and economically. But respect is also something greater than the liminal requirements for politics demanded by Schmittian political theorists like Chantal Mouffe (2000), who see legitimate political engagement as fundamentally agonistic with little room for consideration of the other as a moral equal. Respect, then, reflects the ability to see another as a fellow human being, invested with moral worth and dignity, but does not demand the theological fraternity that some thinkers place at the core of reconciliation. Such a notion of respect prompts us to rethink social interaction in a way that promotes tolerance of others in public and semipublic life and eventual trust in democratic institutions. Reparations can encourage this insofar as they represent normative responses that highlight the moral equality of all, publicly recognizing the dignity and moral worth of victims. In this sense, then, reparations are particularly crucial to victims.

Reparations also signal to the population the need to *reconceptualize a society's sense of itself*, since it forces society to rethink who qualifies as part of the "we." Insofar as survivors are entitled to recognition not only as victims (that is, that their experiences be publicly recognized) but also as *citizens*—as equals with the right to participate in the political, social, and economic life of the nation—all citizens must reconsider how they think of citizenship and how to include erstwhile enemies as partners in a new future (indeed, while they may become opponents, one hopes they will no longer be enemies). Material and symbolic reparations are important to the larger political project of creating a democratic citizenry, for they signal a more inclusive sense of nationhood. They also signal an expanded constellation of responsibility and obligation—to the extent that victims are treated as equals and society is forced to rethink of itself more inclusively, the moral constellation of obligation toward fellow citizens is expanded. Reparations signal that the state recognizes victims as fellow citizens and encourages others to do so as well.

Reparations can also have the effect of strengthening *public trust* in state institutions. In Latin America, where state security apparatuses

[9] Volf calls for something greater than respect, a "will to embrace": "The will to give ourselves to others and welcome them, to readjust our identities to make space for them, is prior to any judgment about others, except that of identifying them in their humanity. The will to embrace precedes any 'truth' about others and any reading of their action with respect to justice. This will is absolutely indiscriminate and strictly immutable; it transcends the moral mapping of the social world into 'good' and 'evil'" (2001, 42).

committed most of the recent violations, reparations highlight the state's commitment to principles of justice, the rule of law, and citizen welfare, as well its rejection of past policies against perceived enemies. This is especially important where state legitimacy is badly tarnished and the successor regime is struggling to gain some degree of popular support. Often, it is the police, military, and judiciary who held particular responsibility for the commission of crimes, and thus reparations, combined with institutional reform, can help generate public trust. Reparations are not enough to renew such trust, which can only be achieved over time, but they can begin strengthening social support for a fledgling democratic state.

Prosecutions are the clearest and most powerful way to identify past actions as violations and to undermine the ideologies of perpetrators. However, reparations also do so, for identifying victims as worthy of recognition implicitly redefines certain events and actions as transgressions. In conjunction with trials and truth-telling mechanisms, such as truth-commission reports, reparations may promote an alternative account of the past. Indeed, recognizing victims as bearers of rights and legitimate claims to dignity helps to *undermine the justificatory narratives of the perpetrators*, narratives that gave legitimacy to their actions. By signaling that espousing these narratives led to actual crimes entailing victims, these narratives are slowly eroded, and the exclusivist political project of the past (ideally) gives way to a more open, humane understanding of plurality and cohabitation, which in turn opens the possibility of status parity.

In a closely related vein, reparations, particularly forms of symbolic acknowledgment of the type identified above, may *promote an alternate, critical interpretation of the past*, insofar as they explicitly recast victims as agents with a moral status equal to that of other citizens. A critical history investigates the assumptions and biases employed in accounts about the past. Such a history eschews what Nietzsche (1997) calls "monumental" histories, where the present is legitimized through unreflective appeal to the past (or any unrealizable transcendental claim that legitimizes any means to achieve it). In cases where earlier historical narratives served to justify violations, symbolic reparations signal to the population that these narratives distorted the past and minimized atrocity, and that a reappraisal of the past is necessary. Of course, the moral force of reparations only helps create a space for interrogating the past—the difficult task of reappraisal occurs over time in the public sphere, may include truth-commission reports, debates among political elites and among the broader public, and may end with changes in educational curricula and the development of new histories.

All of this is a highly contentious business, and reparations can only contribute to it, rather than being the decisive factor. Nevertheless, symbolic reaffirmation of the victims as moral equals limits the range of falsehoods that can be presented as history. And ideally such a reappraisal can contribute to a society's self-reflection, though, as is always the case with issues of transitional justice, we should not set our expectations too high. But while disagreements will persist, the very move toward a reappraisal of the past is an achievement and may promote, in the long run, a "critical truth." Such developments have occurred to some extent in Chile and Argentina, where the legitimacy of the armed forces has suffered and the original justifications given for their dirty wars have lost some purchase (more so in Argentina than in Chile). So in a sense symbolic acknowledgment goes some way in reconceptualizing historical memory and combating unreflective, "monumental" understandings of the past that justify crimes.

I have claimed, then, that official apologies can perform, or at least contribute to, five key tasks. First, they publicly reaffirm victims' moral worth and dignity. Second, they force a society to reconceptualize its sense of "we" when it is confronted with including as equal members those who were maltreated, disparaged, and attacked in the past. Third, reparations may help in creating some public trust in state institutions, institutions that in many cases were responsible for (or at least complicit in) the commission of atrocities. Fourth, by recognizing victims as citizens, reparations contribute to undermining the justificatory narratives given by perpetrators. And finally, along these lines, reparations may also catalyze a public debate around a critical interpretation of history, one that calls for a careful reconsideration that eschews monumental, unreflective understandings of the past.

I have argued that reparatory justice is crucial for societies facing a legacy of political atrocity. Such a theory, as I have outlined it here, seeks to transform victims into citizens—to give them the status that will allow them to live meaningful lives in a new society. A normatively satisfactory theory consists of four ideal-typical dimensions: a typology of acknowledgment that includes symbolic and material components, and a typology of victims that focuses on both collective and individual measures. Such a model provides conceptual clarity to the possibilities and limits of reparations, helping us assess how successful actual programs are. Nevertheless, it must be understood as part of a broader process of engaging legacies of abuse, including facing the past openly and honestly. For a society that continues to live immersed in hidden legacies of violations and denials cannot develop into a culture that treats its members as equals. In the absence of some form of accountability, impunity will continue to poison social relations and breed contempt for fellow citizens, and without the meaningful acknowledgment of victims, survivors are unlikely to receive the dignity and respect they deserve. Shorn of the rule of the law and the commitment to peaceful democratic debate for resolving differences, reconciliation becomes little more than a euphemism for the power of entrenched elites. With such considerations in mind, it becomes evident that reparations are a necessary, though certainly insufficient, element to achieving justice and reconciliation.

References

Arendt, Hannah. 1973. *Origins of Totalitarianism*. New York: Harcourt Brace.

———. 1989. *The Human Condition*. Chicago: University of Chicago Press.

Argentina. 1984. *Informe de la Comisión Nacional sobre la Desaparición de Personas*. Buenos Aires: Editorial Universitaria.

———. 1990. *Law No. 23,852.*

———. 1994a. *Law No. 24,321.*

———. 1994b. *Law No. 24,411.*

Barkan, Elazar 2000. *The Guilt of Nations*. New York: Norton.

Baron, Marcia, Philip Pettit, and Michael Slote (eds.). 1997. *The Three Methods of Ethics*. Oxford: Blackwell.

Benhabib, Seyla. 2002. *Claims of Culture: Equality and Diversity in the Global Era*. Princeton: Princeton University Press.

Benjamin, Jessica. 1998. *The Bonds of Love*. New York: Pantheon.

Biggar, Nigel (ed.). 2001. *Burying the Past: Making Peace and Doing Justice after Civil Conflict*. Washington, D.C.: Georgetown University Press.

Brazil. 1995. *Article 1, Law 9,140.*

Brooks, Roy L. (ed.). 1999. *When Sorry Isn't Enough: The Controversy over Apologies and Reparations for Human Injustice*. New York: New York University Press.

Chile. 1991. *Report of the Chilean National Commission of Truth and Reconciliation*, 2 vols. Notre Dame: University of Notre Dame Press.

———. 1992. *Law Creating the National Corporation of Reparation and Reconciliation, Law No. 19,123.* Reprinted in *Transitional Justice: How Emerging Democracies Reckon with Former Regimes*, edited by Neil Kritz, vol. 3, 685–95. Washington, D.C.: United States Institute of Peace, 1995.

Chile National Corporation of Reparation and Reconciliation. 1996. *Informe Sobre Calificación de Víctimas de Violaciones de Derechos Humanos y de la Violencia Política*. Santiago: Corporación Nacional de Reparación y Reconciliación.

Crocker, David. 2000. "Truth Commissions, Transitional Justice and Civil Society." In *Truth v. Justice: The Morality of Truth Commissions*, edited by Robert Rotberg and Dennis Thompson, 99–121. Princeton: Princeton University Press.

Cuneen, Chris. 2001. "Reparations and Restorative Justice: Responding to the Gross Violation of Human Rights." In *Restorative Justice and*

Civil Society, edited by Heather Strang and John Braithwaite, 83–98. Cambridge: Cambridge University Press.

El Mercurio. 1991. "Aylwin Pide Perdón al Pueblo Chileno." Santiago, Chile. March 5.

Esmas. 2004. "Kirchner Pide Perdón en Argentina." March 24. At http://www.esmas.com/noticierostelevisa/internacionales/352624.html. Accessed November 23, 2005.

Fraser, Nancy. 1997. *Justice Interruptus: Critical Reflections on the "Postsocialist" Condition*. New York: Routledge.

———. 2000. "Rethinking Recognition." *New Left Review* 3: 107–20.

———. 2001. "Recognition without Ethics?" *Theory, Culture and Society* 18, nos. 2–3:21–42.

———. 2003. "Social Justice in the Age of Identity Politics: Redistribution, Recognition and Participation." In *Redistribution or Recognition? A Political Philosophical Exchange*, edited by Nancy Fraser and Axel Honneth, 7–109. New York: Verso.

Goodin, Robert. 1989. "Theories of Compensation." *Oxford Journal of Legal Studies* 9:56–79.

Guatemala. 1999. *Guatemala: Memoria del Silencio: Informe de la Comisión para el Esclarecimiento Histórico*. 9 vols. Guatemala City: Commission for Historical Clarification.

Herman, Judith. 1997. *Trauma and Recovery*. New York: Basic Books.

Honneth, Axel. 1995. *The Fragmented World of the Social: Essays in Social and Political Philosophy*. Albany: State University of New York Press.

———. 1996. *The Struggle for Recognition: The Moral Grammar of Social Conflicts*. Cambridge, Mass.: MIT Press.

———. 2003. "Introduction." In *Redistribution or Recognition? A Political Philosophical Exchange*, edited by Nancy Fraser and Axel Honneth, 1–6. New York: Verso.

Jones, Adam (ed.). 2004. *Gendercide and Genocide*. Nashville: Vanderbilt University Press.

Kant, Immanuel. 1996. "Groundwork of the Metaphysics of Morals." In *Kant's Practical Philosophy*, translated by Mary Gregor. Cambridge: Cambridge University Press.

Korsgaard, Christine. 1993. "The Reason We Can Share: An Attack on the Distinction between Agent-Relative and Agent-Neutral Value." *Social Philosophy and Policy* 10:24–51.

———. 1996. *Creating a Kingdom of Ends*. Cambridge: Cambridge University Press.

Lomasky, Loren. 1991. "Compensation and the Bounds of Rights." In *NOMOS XXXIII: Compensatory Justice*, edited by John Chapman, 13–44. New York: New York University Press.

McCarthy, Thomas. 2002. "Vergangenheitsbewältigung in the USA: On the Politics of the Memory of Slavery." *Political Theory* 30, no. 6: 623–48.

Mouffe, Chantal. 2000. *The Democratic Paradox*. New York: Verso.

Nietzsche, Friedrich. 1997. "On the Uses and Disadvantages of History for Life." In *Untimely Meditations*, translated by R. J. Hollingdale. Cambridge: Cambridge University Press.

Office of Human Rights of the Archbishop of Guatemala. 1998. *Guatemala: Nunca Más: Informe del Proyecto Interdiocesano de Recuperación de la Memoria Histórica*, 4 vols. Guatemala City: Office of Human Rights of the Archbishop of Guatemala.

Okin, Susan. 1999. *Is Multiculturalism Bad for Women?* Princeton: Princeton University Press.

Peru. 2003. "Plan Integral de Reparaciones." Vol. 11 of *Peru: Informe Final de la Comisión de la Verdad y Reconciliación*. At www.cverdad. org.pe. Accessed July 23, 2005. The International Center for Transitional Justice has translated sections of the report, which are available at www.ictj.org.

Roht-Arriaza, Naomi. 2004. "Reparations Decisions and Dilemmas." *Hastings International and Comparative Law Review* 27, no. 2 (winter): 157–219.

Scarry, Elaine. 1987. *The Body in Pain: The Making and Unmaking of the World*. New York: Oxford University Press.

Taylor, Charles. 1989. *Sources of the Self*. Cambridge, Mass: Harvard University Press.

——. 1994. "The Politics of Recognition." In *Multiculturalism*, edited by Amy Gutmann and Charles Taylor, 25–74. Princeton: Princeton University Press.

Tutu, Desmond. 1999. *No Future Without Forgiveness*. New York: Doubleday.

United Nations. 1993. *El Salvador: From Madness to Hope: The 12-Year War in El Salvador: Report of the Commission on the Truth for El Salvador*. United Nations Doc. S/2550, Annex. New York: United Nations.

Van Boven, Theo. 1993. "Study Concerning the Right to Restitution, Compensation and Rehabilitation for Victims of Gross Violations of Human Rights and Fundamental Freedoms." *ECOSOC, Commission on Human Rights, Subcommission on Prevention of Discrimination and Protection of Minorities*, United Nations Doc E/CN.4/Sub.2/1993/8. New York: United Nations.

Volf, Miroslav. 2001. "Forgiveness, Reconciliation, and Justice: A Christian Contribution to a More Peaceful World." In *Forgiveness and Reconciliation: Religion, Public Policy and Conflict Transformation*, edited by Raymond G. Helmick and Rodney L. Petersen, 27–50. Philadelphia: Templeton Press.

Wilson, Richard A. 2001. *The Politics of Truth and Reconciliation in South Africa: Legitimizing the Post-Apartheid State*. Cambridge: Cambridge University Press.

Zimmerman, Michael. 1994. "Compensation and Culpability." *Philosophia* 24, nos. 1–2:29–48.

11

PROSECUTING MILITARY LEADERS FOR WAR CRIMES

LARRY MAY

I believe that leaders should be the primary targets of international prosecution for war crimes. While soldiers can be held individually responsible for violating international humanitarian law, normally it should be difficult to do so unless there was a joint criminal enterprise. Even in such cases, the *mens rea* component of criminal liability will be difficult to prove. It is the leaders rather than the normal soldiers that more often display the kind of mens rea that is looked for in criminal cases. When we come to consider the criminal responsibility of the leaders there are two conceptual problems nonetheless. In this essay I argue that military (and political) leaders should normally be those who are prosecuted for war crimes. To do so I will offer a solution to the two main conceptual problems.

The first conceptual problem concerns how difficult it often is to establish the *actus reus* component of criminal liability, since it is the normal soldiers rather than the commanders who actually do the killing of civilians or torturing of prisoners, for instance. Two strategies are normally employed for solving the actus reus problem, and these strategies correspond to the two main provisions on criminal liability of the International Criminal Tribunal for Yugoslavia (ICTY) Statute. First, issuing orders to do the killing or the torturing, and the like, is itself a criminal act that directly links the commander to the normal soldier. Second, failing to prevent the soldiers from doing what they were known to be doing, or would do, is a failure to act that could also link the commander to the acts of the normal soldier. The second conceptual problem concerns the mens rea component, especially when we are discussing leaders who did not themselves intentionally plan the larger criminal enterprise. The questions concern whether having knowledge is sufficient, and whether negligence can be seen as sufficiently grave to warrant individual criminal liability for violations of international humanitarian law. I will mainly focus on the mens rea issues.

I believe it is mens rea that should be key in war crimes prosecutions, and hence it is the leaders not the minor players who should be the primary subject of prosecution for international crimes. But I will also discuss some serious difficulties in determining the level of mens rea that needs to be proved in order to convict political and military leaders for international crimes. In this respect, I will focus on cases where the claim is that leaders ordered that these crimes occur. I will not consider the somewhat easier cases concerning the criminal liability of leaders for the lesser crimes of aiding or abetting a crime. I will focus on a particular case, namely, that of the prosecution of General Tihomir Blaskic, the commander of the Croatian Defense Council. Blaskic was prosecuted for his part in the mass crimes committed against Muslims in Bosnia, especially for inhumane treatment in the taking of hostages and the use of human shields in 1993 and 1994.

In section 1, I present the key facts of the case and the basis of the ICTY Trial Chamber's conviction of General Blaskic. In section 2, I set out the basis of the ICTY Appeals Court's overruling of the Trial Chamber's decision. In section 3, I focus on the issue of mens rea concerning those who command others to commit such crimes as the taking of hostages and the use of human shields. In section 4, I set out a limited argument in favor of negligence as a type of mens rea in international criminal law. And finally, in section 5, I discuss the relevance of the idea of the theory of joint criminal liability in such cases. Throughout, while arguing in favor of holding leaders responsible for international crimes, I worry quite a bit about what would be a fair standard of mens rea for these leaders.

1. The Case against General Blaskic

General Tihomir Blaskic was one of the few non-Serbs to be prosecuted for war crimes by the International Criminal Tribunal for the Former Yugoslavia. Blaskic

> was appointed commander of the HVO [the Croatian Defense Council] armed forces headquarters in central Bosnia on June 27, 1992 and occupied that position throughout the period covered by the indictment. In this position and pursuant to Article 7(1) of the Statute, he was accused of having, in concert with members of the HVO, planned, instigated, ordered or otherwise aided and abetted in the planning, preparation or execution of each of the crimes alleged ... and that he had not taken the necessary and reasonable measures to prevent the said crimes. (Trial Chamber Judgment 2000, para. 9)

Among the crimes Blaskic is accused of participating in are persecution, unlawful attacks upon civilians and civilian objects, willful killing and serious bodily injury, destruction and plunder of property, destruction of institutions dedicated to religion or education, inhumane treatment, taking of hostages, and use of human shields (paras. 10–16).

The Trial Chamber of the ICTY notes that the Blaskic prosecution concerned "the criminal responsibility of a military commander" (Trial Chamber Judgment 2000, para. 261). Involved in this prosecution are two related forms of individual responsibility. The first is the planning, instigating, ordering, or aiding and abetting of a crime. This is covered under Article 7(1) of the Statute of the ICTY and is not necessarily restricted to "persons who directly commit the crimes in question" (para. 263). Blaskic is not accused of having committed the actus reus of any of the crimes just mentioned. Rather, he is prosecuted for having ordered, planned, or instigated the acts of others who directly committed the crimes in question. It is interesting that the Trial Chamber comments that to be convicted of issuing an order, the "order does not need to be given in writing or in any particular form" and does not need to "be given by the superior directly" to the person who performs the actus reus (paras. 281–82).

Second, Blaskic is accused, in the alternative, of having known that crimes were about to be committed, or had been committed, by a subordinate and having failed to take the necessary steps to prevent or punish the commission of the crime (Trial Chamber Judgment 2000, para. 289). This is covered under Article 7(3) of the ICTY statute. The Trial Chamber then goes on to list the proof required here: proof that

(1) there existed a superior-subordinate relationship between the commander (the accused) and the perpetrator of the crime;
(2) the accused knew or had reason to know that the crime was about to be committed, or had been committed; and
(3) the accused failed to take the necessary and reasonable measures to prevent the crime or punish the perpetrator thereof. (Para. 63)

The Trial Chamber also held that "the commander need not have any legal authority to prevent or punish acts of his subordinates. What counts is his material ability, which instead of issuing orders or taking disciplinary action may entail, for instance, submitting reports to the competent authorities in order for measures to be taken" (para. 302).

One of the key factual findings of the Trial Chamber was that Blaskic ordered an offensive against Loncari and Ocehnici, directly implicating him in the "cleansing" of these areas (Trial Chamber Judgment 2000, para. 590). The Trial Chamber also found that when Blaskic gave these orders "he knew full well that there were criminals in its ranks, the accused [Blaskic] intentionally took the risk that very violent crimes would result from their participation in the offensive" (para. 592). In addition, to mention just one of the crimes, the Trial Chamber also found that Blaskic "ran the risk that many detainees might be taken hostage" (para. 741) and that "Blaskic ordered civilians from Gacice village to be used as human shields in order to protect his headquarters" (para. 743). Thus, Blaskic is found to have ordered many of the atrocities or in the alternative to have run the risk that they might occur and then failed to prevent them.

The Final Conclusions section of the opinion is unusually harsh. The Trial Chamber accuses Blaskic of having given "genuine attack orders" to kill civilians and to slaughter livestock and destroy mosques (Trial Chamber Judgment 2000, paras. 749–50). The Court concluded:

> At no time did he even take the most basic measure which any commander must at least take when he knows that crimes are about to be or have actually been committed. The end result of such an attitude was not only the scale of the crimes, but also the realization of the Croatian nationalists' goals—the forced departure of the majority of the Muslim population in the Las Va Valley after the death and wounding of its members, the destruction of its dwellings, the plunder of its property, and the cruel and inhuman treatment meted out to many. (Para. 754)

For these reasons, the Court, by majority vote, convicted Blaskic and sentenced him to forty-five years in prison, certainly one of the stiffest penalties meted out by the ICTY.[1]

One of the most interesting aspects of this case is the way that the Court tries to prove that orders were given as a way of substantiating Blaskic's individual responsibility under Article 7(1) of the ICTY Statute, and the way that it established the riskiness of his behavior in not intervening when he could as a way of substantiating his individual responsibility under Article 7(3) of the Statute. In both cases, the Court attempts to draw inferences from a somewhat spotty evidentiary record. As in many cases that go before international as well as domestic criminal tribunals, courts look for what is beyond reasonable doubt, not for what is certain. It is thus also very interesting that, as we will see in the next section, the Appellate Court's reversal is unusually harsh.

General Blaskic, as a commander of Croat national forces, clearly had a duty to exercise care in the way that he issued orders. But the question becomes whether he should be held criminally liable for not exercising *extraordinary* care. I am inclined to agree with the Trial Chamber that we should hold commanders to a very high standard. Especially when they know that there are miscreants under their command, commanders must be extraordinarily vigilant not to let these potential criminals engage in abuses and atrocities that have been so common over the centuries during ethnic wars. And with only a bit of hindsight, it also seems reasonable to hold people responsible for what are the obvious problems that result from attempts at ethnic cleansing.

In terms of war crimes, as opposed to prosecutions of crimes against humanity, the command structure should not be something that military leaders can hide behind. For it will indeed be hard to prove that a general order is interpreted in just one way by those who are down the line. But then the very difficult question becomes that of deciding what standard of mens rea to use in such commander cases. Everyone agrees that strict

---

[1] Blaskic Trial Judgment 2000, disposition following para. 802. A life sentence is actually the stiffest punishment, but given that Blaskic was in his late thirties when the crimes alleged were committed, he faced the equivalent of a life sentence.

liability is not sufficient for criminal liability in such cases, that is, that it is not enough merely to show that the general was indeed the commander at the time. At the very least it must also be shown that the general knew a massacre was likely to occur. But at various points the Trial Chamber seems to signal that actual knowledge or intent is not required, only a certain kind of negligence on the part of the general. Yet, as we will see in the next section, it is highly controversial to use a negligence standard of mens rea in criminal law, and it is even more controversial how to understand that standard. It seems to be insufficient to seek a conviction on the ground that reasonable people would have seen the possibility that harms could result from the issuing of various orders, but too much to require that it be certain that such harms would result. In the next section we will see that the Appeals Chamber took issue with the Trial Chamber on just such grounds and ultimately reversed Blaskic's conviction.

2. Blaskic's Appeal

In 2004 the ICTY Appeals Chamber surprisingly ruled that the Trial Chamber in the Blaskic case had made very serious mistakes in law. Based on newly discovered evidence, the Appeals Chamber also voted to exonerate Blaskic of most charges and have him released, based on the eight years he had already served in prison. The main alleged mistake in law that caused this reversal concerned the mens rea component of individual liability for leaders who participate in war crimes. Before I address the important ruling of the Appeals Chamber on negligence as mens rea, I first briefly want to say something about the actus reus issue—namely, whether there was sufficient reason to think that General Blaskic's acts constituted unjustified ordering of the acts that the soldiers under Blaskic's command subsequently committed.

The Trial Chamber had drawn the inference that since the towns in question, especially Ahmici, had no notable military significance, attacking the towns was not based on a military objective. While the Appeals Chamber seems to agree with this assessment, it nonetheless declared that:

> The Trial Chamber gave no significant weight to the argument that the road linking Busovaca and Travnik had strategic significance, and with respect to the fact that AbiH [Muslim] soldiers were reported to be traveling toward Vitez ... additional evidence submitted on appeal shows that there was a Muslim military presence in Ahmici and the neighboring villages, and that Appellant had reason to believe that the AbiH intended to launch an attack along the Ahmici-Santici-Dubravica axis. (Appeals Chamber Judgment 2004, paras. 331 and 333; and see Drumbl 2004)

Thus, the Appeals Chamber concluded that the Trial Chamber had misinterpreted Blaskic's order to attack. Evidence of the imminent Muslim attack and evidence that individuals other than Blaskic gave the order to attack makes Blaskic harder to link to an actus reus and casts reasonable doubt, which a jury could have determined, on Blaskic's criminal culpability in this case.

More important conceptually is the Appeals Chamber's ruling concerning Blaskic's mens rea, especially whether Blaskic was aware that civilians would be killed during the attack on Ahmici. Even if Blaskic did give various orders, the question is what his state of mind was in so acting. Here is how the Appeals Chamber characterizes the relevant mens rea standard:

> In the absence of direct intent . . . a person who orders an act or omission with the awareness of the substantial likelihood that a crime will be committed in the execution of that order, has the requisite *mens rea* for establishing responsibility under Article 7(1) pursuant to ordering. Ordering with such awareness has to be regarded as accepting that crime. (Appeals Chamber Judgment 2004, para. 345)

The Appeals Court reverses the judgment of the Trial Chamber and holds that the orders "at most, [are] sufficient to demonstrate the Appellant's knowledge of the mere possibility that crimes could be committed by some elements" but not "a substantial likelihood that crimes would be committed in the execution of" the order (para. 347).

As I noted earlier, there are two ways to establish the mens rea component of criminal liability of leaders under the ICTY Statute. The first way, which was addressed in the previous paragraph under the rubric of Article 7(1) of the ICTY Statute, concerns whether a commander gave orders that were known to create a substantial likelihood that a crime would be committed. The second way, under Article 7(3) of the Statute, concerns whether reasonable steps were taken to prevent crimes that the commander had reason to know were being committed, or would be committed, by those who were under his or her control. In this second respect, the Appeals Chamber initially agrees that Blaskic had effective control over the military personnel who committed crimes against civilians. But the Appeals Chamber disagrees with the Trial Chamber in the analysis of what it means to say that Blaskic "had reason to know" that crimes were being, or would be, committed.

Previously in the Appeals Chamber Judgment substantial time was spent explaining what it means for a commander to have "reason to know" that a crime would be committed that could be prevented. The Trial Chamber addressed this issue in terms of negligence, which the Appeals Chamber agrees is "likely to lead to confusion of thought" (Appeals Chamber Judgment 2004, para. 63). Indeed, the Appeals Chamber remarks that the International Criminal Tribunal for Rwanda (ICTR) "Appeals Chamber has on a previous occasion rejected criminal negligence as a basis of liability in the context of command responsibility" (para. 63). So in rejecting a negligence standard of mens rea, the ICTY

Appeals Chamber turns to the jurisprudence concerning the idea of "reason to know" as a standard of mens rea for commanders.

The Appeals Chamber adopts the view of the ICTY's Celebici Appeals Chamber that commanders have a duty to be informed of the behavior of their subordinates but that they cannot merely be assumed to have indeed been so informed simply because they occupied a superior position of authority.

> The Celebici Appeal Judgment has settled the issue of the interpretation of the standard "had reason to know." In that judgment, the Appeals Chamber stated that "a superior will be criminally responsible through the principles of superior responsibility only if information was available to him which would have put him on notice of offenses committed by subordinates." Further, the Appeals Chamber stated that "(n)eglect of a duty to acquire such knowledge, however, does not feature in the provision of Article 7(3) (as a separate offense) and a superior is not therefore liable under the provision for such failures but only for failing to take necessary and reasonable measures to prevent or to punish." (Appeals Chamber Judgment 2004, para. 62)

Thus, the Appeals Chamber endorses the appellant's claim that actual knowledge must be proved, not merely a showing of possible knowledge that a reasonable person should have obtained. The criminal liability of a commander requires proof that the commander had actual knowledge of what the subordinates were doing, not mere negligence that the superior should have had such information. As the Court says, the "had reason to know" mens rea standard does not reduce to a "should have known" standard (para. 59).

The Appeals Chamber thus reaches the judgment that General Blaskic was not liable for the criminal acts of those under his control. The Appeals Chamber holds that he did not have knowledge of what his superiors were doing. In addition, the Appeals Chamber concludes that "the Appellant took the measures that were reasonable within his material ability to denounce the crimes committed" and that in any event Blaskic lacked effective control to prevent or punish these crimes (Appeals Chamber Judgment 2004, paras. 420 and 421). For these reasons, the Appeals Chamber exonerates Blaskic of most of the serious charges alleged against him. Thus, the highest-ranking Croat leader to stand trial for mass crimes committed against Muslims in Bosnia was released, with the Trial Chamber receiving a rather stiff admonishment for having incorrectly stated the mens rea standard for commanders in such cases involving Article 7(3) of the ICTY Statute.

The Appeals Chamber Judgment in the Blaskic case is likely to have far-reaching effects in the development of international criminal law. For it is hard to see how the ICTY Appeals Chamber action will not make it harder to convict military (and political) leaders of war crimes. As is true of leaders of corporations, the negligence standard rejected by the

Appeals Chamber has often been seen as the only practicable standard for achieving convictions of leaders in such cases. In the next section I survey the most important mens rea considerations in holding commanders responsible for war crimes and begin to explain why negligence has often been appealed to.

3. The Mens Rea of Leaders

Normally it is thought that the hard part in obtaining convictions of leaders concerns the fact that leaders do not do the proscribed deed, that is, leaders are not the ones who do the actual killing or torturing. But it is also thought that leaders, not soldiers, are the ones who intentionally issue the orders and hence have the mens rea requisite for criminal liability. While this is how it appears, the reality is that it is often very hard to find evidence of orders to kill or torture. Instead, the norm seems to be that there are generalized orders, such as the order to "secure an area" or "clear civilians from an area," and these orders do not appear to be based on a guilty mind, at least not at face value. So, establishing the mens rea of leaders is in many cases harder than it might first be thought. For, as the ICTY Appeals Chamber has said, it does not appear to be fair merely to hold leaders criminally guilty just because they gave generalized orders and a crime occurred on their watch. To take this route would be tantamount to adopting a strict liability standard of criminal liability for leaders, an idea that has generally seemed abhorrent to most.

It is important to try to explain why strict liability, in its various forms, is indeed considered so abhorrent. There are three ways that liability can be strictly assigned. The most severe form concerns a disregard for both mens rea and actus reus. Think of a parent who is held strictly liable for what his or her child does. Under such a scheme, criminal liability is assigned regardless of what the parent did to try to stop the child from acting, and regardless of what the parent's intentions or knowledge were concerning the child's actions. While there may be good reasons to hold parents liable, as a way of motivating them to minimize the risky actions of their children, it does not seem fair to a particular parent then to disregard what the parent has done, or intentionally tried to do, to minimize these risks.

Perhaps it could be argued that parents have indeed done something to warrant liability, namely, they have procreated, thereby creating the child, and but for the act of procreation there would be no child whose harmful or risky behavior is now at issue. On this view, even this form of strict liability is not completely strict, since it is still based on something the parent did, and perhaps even something that the parent did intentionally or with knowledge of the risks being created. But this is not the normal kind of action that connects a perpetrator to a harm and triggers possible criminal liability. For we normally look for proximate rather than remote causal influence. Remote causal influence, extended to its limit, would involve so many people's actions in harms that liability would be diffused beyond recognition, perhaps extending back generation upon generation, holding all living relatives responsible for what the current child has done. So, the liability that is most strict has made little sense, at least as a form of criminal liability.

A second form of strict liability is one that disregards only the intentions of the person held liable but that still requires action that is not remote. A classic example of this form of strict liability concerns the manufacture of explosives. We might hold the manufacturer criminally liable for anyone who is injured in the manufacturing process, no matter how careful the manufacturer is, and regardless of the fact that it was no part of the manufacturer's intention that people would be harmed during the manufacturing process. Again, it seems that this is unfair, since the manufacturer hasn't tried to harm anyone and may even have tried exceptionally hard to minimize the likelihood of harm. On the assumption that the manufacturing was indeed considered a trigger for criminal liability, it is true that the manufacturer did something wrong, hence establishing actus reus. But the lack of any mens rea seems to mean that there isn't the kind of willfulness that is often thought to be the hallmark of responsibility, the larger category under which liability falls.

Criminal liability, unlike civil liability, involves the risk of loss of liberty. To warrant loss of liberty it is normally thought that willful misconduct is required, not merely accidental misconduct, as it were. For if an agent caused harm but did so intending to do good, or perhaps without even understanding that his or her conduct could cause harm, it seems to be unfair then to take liberty away from the agent. Punishment to be fair requires responsibility, and yet responsibility is blocked when an agent did not act willfully. Again, it might be appropriate to levy a fine for accidentally harmful behavior, but punishment, and its attendant loss of liberty, seems to require more from the agent than mere action without any guilty mental state.

The third kind of strict liability concerns liability that disregards only the actions of a person, focusing instead on the person's intentions and knowledge. This is indeed the form of strict liability that normally is assigned to leaders. For as I said above, the leader normally doesn't do the killing or the torturing but may nonetheless have come up with the plan that called for just such actions by others. But, despite the fact that the leader did not commit the guilty action, we might hold him or her criminally liable based on intentions and planning alone. For it seems that having a guilty mind is the most important dimension to being guilty. Yet, even if this is true, there seems something odd in not requiring proof of some sort of action on the part of the accused, since without requiring action we would start down the slippery slope that might end in the punishment of mere thoughts.

The way to avoid sliding down this slippery slope is to require some action, even if the action is relatively remote from the actual perpetration of the killing or the torturing. So, in many contexts the issuing of a command or the actual drafting and dissemination of a plan, no mater how long before, is thought to be enough of an actus reus to let mens rea dominate in the assigning of criminal liability. But in such a case, since there is both action and intention, we are not really in the domain of strict liability at all anymore. In the Blaskic case, the prosecution tried to prove that General Blaskic did indeed issue an order to assault the civilian population, and in the alternative that Blaskic failed to act, an act of omission, to prevent what he knew, or should have known, would result. These acts, of commission or omission, stop the possible slide down the slippery slope. But the Appeals Chamber still thinks there is a problem.

The Appeals Chamber focuses on another issue that arises in cases concerning the mens rea of leaders, namely, whether potential knowledge is ever sufficient to constitute a guilty mind. By virtue of being a military commander, Blaskic was in a position to know certain things and even had a duty to come to know what his troops were doing or were about to do. The Trial Chamber held that it was sufficient to establish that the knowledge was available and that Blaskic had a duty to obtain the knowledge. But the Appeals Chamber reverses this view and holds that actual knowledge had to be proved. The main reason for this reversal has to do with the fact that the actus reus was already so diminished, and the intent part of mens rea was similarly seen as being of diminished importance. To get a better grip on this matter, we next turn to the question of whether negligence should be sufficient to generate criminal liability in international tribunals.

4. Negligence in International Criminal Law

Negligence has played only a limited role in criminal law, although it has played what is probably a disproportionate role in the few cases of chief executives prosecuted for white-collar crimes. The main reason for this general neglect of negligence in criminal law, as I explained above, is the view that punishment cannot be administered in all fairness if the accused has not willfully done something. Not only is negligence not willful, it is unclear that negligence is even a state of mind at all, rather than merely the absence of a certain state. The terms *carelessness* and *inadvertence*, sometimes thought to be synonyms for negligence, clearly indicate a lack, that is, care-less-ness and in-advertence, the mere negation of states of mind rather than guilty states of mind themselves. In this section I will explore the idea of negligence in international law, especially international criminal law.

A recent textbook in international criminal law by the renowned jurist Antonio Cassese, but written before the Blaskic Appeals Chamber judgment, argues that there has been a

> broadening of the range of acts amenable to international prosecution ... in keeping with the general object and purpose of international humanitarian law. This modality of *mens rea* [gross or culpable negligence] may for instance apply to cases of command responsibility where the commander should have known that war crimes were being committed by his subordinates. (Cassese 2003, 58)

Cassese admits that mere "negligence is the least degree of culpability. Normally, it is not sufficient for individual criminal liability to arise" (172). Given what is at stake in international criminal prosecutions, only gross or culpable negligence will generally meet the standard of mens rea. Gross or culpable ignorance arises, according to Cassese, when the person

(i) *is expected or required to abide by certain standards of conduct or take certain specific precautions,* and in addition
(ii) is aware of the risk of harm and nevertheless takes it, *for he believes that the risk will not materialize owing to the steps he has taken or will take.* (172)

Furthermore, for international prosecutions there must be "some specific conditions relating to the objective elements of the crime, that is, the *values* attacked are fundamental and the *harm* caused is serious" (172).

So, while Cassese argues that there has been a broadening of how mens rea is understood, he nonetheless recognizes that negligence is used in a fairly limited set of criminal cases. Cassese does argue, though, that in some cases a superior can be held criminally liable for the acts of his subordinates "if he did not know, but 'should have known' that they were about to commit, or were committing, or had committed crimes" (2003, 173). As we saw above, this analysis is at odds with the analysis provided by the Blaskic Appeals Chamber, which clearly required more than proof that Blaskic "should have known" what his subordinates did, or were about to do. Rather, the Appeals Chamber required proof of actual knowledge of what the subordinates did, or were about to do. In effect, the Appeals Chamber said that negligence in any form would not be sufficient for international criminal liability. By requiring actual knowledge, the ICTY effectively required at least recklessness for mens rea, not merely culpable negligence.

Admittedly, the border between gross or culpable negligence, on the one hand, and recklessness, on the other hand, is often difficult to see, and even harder to prove. In corporate cases, proof of what a CEO knew is often very hard to fathom, especially since CEOs often either intentionally blind themselves to what their subordinates are doing or make sure that there is no paper trail concerning what they have been informed about. For this reason, the standard often employed is what a "reasonable" CEO would and should have known. This moves us more toward negligence, though it is often a standard used when there is suspicion that a CEO was in fact reckless but proof of the CEO actually having knowledge is just too difficult to get, especially when CEOs are well insulated from observation by their subordinates.

I wish to spend the rest of this section discussing whether there are good normative grounds for not allowing gross or culpable negligence to satisfy the mens rea requirement of criminal liability for commanders as regards war crimes. Gross or culpable negligence is often morally serious enough for us to think that those who have this "mental state" are guilty in some sense. Think here of the case of those given the task of caring for children who have been separated from their parents. If those put in the position of standing in for the parents disregard the needs of the children, why would we need to show that these people actually knew that disregarding their needs would produce suffering in the children? Isn't it enough to show that they certainly should have known?[2]

Yet even in the case just sketched it is unclear whether what was described was gross negligence or recklessness. For those in charge of the children not only *should* have known that the children would suffer but in some sense *must* have known as well. "Must have known" is of course somewhere between "did know" and "should have known." While it would be reckless to know information and yet not act on it, it is only gross negligence not to know what one should have known and not act on it. But "must have known" does not fit into this divide. One of the reasons why gross negligence does indeed seem to be sufficient to many people is because they believe that a defendant actually did know because anyone in that situation must have known, but it merely couldn't be proven.

The normative question is why we would demand it be proven that a superior actually did have the knowledge that we assume he had and any normal person would have had in these circumstances. At least part of the answer to this question has to do with what criminal trials are generally supposed to be about—namely, the unique facts of a case rather than the general tendencies of human nature. Indeed, in criminal trials in the Anglo-American system of law, talk of tendencies of how people behave is generally excluded by the rules of evidence. What must be proven is what the defendant did or knew at the time of the incident in question. It is generally considered irrelevant to discuss what others knew or what people generally would have known. This seems to be the basis of the judgment by the Blaskic Appeals Chamber.

---

[2] Cassese 2003, 203, cites the case of Heinrich Gerike and Others (the Velpke Baby Home trial) where a British court found the defendants guilty on grounds of gross negligence in a case similar to the one I have just sketched.

Normatively, the principle is that criminal liability only attaches to willful acts. It could be contended that if a superior is required to know certain things and does not come to know them, then this looks as though "not knowing" is a willful act. But the difficulty is that it would only be willful if it could be shown that the superior chose not to know what he or she should have known. If instead the superior simply forgot, or was not alert, then his or her failure to learn the required information is not necessarily willful. And while we may want to make an exception to the general principle requiring willfulness, we must recognize that such an exception will render the criminality, and subsequent punishability, of the defendant suspect as well.

Let me say just a few more words about why the principle requiring willfulness is so important in criminal liability. At least in part such an investigation might discover in which areas exceptions might be more justifiable than in other areas. Since the time of the ancient Greeks it has been thought that responsibility and punishment attach to the willful acts of agents. If the agent had no choice in the matter, or acted accidentally, the agent is typically not held morally responsible for his or her behavior and its consequences. Similarly, only once a choice has been made to cause, or risk, harm does it make sense to hold someone criminally liable. If the behavior and its consequences were not the result of a willed action, there was no clear decision to do something wrong and hence no clear reason for assigning responsibility or punishment. What we should hold people morally and criminally responsible for is freely choosing to do something wrong. Without the act of will, it is hard to see why punishment would be justified.

The key component in any defensible use of negligence as a mens rea condition in international criminal law has two elements: not only should the commander have acted as any normal person would have acted, the commander also had to have the capacity so to act but chose not to act. We can bring willfulness back into the equation of mens rea in cases of negligence by proving that the commander knew that he or she had a duty to act in a certain way—for instance, to supervise carefully his or her subordinates—and had the capacity to meet his or her duty, and yet chose not to do so. The difficulty is to show that the omission to do, as H. L. A. Hart puts it, "that which any ordinary reasonable man could and would have" done, namely, "a standard requiring him to take precautions against harm," was chosen (Hart 1968, 147, 148).

One of the most difficult normative problems is whether it is sufficient to prove that there was information that could have been available and should have been known, but was not actually known, by the accused. Is it sufficient to prove that there was a duty to get this information but it wasn't obtained, or must it be proven that there was specific information available that was disregarded? In the Blaskic case, the Appeals Chamber required a showing that General Blaskic had knowledge of the likely bad conduct of some of his subordinates. Why wasn't it enough to show that a reasonable person would have and should have known this information? This is really a question, as I mentioned earlier, about whether something very close to recklessness is required, rather than simple negligence.

I am of two minds about this issue, and as a result I am inclined to proceed cautiously. On the one hand, I think there can be clear willfulness in choosing not to be informed even though one should have become informed, or in choosing not to supervise one's subordinates when one should have been supervising them. For this reason, I do not see any reason in principle to rule out negligence as a mens rea standard. But on the other hand, I do not think that it is sufficient merely to infer such willfulness from someone's failure to do that which he or she had a duty to do. For, in law if not also in morality, I think we do need to distinguish inadvertence from negligence, where the difference is not merely whether one had a duty in the latter case but not in the former. From the mere lack of doing x it does not follow that one has omitted to do x in the sense of having willfully chosen not to do x. We should not be too quick to draw the inference that someone has chosen to omit to do x rather than that he or she has merely inadvertently not done x.

Hart argues that "negligence is gross if the precautions to be taken against harm are very simple, such as persons who are but poorly endowed with physical and mental capacities can easily take" (1968, 149). He gives the example of a workman who does not look to see who might be below before throwing slates from the top of a construction site to the ground below. Hart thinks that this is a case of gross negligence that could form the basis for the mens rea element in a criminal prosecution of the workman. So long as there was no incapacity, a person "can be punished in effect for a failure to exercise control" (153). Hart then posits a two-pronged test for when negligence is criminally punishable:

   (i) Did the accused fail to take those precautions which any reasonable man with normal capacities would in the circumstances have taken?
   (ii) Could the accused, given his mental and physical capacities, have taken those precautions? (154)

The question I am raising is whether we need in addition to ask a third question: Did the accused choose not to take those precautions?

One way to address this test, made popular by Hart, is to ask whether we are demanding more than we would demand when the mens rea standard is intentional wrongdoing rather than negligence. Hart says that just as the workman could say, "My mind was a blank," so the murderer could say, "I just decided to kill" (1968, 151). But while this argument works well against those who think that negligence is not sufficiently a mental state at all, it also works against the claim that negligence might not manifest sufficient willfulness to be culpable. The question that I am raising is not whether negligence could be a mens rea standard by being a state of mind but whether it is sufficiently willful to be regarded as a culpable state of mind upon which a criminal prosecution could be based. My general answer is that it could be, but that what is needed is to prove that the neglect was chosen, and yet this is incredibly difficult to show in most cases, although not in all, as we will see in the next section.

Hart thinks that it is often hard to prove that a person chose to commit murder as well. It is possible that the person was forced to do so, or couldn't help but kill. But this would be very odd, barring special circumstances. We would want to know what could possibly have motivated him or her to kill and how it could possibly be that he or she killed without foresight. Similar kinds of things can be said, Hart thinks, about the person who omitted to do what any reasonable person would and should have done. Again, barring special circumstances, we want to know what could have been the motivation not to do what was plainly one's duty to do.

But the lack of a motivation does not of itself allow us to infer that a person had willfully chosen to omit what he or she should have done. A compromise has sometimes been proposed in which only gross negligence will count as satisfying the mens rea requirement of criminal liability. This is roughly what the Model Penal Code attempted when it gave the following qualification:

> The risk must be of such a nature and degree that the actor's failure to perceive it, considering the nature and purposes of his conduct and the circumstances known to him, involves a gross deviation from the standard of care that a reasonable person would observe in the actor's situation. (Model Penal Code, 1962, sec. 2.02[2][d], and see Fletcher 1998, 114–17)

But questions still arise about whether and when we should be entitled to infer willfulness even in gross deviations from what reasonable people would do. Can't even such gross deviations be due simply to lack of thought, that is, to thoughtlessness of the kind that is nonculpable?

The debate about whether negligence should count as a sufficient mens rea for criminal liability is at least in part a debate about whether neglect can be presumed to be willful. Neglect can certainly be willful, but it is often not clear whether it is or not in a particular case. Neglect can be due merely to an absence of thought or it can be due to a decision not to act. If one has a duty to act, then it is more likely that one's failure to act is willful, but this is not always the case. So here is the problem in a nutshell: mere neglect or negligence is not clearly willful and hence not clearly something for which the agent should be held responsible. And because criminality carries with it such serious consequences, I am cautious about holding leaders responsible for what subordinates do unless there is some indication that the leaders *chose* to neglect their supervisory roles. In the next section I will discuss a possible way to get around this problem concerning negligence, although not a foolproof way.

5. Benighting Acts, Willfulness, and Precommitment

When it is unclear what role each person plays in a concerted effort, it is sometimes easier to parse guilt and blame if it is clear that all parties entered into an enterprise together, realizing what was likely to happen and how each person's part would contribute to the joint effort. In military matters, as in corporate matters, often all of the members voluntarily and willfully join in a common undertaking. In these cases certain questions about particular responsibility or liability are not quite as difficult, because of the willful act of joining in the enterprise. When a negligent or benighting act occurs later, it may be easier to infer willfulness.[3] As we will see in this section, the use of the joint-enterprise liability theory can help us resolve some of the problems we identified above concerning the liability of military leaders for what their subordinates have done or are doing. Problems will still remain, but most of the problems will become somewhat easier to solve.

The main difficulty with a negligence standard of mens rea, within a general theory of command responsibility, is that normally we can only infer, not prove, that omitting is indeed willful; and yet if omissions are not willful, then it is not clear why they entail sufficient guilt to be the subject of criminal liability and punishment. But if people have joined in an enterprise and clearly committed to do certain things identified as their duties, then it seems to be more justifiable than not to infer that when they fail to do their duties it is because they have chosen this path. It is still possible that in a given case the reason a person didn't do *x*, even though he or she had committed to doing *x*, was not that he or she chose not to do *x* but that he or she was at a given moment behaving thoughtlessly.

But the most important question, as Holly Smith has shown, is whether there was a culpable act that preceded the benighting or negligent act, a preceding act that itself colored the benighting act, the ensuing unwitting act that followed and caused harm. Let us take an example to illustrate the general problem. Consider a commander who fails to discover that his troops are planning to cause harm, and as a result the commander does not move to prevent them from doing harm to civilians

---

[3] Holly Smith (1983) first uses "benighting" in this way when she discusses the first act of doing what would make one ignorant of certain facts that later prove important in one's harmful behavior. *Webster's New Twentieth-Century Dictionary*, unabridged, 2d edition, gives this as its third definition of "benight": "to involve in moral darkness or ignorance, to exclude from intellectual light; as absorbtion in routine benights of the mind." Smith often uses the term also to mean the first act that then colors all others, calling to mind a kind of "knighting" act that colors the rest of one's actions.

and only goes about his job as he otherwise should, and the soldiers cause harm. The initial failure to discover information is the benighting or negligent act. The failure to prevent harm is an unwitting act that gives rise to, or at least significantly contributes to, the perpetration of harm. The main question, as Smith formulates it, is whether the benighting act is both objectively wrongful and also culpable. It is objectively wrongful insofar as it is a violation of a duty that the commander had. But it is unclear whether it is culpable, since we do not know whether the commander had bad motives in not doing his duty.

Two things could make a difference. One is the motive behind the benighting act. The other is whether there was a prior act that so greatly colored the benighting act as to make the benighting act culpable. Smith focuses on the former, pointing out that it is not merely a question of whether at the time of the benighting act the agent had reprehensible motives but also a question of whether the agent had "reprehensible motives at the time of some earlier act that indirectly gave rise to the unwitting act and which render it blameworthy" (Smith 1983, 566). I will focus on the latter factor that could make a difference. If I promise to do x, realizing that failure to keep my promise will cause harm, and then forget that I made the promise and act in an otherwise blameless way, my previous promising act, which is not itself blameworthy, colors the situation to such an extent that the subsequent act is clearly blameworthy because it is an instance of promise breaking that I previously realized was something that would cause harm.

My view, which takes off from Smith's but then diverges from it, is that the key to using negligence as a form of mens rea for criminal liability turns on whether the act of negligence is preceded by an act, or set of acts, that makes the negligence blameworthy, independent of whether we can prove anything about the state of mind of the agent at the very time the act of negligence occurs. Think of one of Smith's own cases: a doctor ought to have read his medical journals but did not, and as a result he did not know that the use of high concentrations of oxygen causes severe eye damage. On Smith's analysis, the prior act that colors the rest, the failure to read the medical journals, is wrongful, if it is wrongful, because it displays a wrongful motive. The key question for Smith is whether the doctor had reason to foresee that his earlier act would spill over to color his later acts and yet took that risk (1983, 554). My own take on this case is somewhat different from Smith's, and in setting out those differences here I will also begin to sketch my own view. I will then connect that view to the theory of joint criminal enterprise liability.

I would argue that the key is whether there is a willful act that is causally connected to the negligence that then caused the harm in question. For regardless of whether the willful act is itself blameworthy, it is the willfulness that transfers, at least in some cases, to the negligent act, making of the negligent act not merely something done thoughtlessly but something done willfully. The doctor has the duty to read the medical journals because of his role as a physician, and perhaps also because of a specific duty based on his maintaining board certification in his specialty. In any event, what is key is that he has committed himself to read these journals. The wrongness of his failure to read them can be construed independently of whether he recognized the risk to his patients of not doing so. So, when he fails to read the journals the wrongness of his doing so turns on the violation of a duty he has expressly committed himself to perform, rather than on the foreseeability of the risk.

In the cases we considered earlier, the key question was whether the negligent act displayed wrongfulness, and I understood that to mean a willful choosing. The problem that needed to be resolved was whether the negligent act was neglect caused by thoughtlessness or by something willful. But it isn't necessary that the willful act itself be wrongful, or even that the benighting act encompass the risk in the sense that the perpetrator of the benighting act recognized the risk at the time. On my analysis, what is wrong is that by not reading the journals the physician violated a duty he had committed himself to serve. In typical commander cases, commanders commit themselves to be part of a larger campaign of a certain sort and to follow certain rules of war. As in the case of the physician, it does not matter that they can or cannot foresee that harms will result from their not following the rules. Rather, it is the violation of duty that is key.

Of course, one could still wonder whether the violation of duty is itself willful or merely thoughtless. The physician might say that he just didn't think. But as in the case of the person who makes a promise and then fails to keep it, the defense or excuse of just not thinking is generally not applicable if one has committed oneself in advance, where precommitment means, among other things, that such a defense or excuse will not be recognized. This is a kind of strict liability, to return to one of the ideas expressed earlier, but perhaps not one that is especially obnoxious, since it is one that the agent could have avoided completely on his or her own merely by not engaging in the precommitment.

Let us turn finally to the idea of joint criminal enterprise liability. One way to understand joint criminal enterprises is as large-scale instances of precommitment. People in a joint enterprise commit themselves to the goals of the enterprise by making the collective goals of the enterprise their own personal goals. And this means that they precommit to do what it takes to achieve the goals of the group enterprise. When, later, individuals unwittingly act to advance those goals by simply doing what they are told, or if they fail to do things that turn out to advance that goal, they are linked to those goals almost as surely as if they had intended that their acts would advance those goals. Once it is proven that there was a joint criminal enterprise, it is significantly easier to show that the failure to supervise is not merely a thoughtless act, especially in those cases where that failure facilitates the achievement of the goals of the enterprise.

Let us return to the Blaskic case. If the general was part of a joint enterprise, whereby some people in the joint enterprise put miscreants into positions where they could terrorize camp prisoners and other civilians, and where not properly supervising these miscreants was part of the plan, then when the miscreants are in fact not supervised it certainly no longer looks like simple negligence based on thoughtlessness. And even if it truly is thoughtlessness, it still looks as though the precommitment counts in allowing us to disregard the thoughtlessness and hold Blaskic strictly liable nonetheless. But, again, this is not an especially obnoxious kind of strict liability, for in effect the general had by his own earlier acts endorsed just such a scheme of liability as had the promise maker.

Another route leading to the same result is that the commander by accepting the assignment as commander also precommits to follow the rules of war. Such precommitment also acts as a kind of license to others to hold commanders strictly liable for following this self-assumed duty. It may still be true that some generals and other commanders act out of thoughtlessness rather than willful wrongness when they do not properly supervise their subordinates. But the precommitment to follow the rules of war, including the proper supervision of troops to make sure that they do not commit war crimes, looks like a transferred willfulness as regards the later negligence. The category of willful negligence sounds like an oxymoron until it is recognized that the willfulness comes earlier and the benighting or negligent act comes later. We still do not have willfulness at the same time as the benighting or negligent act occurs, or else it wouldn't really be negligence. But the earlier willfulness involved in precommitment does in fact color the negligence and makes of it something culpable.

So, I agree with the ICTY Appeals Chamber that there are significant hurdles to overcome in cases like that of General Blaskic, requiring moves different from those employed by the Trial Chamber. But I have tried to indicate how a commander like Blaskic could still properly be prosecuted for war crimes even if it turns out that he simply didn't think when he left miscreants unsupervised to kill and torture civilians in Bosnia. Blaskic's negligence could still be based on willfulness, although admittedly much earlier in time than the act of negligence of not supervising would be. This is a form of transferred willfulness, or even of strict liability if you like, for in a sense Blaskic has little defense open to him concerning the acts of negligence. But it is important also to recognize that the reason Blaskic would not have these defenses or excuses open to him has to do with his own acts in joining the criminal enterprise, or in simply agreeing to be a commander in the first place. So, while this strategy does not solve all of our problems, it does allow us possibly to hold Blaskic criminally liable even though his most important acts may not have arisen out of willful malice at the time.[4]

---

[4] This essay is drawn from chapter 12 of my book-length manuscript, "War Crimes and Just Wars."

References

Appeals Chamber Judgment of the ICTY, *Prosecutor v. Tihomar Blaskic*. 2004. (July 29.) Available at http://www.un.org/icty/blaskic/appeal/judgement/index.htm

Cassese, Antonio. 2003. *International Criminal Law*. Oxford: Oxford University Press.

Drumbl, Mark A. 2004. "ICTY Appeals Chamber Delivers Two Major Judgments: Blaskic and Krstic." *ASIL Insights* (August 18).

Fletcher, George P. 1998. *Basic Concepts of Criminal Law*. Oxford: Oxford University Press.

Hart, H. L. A. 1968. "Negligence, *Mens Rea*, and Criminal Responsibility." In his *Punishment and Responsibility*, 136–57. Oxford: Oxford University Press.

Model Penal Code, Section 2.02(2)(d). 1962. New York: American Law Institute.

Smith, Holly. 1983. "Culpable Ignorance." *Philosophical Review* 92 (October): 543–71.

Trial Chamber Judgment of the ICTY, *Prosecutor v. Blaskic*. 2000. (March 3.) Available at http://www.un.org/icty/blaskic/trialc1/judgement/index.htm

12

RETHINKING THE LEGITIMACY OF TRUTH COMMISSIONS: "I AM THE ENEMY YOU KILLED, MY FRIEND"

NIR EISIKOVITS

South Africa's Truth and Reconciliation Commission (TRC) was a bold, controversial experiment in transitional justice. The most contentious aspect of the commission's work concerned its amnesty-granting powers: in return for full disclosure about their crimes, the TRC was authorized to release perpetrators of gross human rights violations from both criminal responsibility and civil liability. This essay takes up the thorny question of how such a commission might be morally justified. Part 1 discusses the political circumstances that led to the creation of the TRC. Part 2 provides a critical survey of some previous attempts to justify the commission's work. Part 3 offers a new justification, grounded in Adam Smith's notion of sympathy; after outlining some of the benefits of sympathy for political reconciliation, I argue that the work of a South African–style truth commission can promote sympathy between former enemies.[1]

Part 1: South Africa's TRC and the Problem of Political Legitimacy

The TRC was the result of a political compromise between Frederik de Klerk's outgoing National Party (NP) and Nelson Mandela's incoming African National Congress (ANC). South Africa's interim constitution of 1993, which set the terms for the transition from apartheid to democratic rule, contained a "postamble" stipulating amnesty for crimes committed during the era of white rule. It read: "In order to advance . . . reconciliation and reconstruction, amnesty shall be granted in respect of acts, omissions, and offenses associated with political objectives and committed in the course of the conflicts of the past" (quoted in Meredith 1999, 20–21). Many ANC supporters, who wanted to see Nuremberg-style war-crime tribunals, were understandably upset by the arrangement. Mandela, who insisted on the

[1] The quotation in my subtitle is taken from Wilfred Owen's poem "Strange Meeting" (1917). I am grateful to David Lyons, Aaron Garrett, Hugh Baxter, Charles Griswold, David Roochnik, Maria Granik, Rivka Eisikovits, Jamie Kelly, Tony Reeves, Shai Biderman, and Fred Tauber. Many thanks to Simon Keller and the other members of the Boston-area ethics reading group for the opportunity to present an earlier draft of this essay in spring 2006.

importance of steering clear of "victors' justice," remained adamant about the need for some kind of accountability for apartheid's crimes. Without such reckoning, he threatened, the unaddressed atrocities of the past would live with South Africans like a "festering sore" (Meredith 1999, 18).

The convergence between these two commitments—to amnesty on the one hand and to accountability on the other—was to shape the TRC's mandate. The commission would respect the ANC's promise to offer amnesties, but the reprieve would not be granted automatically. It would, rather, be linked to a demand for full disclosure from perpetrators. Those seeking amnesty would have to apply for it, provide complete details about what they had done, and establish that their activities were politically motivated (rather than the result of greed, sadism, and so on).[2] Applicants would not, however, be required to apologize or otherwise express regret. Furthermore, the arrangement would eliminate not only criminal responsibility but also civil liability.[3] Successful applicants could be neither charged nor sued for their conduct during the apartheid years.

Not surprisingly, the main controversy surrounding the commission's work concerned its amnesty-granting powers. The opportunity for perpetrators of egregious human rights abuses to walk away from prosecution enraged many black South Africans who wanted to see those who had tormented them and their families put behind bars. Consequently, much of the scholarly literature on the TRC centers on the question of justification, on the attempt to locate a rationale that might make sense of an arrangement that goes against a great deal of our untrained intuitions about justice. "If justice requires the prosecution and punishment of those who commit gross human rights violations," writes Elizabeth Kiss, "then the amnesty offered by the TRC violates justice. Can the TRC be defended against, or in spite of, this criticism?" (2000, 143). Similarly, Amy Gutmann and Dennis Thompson point out that "in a democratic society, and especially in a society that is trying to overcome injustices of the past, trading criminal justice for a general social benefit such as social reconciliation requires a moral defense if it is to be defensible" (2000, 22).

In the next section I consider some of the most important attempts to justify the work of the TRC. These include the view that the commission embodies important tenets of deliberative democracy, that it promotes justice as recognition, and that it is more suitable than trials in providing an account of past human rights violations.

A note on the scope of the argument is in order before we proceed. The South African TRC attracted more attention than other truth commissions because of its broad mandate, the celebrity of its chairperson (Archbishop Desmond Tutu), and the very public nature of its hearings.

---

[2] For a more specific account of the criteria used to determine whether an act was "politically motivated" see Hayner 2002, 274 n. 32.

[3] For more detail see Minow 1999, 56, and Kiss 2000, 68.

Since the TRC has become paradigmatic of this kind of transitional instrument, I shall direct most of my comments in this essay to its work. I believe that the argument put forth here applies to any truth commission with comparable powers.

Part 2: Justifications of the TRC

2.1 Deliberative Democracy

Amy Gutmann and Dennis Thompson argue that the justification of a truth commission needs to meet three criteria that any attempt to justify a democratic institution must satisfy: it must be moral in principle, be inclusive, and be moral in practice. The first condition rules out what the authors call the *realist* justification, the claim that the TRC was the only politically feasible way to ensure a peaceful transition. The second demands that the justification employ reasons that are "broadly accessible and therefore inclusive of as many people as possible" (2000, 23). The last requirement stipulates that the justification be based on the kind of reasons that "are to the extent possible embodied or exemplified by the commission's own proceedings" (23). The justification that most fully meets these three requirements, argue the authors, is one rooted in the idea of deliberative democracy and its constituent notion of reciprocity. Central to deliberative democracy is "the idea that citizens and officials must justify any demands for collective action by giving reasons that can be accepted by those who are bound by the action" (35–36). This, in turn, presupposes the notion of reciprocity "which asks citizens to try to justify their political views to one another, and to treat with respect those who make . . . efforts to engage in this mutual enterprise even when they cannot resolve their disagreements" (36).

Insofar as a truth commission tries to foster this sort of reciprocal exchange, it is justifiable on moral grounds, because such an exchange is, in itself, a moral good. The first condition is thus met. A commission grounded in a conception of deliberative democracy is inclusive because the principle of reciprocity involves locating the kind of reasons that appeal to a relatively large number of citizens. "The standard of reciprocity also satisfies the second requirement of justification by providing an inclusive perspective. A reciprocal perspective is one that cannot be reasonably rejected by any citizen committed to democracy because it requires only that each person seek terms of cooperation that respect all as free and equal citizens" (37). Finally, a commission based on the principle of reciprocity is likely to operate through procedures that embody that principle. "Such a commission practices what it preaches about the democratic society that it is trying to help create. Reciprocity serves as a guide . . . for the commission itself, calling on the commissioners and the testifiers to practice some of the skills and the virtues of the democratic society they are striving to create ... the openly participatory process by which members and staff of the TRC were appointed, and the generally public process in which its proceedings were conducted, demonstrated its own commitment to democratic practices" (37).

Reciprocity, claim Gutmann and Thompson, dictates another commitment—to the principle of "the economy of moral disagreement." Citizens must justify their positions by using the least controversial rationale available to them. The principle of economy encourages those engaged in deliberation to look for the kind of justifying rationales that overlap with rather than completely contradict beliefs held by others. To be morally justifiable under a conception of deliberative democracy, a truth commission needs to economize, as much as possible, on disagreement. An example of such economizing in the work of South Africa's TRC is the decision not to grant blanket amnesties and to insist on the punishment of some of the worst perpetrators.

2.1.1 Critique

The deliberative-democracy-based justification of the TRC presents several difficulties. First, and most generally, it presupposes that a justification of truth commissions must meet the same demands that justifications of existing democratic institutions need to satisfy. This assumption strikes me as overambitious. A truth commission is not a democratic institution but, rather, an institution that is meant to facilitate the transition of a society to democracy. Most often, countries undergoing such transitions lack a democratic tradition, have no history of significant public dialogue, and have not secured the minimal economic conditions required for meaningful political participation. Under these circumstances, expecting truth commissions to reflect and promote the ideals of deliberative democracy might be asking for too much.

Second, the justification does not seem to be specific enough. In other words, it is not clear why deliberative democracy, and its accompanying attributes of reciprocity and minimizing disagreement, justify truth commissions any more than they justify other transitional instruments. Thus, for example, a war-crimes tribunal may generate as much public discussion as a truth commission, it may be based on reasons or principles as widely accessible as those underlying a truth commission, and it may insist on trying only the worst offenders, thus economizing on moral disagreements. It seems, in other words, that the deliberative-democracy-based argument justifies too much.

Finally, I am skeptical whether the TRC can be justified through a deliberative-democracy rationale at all. The commission simply did not embody an especially open, deliberative stance in its operation. Though many of the hearings of the TRC's three committees were public, some of the important procedures associated with them were confidential by default. Thus, for example, the proceedings of the amnesty commission were public, but the amnesty applications themselves, as well as the documentation submitted to support them, remained confidential until declassified by the commission. Furthermore, it must be remembered that the commission was exempt from standard rules of legal procedure and evidence. Perpetrators who were named in the testimony of victims, or in the testimony of other perpetrators, were not given an opportunity to defend themselves; second-hand information, which would have been ruled out of court as hearsay, was admitted, and so forth. I think a commission making these sorts of exceptions to the precepts of procedural justice can still be justified (for example, by showing that these exceptions were necessary for establishing the chain of responsibility leading to the higher ranks of government). I do not, however, think that the best way to justify such a commission is by invoking a conception of deliberative democracy. For public deliberation to be meaningful and substantial, robust protections of procedural justice must be in place. As I have mentioned, these were lacking in the case of the TRC.

2.2 Justice as Recognition

A second justification of the TRC holds that truth commissions, by focusing as they do on victims and providing them with the opportunity to tell their stories in an uninterrupted fashion in front of a sympathetic forum, recognize victims as moral agents with stories worth telling. As Kiss puts it, "Providing a platform for victims is one of the core tasks of truth commissions, not merely as a way of obtaining information but also from the standpoint of justice. . . . Those whose lives were shattered are entitled to have their suffering acknowledged and their dignity affirmed, to know that their 'pain is real and worthy of attention.' . . . We affirm the dignity and agency of those who have been brutalized by attending to their voices and making their stories a part of the historical record" (2000, 73).

The TRC did not adhere to the strict, skeptical approach to witnesses prevalent in law courts. Many of the standard laws of evidence were suspended. Commissioners offered gestures of acknowledgment, such as rising when the witnesses entered the courtroom, visiting the sites of atrocities with them, and participating in public reburials and commemoration ceremonies (Kiss 2000, 73). These arrangements and exceptions to the standard rules of procedures were designed to make the process be *about* the victims of apartheid; witnesses were assumed to be speaking the truth, and they were treated as people who had been through hell and had come back to tell their tale, rather than as containers of information.

2.2.1 Critique

The justification of the TRC sketched above is a powerful one. A transition from mass atrocity into civil society, if it is to be stable and lasting, requires that the value of the individual lives of an entire class—the class of victims—be affirmed. By allowing victims to testify in an uninterrupted manner, and by creating a setting in which their testimonies were presumed to be true, the hearings of the TRC in South Africa went beyond establishing the crimes of the security forces or presenting the hardships of everyday life under apartheid. They also posited blacks, for the first time, as persons whose stories ought to be heard with care and respect. In other words, not only the content of the testimonies before the TRC was of significance; the mere act of blacks testifying was transformative as well. The members of the white class, the majority of whom had supposed that a black man or woman cannot be the bearer of legitimate, significant information, were made to think again.

However, the argument from recognition raises a serious difficulty. Some victims may legitimately claim that the restoration of their sense of dignity requires that those who have hurt them be punished; that in order to feel like moral agents worthy of respect, they must know their injuries merit the criminal law's protection. For such agents, dignity and individual worth are manifested not (or at least not solely) in the capacity to testify but in the commitment of the state to apply its coercive power on their behalf. For such victims, the currency of recognition may include punishment rather than mere storytelling; it may consist first and foremost in knowing that one has reentered a civic zone protected by law, where the use of violence against one is met with strict, reliable sanctions.

2.3 More Truth

Proponents of truth commissions argue that the commissions are better than trials at producing detailed, comprehensive accounts of past abuses. This superiority, they say, justifies compromises in retributive justice. In the case of the TRC, it was not only the dismissal of regular rules of evidence that allowed commissioners to unearth more information. The commission's amnesty-for-truth mechanism created an incentive for perpetrators to come forward. Once they started to do so, a domino effect resulted: offenders who were exposed in the testimony of their colleagues rushed to testify lest they be indicted. The chain reaction quickly led to the highest rungs of the apartheid regime. Furthermore, because the commission was authorized to deny amnesty to anyone who had not provided full disclosure, those who came before it tried to give as much detail as they could.

2.3.1 Critique

The "more truth" justification is a strong one. Two observations are, however, in order. First, as several critics of the TRC have noted, its choice to focus on gross human rights violations—on dramatic, specific stories of suffering—has obscured some of the institutional aspects of apartheid. Thus, the interconnections between business and the security forces, the wildly discriminatory practices of many workplaces, and the support that many white media outlets lent authorities in masking the practices of apartheid were largely overlooked by the commission's work. Insofar as these, too, are aspects of the truth, they were not revealed by the TRC.

Second, the fact that the TRC was the result of a political compromise meant that there were some areas in which it proceeded very cautiously. Quite a few cans of worms remained unopened. In a recent book on the history of apartheid, South African journalist Terry Bell (2003, 4) mentions one spectacular example: as Frederik de Klerk, South Africa's last white leader, was heading for Oslo to receive the Nobel Peace Prize in 1993, he ordered a strike on a house allegedly housing militants from the Pan-African Congress liberation group. A police death squad ended up killing five teenagers sleeping in a private home in the town of Umtata. The incident was never investigated by the TRC. Bell (2003, 245) also points to some rather obvious investigative avenues the commission did not pursue. One of the TRC's researchers proposed to make a list of where and when members of apartheid security forces had served and to crosscheck it with a list of cases of human rights violations in which the identity of perpetrators was not known. This strategy would have allowed the commission to identify perpetrators on its own, rather than wait for them to be named in the testimony of others. Nevertheless, the idea was ruled out by senior commissioners. Although such an approach would have been time consuming, it seems that time constraints were not the primary consideration for rejecting it. The sort of aggressive investigating it involved had the potential to destabilize the commission's already shaky standing with whites. The commissioners decided not to take the risk.

Part 3: A Sympathy-Based Justification of the TRC

The work of truth commissions involves the kind of moral compromises that require justification. The preceding survey suggests that this project of justification needs all the help it can get. In this section I try to show that a South African–style truth commission can be justified because it creates the preconditions for what Adam Smith called sympathy—the ability to project oneself imaginatively into the circumstances in which others operate and to view the world from their perspective. After providing a brief outline of what Smith meant by sympathy, I proceed to enumerate some of its benefits for political reconciliation, and I conclude by explaining how truth commissions can promote it.

3.1 Sympathy and Its Benefits for Political Reconciliation[4]

For Smith, to sympathize with someone is to understand her sentiments or actions as a function of the situation she finds herself in. It is to think that I might have felt or done the same under similar circumstances. It is this sympathetic ability, he claims, that is at the heart of moral judgment. We only deem an action or emotional response morally right if we imagine we would have acted or felt similarly if placed in a similar situation. As Smith puts it: " If, upon bringing the case home to our own breast, we find that the sentiments which it gives occasion to, coincide and tally with our own, we necessarily approve of them as proportioned and suitable to their objects; if otherwise, we necessarily disapprove of them, as extravagant and out of proportion" (1976, I.i.3.9). To sympathize with X, then, is to imagine myself in X's circumstances and to try to think, as independently from my own contingent attributes as possible, what I would have felt and done in his place. This results in a suspension of moral judgment of another's actions or emotional comportment until after an imaginary exchange has been attempted.

Crucially, sympathy depends on exposure to details, on familiarity with specifics. To project myself into the circumstances in which somebody else operates, I need to know as much as possible about those circumstances. Sympathizing does involve an imaginary projection, as Smith insists. But the imagination needs something to work with. It needs data. An imagination uninformed by details is bound to produce shallow, romanticized versions of the realities on which it reflects.

The importance of sympathy for conflict resolution should not be exaggerated. Political reconciliation consists not only, perhaps even not primarily, in the inculcation of sympathetic attitudes. For any peace process to get off the ground, formal questions—those pertaining to the rights and responsibilities two groups have against and toward each other—must be fairly addressed. Such "formal" disputes typically revolve around land ownership, ethnic self-determination, and civic enfranchisement. Strife between India and Pakistan will not end before a determination can be made about the ownership of Kashmir. The apartheid regime could not have been extinguished without a comprehensive empowerment of the black population with basic civil rights. The Israelis and the Egyptians could not have signed a peace accord without settling outstanding questions regarding rights to the Sinai Desert and the

---

[4] For a fuller account of the benefits of sympathy for political reconciliation see Eisikovits 2004.

Suez Canal. To claim that sympathy alone—the ability imaginatively to switch places with a former enemy and consider her commitments from her own position—can resolve such conflicts is worse than naïve; it is plain silly.

And yet sympathy does have a significant role to play in peacemaking. For one thing, it can be extremely useful in negotiation processes. Roger Fisher, the founder of Harvard Law School's Program on Negotiation, insists that reaching agreement between two rivals depends, crucially, on the ability of each imaginatively to switch places with the other (1996, 21). Sympathy is so important in negotiations because it provides the means for breaking out of seemingly intractable disagreements. Negotiations scholars like to distinguish between "interests" and "positions" (see, for example, Lax and Sebenius 1991). The former represent the long-term, essential aims and principles a party holds. The latter stand for the specific claims or demands made during the talks. One of the main impediments to fruitful negotiations can be a tendency on both sides to focus on positions rather than interests. Indeed, very often parties don't think in terms of interests at all, rigidly sticking to preprepared stances. The imaginative exchange constitutive of sympathy creates the basis for moving beyond positions. Through sympathizing, each side can try to ascertain what it is that really matters to the other. A serious attempt at sympathy can put an opponent's *interests* in view. This not only makes it easier to come up with new, more congenial positions to answer these interests; it also has the potential of making the negotiations primarily *about* interests for the first time.

Second, sympathy might be instrumental in combating what might be called "moral blindness." War is sustained, in part, by a certain kind of blindness to detail. Michael Ignatieff (1997a) claims that in ethnic conflict our ability to perceive separate human beings is replaced by an insistence on seeing groups. In Croatia, former neighbors who knew each other as barber and customer, doctor and patient, lawyer and client began referring to each other as Serbs and Croats and thus, suddenly, as enemies. The same dynamic held in Rwanda, where former business partners and colleagues started regarding each other primarily as Hutus and Tutsis. Ethnic identities, which before the war were either secondary or altogether marginalized, became, once the war started, the lens through which each side perceived the other.

Sometimes, though, war makes us blind even to the existence of ethnic groups, inducing us to see nothing instead. Prominent figures on the moderate Israeli right have been claiming for years that "there is no such thing as the Palestinian People" (the justification usually being that Palestinian nationalism did not exist prior to Israel's existence and can certainly not be traced back to biblical times). They take this position even though almost four million people inconveniently insisting that they are Palestinians live no more than ten kilometers away from most major

Israeli cities. The Palestinian claim for an actual, practical, nonsymbolic "right of return" to the center of Israeli cities demonstrates the same myopia, the same refusal to *see* people, groups, and changed circumstances.

If so much of what happens in war is due to such blindness—to the propensity to look through people, to act as if what we do has no specific impact on specific human beings—sympathy is a retraining of sight. Because it begins not with principles but with simple exposure to the conditions and circumstances under which others operate, it is essentially about *seeing*. And seeing makes it harder to sustain war. The more information you have about someone you kill, about what he does, where he lives, what books he owns, how many children he has, what his living room looks like, the harder it becomes to kill him. Detail turns out to be the antidote to moral blindness—and, eventually, to war itself.[5]

Finally, sympathy can help us avoid tendencies toward moral absolutism, the belief that nothing less than a comprehensive acceptance of our claims against others can fairly address our grievances against them. An insistence on absolute justice might lead to absolute injustice. Rigid, unwavering demands to receive everything that is due to us, whether such performance is practical or not, very often leads to catastrophe.

The Palestinian refugees may be morally justified in claiming a right of return to the properties they left behind in 1948. But insistence on straightforward implementation of this right may be destructive. Many of the places Palestinians want to "return" to are now populated by Jews. Removing the Jewish inhabitants would address one tragedy by creating another. Furthermore, the unyielding demands for a right of return are one of the factors blocking the prospects for peace in the region. For Israelis "return" is code for creating an Arab majority in their territory, thereby eradicating the Jewish nature of their state. That is an idea that even the most moderate Israelis, those who are both willing to accept some responsibility for the plight of Palestinian refugees and to participate in a compensation program, cannot commit to.

A similar problem frequently comes up in designing new institutions for countries emerging from oppressive rule. Survivors, families of victims, and the international community often demand that the new administration be purged of officials who worked for the old one. This is a justified demand. But it can also be quite impractical. In many cases, there are simply not enough people who were not involved in one way or another with the previous regime. Put more simply, if the new state wants to have a functioning army, police force, judiciary, and civil service, it will probably have to leave in place at least some of those who previously held

---

[5] As Ignatieff puts it, "Moral life is a struggle to see—a struggle against the desire to deny the testimony of one's own eyes and ears" (1997b, 29).

such positions. This was the case in Germany, Argentina, and South Africa and will most likely happen eventually in Iraq. Painful, disgusting, and unjust as this maybe, a legitimate regime reduced to anarchy through lack of personnel to run it is not a prettier sight.

Sympathy, with its focus on particulars, can be a very useful buffer against the temptations of absolute justice. Suppose that Samir, a resident of the Dir Balah refugee camp in Gaza, meets the Hanin family, now living on the plot of land his parents were expelled from in 1948. Then it was called Beit Mizmil. Today it is called Kiryat Yovel, and it is a southern suburb of Jerusalem. Suppose Samir became aware of the fact that the Hanins have two children attending grade school, that they have a mortgage, and that they vote for the Labour Party. Suppose he learned that the Hanins' own parents were Egyptian Jews, expelled from their stately house in the suburbs of Cairo after Israel's inception. While we are at it, imagine that the Hanins talk with Samir for an hour and find out that he still keeps the key to his father's old house. That he keeps the original copy of the deed laminated in his bedside drawer. That even though he has never really been there, his neighbors at the camp refer to him as Samir from Beit Mizmil, just as he refers to them by the places from which their families were expelled. Suppose this kind of mutual exposure to detail did take place. How easy would it be for Samir to keep claiming that there can be absolutely no other remedy for his grievance except to receive actual control over his father's land? How likely would it be for the Hanins to refuse to participate even in theoretical discussions about the right of return?

3.2 Becoming Sympathetic

Rosa and Drago Sorak, their son Zoran, and his pregnant wife, all Serbs, shared an apartment in the largely Muslim enclave of Gorazde in Bosnia. In 1992, after ethnic warfare broke out and the Serbs began bombarding the city, the Muslim police arrested Zoran. Soon after, his wife gave birth to a girl. The continuous shelling of the city resulted in severe food shortages, and the Soraks began worrying that the baby would starve. They could not leave the apartment, even when the air raids subsided, for fear of being lynched by angry Muslims. They fed the baby with tea for several days, but she grew progressively weaker. Then one morning Fadil Fejzic, a Muslim farmer, appeared at the door with half a liter of milk. He came the next day, and the day after, and for the next 439 days. He persisted in spite of the fact that only one of his cows survived the bombings, in spite of the fact that he could have sold the milk for a hefty sum, and in spite of the scorn of his Muslim neighbors. By the time the war ended the Soraks had lost both their sons, but their granddaughter had managed to survive. Fejzic, the illiterate Muslim farmer, had saved her (see Hedges 2002, 50–53).

How does one become a Fadil Fejzic? How does one widen the scope of one's concern and curiosity beyond the traditional boundaries of family, neighborhood, and ethnicity? What is involved in maintaining an interest in someone you have been conditioned to hate? What, in short, does it take to sympathize with an enemy?

If sympathy is, as I have been claiming, conducive to political reconciliation, the question of its inculcation—the attempt to understand the conditions under which adversaries can actually sympathize with each other—becomes one of the most important problems of peacemaking. In what follows I shall try to answer this question. In a nutshell, I shall argue that sympathizing with an enemy requires acquiring detailed knowledge about the way she lives, and that the willingness to collect such information depends on something like political generosity.

3.2.1 Detailed Exposure

Sympathy requires "raw material." In order to consider what it is like to be a Christian in Gorazde, a non-Arab in the Darfur region of the Sudan, or a refugee in a camp in southern Lebanon, one needs to know as much as possible about the living conditions obtaining in these places. Simply put, human beings are moved by and react much more easily to presentations involving specific, graphic details.

David Hume captures this psychological truism compellingly. We are more likely, he tells us, to be moved by the plight of a distressed ship we can actually see than by the misfortunes of a more distant vessel. "Suppose the ship to be driven so near me, that I can perceive distinctly the horror, painted on the countenance of the seamen and passengers, hear their lamentable cries, see the dearest friends give their last adieu, or embrace with resolution to perish in each others' arms: No man has so savage a heart as to reap any pleasure from such a spectacle, or withstand the motions of the tenderest compassion and sympathy" (1978, 3.3.2).[6]

Contemporary reports of those who have witnessed war serve to confirm this point further, if further confirmation is necessary. Republican senator Bob Dole of Kansas began denouncing the human rights record of Yugoslavia in the U.S. Senate as early as 1986. But a visit to Pristina in 1990 endowed his efforts with a previously lacking sense of urgency. Through the windows of a bus carrying him and several other members of the Senate through the countryside, he saw dozens of Albanians chanting "USA, USA" as they were clubbed

---

[6] There is, of course, a significant difference between what Hume and Smith mean by "sympathy." Nevertheless, it strikes me as quite safe to assume that Hume agrees about the importance of vivid detail for the operation of the imagination.

and beaten by Serb security forces. Very soon after returning home, Dole addressed his Senate colleagues in no uncertain terms: "The United States cannot sit this out on the sidelines, we have a moral obligation to take a strong stand in defense of the rights of Albanians and all of the people of Yugoslavia." What Dole had seen had completely changed his level of commitment. His foreign-policy adviser, Mira Baratta, summed up the transformation her boss had undergone: "It is one thing to have a natural inclination to care about human rights, but it is another thing entirely when you see people who only want to wave at Americans getting pummeled before your own eyes. Once you have seen that you just can't look away" (quoted in Powers 2002, 255).

Details give our imagination something to work with. Imaginative identification with our family and kin comes as easily as it does because we know a good deal about them—because we know, quite specifically, what it is like to *be* them. When a mother feels deeply saddened to learn that her son was rejected by his peers at his elementary school, it is not only because the child is *hers*. Rather, the fact that he is hers allows her to know exactly what makes him tick: she knows how important it is for him to feel he belongs, how much time he spends thinking and worrying about belonging, what kind of tricks and strategies he has devised to make his friends like him more. It is such intimate knowledge that creates the backdrop against which the boy's rejection comes to mean so much to her. It is this immersion in context that makes the child's pain so palpable. As we move farther away from our immediate surroundings, this sort of context naturally becomes thinner. The raw material required for sympathy is no longer simply there, all around us. It must, rather, be collected.

3.2.2 Political Generosity

The preceding discussion does not take us far enough. Even if it is agreed that details are a precondition of sympathy, one might legitimately ask what it takes to be willing to collect details. To sympathize with an enemy you must know enough about what her life is like. But what does it take to be willing to find out? What kind of person is disposed to pay such attention to an enemy?

What did it take for Fadil Fejzic even to notice that his Christian neighbors' granddaughter was crying? How was he different from others who had either ignored the girl or somehow rationalized away her suffering? Sympathizing with an enemy requires detailed, graphic, dramatic exposure to the manner in which he lives, and such exposure, the willingness either to collect or to submit oneself to such information, is made possible by a specific moral motivation. I believe this motivation, or attitude, is best described by the term "generosity." In what follows I shall explain what I mean by generosity, why I think it is realistic to expect something like it in the context of group conflict, and what benefits it might have, beyond its potential to generate sympathy.

3.2.2.1 What Is Political Generosity?

Six years into the Peloponnesian War, in 425 B.C., Sparta made Athens a peace offer. Thucydides relates that the Spartan envoys began their offer by warning the Athenians against hubris: "The prosperity which your city now enjoys, and the accessions that it has lately received, must not make you suppose that fortune will be always with you. Indeed, sensible men are prudent enough to treat their gains as precarious, just as they would also keep a clear head in adversity, and think that war, so far from staying within the limits to which a combatant may wish to confine it, will run the course that its chances proscribe; and thus, not being puffed up by confidence in military success, they are likely to come to grief and most ready to make peace, if they can, while their fortune lasts." After this introduction, the Spartans proceeded in an unequivocally conciliatory tone "[We] . . . invite you to make a treaty and to end the war, and offer peace and alliance and the most friendly and intimate relations," they told the Athenian assembly. "*If great enmities are ever to be really settled we think it will be not by the system of revenge and military success, and by forcing an opponent to swear to a treaty to his disadvantage; but when the more fortunate combatant waives his privileges, and, guided by gentler feelings, conquers his rival in generosity and accords peace on more moderate terms than expected. From that moment, instead of the debt of revenge which violence must entail, his adversary owes a debt of generosity to be paid in kind, and is inclined by honor to stand by his agreement*" (Thucydides 1998, 1.76; my italics).

The Athenians rejected Sparta's overture. They had just scored a major naval victory and did not want to quit while they were ahead. Twenty-one miserable years later, their legendary navy all but destroyed, they surrendered to Sparta on humiliating terms. The walls of their city were torn down, the fortifications of their port were destroyed, and their popular assembly was dissolved.

Generosity, as I shall be using the term, amounts to something quite similar to what the Spartans had in mind. It consists in the willingness to forgo, at least to some degree and at least for a short time, the vindictive dynamics of action: reaction, grievance and countergrievance, injury and reprisal so typical of political conflict. The willingness to do this is very often accompanied by, or made possible through, two further dispositions: first, the ability to move one's focus of attention, at least partially and temporarily, from one's self, and, second, the readiness to offer an enemy more, even slightly more, than she can minimally expect: to depart, or at least take respite from, what we might call a "politics of shop keeping," in which each party takes the greatest care never to offer any concession that it has not been offered itself. Any one of these three dispositions—stepping outside the cyclical dynamic of injury and retaliation, shifting part of one's focus away from one's self, and the readiness to give up more than one absolutely has to—amounts to generosity in politics.

Had Athens agreed to the Spartan peace offer, its consent would have been generous, because its power allowed it, at least at the time, to seek more advantages from war. Accepting peace would have thus been generous in the third sense we have just discussed—giving up more than one absolutely must. But this would also probably have implied generosity in the first sense—the willingness to forgo retaliation for the last Spartan attack suffered—as well as generosity in the second sense—shifting part of one's focus from one's self, in this case from how decisively Athens was winning and what kind of spoils victory could have afforded it.

Fadil Fejzic was obviously generous in the first sense. It is hard to imagine anything less vindictive than saving a Serbian infant while Serbian forces are shelling your hometown. He was also generous in the second sense. Paying attention to the baby girl, actually being able to see that she was in danger, required shifting the focus of his attention, at least partly, from the risks the war had created for him and his family members, from the economic and psychological strains they were subjected to, from the profits he could have made by selling the milk he ended up giving to the baby, and so on. Finally, Fejzic was generous in the third sense: by bringing the child a liter of milk every day for 440 consecutive days, he did more, much more, than her grandparents could have expected. After all, the politics of shop keeping dictate never helping anyone who hasn't helped you. One can easily imagine Fejzic's Muslim relations asking, "What are you doing saving *their* kids while they are busy killing *ours?*"

There are two reasons why I think the conception of generosity just expounded is attractive. First, it is developed in the context of war. As such it is unlikely to be overambitious. Indeed, as the speech of the Spartan envoys suggests, the motivation for political generosity has more to do with modesty than with pureness of heart or the ability to love one's enemies. It is based on the understanding that one's privileged position of power may very well be short lived. Generosity between enemies, in other words, does not spring from Christian "love," Kantian "duty," or a condescending victor's grace. It is a result of level-headedness, of the understanding that one's military advantages, one's ability to inflict damage, are not necessarily the result of anything except good fortune, and as such are always precarious. The Spartans can be accused of many things. A bleeding heart is not one of them. The advantage of basing a conception of political generosity on their proposal to the Athenians is that it might actually work.

Second, the account of generosity put forward by the Spartans helps explain an important intuition about sympathy: if sympathy is a constitutive part of political reconciliation, surely there must be cases where the burden of sympathizing is not symmetrical, where it is placed mostly, or more significantly, on one side. We tend to assume, for instance, that whites should do most of the sympathizing in the South African case, and that Germans needed to do most of the sympathizing after World War II. Why? If sympathy requires generosity, as I have been arguing here, it is much easier for "the more fortunate combatant"—the side that has suffered less, lost less—to be generous. This is not, or not only, a question of justice. Generosity, as we have characterized it, requires a readiness to pay attention, to see what has befallen others, without the absolute certainty that one will receive the same kind of consideration in return. It requires the willingness to dedicate at least some of one's resources—in this case attention and curiosity—to an enemy's fate. In conflicts involving vast discrepancies of power, the stronger side simply has more of those resources to give. It literally has more of itself left, more actual substance with which to be attentive and curious.

The point I have been trying to make so far in part 3 can be summed up thus: sympathy is conducive of political reconciliation. But sympathy requires obtaining detailed knowledge about the manner in which our enemies live. Without such detail, the imaginative exchange underlying sympathy is either difficult or impossible. In order to be willing to obtain such knowledge, in order to notice what actually happens to one's enemies, one must be generous in the ways just described. But is generosity really an option between enemies? If the argument provided above is going to be successful, it must be defended against what we might call the "realist challenge"—the claim that talking about generosity in the context of political conflict is naïve, perhaps even dangerous.

3.2.2.2 The Realist Challenge

Realists see the international system as an essentially anarchic environment in which competing groups are engaged in a never-ending contest for resources and dominance. The position's paradigmatic (though by no means first) statement can be found in chapter 13 of Hobbes's *Leviathan*: "In all times kings and persons of sovereign authority, because of their independency, are in continual jealousies, and in the state and posture of gladiators, having their weapons pointing, and their eyes fixed on one another; that is, their forts, garrisons, and guns upon the frontiers of their kingdoms, and continual spies upon their neighbors, which is a posture of War" (1994, 78). Machiavelli is most often taken to be the other protorealist thinker. Idealism has no place in politics and international relations, he tells us, because "it must ... be taken for granted that all

men are wicked and that they will always give vent to the malignity that is
in their minds when opportunity offers" (1974, 112). A more recent
statement of the realist creed holds that "success is the ultimate test of
policy, and success is defined as preserving and strengthening the state"
(Waltz 1979, 117). For our purposes, a more detailed discussion of the
different nuances and trends within international realism is not required.
Suffice it to say that the name "realism" denotes a theory or a group of
theories that construe the international arena as dangerous and treacher-
ous and, consequently, are deeply skeptical about any principled approach to intergroup relations.

It is easy, then, to imagine the realist response to the account of
generosity just offered. It would proceed along the following lines:
"Generosity? Between enemies? Such lofty suggestions are dangerous in
the extreme! Not only do they result in giving the enemy more than is
absolutely necessary; they also signal a weakness of resolve which might
embolden one's foes to engage in further attacks." Consider, for example,
this excerpt from an opinion piece Daniel Pipes wrote for the *Los Angeles
Times* of 17 October 2000 shortly after the Intifada eruption: "Israel gets
precious little in return for its willingness to turn over land and other
benefits. And rather than win goodwill from enemies, it prompts them to
despise Israel and find it weak. Magnanimity leads not to friendship but
to a dangerous mood of exhilaration and ambition."

The realist take on political generosity may sound sensible, but I think
there are good empirical as well as policy-based reasons to reject it.
Empirically, there are important examples in which generosity has proven
to be remarkably effective in politics. Such historical evidence, if sound,
counters the argument from realism with what we might call an argument
from reality. On the policy level, generosity has the potential to produce
significant benefits, over and above its role in allowing for sympathy. Let
us examine these two defenses of political generosity in more detail.

In the autumn of 1977, after fighting four wars with Israel, and in spite
of violent opposition at home, Anwar Sadat, president of Egypt, decided
to travel to Jerusalem and directly address the Israeli public about the
need for peace. Many Egyptians were appalled, seeing their president's
trip as a humiliating concession to the Israelis. After the resounding
defeat that Egypt, Syria, and Jordan had suffered during the Six Day War
in June 1967, Egyptians felt that some of their country's prestige had been
regained during the 1973 campaign against the Jewish state. Why on earth
should *their* president go to the Israelis? Egypt's military chiefs were
similarly dismayed, warning against what they perceived as a show of
weakness. And yet Sadat went. On 19 November he addressed Israel's
parliament, the Knesset, with the following words: "In all sincerity I tell
you we welcome you among us with full security and safety. . . . We used
to reject you. We had our reasons and our fears, yes. . . . Yet today I tell
you, and I declare it to the whole world, that we accept to live with you in

permanent peace based on justice. We do not want to encircle you or be encircled ourselves by destructive missiles ready for launching. . . . I have announced on more than one occasion that Israel has become a fait accompli, recognized by the world. . . . As we really and truly seek peace we really and truly welcome you to live among us in peace and security."[7]

On the plane that took him to Israel Sadat told *Time* magazine's Wilton Wynn, "What I want from this visit is that the wall created between us and Israel, the psychological wall, be knocked down" (*Time*, 2 January 1978). The impact of the president's speech on Israelis was indeed profound. At one bold stroke it introduced a conciliatory tone into Israeli public opinion. Sixteen months later, Sadat, Israeli prime minister Menachem Begin, and U.S. president Jimmy Carter were shaking hands on the White House lawn.

On 16 March 1997, King Hussein, the Hashemite monarch of Jordan, stepped into a small apartment in the Israeli town of Bet Shemesh, knelt before a woman sitting on the floor, took her hand, and apologized. He repeated this gesture in six other homes, personally expressing regrets for the killing of seven Israeli schoolgirls by a Jordanian soldier. "I looked in his face and I saw that he was ashamed, and he had tears in his eyes, and he was honest," one of the mothers told reporters.[8] The king did not express official condolences, as diplomatic decorum requires. He did not limit himself to promising that the perpetrators would be brought to justice. He went from home to home, got down on his knees, and said he was sorry. The tension over the incident, which had the potential to destabilize the relationship between Jordan and Israel, was dissipated.

Sadat's initiative was generous in the second sense we have been discussing: it indicated a propensity to consider the interests, concerns, and fears of an enemy—in this case Israel's apprehension about never being recognized or accepted by its Arab neighbors. The decision to visit Jerusalem was also generous in the third sense: it marked a departure from the calculative, small-minded line touted by the Egyptian president's advisers, who were outraged at the prospect of Egypt reaching out to its archrival rather than being courted by it.

King Hussein's gesture was generous in the second meaning of the term: it exhibited an attunement to the grief of particular parents as well as an understanding of the wider suspicion and trepidation Israelis felt in the wake of the Jordanian soldier's attack. It was also generous in the third sense, insofar as it was a departure from protocol. After all, there would have been nothing formally wrong—the Israelis would have had nothing to complain about—had the king refrained from genuflecting

---

[7] The full text of Sadat's speech is available online at the Web site of the Jewish Virtual Library: http://www.jewishvirtuallibrary.org/jsource/Peace/sadat_speech.html

[8] See "Hussein, on His Knees, Begs Forgiveness for Massacre; Jordanian King Visits Families of Slain Israeli Girls," by Barton Gellman, *Washington Post*, 17 March 1997.

before the bereaved mother and elected to convey his condolences in writing instead.

Having provided some examples to establish that generosity actually works, I move to the other part of my reply to realism—specifying some important public-policy benefits that political generosity has, in addition to its previously explained role in generating sympathy.

First, acts of generosity can work to weaken or even dislodge stereotypes. On 17 August 1999 a powerful earthquake struck north-eastern Turkey, killing more than seventeen thousand people and leaving many more homeless. Within less than twenty-four hours, Greece, historically Turkey's sworn enemy, sent a substantial amount of financial aid, military rescue teams, sniffing dogs, blankets, and medicines. Responding to a call by their mayor, residents of Athens began collecting clothes and blankets for Turkish survivors.[9] In the following weeks, quite a number of the Turks interviewed by the foreign media sounded as if they had undergone a change of heart about their Greek neighbors. After all, it is harder to believe that all Greeks are brutes when you are wearing clothes sent by residents of Athens and taking malaria pills financed by the Greek government.

Generosity can help change the dynamics of a conflict. It can introduce new elements, such as gratitude or trust, into the intergroup relationship. An act of generosity can be like a stick inserted into the spinning wheels of war. Being so far removed from the predictable, petty, gruesome dance of blow and counterblow characteristic of ethnic strife, it has the potential to make both sides stop and think. Once this happens, there is even a chance that the proverbial wheels might start spinning in the opposite direction. As the Spartan envoys put it, once one of the combatants had displayed generosity, "instead of the debt of revenge that violence must entail, [an] adversary owes a debt of generosity to be paid in kind, and is inclined by honor to stand by his agreement."

Second, acts of generosity make for a good deal of symbolic capital. They can be "exploited" in the politics of peace. The image of Anwar Sadat standing behind the podium in the Knesset, the picture of the king of Jordan kneeling before a grief-stricken Israeli mother, or that of a Greek rescue worker extracting a Turk from the rubble could all serve as powerful, positive symbolic loci to which the public can have easy access, and which can be employed to great benefit in what Martin Luther King Jr. called "the propaganda of peace."

Two further benefits of political generosity have to do with the international legitimacy it can confer. Acting generously toward an enemy has the potential to enlist the support or approval of other states; such support often results in the extension of palpable benefits, the

---

[9] See the BBC report "Historic Enemy Offers Full Support," 19 August 1999, which can be accessed online at: http://news.bbc.co.uk/1/hi/world/europe/424465.stm

mounting of pressures on the more intransigent side, or both. Thus, for example, the fact that Israel's leaders had agreed to the U.N. resolution to divide Palestine in 1947 (though the resolution had granted them considerably less territory than they had hoped for), whereas all Arab states rejected it, was instrumental in procuring international support and financial aid for the fledgling Jewish state.

Finally, generosity can lay the groundwork for the legitimate use of force. Once one side has done everything it can to reach a fair resolution of a conflict with its adversary, and continues to encounter obduracy, the use of force against that enemy gains legitimacy. In 1999 Prime Minister Ehud Barak of Israel took the Israeli Defence Force (IDF) out of southern Lebanon in spite of the fact that peace talks with Syria (which effectively controlled Lebanon at the time) had broken down. Israel had thus given up an important bargaining card in future negotiations with the Syrians. Immediately after the IDF had withdrawn, the United Nations certified that the Israelis had fully retreated to the international border. Once this had happened, Israel's harsh reactions to cross-border attacks by Hizballah, Syria's guerrilla proxy, gained a new degree of legitimacy.

3.3 Truth Commissions and Sympathy

I would like to conclude this essay by arguing that South Africa's TRC (or any comparable commission) is morally justified because of its ability to promote sympathy between former enemies: insofar as the TRC provided detailed accounts of life under apartheid, and to the degree it created an atmosphere of political generosity, it put in place both conditions for the inculcation of sympathetic attitudes.

3.3.1 Detailed Exposure

During its two-and-a-half-year tenure, the TRC collected testimony from more than twenty-two thousand victims of human rights abuses. More than two thousand of them were heard in public. Many of the hearings were carried live on television and radio. Daily and weekly television journals provided lengthy synopses of the proceedings. Newspapers, including those owned and read by whites, printed extensive reports—often dedicating separate pages to each story.

For the first time a flood of detailed, graphic information about the indignities, abuses, and atrocities perpetrated by the apartheid authorities became completely public. Whites, many of whom either did not believe or comfortably ignored the level of their government's cruelty, were faced with the full extent of it. At the same time, and more controversially, the commission heard testimonies from the victims of attacks perpetrated by members of the ANC.

I have argued that sympathy requires raw material, that if we are to perform an imaginary exchange with others a specific dramatic presentation of the manner in which they live is necessary. The commission's hearings provided just this sort of detail: from Lalloo Chiba, a member of the ANC's military wing, whites heard what it was like to be beaten until one's ear drums are ripped, have a wet sack placed on your body, and be hit with electric shocks (Meredith 1999, 116). From Abdulhay Jassat they heard what it was like to be dangled by the ankles from the third-floor window of a police station after being subjected to electric shocks (Meredith 1999, 117). From Thandi Shezi, a female member of the ANC's youth league, they heard what it was like to be chained, beaten, electrocuted, and then gang raped by four police officers.[10]

Blacks heard what it was like for Dawie Ackerman, whose wife had been shot during an ANC raid on a white church, to step over the bodies of other worshipers, hoping against hope that she was only injured, to find her limp body at the other side of the hall.[11] Beth Savage, a white librarian who survived an attack by the Azanian People's Liberation Army, told the mostly black audience at her hearing how she watched four close friends die from gunshot and grenade wounds, and how her father, a staunch opponent of apartheid, sank into depression and died after the incident. If sympathy requires details, the commission's hearings provided them in gruesome, relentless abundance.

At this point it may be objected that the TRC's focus on egregious human rights violations was not appropriate for providing a picture of everyday life under apartheid. As Meredith puts it, "The commission's focus was limited to the investigations of gross violations of human rights … these violations were defined as the killing, abduction, torture, or severe ill treatment of any person, or any attempt, conspiracy, incitement, instigation, command, or procurement to commit those acts. Thus the wider injustices of the apartheid system—such as the forced removal of some 3 million people from their homes, the imprisonment of millions for pass-law offenses, and the widespread use of detention without trial—would not be addressed. Only the extreme of apartheid would be examined, not its normality" (1999, 20). If this criticism is sound, my argument that the commission's work provided the raw material for sympathy becomes suspect. An exclusive focus on particular egregious human rights violations obscures not only the structural inequities that sustained apartheid but also the nature of everyday life under it—the more mundane, humdrum indignities and humiliations that so many

---

[10] See also Frances Reid and Deborah Hoffman's documentary on the TRC, *Long Night's Journey into Day* (Iris Films, 2000).

[11] For a detailed account see Bill Moyer's documentary *Facing the Truth* (Public Affairs Television for PBS, 1999).

blacks had to face in their regular dealings. If sympathy requires gathering details about the everyday lives of those we are to sympathize with, then, so the argument goes, the truth commission did not provide such information.

This criticism is unfounded. It must be addressed on two levels. First, the egregious violations of human rights *were* part of blacks' everyday lives. Under a system of social subjugation as pervasive as apartheid was (especially during the 1980s and early 1990s), most blacks were likely either to experience extreme abuse first hand, to be related to someone who had, or to be close friends with such a victim. Apartheid generated an environment in which severe violence was an ever-present possibility. One was always thinking about it, worrying that it would catch up with one's children, trying to avoid it, recovering from it oneself, trying to help friends or relatives who had suffered under it.

Second, what Meredith calls the "normality" of apartheid often came up during testimony about its "extremes." Many of those who ended up severely tortured were first harassed by the police and imprisoned without trial. Thus the kinds of detailed contextualized testimony gathered by the truth commission very often included descriptions of these more "benign" mistreatments.

3.3.2 Generosity

Recall that a policy or a political action can be described as generous (1) if it forgoes, at least to some degree and at least for a short time, the vindictive dynamics of injury and reprisal so typical of political conflict; or (2) if it involves at least a partial and temporary shift of attention away from oneself, from one's interests or the grievances one has suffered, to the interests and grievances of someone else; or (3) if it involves the readiness to offer an enemy more, even slightly more, than he can minimally expect.

Unlike the examples discussed a bit earlier, the political generosity displayed in South Africa was, at least to some degree, two-sided. Its essence was this: black South Africans would demand less than they could have demanded; they would forgo the retributive justice that the crimes of apartheid merited. Whites would deliver more than they minimally had to; those who participated in the regime's crimes would divulge more information than they would be required to during a criminal indictment. More people would implicate themselves in having done worse things than could ever be found out by criminal proceedings.

This exchange constitutes generosity on the part of both sides in the third sense of the term: demanding less (or giving more) than one is entitled (or required) to. But it also represents generosity in the second sense. Black support for the TRC meant that many of apartheid's victims were willing to divert at least part of their attention from their own injuries to thinking about what was best for a peaceful, multiracial South Africa. Furthermore, the TRC hearings found blacks not only concentrating on what had been done to them but also, for the first time, listening to the testimony of white victims of ANC attacks. More significantly, it found at least part of the white "silent majority"—those who did not actively enforce apartheid but did not resist it either—shifting some of their focus from attempts at self-justification ("Fighting the ANC was part of the global war on communism," "We didn't know exactly how bad things were," and so on) to listening to what the apartheid regime had done to blacks in their name. Some white members of the security forces similarly shifted at least some of their resources from frantic attempts at self-exoneration to complying with the requests of victims for more details about the circumstances surrounding their torture or the deaths of their family members.

Finally, and rather more obviously, the amnesty-for-truth arrangement was generous in the first sense of that term: it consciously rejected the legitimacy of revenge. As the postamble to South Africa's 1993 interim constitution states, the commission's mandate was based on the understanding that there was "a need for understanding but not vengeance, a need for reparation but not retaliation" (in Meredith 1999, 20).

Now it may be objected that, at least in the case of South Africa, the amnesty-for-truth arrangement was a political compromise; that it was strictly the function of necessity, of the fact that whites were no longer sufficiently strong to control an unruly black majority but still strong enough to make a peaceful transition impossible. On this view the TRC arrangement had nothing to do with generosity and everything to do with political expediency and necessity. Two observations are in order. First, this claim rests on the oversimplified assumption that political expediency and generosity are mutually exclusive. They are not. The fact that a certain arrangement is the result of a political compromise does not imply that those who signed it had no principled, moral motivations to do so. Quite a few black leaders, not only those with deep Christian commitments, honestly believed that finding a way to forgo victor's justice while exposing as much as possible of apartheid's crimes really was the right (as opposed to the only possible) thing to do. Second, and much more important, the moral significance of a given institution is not exhausted by the intentions of its originators. Neither King John nor the noblemen who agitated against him conceived of the Magna Carta as an expression of pure constitutionalism. John's barons wanted the onerous financial demands the king had imposed on them lifted. John, who had just lost London to the rebellious barons, realized he could not subdue them. The Magna Carta was a political compromise if there ever was one. And yet it became emblematic of the principle of the rule of law, subjecting even the king to the laws of the land.[12]

Even if the TRC arrangement was set up on the basis of nothing but cynicism, its premise and the manner in which it operated allowed for political generosity. This, in turn, made it easier for populations formerly hostile to one another to absorb the kind of data required for sympathetic identification.

Conclusion

The TRC rendered an invaluable service in spite of all its drawbacks—the murderers it set free, the thorny issues it refrained from investigating, its narrow focus on the last decades of white rule, its inability to expose the role of institutional players, and the meager compensation funds it doled out. Its proceedings and its final report painted a detailed, ghastly picture of life under apartheid. Its exercise in political generosity—the forgoing of retributive justice in return for full disclosure—helped create an atmosphere that allowed people to take a long hard long look at that picture.

Needless to say, this achievement falls painfully short of political reconciliation. Sympathy is only part, probably the smaller part, of peacemaking. South Africa is riddled with a formidable public-health crisis, soaring crime rates, and record-breaking unemployment. Some 11 percent of South Africans are HIV positive. Years of government refusal to introduce antiretroviral drugs (President Thabo Mbeki famously doubted whether HIV causes AIDS) have resulted in the death of more people than were killed by all apartheid governments. The country has the highest murder rate for any nation not involved in active warfare: fifty-five murders for every one hundred thousand people. Depending on one's method of calculation, between 28 percent and 40 percent of the population is unemployed. The good news is that Mbeki's government has started tackling these problems in earnest. A program to collect illegal weapons has been put in place. AIDS "cocktails" are slowly being distributed. The economy is gradually being diversified to rely on services and tourism in addition to the country's traditional strength in gold mining. New plans for building roads, ports, and energy plants provide hope for shrinking the ranks of the unemployed.

Amazingly, throughout all of these crises, South African politics has been stable during the past decade. The political violence that accom-

---

[12] I take this point from Allen (1999, 332), who writes: "The fact that an institution is the product of a political negotiation in which the parties were intent on self-interested goals, narrowly conceived, does not demonstrate that the institution does not *also* and in spite of the participants' goals, express morally defensible values." I chose to use the Magna Carta as an illustration over Allen's use of the U.S. Constitution. The Constitution's proslavery clauses made sure that it did not "express morally defensible values" for quite a while.

panied the country's first democratic election in 1994 has almost vanished. Interracial tensions as well as tensions between supporters of the Zulu Inkatha Freedom Party and backers of the ANC have eased. Democratic institutions, including a liberal constitution, a free press, and a strong legal system are firmly in place.[13] That South Africa enjoys underlying political robustness in spite of the difficulties just enumerated may, at least in part, be due to the moderating effects of sympathy—to knowing a bit more specifically who one's neighbors are, what they have been through, and what it is like to be them.

References

Allen, Jonathan. 1999. "Balancing Justice and Social Unity: Political Theory and the Idea of a Truth and Reconciliation Commission." *University of Toronto Law Journal* 49, no. 3:315–53.

Bell, Terry, and Ntsebeza Dumisa Buhle. 2003. *Unfinished Business: South Africa, Apartheid and Truth*. London: Verso.

Eisikovits, Nir. 2004. "Forget Forgiveness: On the Benefits of Sympathy for Political Reconciliation." *Theoria* 52, no. 1:31–63.

Fisher, Roger, Elizabeth Kopelman, and Andrea Kupfer Schneider. 1996. *Beyond Machiavelli: Tools for Coping with Conflict*. New York: Penguin.

Gutmann, Amy, and Dennis Thompson. 2000. "The Moral Foundations of Truth Commissions." In *Truth v. Justice: The Morality of Truth Commissions*, edited by Robert Rothberg and Dennis Thompson, 22–44. Princeton: Princeton University Press.

Hayner, Priscilla. 2002. *Unspeakable Truths: Facing the Challenges of Truth Commissions*. London: Routledge.

Hedges, Chris. 2002. *War Is a Force That Gives Us Meaning*. New York: Public Affairs Books.

Hobbes, Thomas. 1994. *Leviathan*. Indianapolis: Hackett.

Hume, David. 1978. *A Treatise of Human Nature*. New York: Oxford University Press.

Ignatieff, Michael. 1997a. "The Narcissism of Small Difference." In *The Warrior's Honor: Ethnic War and the Modern Conscience*, 34–71. New York: Owl Books.

———. 1997b. "Is Nothing Sacred? The Ethics of Television." In *The Warrior's Honor: Ethnic War and the Modern Conscience*, 9–33. New York: Owl Books.

---

[13] The data are taken mostly from the *Economist*'s invaluable archive on South Africa. Of special help were the following pieces: "A man of two faces" (22 January 2005), "Guns in South Africa" (27 January 2005), "Good economic news from South Africa" (28 October 2004), "Ten years of democracy in South Africa" (8 April 2004), and "AIDS and generics in South Africa" (25 March 2004).

Kiss, Elizabeth. 2000. "Moral Ambition Within and Beyond Political Constraints: Reflections on Restorative Justice." In *Truth v. Justice: The Morality of Truth Commissions*, edited by Robert Rothberg and Dennis Thompson, 68–98. Princeton: Princeton University Press.

Lax, David, and James Sebenius. 1991. "Interests: The Measure of Negotiation." In *Negotiation Theory and Practice*, edited by William Breslin and Jeffrey Rubin, 161–80. Cambridge: PON Books.

Machiavelli, Niccolò. 1974. *The Discourses*. New York: Penguin.

Meredith, Martin. 1999. *Coming to Terms: South Africa's Search for Truth*. New York: Public Affairs Books.

Minow, Martha. 1999. *Between Vengeance and Forgiveness*. Boston: Beacon Press.

Powers, Samantha. 2002. *A Problem from Hell: America and the Age of Genocide*. New York: Perennial.

Smith, Adam. 1976. *The Theory of Moral Sentiments*. New York: Oxford University Press.

Thucydides. 1998. *History of the Peloponnesian War*. New York: Free Press.

Waltz, Kenneth. 1979. *Theory of International Politics*. New York: McGraw-Hill.

13

ACKNOWLEDGING AND RECTIFYING THE GENOCIDE OF AMERICAN INDIANS: "WHY IS IT THAT THEY CARRY THEIR LIVES ON THEIR FINGERNAILS?"

WILLIAM C. BRADFORD

> Why is it that the Apaches wait to die. . . . That they carry their lives on their fingernails? They roam over the hills and plains and want the heavens to fall on them. The Apaches were once a great nation; they are now but few, and because of this they want to die and so carry their lives on their fingernails.
> —Cochise (Chiricahua Apache), c. 1872[1]

Introduction

So that the millions of people who were dragged from their homes, brutalized, caged, and murdered during World War II solely for their membership in human collectivities organized around a common religion, ethnicity, race, and history should not have died in vain, Raphael Lemkin coined the term "genocide":

> Generally speaking, genocide does not necessarily mean the immediate destruction of a nation, except when accomplished by mass killings of all members of a nation. It is intended rather to signify a coordinated plan of different actions aiming at the destruction of essential foundations of the life of national groups, with the aim of annihilating the groups themselves. The objectives of such a plan would be the disintegration of the political and social institutions, of culture, language, national feelings, religion, and the economic existence of national groups, and the destruction of the personal security, liberty, health, dignity, and even the lives of the individuals belonging to such groups. Genocide is directed against the national group as an entity, and the actions involved are directed against individuals, not in their individual capacity but as members of a national group. (Lemkin 1944, 79)

Although the victorious Allies did not include genocide—in effect, the first "hate" crime—within the jurisdiction of the Nuremburg Tribunal, choosing instead to prosecute genocidal acts as crimes against humanity,

---

[1] Available at http://www.chiricahuaapache.org/Chiricahua_Apache.htm

genocide rapidly assumed the status of the ultimate transgression. The phrase "Never again!"—spoken in the steely conviction that the world would never again stand idly by—became the unofficial motto of the State of Israel, while the Genocide Convention (1948) rendered the legal judgment of the international community that a parade of horrors—murder, serious physical or psychological harm, forced contraception, and abduction of children—when committed with the "intent to destroy, in whole or in part, a national, ethnical, racial or religious group, as such"—was so far beyond the moral pale that the duty to prevent and punish their commission was incumbent upon all states.[2]

Sadly, the promise "Never again!" has been broken seriatim. A train of genocides in Timor, Cambodia, Iraq, Bosnia, Rwanda, Congo, and now the Darfur region of the Sudan is written in blood upon the pages of post–World War II history. Why, sixty years after the liberation of Auschwitz, does genocide remain too much with us? Anthropologists conclude that humankind is atavistic, and that genocide will bedevil us for so long as resources are finite upon earth and contending human collectives battle over them (Malthus 1993, 3). Lawyers advise us that enforcement of the prohibition of genocide requires effective rules and institutions, and that above all perpetrators must be apprehended and brought to justice (Bradford 2005, 1243). Political scientists explain inactivity in the face of genocide as a rational response to an absence of actionable interests: simply put, what happens to peoples in far-flung corners of the earth is inconsequential so long as it does not threaten the physical security or economic well-being of the West. Perhaps all are correct, or none; at any rate, Kuwait is spared, but Bosnia is bled white before it is rescued, and Rwanda and the Sudan are left to burn. "Never again!" is at best a bromide quaffed to assuage the consciences of those made uncomfortable, but not too uncomfortable, by the reprise of mass murder motivated by hatred of a targeted group. Lemkin's contribution to the lexicon of law and moral philosophy is a bust.

Can we do better? Is it possible to reinvigorate our commitment to eradicating the ultimate crime or, at the very least, to punishing and, better still, deterring would-be perpetrators? If the lessons of Nuremburg have been smothered under a mountain of killings like those at Srebrenica—a village in Bosnia where, in 1995, Bosnian Serb forces machine-gunned eight thousand Muslim men and boys for the crime of being Muslim—what reason is there to repose our hopes in the International Criminal Court, a permanent tribunal with the jurisdiction to punish the authors of genocide?[3] Unless we can awaken the moral indignation that

[2] Convention on the Prevention and Punishment of the Crime of Genocide ["Genocide Convention"], United Nations Treaty Series 78, 277ff. (Dec. 9, 1948), Art. II (a)–(c) and Art. 1 ("The Contracting Parties confirm that genocide, whether committed in time of peace or in time of war is a crime under international law which they undertake to prevent and to punish.").

[3] For a discussion of the Srebrenica massacre, see Rhode 1997.

encouraged the Allies to hang the architects of the Holocaust by the neck until they were dead, how will we inspire the contemporary community of states to commit their blood and treasure to defending the objects of genocidal instinct from their attackers?

If genocide is simply an immutable aspect of the human condition because humankind is inherently evil or the scarcity of resources is so profound that we are doomed to fight and only the strong will survive, then our work is done. We are observers of, not active participants in, our own futures. But if genocide is not inevitable, we must summon the will to intervene. To do this is largely a prospective challenge: we cannot change what has gone before, much as we wish to do so; we can only devise a future in which genocide is deterred, and when it cannot be deterred it is checked, and when it is not checked in time its practitioners are prosecuted and punished. If we are to rise to this challenge, we must recognize that the integrity of the moral norm at the core of the legal prohibition against genocide is, to some degree, a function of the seriousness with which we respond to its violation. Each genocide tolerated makes the counterargument against its prohibition: Isn't killing the enemy what war is all about, and isn't genocide the most effective way of winning wars (and preventing the possibility of future wars, at least with the eliminated groups)? In other words, a genocide-free future demands vigilance and the willingness to put force in service to the vow "Never again!"

Yet even this expression of commitment may be inadequate. So long as the present consequences of past genocides go unrecognized and unremedied, their ghosts will haunt our present. Worse, as we see from the recent histories of the Balkans, the Middle East, and Africa, nothing is more likely to motivate the descendants of yesterday's victims to become tomorrow's perpetrators than a stubborn refusal to acknowledge and repair the damage. The risk extends to the spectator class as well: with each successive genocide that slips by with little notice, less intervention, and all but no justice, we become more experienced at "living" with genocide. The attendant moral hazards require, in short, that we think not just prospectively but also retrospectively if we wish to avoid them, do justice, and bring about the end of history, at least insofar as genocide is concerned.

Where do we begin? Many genocidal episodes stain the sands of time: the Nazi butchery of European Jews, the Japanese Rape of Nanking, the Ottoman murder of Armenians, the Mongol devastations of Central Asia, the Roman eradication of Carthage, and the Hebrew destruction of the Canaanites, to name but a few. The unique experience of American Indians presents a logical heuristic whereby to assess more broadly the requirements of justice following genocide.[4]

---

[4] "Indian" is the preferred term to denote the indigenous inhabitants of the United States. See Porter 1997, 235, 236 n. 7.

The brutal reality of invasion, murder, slavery, land theft, ethnocide, and sterilization has not percolated deeply into contemporary understandings of the history of Indians in the United States. The role of the United States in the deliberate destruction of Indian populations, property rights, and cultural patrimonies is for most Americans a hidden history. Because the genocide of American Indians is neither broadly acknowledged nor deeply understood, this first part of this essay will provide historical foundation. The second part will present and evaluate several theories of justice with respect to the Indian claim for redress. And the third part will counter these theories with an indigenist theory intended to accord the full measure of relief to Indian claimants consistent with the requirements of justice for all peoples.

1. The Genocide of American Indians

American Indian genocide assumed varied forms: aggressive war, murder, land theft, ethnocide, and forced sterilization.

A. Aggressive War

In May 1493 Pope Alexander VI ordered Spanish *conquistadores* to discover new lands in the Americas in order to draw "barbarous nations" to Christianity (Washburn 1995, 5). The subsequent invasion of the Western Hemisphere, predicated upon the assumption that its indigenous inhabitants were a distinctly inferior species, was governed by the international legal principle, invented specifically to address the phenomenon of the European encounter with the Americas and contrary to existing principles proscribing aggressive war, that a European nation became sovereign of territory its agents "discovered," provided it subjugated the population and annexed its lands. To justify the dichotomy between the law applicable to Indians and the law applicable to nonindigenous peoples, and to enable the lawful use of force against the former, European legal scholars proclaimed that indigenous peoples were subhumans devoid of legal personality—fit for legal protection only if they submitted to European rule, fit for the sword otherwise (Rosen 1997, 242). It is no wonder that the next four centuries are known as the Age of Genocide.

B. Murder

The precise number of victims evades quantification. Estimates of the pre-Columbian population in what later became the United States range from five million to ninety-four million, yet by 1880 disease, slaughter, slavery, and aggressive wars had reduced their number to three hundred thousand—and declining (Sterba 1996, 424–25). Initially, a legislative approach effected the physical removal of Indians from ancestral lands;

ultimately, the United States turned to forcible relocation. The removal of
the Cherokee Nation from the Eastern Woodlands is perhaps the most
infamous relocation. With a federal statute explicitly overruling a contrary Supreme Court opinion, the entire Cherokee Nation was forced, in
the dead of winter, on a thousand-mile "Trail of Tears" trek to
Oklahoma. More than four thousand Cherokees died of exposure and
starvation (Borewich 1996, 47). Taking a cue from the federal government, several states adopted Indian genocide as their official policy; even
the private sector joined in, with contractors hired to induce deliberate
starvation by destroying the buffalo (Prince 1993, 186).

In the aftermath of the Civil War, the might of the U.S. Army was
directed toward Indian eradication, and one by one the tribes were
pursued, cornered, and murdered. A series of "massacres" were written
in Indian blood on the pages of American history: Blue River (1854), Bear
River (1863), Sand Creek (1864), Washita River (1868), Sappa Creek
(1875), Camp Robinson (1878), Wounded Knee (1890), and more than
forty others. Gruesome exterminations of defenseless women and children were perfectly legal exercises of state and federal authority as the law
then stood. By the conclusion of the "Indian Wars," the Indian population had been reduced by as much 98 percent (Sterba 1996, 430). The
fraction that survived was corralled on reservations infested with vermin
and disease and lacking in adequate shelter and food.

The struggle of the Chiricahua Apaches is representative. In 1886 the
surviving three hundred members, suffering from starvation and the
murder of three thousand relatives, became the last Indian tribe to
surrender. Every Chiricahua—man, woman, and child—was incarcerated
for a generation in military prisoner-of-war camps in which the population
was reduced to less than half by disease, hunger, and exposure. Upon their
release in 1913, the Chiricahuas were divided in two and relocated to
reservations far from ancestral lands, where they were surrounded by
traditional rivals and provided inadequate food, housing, and medical
care. Many more perished (Lieder and Page 1997, 49).

C. Land Theft

The relationship between the land and the Indian people is fundamental
to their physical and cultural survival as autonomous groups. Indian land
is constitutive of identity and designative of the boundaries of the Indian
cultural universe (Deloria 1992, 122). Indians proclaim a sacred responsibility to preserve and transmit land, and with it identity, religion, and
culture, to successive generations. The depopulation of Indian land by
murder proved a highly efficient means to facilitate the annexation of
territory, and the seizures that followed constitute an independent
element of genocide.

The United States acquired most Indian land prior to 1865 by fraudulent treaty negotiations and by legal perversions in its own courts, and although these processes were arguably genocidal, the case is stronger with respect to subsequent outright thefts.[5] In the first three post–Civil War decades, the U.S. Army prosecuted a sequence of aggressive wars to divest Indians of land. After each homicidal campaign, a dwindled, harried, and hungry Indian nation sued for a peace that surrendered vast tracts and subjected its members to confinement on resource-deprived, alien land remnants. The United States employed murder and threats to acquire one-fourth of the land within its modern contiguous boundaries for distribution to non-Indian settlers, and by 1890 the army had fulfilled American Manifest Destiny and crushed the last obstacles to the Pacific. A series of laws fragmented what remained of Indian lands and facilitated their transfer to non-Indians over the next half-century. By 1934, of the two billion acres that once was Indian, all that remained was a fragmented, forty-seven million acre mosaic of tribal lands, plots owned in fee simple by whites, and plots held by Indian individuals no longer enrolled in any tribe. Ninety-five thousand Indians were landless (Bradford 2002–03, 38–39).

D. Ethnocide

Once Indians had been defeated, culled, and caged, the United States undertook to divest them of their ethnicity by liquidating their culture and forcing their assimilation.

1. Cultural Liquidation

Of all the processes engineered to strip away Indian culture, perhaps the most nefarious was congressional funding of religious schools geared toward the substitution of Euro-American, Christian culture in its stead. Beginning in the late nineteenth century, Indian children were spirited off to boarding schools where their hair was cut, their tribal clothing was exchanged for Western garb, and harsh abuses were meted out for speaking tribal languages or engaging in Indian religious practices (Noriega 1992, 380–82). During their residence, children were prohibited from visiting their relatives, whom, as a result, they often did not see for years. Removed Indian children, and generations of their descendants, lost the use of their languages and knowledge of their cultures (Pritchard 1998, 263).

While Indian children underwent forced conversions, the United States posted missionaries to the reservations with orders to Christianize Indians. Congress criminalized traditional Indian family relationships, property rights, and religious practices. For most of the twentieth

---

[5] For a discussion of seizures of Indian land through fraudulent dealings and by judicial decisions, see Bradford 2002–03.

238 WILLIAM C. BRADFORD

century, the exercise of Indian religion was illegal. Despite the 1978 passage of the American Indian Religious Freedom Act establishing the policy of the United States to "protect and preserve for American Indians their inherent right . . . to believe, express, and exercise . . . traditional religions,"[6] in practice Indian religions—particularly when they involve the hunting of charismatic fauna, such as whales or eagles, or the use of controlled substances, such as peyote—are too enigmatic for non-Indian jurists to admit within the meaning of "religion" as enunciated in the U.S. Bill of Rights. Simply put, Indians may not celebrate the sacraments of their faith without threat of prosecution for violation of controlled-substance or species-protection laws.

2. Forced Assimilation
Early treaties between the United States and Indians did not contemplate incorporation of Indians as U.S. citizens, and later treaties incorporated only "detribalized" individuals who assumed the "characteristics and mannerisms of a civilized person" (Porter 1999, 111–12). Against the force of a clear preference for a primary affiliation with tribal institutions, federal Indian policy has subsumed Indians within the body politic, facilitating the seizure of tribal lands and resources and the elimination of competing objects of political loyalty. The first such assimilative measure, Allotment, divested many Indians of land and created great physical and social distance between them and their tribes. The imposition of U.S. citizenship in 1924 added legal momentum by foisting an awkward dual allegiance upon Indians and pressuring them to transfer loyalties to the United States.

a. Termination
Although assimilationist pressure abated during World War II, with the onset of the cold war and mounting fears of enemies within the preservation of distinct political communities within U.S. boundaries became too offensive for many non-Indians to tolerate. House Concurrent Resolution 108 ("Termination") ended the U.S. trust relationship with more than a hundred tribes, curtailed federal benefits and services, dissolved tribal governments, and distributed former tribal lands and assets on a per capita basis.[7] By legislatively disappearing tribes, Termination stripped Indian people not only of Indian citizenship but also of sacred sites and other fonts of cultural renewal. Assimilationist pressure mounted, and in 1954 Public Law 280, by according states extensive jurisdiction over Indians, granted non-Indian institutions of social control the legal authority to adjudge and condemn Indian domestic relations

[6] American Indian Religious Freedom Act, Pub. L. No. 95–341, 92 Stat. 469 (1978).
[7] See H.R. Con. Res. 108, 67 Stat. at B132 (1953).

and employment practices.[8] In perhaps the most egregious exercise of such jurisdiction, state health departments seized Indian children and placed them with non-Indian parents on the culturally bound theory that traditional Indian parenting, reliant on extended kinship groups for monitoring and nurturing children, was tantamount to neglect (Pritchard 1998, 259).

b. Relocation

Predicated upon the misapprehension that the emerging "Indian problem" was rooted in segregation and parochialism rather than a cascade of assimilative legislation, Public Law 959 ("Relocation")[9] directly targeted Indian culture. At a time when reservations were increasingly unable to provide material necessities, Relocation, by portraying "contented Indian[s] working at good jobs and sitting beside televisions and refrigerators [in Northern cities]," induced an exodus to select urban magnets (Barsh 1991, 159). A generation of the Indian best and brightest were dumped into substandard housing and menial employment and subsumed in the American melting pot. By 1970 reservation populations had dwindled so far that a final solution to the Indian problem appeared at hand, and yet the "stubborn [Indian] refusal to . . . become simply another American citizen" has sustained tribalism against a malign tide of assimilationism up to the present. (Relocation continues as federal policy, albeit outside the legislative orbit of Public Law 959.) Although Indians currently possess both tribal and federal citizenship, meaningful "dual citizenship"—predicated upon the assumption that tribal and federal governments exercise separate, if overlapping, spheres of authority in good faith—is a legal fiction. For many Indians, this forced "split identification" is a genocidal act, and few believe that tribal and national political participation can coexist when Indian tribes are perceived as threatening U.S. territorial integrity (Porter 1999, 266–68).

E. Forced Sterilization

Having murdered and forcibly assimilated Indians' ancestors, the United States set about preventing the birth of their descendants. From the late nineteenth century to the mid-1970s, the Indian Health Service sterilized more than one thousand Indian women per year (Shapiro 1985, 91). As many as 42 percent of Indian women of child-bearing age were secretly subjected to nonconsensual sterilization, a cognizable war crime at Nuremburg and under Article 8(2)(b)(xxii) of the Rome Statute of the International Criminal Court.

[8] Act of Aug. 15, 1953; Pub. L. No. 83–280, ch. 505; 67 Stat. 588, 588–90.
[9] Act of Aug. 3, 1956, Pub. L. No. 84–959, 70 Stat. 986, 986 (1956) ("Relocation").

Summary: American Indian Genocide

The United States murdered millions of Indians so as to depopulate their land and eliminate rival polities within a colonial state constructed on it. The survivors and their descendants—those who somehow managed to be born—have been under cultural assault to this day. This malign history had rendered Indians the most materially deprived and legally exposed group in the nation, and the scars of this genocide are manifested in an ongoing cycle of unemployment, infant mortality, suicide, homicide, substance abuse, homelessness, and poor health. It is perhaps impossible to overstate the magnitude of the human injustice: indeed, the severity and duration of the harms endured by the original inhabitants of the United States may well rival those suffered by any other group, domestic or international. The next section will review existing theories of justice that suggest avenues toward the remediation of the genocide of American Indians.

2. The Indian Claim for Redress: Existing Theories of Justice

Extant theories cluster around three distinct approaches: supersession, compensation, and restoration.

A. Justice as Supersession

While the historical record establishes a factual predicate presumptively obligating the United States to remedy the genocide of Indians, proponents of the Justice as Supersession (JAS) theory reach a very different conclusion. JAS theorists treat the land-theft element of the Indian claim as the only aspect of moral relevance and dismiss the rest.

Even with respect to the question of land theft, JAS theorists reject as foolishly naïve a "natural way of reasoning" that would require that lands illicitly taken by colonial invaders and passed on to their descendants nonetheless be returned (Lyons 1977, 252). Although JAS theory recognizes that the historical record has an important place in a theory of justice, for JAS theorists the historical injustices must be weighed against the current injustice that would be inflicted upon innocent owners now in possession of erstwhile Indian lands if those lands were stripped away and restored to Indian ownership (Waldron 1992a, 27). To sanction a moral understanding that demands restoration of Indian lands would have practical effects, foremost among them the dispossession and impoverishment of non-Indians (Lyons 1977, 252). To avoid this, JAS theorists urge us to reconceive of the historical injustices suffered by Indians as a "dead history" and to accept that Indian claims for redress have been superseded by demographic and ecological transformations—in other words, while injustice may have been inflicted in centuries past, injustice is perishable, and the accreting rights of non-Indians in Indian land have incrementally extinguished any present claims for its restoration (Lyons 1977, 257).

JAS proponents defend what they further concede is very much a prospective theory by asserting that only a deliberate discounting of the past can possibly ensure that resources are allocated in a manner that is "fair to all of [the world's] existing inhabitants" (Waldron 1992a, 27). Because they now constitute the overwhelming majority, non-Indians are the primary reference point. For JAS theorists, even had non-Indians not come by their current entitlements through fraud and force they would at present be entitled to a share of Indian lands proportionate to their numbers by simple virtue of their existence and legitimate need here in North America (Waldron 1992a, 25). Thus, although JAS theorists accept that symbolic recognition and remembrance of historical injustices may often be morally appropriate and that Indians are entitled to a more equitable distribution of the panoply of resources generally available within society, these theorists categorically reject all proposals that would "actually . . . rectify past wrongs" either by retransferring lands or by paying their full, rather than their symbolic, value in compensation (Waldron 1992a, 66). Compensation is thus, at best, an act of grace; at worst it is an undeserved handout to the losers of a long-ago struggle for the continental landmass that may threaten non-Indians and justifiably provoke resentment.

With regard to the ethnocide element of Indian genocide, although JAS theorists accept in theory that individuals have the basic human need to belong to groups "united by some common links—especially language, collective memories, continuous life upon the same soil," and perhaps "race, blood, religion, [and] a sense of common mission" (Berlin 1980, 252, 257), the theorists reject Indian tribes as mere "partisans of small-scale community" lacking in any entitlement to "special support or assistance or to extraordinary provision or forbearance" from the United States (Waldron 1992b, 778). Rather than encourage an "artificial" commitment to tribalism, JAS theorists would require Indian cultures to "wither away," to "amalgamate with other cultures," and to "adapt themselves to geographical or demographic necessity" (Waldron 1992b, 787). Further, rather than accept that Indian culture and tribes are worthy of preservation and that injuries to either give rise to obligations to afford redress, JAS theory demands that Indians submit to a "'mongrelization' of [their] identity" in service to a cosmopolitan vision that broadens the scope of individual life possibilities and serves as a more "authentic response to the world in which we live" (Waldron 1992b, 787). Although JAS theory does not go so far as to immunize ethnocide, it suggests strongly that the historical processes responsible for the loss of culture and the right to self-govern are at worst a trivial moral or legal consequence and at best even promote the individual rights and life possibilities of individual Indians.

In sum, JAS theory holds that while the United States may be obligated to negotiate symbolic redress, any retrospective proposal to

restore lands, pay market value for expropriations, or transform existing
legal regimes to lend genuine political and material support to Indian
culture would inflict great injustices upon living non-Indians while
simultaneously interfering with the opportunities of living Indians to
partake of the superior virtues of Western liberal cosmopolitanism.

B. Justice as Compensation

Justice as Compensation (JAC) is similarly landcentric. JAC theorists
ignore the process whereby Indian land was depopulated and contend
quite simply that where land has been acquired unjustly through fraud or
force, either it must, regardless of whether or not it has subsequently been
lawfully transferred, be restored to its rightful owner or full compensation
must be paid (Nozick 1974, 152). Where sacred lands are concerned, the
obligation to restore is at a zenith, and where restoration would require
the dispossession of non-Indians, Indians must be granted rights of way
to such sites (Thompson 2002, 63). By accepting the duty to restore or
compensate and thereby settling the normative question, JAC theorists
are free to direct their energies to prudential issues, such as membership in
the remedial class, the form that compensation is to assume, and the
identities of the parties from whom restoration or compensation must
issue. JAC theorists accept the argument that the historic deprivation of
Indian lands is causally related to the material deprivation currently
experienced by Indians and consequently view compensation for expropriation as "an example of ordinary corrective justice" that, coupled with
"some form of group-based political autonomy"—whether exemptions
from taxes or other group-specific entitlements—befits the redress of
Indian claims (Posner and Vermeule 2003, 733–34).

Nevertheless, many who would otherwise recognize the duty to afford
redress to Indians for land expropriation point to relevant treaties and
statutes, the Indian Claims Commission (ICC), and a host of federal
Indian benefits programs as evidence that compensation has already been
paid and claims settled (Harris 2003, 445).[10] Even those JAC theorists
who would accept that further measures of compensatory relief are still

---

[10] In 1946, embarrassed by Nazi comparisons of *Lebensraum* and death camps to
Manifest Destiny and reservations, Congress created the ICC, providing a forum for
adjudication of Indian treaty violations and broad moral "claims based upon fair and
honorable dealings that are not recognized by any existing rule of law or equity." 25 U.S.C.
70–70(v)(3). The ICC was charged with assessing damages in accordance with the factual
history of the tribe, relative U.S. responsibility, and price per acre at the time of
expropriation (ibid.). Although the ICC found that 35 percent of the United States—750
million acres—is legally Indian land, it read the "fair and honorable dealings" clause out of
its organic statute, the text of which prohibited *in natura* restitution (ibid.). Ultimately,
before its legislative demise in 1978 the ICC redressed fewer than one-third of land seizures
with cash only, most at rates far below a just level of compensation. For a discussion of the
ICC, see Rosenthal 1990.

THE GENOCIDE OF AMERICAN INDIANS

due Indian claimants insist that amounts be negotiated through the political process rather than be determined in accordance with some rational, objective standard (Tully 1994, 157). Some insist that a "commitment device" be engineered that would definitively resolve Indian land claims and prevent their reopening even if justice should so require at a later date (Posner and Vermuele 2003, 745).

Most significantly, JAC theory is silent as to the deprivation of Indian lives and culture. A mode of redress morphologically identical to reparations, JAC theory is ultimately a narrowly tailored approach to justice, whether as the result of a presumption that cash cannot compensate these deprivations, a limited remedial reach, assimilative preferences, or an ignorance of these equally, if not more, compelling elements of the Indian genocide claim.[11]

C. Justice as Restoration

Justice as Restoration (JAR) aims at a more holistic approach. For proponents of JAR, in-kind compensation, even if theoretically equivalent in value to that which was taken, is insufficient to rectify the original injustice; restoration of the illicitly appropriated property itself is essential to "set unjust situations right." Even more significantly, JAR does not limit its remedial scope to the issue of land rights: rather, it extends to those "injustices that may in fact loom larger in the minds of the victims or their descendants—murder, torture, enslavement, discrimination and degradation" (Corlett 2002, vix). Because restoration of land alone does not restore moral parity, JAR theorists insist that a full settlement of claims necessitates that the United States publicly acknowledge and apologize for specific past acts and then accept some form of social punishment (even if sanctions are limited to moral judgments). Many JAR theories rely on truth and reconciliation commissions (TRCs), tribunals that investigate and publicize the gross human injustices of previous regimes, as integral to this process.[12]

Furthermore, JAR contends that theories which purport to remedy a genocidal history solely "through the language of missing property" forfeit transformative opportunities whereby to reconcile victims and wrongdoers. Accordingly, in conjunction with land restoration and

---

[11] Reparations are a tort-based mode of redress "where a guilty party makes up for an injustice by paying or otherwise benefiting a victim" (Wheeler 1997, 301).

[12] Since 1974 more than twenty TRCs have been initiated in Argentina, Bolivia, Chad, Chile, El Salvador, Ethiopia, Germany, the Phillippines, Malawi, Rwanda, South Africa, Uganda, and Zimbabwe, and still more have been demanded for Bosnia, Mexico, South Korea, Honduras, and Sri Lanka. See Christie 2000. Though a lack of cash and courage has hampered them, several TRCs have aided reconciliation. See Christie 2000, 54–55 (table 2.1), 58–59 (table 2.2) (providing dates, objectives, and accomplishments). TRCs typically publish an open record or final report, and in the interests of transparency public hearings are often broadcast on national media. See Wacks 2000, 195, 207.

apologies, JAR theorists call for rehabilitative measures designed to heal the injured psyches of individuals and groups. Some JAR theorists cast promotion of self-determination as a necessary condition precedent to the moral relegitimization of the nation (Yamamoto et al. 2003, 1272). Still, although some JAR theorists would reinvest a significant degree of land and political autonomy in beneficiary groups and liberate them from the cultural and physical control of the majoritarian legal and political system, either through limited legislative dispensations or through some process of formal secession, most propose far more limited agendas that would provide beneficiary groups little more than a package of grants, subsidies, and tax incentives (Daly 2003, 403).

D. Analysis

At its core, JAS theory is a not terribly subtle justification for genocide. While JAS theorists may highlight the pragmatic and utilitarian approach to preserving the interests of the non-Indian majority, stripped of its academic veneer JAS theory is little more than the medieval dogmas once enunciated by conquistadors as justification for their adventures in the Americas. Incredibly, the indispensability thesis—that formerly Indian lands are indispensable not to Indian survival but to non-Indians currently in possession, who would suffer impoverishment and uprooting were they stripped of title—marshals the fact that some Indians survived genocide as evidence against their claim: had Indians been extinguished as the consequence of the expropriation of their lands, then and only then would JAS concede that Indian lands were indispensable to Indians, but then there would be no claimants left. In other words, Indians have proven that they can do without Indian lands, but non-Indians cannot or should not have to make the same showing. The only explanations JAS theory offers to support its differential treatment are two: (1) that was then, and this is now; and (2) the fundamental precept of Western liberal jurisprudence, that like cases are decided alike, does not apply to Indian claims.

In other words, rather than present a theory of justice, JAS theorists inform Indians that "our culture is superior to yours, that's why we won the war, and to the victors go the spoils, so either content yourselves with scraps we throw you savages or, better yet, shed your anachronistic Indianness and embrace our modern civilization, but either way stop bringing up the past—it poisons our national body politic and scares us nice non-Indian people." Simply put, JAS categorically rejects any moral or legal obligations flowing from genocide. In the face of the claim that the theft of Indian land and the murder of Indian people are neutral facts, Indians might be forgiven for concluding that the only path to justice is down the very same road whereby lives, lands, and cultures were taken.

JAC theory, in contrast, rejects the premise that history is dead insofar as the obligation to render justice for past wrongs is concerned and that the passage of time can and has rendered good a thief's title.[13] Compensating Indians would alleviate grinding poverty and, if accompanied by expressions of regret and remorse, might demonstrate to future generations the continuing vitality of moral duties to refrain from genocide. The infusion of significant sums into tribal institutions might even create the financial preconditions for genuine self-determination and enable land restoration.

However, JAC theory is far too quick to assume that cash and Indian land are commensurable and far too susceptible to counterclaims that sufficient compensation either has been or will be paid to discharge the obligation to remedy all the injustices visited upon Indians. Simply put, money can play at best an indirect part in the remediation of these harms: most Indians desire above all not to be made whole financially but rather to exercise their rights to express their unique cultures and religions upon sacred ancestral lands (Cornell 1988, 152–56). Only land restoration and legal transformations that permit the (re)development of separate and secure political identities can relieve the pain Indians bear and transmit intergenerationally. No amount of money can compel unwilling sellers, public or private, to reconvey formerly Indian lands, and no dollar figure will induce tribes to trade their right to self-government. Cash, however beneficial to its recipients, cannot restore to Indians the capacity to self-determination on their aboriginal landmass, nor can it bring dead ancestors back to life.

Even if Indian tribes could be persuaded to surrender their claims for cash, the fair value would be so great as to threaten the national fisc and spark a racialized political firestorm. Indian tribes currently control only fifty-two million acres, or 2.6 percent, of the U.S. continental landmass. The ICC, charged with assessing relative U.S. responsibility for expropriation of Indian lands, estimated that 35 percent of the two billion acres making up the United States—a total of 750 million acres—is legally Indian land (Newton 1992, 776–84). Assuming, *arguendo*, that the median value of an acre is $1,000, the fair market cost to compensate Indians would exceed $750 billion. Even assuming that nothing close to fair market value would be paid, and even if the award were reduced by the amounts paid through federal benefits programs or by the ICC, the enormity of any proposal that would offer even "payment on the cheap" would still have macroeconomic consequences. If one factors into the

---

[13] At common law, a thief's title to property is void, and the thief cannot convey good title even to a subsequent good-faith purchaser. See, e.g., *Schrier v. Home Indem. Co.*, 273 A.2d 248, 250–51 (D.C. 1971). The rule is intended to protect property against thievery; for if a thief could convey good title "there must be an end of all social commerce between man and man, unless private possessions be secured from unjust invasions: and, if an acquisition of goods by either force or fraud were allowed to be a sufficient title, all property would soon be confined to the most strong, or the most cunning; and the weak and simpleminded part of mankind (which is by far the most numerous division) could never be secure of their possessions." Blackstone 2002, 3:145.

compensatory scheme additional moneys for the wrongful deaths of at least five million Indian ancestors at a paltry rate of $100,000 for each decedent—and JAC theory is further to be faulted for failing to extend its remedial reach to this element of genocide—the total cost to taxpayers would exceed one trillion dollars. Those ignorant of the historical predicate behind the demand for justice might mistakenly equate compensation with revenge; others, merely self-interested, will be unwilling to effect such a radical redistribution of wealth. Either way, many Indians, concerned that application of JAC theory would lock Indians and non-Indians in bitter political combat, join with non-Indians in opposing this approach to justice.

Finally, JAC theory completely fails to account for the most important variable in the remedial equation: law. Congress has nearly absolute and unreviewable dominion over Indian tribes, and this plenary power proscribes judicial review of takings, insulates violations of treaty provisions, and withdraws Indian property, culture, and religion from the protection of the Constitution (Bradford 2002). Moreover, that which Congress can give, Congress can take away. Any settlement of Indian claims will therefore depend upon the inconstant will of a majority of its legislative branch. Under the current legal regime, should a future Congress elect to reclaim moneys paid as compensation, take property purchased with such moneys without paying compensation, or even terminate each and every Indian tribe, dissolve each and every reservation, and criminalize every aspect of Indian culture, nothing—save for any resulting moral outrage—will stand in its way. Federal Indian law—barren terrain for the expression of Indian claims—is structurally incapable of ensuring the finality of any compensation agreement, even in the decidedly unlikely event that an agreement could ever be fashioned that would reach most, or even some, of the elements in the Indian claim for genocide. Power is as yet the only currency fully negotiable in intercourse between the United States and Indians.

Of the three theories, only JAR embraces restoration of Indian land, and only JAR is theoretically amenable to consideration of the non-material injuries that occupy a central place in the Indian claim for redress for genocide. Furthermore, only JAR would hold the United States accountable under moral, as opposed to strictly legal, principles, and only JAR would even attempt to induce the United States to repudiate past acts of egregious injustice. Quite distinct from JAS and JAC theories, JAR recognizes that justice is not merely a settlement of historical accounts but an opportunity to reconcile and relegitimize the nation in its relations at home and abroad. Finally, JAR is, if not positively encouraging, at least not hostile to the notion that self-determination, in whatever form it comes to assume, is the legitimate objective of Indians in their relations with the United States, and that the United States has an obligation to assist them in this endeavor.

Still, while JAR is the most normatively attractive of the three theories, it is not the final stop on the journey to justice. Compelling as the argument may be that non-Indian landowners are obligated to vacate their entitlements in favor of the descendants of their Indian predecessors-in-title, principles of equity *should* proscribe the wholesale evacuation of millions of acres of land and the forced relocation of innocent and newly homeless non-Indians to places uncertain. Even if equity alone is not sufficient to counsel prudence, the prospect that non-Indians threatened in the security of their property interests might organize to induce political action resulting in further abridgement of Indian resources and rights must be accounted for in any theory of Indian justice. If the only remedy for a past injustice is a present injustice, a perpetual cycle of bloody conflict is inevitable.

However, the most radical JAR theorists are oblivious to the broad externalities the application of their theory might spawn: despite warnings that it is now much too late to "give back Manhattan," some insist that nothing short of the dissolution of the United States will suffice if we are to "tak[e] seriously ... morality and justice" (Corlett 2002, 155). If politics is the art of the possible, a theory that insists on the dismemberment of the United States or other forms of "radical social surgery" is too fantastic to be given serious consideration. Furthermore, if JAR may conceivably go too far in pressing for land restoration, like JAC theory it does not go far enough, because it does not recognize, let alone engage, federal Indian law as the primary variable preventing the balancing of the moral equation. Compensation and apologies, gestures potentially part of an amicable settlement, do not reinvest sovereignty, physical security, and cultural integrity in Indian tribes. Only a comprehensive program of legal reform that dispenses with doctrines and precedents perpetuating the denial of Indian rights will create the preconditions for justice. As law, more than any other social variable, has (re)produced the subordination of Indians, legal reform occupies central position in a theory of Indian justice. Thus, while much of JAR is germane, neither it nor the other theories surveyed afford the full measure of relief. The next section offers an alternative.

3. Justice as Indigenism

A. General Theoretical Premises

Because the rapacious, bloody, dishonorable history of United States–Indian relations is a factual and moral predicate to the Indian claim, Justice as Indigenism (JAI) maintains that development and application of a theory of Indian justice cannot be undertaken except in full cognizance of this history.

Second, JAI ventures into terrain heretofore unmapped by insisting that legal reforms designed to make the nation safe for the peaceful coexistence of basic value differences are a necessary, if not sufficient, step toward the attainment of justice for Indians. Thus, legislation and even constitutional amendments to strengthen protection of Indian cultural and property rights are within its contemplation.

Third, although it challenges the legitimacy of U.S. dominion over Indians, JAI rejects the substitution of one ethnocentric perspective on justice for another: without compromising Indian rights, JAI treats reconciliation between disparate yet interdependent peoples, rather than prescription of a formula for the distribution of social resources or the administration of punishment or vengeance, as the appropriate teleology. For JAI, the healing of the American nation and the joint authorship of a harmonious future——not simply the redress of genocide——are crucial objectives.

Fourth, although it rejects the tendency to essentialize Indians as an undifferentiated population with a uniform bloc of interests, JAI contends that a pan-Indian consensus exists as to a set of objectives the attainment of which is central to the project of Indian justice, and that the most important of these are a just resolution to Indian land claims and the investment of the notion of Indian self-determination with real meaning. At the same time, generalization to the question of justice on behalf of other groups that have been subjected to genocide must proceed with caution and the benefit of rigorous contextual research and analysis.

Fifth, and perhaps paradoxically in light of the preceding proposition, JAI cautions that the application of a theory of Indian justice generates moral consequences internationally. JAI insists that if its political and legal system cannot or will not afford justice to its original inhabitants, the United States, no matter how currently committed to justice on behalf of other foreign and domestic social groups, must concede that the aspirations of its founders to "establish Justice" in a republic in which "all men are created equal" before the law and into which they invested their "sacred Honor"[14] have been sacrificed at the altar of an avaricious Indian policy. In other words, JAI theory posits that the legitimacy of the United States and its international leadership is a function of the extent to which it affords justice to Indians and, more specifically, remedies for Indian genocide.

B. JAI Applied: The Redress of Indian Genocide

As applied, JAI commits its practitioners to an eight-stage sequential process: acknowledgment, apology, peacemaking, commemoration, compensation, land restoration, legal reformation, and reconciliation. Only upon reaching the final destination—which is in reality the promise of a shared journey—is JAI complete.

[14] See U.S. Constitution, Preamble, The Declaration of Independence, paras. 2, 32 (U.S. 1776).

Acknowledgment

Although most Americans disavow the malignant racism that inspired their forefathers, they remain a remarkably presentist people, particularly with regard to the events marking the "discovery," formation, and expansion of their nation. This ahistoricism has dire consequences. Without a firm understanding of the nexus between past acts of injustice and the Indian claim for redress, it is all too easy to dismiss Indian claims as pleas for distributional justice rather than as legitimate moral arguments demanding the internalization of the consequences of this unjust history. Displacement of a mythical version of national genesis and development in favor of the truth is thus a necessary condition precedent.

Therefore, the first step in applying JAI theory is the reenvisioning of United States–Indian relations. Indian oral histories that contextualize and humanize the Indian experience of genocide while revealing the inadequacies of the record as it has been constructed can be a powerful source of liberation for all Americans. To enable national demythification, Congress should establish and fund an independent TRC charged with (1) investigating Indian claims afresh; (2) allowing Indian voices to enrich and debunk the sanitized national record with their oral histories; and (3) persuading the United States formally to acknowledge the wrongs inflicted upon Indians since 1776.

Membership of the American Indian Reconciliation Commission (AIRC) would consist of equal numbers of Indians and non-Indians and include tribal chairpersons and nationally elected officials; jurists, lawyers, and scholars versant in federal Indian law, tribal legal systems, and indigenous-rights regimes; and clergy. Drawing upon the experiences of precedent TRCs, AIRC would identify sites across the United States—Indian reservations, major urban centers with significant Indian populations, and universities—where forums would be established in which tribes and individual Indians would testify. AIRC would broadcast testimony on public media and a Web site, and transcripts would be circulated in newspapers to facilitate the wide dissemination of Indian stories. Victims would receive a certificate recognizing their contribution to truthtelling and reconciliation. Upon conclusion of its hearings, AIRC would send a Final Report to Congress and the president with nonbinding remedial recommendations, to include apologies, compensation, land restoration, and other measures to promote and protect self-determination.

Apology

JAI assumes that the AIRC hearings would be likely to cause many citizens to experience the moral taint of the history of U.S. treatment of Indians for the first time. After persuading many citizens to acknowledge harm to Indian tribes and individuals, AIRC should recommend in its Final Report that the U.S. government issue a formal apology, on behalf of the United States and all its citizens past and present, as symbolic recognition of the role of public and private actors in past acts of genocide.[15] National church and corporate boards might apologize for acts in which these institutions were complicit. An appropriate apology must incorporate recognition of a corresponding moral obligation to negotiate the next stage of JAI: peacemaking.

Peacemaking

If a theory of justice is to span the chasm between peoples, it will require negotiation. Although the resilience of Indian tribes is unquestionable, the tribes are now too numerically and militarily inferior to impose solutions by force; on the other hand, reason, principle, moral obligations, and the aspirational values of a constitutional republic erected upon prior sovereigns, with whom it is interdependent, conspire to restrain the United States. While the conflict has been waged primarily on battlefields and in courtrooms, the origins are rooted in cultural differences difficult to exaggerate: the "problem of learning how meaning in one system of expression is expressed in another is one of the most difficult tasks we confront in a multicultural world" (Williams 1997, 112). Recognition of mutual sovereignty will require a cross-cultural hermeneutics that clears communication barriers and shares fears, hopes, and dreams. By tutoring both parties in the common humanity of each other, United States–Indian negotiations can usher in a new era of peace and justice.

A United States–Indian Peace Conference (USIPC) might enlist the most respected elder Indian and non-Indian statesmen as peacemakers to supervise, lead, and guide negotiations as to remedies for the redress of Indian claims. Such persons would collect and merge spiritual and secular values common to both cultures and urge negotiators to envision a future when all U.S. citizens are full and equal members of one great nation. Peacemakers would urge the United States to suggest remedies that would restore dignity and demonstrate a genuine desire to live up to the highest values enshrined in the Declaration of Independence. USIPC might meet at a series of venues, including sacred tribal lands and U.S. retreats, such

---

[15] An apology need not address contemporary effects of past discrimination to initiate reconciliation; to do so might trench upon terrain too sensitive for a present-day majority whose willingness to concede national fallibility may be merely retrospective. An apology might track with the letter accompanying compensation to Japanese Americans, perhaps as follows: "The United States acknowledges the historic significance of its illegal and immoral actions and expresses its deep regret to the Indian peoples. Money and words alone cannot restore lost ancestors or lands, or erase painful memories; neither can they fully convey American resolve to rectify injustice, but the United States recognizes that serious injustices were done to Indians over the course of the creation and expansion of the United States. In enacting a law calling for restitution and reconciliation and offering a sincere apology, your fellow Americans have, in a very real sense, renewed their traditional commitment to the ideals of freedom, equality, and justice. The Nation humbly asks for your forgiveness."

as Camp David. Although USIPC's recommendations need not be binding, remedies agreed upon could be transmitted to Congress as the basis for legislative action.

Commemoration

The next step—commemoration—is necessary to ensure that future generations will neither forget nor perpetuate the past. Erection of monuments at sites of Indian genocide and on the National Mall, naming of public buildings and parks after Indians of historical significance, and creation of a wing in the National Museum of the American Indian with specific focus on Indian genocide will serve these transformative and deterrent purposes.[16] Posthumous pardons should be granted to Indians executed for resisting genocide. Establishment and funding of cultural, historical, linguistic, and religious centers will regenerate sources of tribal cohesion while offering non-Indians the opportunity to adjust their perceptions of Indian culture toward understanding and tolerance.[17] Although the object is to unite rather than divide peoples, the mythical version of history from which the genocide of Indians has been redacted no longer functions as political adhesive. Memorials can restore the gravitational force between disparate groups in the American polity by concretizing the findings of AIRC and USIPC and inscribing the unvarnished history of United States–Indian relations in the minds and hearts of successive generations.

Compensation

It is impossible objectively to quantify the value of the injuries inflicted upon Indian people over history, and morally odious to try. The harm suffered is inestimable to peoples for whom ancestors, land, and culture are spiritually interwoven. Moreover, compensation cannot reach, let alone discharge, the wrongful deaths of ancestors, the denial of the use of tribal lands and resources, and the legal assaults on Indian religions,

---

[16] The National Holocaust Museum might serve as a model for a Genocide Wing of the National Museum of the American Indian. Exhibits might include original copies of United States–Indian treaties along with subsequent histories and specific dates and circumstances of U.S. breaches. Histories of tribes, from first contact to dispossession and genocide to the present, could be preserved in rich detail. Names of Indians murdered might be inscribed on a national register, and certificates could be issued to descendants of each victim commemorating the circumstances of his or her death.

[17] Certain existing institutions, such as the D'Arcy McNickle Center for American Indian History of the Newberry Library, might discharge some of these functions, possibly as a central archive with satellite branches across the United States and in consortium with tribal colleges. Moreover, as the cost of higher education is the greatest obstacle to Indian students, scholarship grants to attend the thirty-four Indian tribal colleges and universities would be appropriate. The American Indian Higher Education Consortium, an organization founded in 1972 to support Indian higher education, might be tapped to administer an Indian Educational Trust. See http://www.aihec.org

languages, and cultures. Worse, any proposed sum might stoke the perception of greed or suggest that the real motivation for redress is vindictive. Thus, JAI theory would regard any wealth transfer as a symbolic act undertaken in further recognition of moral responsibility, rather than a settlement of claims for loss, grief, and trauma. Although endowment of a fund sufficient to allow tribes to repurchase lands and to infuse the social-support net for the poorest Indians would not be incompatible with JAI, money is a relatively unimportant, and potentially even a dispensable, element.

Land restoration
One of the most difficult stages in applying JAI theory will be land restoration. Even if preceding stages commit the United States and its people in theory to do "justice," it will prove far more difficult in practice to reach an agreement as to what measures must be implemented to yield a "just" result, and still more difficult to cobble together legislation implementing agreed-upon measures without catalyzing opposition. For much of the non-Indian majority, land restoration represents an existential threat. Non-Indians are Americans too, and they have nowhere to go if transformations in land-tenure regimes evict them from their homes. Broaching the subject of land restoration with a non-Indian can trigger a defensive backlash: as a white businessman huffed, "I didn't persecute anybody at Plymouth Rock. . . . This is the 1990's. We didn't do anything to them, and we don't owe them anything" (Egan 1998, A1).

Nonetheless, while JAI concedes that centuries after the facts of expropriation it is too late to cast clouds over most of the land titles in the United States, it insists that Indians are entitled to the restoration of their ancestral lands to the furthest limits of reason and equity. A necessary precondition for personal security, the exercise of the powers of self-government, and the safe propagation of culture is the possession of a physical space upon which to center these forms of human endeavor and from which it is possible to exclude others hostile to these activities. Where Indians have ceded lands in a process free from coercion, fraud, or duress, such cessions are to be respected categorically, along with the private entitlements of those currently in possession of such lands. However, where Indian lands were seized by force of arms or by coercive, duressive, or fraudulent dealings, or where the lands in question are sacred to a tribe, JAI requires as a general rule that those specific lands be restored to the ownership of the tribes from which they were taken. Only where this restoration would prove so disruptive to the settled expectations of blameless present owners that it would threaten social peace or otherwise inflict gross injustice would alternative arrangements be considered.

That restoration of rights in Indian lands will inflict unwarranted hardship on non-Indian possessors is, however, not to be presumed lightly. Even if the United States becomes genuinely committed to this project of land restoration, no serious person believes that the United States is "about to divest itself or its non-Indian citizens of large acreage in the name of its own laws."[18] One need not subscribe to the critical legal studies premise that "law is politics" to recognize that the conceptual boundaries between law and politics break down rather easily before the question of Indian land rights. Moreover, although the fear of many non-Indian possessors of residential real estate, family farms, and small businesses is that the assertion of Indian claims to land will eventually lead to their ejection and impoverishment, this concern need not be justified in practice, for JAI unequivocally proscribes the involuntary dispossession of non-Indians, as well as the uncompensated taking of their improvements. Although JAR is unabashedly disinterested in the fate of non-Indians now residing upon lands claimed by Indians, JAI regards non-Indian interests as morally relevant.

Accordingly, JAI insists that the transfer of sovereignty over territory need not disturb private land titles: Indian tribes reinvested with powers of public sovereignty over lands now settled by non-Indians are free to recognize all of these private titles, and JAI theory discourages the notion that a change in sovereignty is destructive of the system of land titles established by the prior sovereign. Public sovereignty—the ultimate dominion over territory and the power to make and enforce laws—is conceptually and practically distinct from private "ownership"—the power to make individual decisions as to the use and alienation of land. As a general rule, JAI envisions that land restoration will be undertaken in the least disruptive fashion possible: non-Indians are encouraged to remain in possession on the sole condition that they agree to live in peace with their Indian neighbors under Indian sovereignty. Non-Indian titles would either be left totally undisturbed or non-Indians would be entitled to just compensation for the taking of their property.[19]

Furthermore, should non-Indians elect not to accept Indian sovereignty subsequent to the program of restoration, JAI proposes that, rather than bring actions in ejectment, tribes grant these parties long-term leases on fair market terms, thereby granting de facto autonomy to the extent compatible with Indian sovereignty.[20] Such lease agreements might incorporate terms providing compensation for lost rental earnings and

[18] Brief for Petitioner in *County of Oneida v. Oneida Indian Nation*, 470 U.S. 226 (1985).

[19] Responsibility for payment of just compensation to non-Indians should attach to the United States, the party responsible for the original dispossession of Indians. In addition to compensation for acts of expropriation, non-Indians suffering loss of property interests might be granted other measures of relief, including tax remission on income or property situated elsewhere.

[20] Only the refusal to accept reasonable lease terms should trigger the exercise of U.S. powers of eminent domain to condemn properties held by non-Indians. See, e.g., Seneca Nation Settlement Act of 1990, 25 U.S.C. §§1774f. (2000).

damages for prior trespass and might have the effect of terminating all
prior claims relating to the leased parcels. Still, where restoration would
clearly inflict gross injustice upon blameless non-Indian possessors, and
the land in question is not sacred, JAI is prepared to accept in-kind grants
from federal landholdings in lieu.

In sum, recovery of a land mass sufficient to create the material
preconditions for the preservation of physical security and cultural
integrity is crucial, and thus JAI proposes land restoration to the furthest
limits possible short of imposing injustice on non-Indians. By negotiating a
creative strategy for identifying appropriate lands wherein to transfer some
quantum of sovereignty, and by jointly committing to preserve the private
property rights of non-Indian residents of lands over which sovereignty is
transferred, Indian tribes and the United States can devise a restorative
program that will prevent or internalize demoralization costs and preserve
the political and territorial integrity of the United States.

Legal reformation

If land restoration portends challenges, the penultimate step of JAI
promises even more. JAI, unlike existing theories of justice, specifies a
program of legal reformation as the critical stage in concretizing other
remedies. Taken together, the legal doctrines of discovery and conquest,
as incorporated in domestic law, as well as the almost absolute legislative
power of Congress, constitute an interconnected matrix of legal disability
that refers Indian rights to liberty, property, and culture to perpetual
reinterpretation and suppression by non-Indian majorities and hostile
judges.[21] Accordingly, legal reform, oriented toward the protection of this
bundle of Indian rights against non-Indian majorities, occupies the apex
of the remedial pyramid. Practically speaking, the project of legal
reformation needed to secure Indians against future genocide will require
four major commitments: (1) government-to-government negotiations
toward formal issue-area autonomy, (2) passage of federal legislation
creating judicially enforceable protections for Indian culture—including
the hunting of species protected by federal legislation or the use of
substances otherwise prohibited by state and federal laws, (3) incorporation of international legal principles defensive and promotive of the rights
of indigenous peoples,[22] and (4) Constitutional amendments cabining the
power of Congress and of the states with regard to Indian tribes.[23]

---

[21] For a discussion of the numerous legal disabilities that plague Indians, see Bradford
2005.

[22] See, e.g., U.N. Draft United Nations Declaration on the Rights of Indigenous Peoples,
(Oct. 28, 1994), 34 I.L.M. 541, 550 (codifying customary international legal principles that
recognize a broad array of rights inhering in indigenous peoples, including life, culture, and
property, and impose affirmative duties upon states to protect these rights).

[23] For a discussion of the specifics of such a constitutional reform proposal, see Bradford
2005.

Reconciliation

The execution of the first seven stages will implicate non-Indian interests, and may well compromise the universalist approach to conceiving of, promoting, and protecting rights. JAI will therefore invite contestation over its form, pace, and scope. However, if the United States acknowledges, recognizes responsibility for, and as far as possible repairs genocide and the effects of genocide that Indians have suffered over the course of its creation and expansion, JAI obligates Indians to find it in their hearts and minds to forgive. A new regime of peace and justice worthy of emulation and export must be rewarded with the most precious gift Indians can bestow: forgiveness. By forgiving the United States and its people in a solemn ceremony symbolizing the dawn of this new relationship, Indians will finally be allowed to heal, and all Americans will be released from the chains of history.

4. Conclusion

It may be naïve to believe that genocide—like smallpox—can ever truly be wiped from the face of the earth. Yet, so high are the stakes, unfavorable odds must not prevent us from trying. The Genocide Convention commits member states to prevent genocide or, failing prevention, to punish those responsible for it, and the ad hoc international criminal tribunals, along with the establishment of the International Criminal Court, constitute important steps toward honoring this commitment. However, based on the record of the past half-century, genocide is not even in remission. Cambodia, Bosnia, Rwanda, the Congo, Darfur—each calls into question whether an episode of genocide is less analogous to the outbreak of a dread disease than to a bus: it seems that there is always another one coming down the street.

Clearly, the commitment to the principle of "Never again!" is incomplete. Perhaps too few perpetrators are brought to justice to enable deterrence, or they are not sufficiently punished, or those who would commit genocide simply cannot be dissuaded by the specter of anything we might visit upon them in the unlikely event that they should be captured. Prevention seems to have been abandoned in favor of the presumption that genocide is an inevitability, and thus nothing about which to get (truly) exercised. The great and powerful nations have the capacity to prevent genocide; genocides are not in short supply; therefore, the legal prohibition against genocide is either not *really* law or there is simply no moral imperative at the heart of the law that is worth championing.

The failure to remedy past genocides reinforces the perception, spawned by contemporary great-power inertia, that mass murder, deportation, enslavement, and ethnocide are, have always been, and will therefore always be an inherent, albeit disagreeable, part of the human condition. If this is true, then we can rest assured that, just as we manage to get by without admitting or remedying the sins of yesteryear, so someday will we look back on the present day without qualms and without remorse, for after all, nothing was terribly, insufferably awry. We will take comfort in the knowledge that there was a cure for neither the common cold nor genocide; one could only hope to treat the symptoms. The occasional Serb or African served up for trial was the best we could do. We need feel no shame.

Despite its imperfections, the United States is an exceptional nation, and the greatest exponent of liberty the world has ever known. The United States has done more than any other country to prevent genocide and punish its perpetrators. Still, its moral legitimacy has of late been called into question by those critical of its 2003 invasion of Iraq who accuse the United States of attempting to establish global hegemony and undermine human rights. Even if one rejects both charges as without merit—and there is good reason to do so—in its current geopolitical posture, the United States has drawn upon itself increased scrutiny of its own record regarding the promotion and protection of rights. Accordingly, failure to afford the full measure of justice due its indigenous peoples casts a shadow over U.S. foreign relations and makes it easier for its many critics to query, "Why do we invade Iraq to kick it out of Kuwait and again to depose its dictator but not do justice at home?" Just a few short years after September 11th, the moral coherence of the United States in the watchful world it so frequently seeks to mold is at stake.

A serious commitment to redressing the genocide of American Indians, however, might remind contemporary critics of the inherent goodness of the United States, legitimate its international leadership during these most troubled of times, and announce that the most powerful nation in history is firmly committed to the defense of the moral truth that genocide is so abominable that each and every state is obligated to commit resources and people not merely to its criminalization but also to its prevention. Justice as Indigenism, by declaring that the genocide undertaken by the United States against its original inhabitants demands a comprehensive program that remedies all its constituent elements, challenges non-Indians to revisit a dishonorable chapter in the history of their own nation. Yet in so doing, it beckons them not only to look back in time but also to seize the day and prove the moral fitness of the United States to lead a world desperately in need of leadership into an era in which there will be no shortage of utterly malevolent actors to whom the lives of whole peoples and nations are far too cheap to be permitted to stand in the path of their ambitions. Our past need not be our prologue. We can and must do better. Far too many have carried their lives on their fingernails for far too long.

References

Barsh, Russel L. 1991. "Are We Stuck in the Slime of History?" *American Indian Quarterly* 15, no. 1 (winter): 59–64.

Berlin, Isaiah 1980. "Benjamin Disraeli, Karl Marx and the Search for Identity." In his *Against the Current: Essays in the History of Ideas*, edited by Henry Hardy, 252–86. Princeton: Princeton University Press.

Blackstone, William. 2002. *Commentaries on the Laws of England: A Facsimile of the First Edition of 1765–1769*. Four volumes. Chicago: University of Chicago Press.

Bordewich, Fergus M. 1996. *Killing the White Man's Indian: Reinventing Native Americans at the End of the Twentieth Century*. New York: Doubleday.

Bradford, William. 2002–03. "With a Very Great Blame on Our Hearts: Reparations, Reconciliation, and an American Indian Plea for Peace with Justice." *American Indian Law Review* 27:1–176.

———. 2004. "In the Minds of Men: A Theory of Compliance with the Laws of War." *Arizona State Law Journal* 36 (winter): 1243–44.

———. 2005. "Beyond Reparations: An American Indian Theory of Justice." *Ohio State Law Journal* 66:1–110.

Christie, Kenneth. 2000. *The South African Truth Commission*. Basingstoke: Palgrave Macmillan.

Corlett, J. Angelo. 2002. "Wrongdoing, Reparations, and Native Americans." In *Injustice and Rectification*, edited by Rodney C. Roberts, 147–64. New York: Peter Lang.

Cornell, Stephen. 1990. *The Return of the Native: American Indian Political Resurgence*. Oxford: Oxford University Press.

Daly, Erin. 2003. "Reparations in South Africa: A Cautionary Tale." *University of Memphis Law Review* 33 (winter): 367–408.

Deloria, Vine, Jr. 1994. *God Is Red: A Native View of Religion*. 2nd edition. Golden, Colo.: Fulcrum.

Egan, Timothy. 1998. "Backlash Growing as Indians Make a Stand for Sovereignty." *New York Times* (9 March): A1.

Harris, Lee A. 2003. " 'Reparations' as a Dirty Word: The Norm Against Slavery Reparations." *University of Memphis Law Review* 33 (winter): 409–48.

Lemkin, Raphael. 1944. *Axis Rule in Occupied Europe: Laws of Occupation, Analysis of Government, Proposals for Redress*. Washington, D.C.: Carnegie Endowment for International Peace, Division of International Law.

Lieder, Michael, and Jake Page. 1999. *Wild Justice: The People of Geronimo vs. the United States*. Norman: University of Oklahoma Press.

Lyons, David. 1977. "The New Indian Claims and Original Rights to Land." *Social Theory and Practice* 4:249ff.

Malthus, Thomas Robert. 1993. *An Essay on the Principle of Population*. Oxford: Oxford University Press. Originally published in 1798.

Newton, Nell Jessup. 1992. "Indian Claims in the Courts of the Conqueror." *American University Law Review* 41 (spring): 753–854.

Noriega, Jorge. 1992. "American Indian Education in the United States: Indoctrination for Subordination to Colonialism." In *The State of Native America: Genocide, Colonization, and Resistance*, edited by M. Annette Jaimes, 371–402. Boston: South End Press.

Nozick, Robert. 1974. *Anarchy, State, and Utopia*. New York: Basic Books.

Porter, Robert B. 1997. "Strengthening Tribal Sovereignty Through Peacemaking: How the Anglo-American Legal Tradition Destroys Indigenous Societies." *Columbia Human Rights Law Review* 28: 235–96.

———. 1999. "The Demise of the Ongwehoweh and the Rise of the Native Americans: Redressing the Genocidal Act of Forcing American Citizenship upon Indigenous Peoples." *Harvard Blackletter Law Journal* 15:107–83.

Posner, Eric A., and Adrian Vermeule. 2003. "Reparations for Slavery and Other Historical Injustices." *Columbia Law Review* 103, no. 3 (April): 689–747.

Prince, Steven J. 1993. "The Political Economics of Articulation: Federal Policy and the Native American/Euroamerican Modes of Production." Doctoral dissertation, University of Utah.

Pritchard, Sarah. 1998. "The Stolen Generation and Reparations." *University of New South Wales Law Journal* 21:259ff.

Rohde, David. 1997. *Endgame: The Betrayal and Fall of Srebrenica, Europe's Worst Massacre since World War II*. Boulder, Colo.: Westview Press.

Rosen, Lawrence. 1997. "The Right to Be Different: Indigenous Peoples and the Quest for a Unified Theory." *Yale Law Journal* 107, no. 1 (October): 227–59.

Rosenthal, Harold D. 1990. *Their Day in Court: A History of the Indian Claims Commission*. Philadelphia: Taylor and Francis.

Shapiro, Thomas. 1985. *Population Control Politics: Women, Sterilization, and Reproductive Choice (Health, Society, and Policy)*. Philadelphia: Temple University Press.

Sterba, James P. 1996. "Understanding Evil: American Slavery, the Holocaust, and the Conquest of the American Indian." *Ethics* 106, no. 2 (January): 424–48.

Thompson, Janna. 2002. *Taking Responsibility for the Past: Reparation and Historical Injustice*. Cambridge: Polity Press.

Tully, James. 1994. "Aboriginal Property and Western Theory: Recovering a Middle Ground." In *Property* Rights, vol. 11, part 2, *Philosophy and Policy*, edited by Ellen Frankel Paul, Fred D. Miller, and Jeffrey Paul, 153–80. Cambridge: Cambridge University Press.

Wacks, Jamie L. 2000. "A Proposal for Community-Based Racial Reconciliation in the United States Through Personal Stories." *Virginia Journal of Social Policy and Law* 7:195–225.

Waldron, Jeremy. 1992a. "Minority Cultures and the Cosmopolitan Alternative." *University of Michigan Journal of Law Reform* 25 (spring and summer): 751–94.

———. 1992b. "Superseding Historic Injustice." *Ethics* 103, no. 1 (October): 4–28.

Washburn, Wilcomb E. 1995. *Red Man's Land/White Man's Law: The Past and Present Status of the American Indian*. Norman: University of Oklahoma Press.

Wheeler, Samuel C. III. 1997. "Reparations Reconstructed." *American Philosophical Quarterly* 34, no. 3 (July): 301–18.

Williams, Robert A., Jr. 1997. *Linking Arms Together: American Indian Treaty Visions of Law and Peace, 1600–1800*. New York: Oxford University Press.

Yamamoto, Eric K., Susan K. Serrano, and Michelle Natividad Rodriguez. 2003. "American Racial Justice on Trial—Again: African American Reparations, Human Rights, and the War on Terror." *Michigan Law Review* 101, no. 5 (March): 1269–337.

14

EPILOGUE:
RECONCILIATION IN THE AFTERMATH OF GENOCIDE

ARMEN T. MARSOOBIAN

I begin these thoughts on a rather personal level. While recently attending a workshop featuring the research of Armenian and Turkish scholars on the most controversial and traumatic period in their shared history, I had an unsettling encounter during one of the customary social breaks that mark all such gatherings. Over drinks and hors d'oeuvres a young woman turned to me and asked, "Do you hate me?" Overcoming my initial shock, I hesitatingly asked, "Why would I hate you?" The woman, who later informed me that she was a doctoral student at New York University, responded that she was Turkish and that since I was Armenian—an easy guess, given my nametag—I should be expected to hate her for what her ancestors had done to mine during the Armenian genocide of 1915–1923. After I assured her that hate was not an emotion I felt toward her or any other Turks I have encountered in my life, the conversation soon moved on to the sorts of exchanges customary in such academic social encounters—What's your research? Who are you working with? How far along are you? And so forth. This encounter lingered in my memory as later that week I began to review the essays for this collection in anticipation of writing a draft of the Introduction. Reading Marina Oshana's essay, "Moral Taint," drew me back to that moment with the Turkish graduate student. Were her words a reflection of the guilt that emerges from the moral taint associated with those whose group identities tie them to the sins of their forebears? More generally, I was prompted to ask what the possibilities are for genuine reconciliation between the descendants of the victims of genocide and the descendants of the perpetrators of genocide. What must individuals do to repair the wounds of genocide? These are difficult questions, ones I do not propose to answer in any definitive sense here. But with the help of some of the insights garnered from the essays in this volume, I hope to explore some possibilities.

My concern here is not with the actual perpetrators of genocide, nor with those who directly aided and benefited from their acts. These are more matters of justice and international criminal law. Progress has been made, though often fitfully, with bringing such individuals to justice. The Nuremberg and Tokyo Trials, while not as comprehensive as some would have liked, began the process of holding perpetrators responsible for their actions. Skeptics might call these beginnings "victor's justice," yet they did plant the seeds for the growth of international humanitarian criminal law and the mechanisms to enforce it. The trials currently taking place in The Hague, Rwanda, and Cambodia are the fruition of this fifty-year effort.[1] My concern is primarily with issues of intergenerational responsibility and repair. For the most part these are moral concerns, though if one considers the issue of genocide denial, they do bring up legal issues in certain European countries where denial of the Holocaust is criminally punishable.[2] As has been pointed out by a number of the authors in this collection, individuals are traditionally found blameworthy or praiseworthy for their *actions*, not for who they are. On first gloss there seems to be no culpable action when we think of the behavior of the descendants of genocide perpetrators. On one level this may be true, though, as we have seen in a number of the preceding essays, one's moral burdens do not end at the point of intentional action. But before exploring this aspect of responsibility, we need to examine more closely what we mean by the phrase "descendants of genocide perpetrators."

The descendants of genocide perpetrators are not necessarily descendants in any genealogical sense, though they may be. Blameworthiness does not rest on familial ties, though, as Oshana has pointed out, having a relative who has committed some evil act may place a moral burden upon a relative (for example, see her discussion of David Kaczynski, the brother of the Unabomber). In the broadest sense, a descendant is one whose ancestors were members of a community, usually an ethnic community, some of whose members committed acts of genocide. An ethnic German whose parents or grandparents lived in Nazi Germany or, as in the case of my Turkish graduate student, a Turk whose grandparents lived in Ottoman Turkey during the period of the Armenian genocide of 1915–1923 would qualify as such a descendant. Again, being the grandchild of Talât Pasha or Hermann Goering is not my focus; rather, I wish to focus on the grandchild's current relationship to his or her ethnic community. Moral assessment, whether it is a self-assessment or a judgment by others, arises out of the nature of one's relationship with one's ethnic group. What counts is the relation between oneself and one's society.

Yet, we must ask if *mere* membership in an ethic group historically identified with genocide carries with it certain moral burdens or moral

---

[1] With regard to the philosophical foundations of humanitarian international law, I would highly recommend a book written by one of our contributors: Larry May, *Crimes Against Humanity* (Cambridge: Cambridge University Press, 2005).
[2] A recent bill passed in the French National Assembly, which needs Senate approval before it becomes law, would criminalize denial of the Armenian genocide.

taint. Oshana has persuasively argued in the affirmative: "I think deserved moral taint, and with it genuine liability and the justified expectation of a level of shame, can be inherited, like a flawed gene." While moral taint can be inherited, Oshana is cognizant of the fact that this does not necessarily lead to our ordinary sense of blameworthiness for wrongdoing. A common rejoinder from descendants of genocide perpetrators is that they can't be blamed for the actions of their forefathers, because they were not there; and in any case, what is past is past and can never be changed. But this misses the point; blameworthiness does not arise out of a relationship with past events *per se*. We are responsible for who we are today, yet paradoxically, who we are today is inextricably bound up with our ancestral heritage.

This is where the analysis provided by Karen Kovich can be helpful. We see that for her more is required than mere membership in an ethnic group. She argues that it is the "alignment" of oneself with one's ethnic community that has implications for moral responsibility. One's shared ancestry opens up a space in which one acts in concert, whether intentionally or not, with the "idea of the group." One acts and responds "emotionally as a member of the group." The particularities of this alignment can vary greatly, from the relatively trivial to the profound—from one's tastes in cuisine to one's deeply felt religious beliefs. Moral taint may be inherited, but, as is the case with a defective gene, the consequences of this inheritance are what count. While it is not true for all genetically inherited disorders, one can think of the analogy of the individual who has inherited the gene for alcoholism but whose behavior is not that of an alcoholic. Blissful ignorance of one's inheritance is not what I have in mind here; rather, I'm thinking of the constant struggle to accept one's inheritance while at the same time remodeling oneself as a sober, moral self. Oshana herself recognizes this sense of responsibility. It is a responsibility in which we account for who we are:

> What there is to account for as well as to attribute to the agent, and to praise or blame her for, is (to borrow from Jaspers and May) *authenticity with respect to one's self-conception.* ... Authenticity consists in truthfulness toward oneself and about oneself in word and in deed. One who is authentic "meets head on his or her faults, or those of one's fellow community members, and regards oneself as at least partially responsible for them" (May 1991, 243). ... Similarly, one is inauthentic when one refuses to take a stance about one's position in the world in circumstances that pressure one to do so. Inauthenticity marks a kind of dishonesty with respect to one's self-conception.

My own concern here is with those aspects of this "idea of the group" that fueled aggression and genocidal violence in the past and continue to be actively present in the ethnic identities of today. We have seen much evidence of this in many of the ethnic conflicts that have culminated in genocides during the past hundred years, recent examples of which were the wars in the former Yugoslavia. A necessary condition for genuine reconciliation between the descendants of perpetrators and the descendants of victims is sincere moral assessment, on each one's part, of the alignment of oneself with one's ethnic identity group. This self-assessment, often aided by others, is crucial to moral authenticity (see May 1991).

What, then, is required to create the space in which such moral self-assessments can take place? I would propose that a crucial component for successful moral self-assessment is openness in the society in which one lives. A society in which individuals are able to participate in healthy, open, and critically vigorous debate, a society with free and diverse news media, and, most important, a society whose educational institutions promulgate an open marketplace of ideas—all are central to the openness necessary for the moral self-assessment required for reconciliation. It was John Dewey who argued that democracy is not a formal structure of governance with elections at its core but is, rather, a way of life. It is an often-repeated truism that democracies do not commit genocides. I would qualify this claim by stating that it is true only for *healthy* democracies, ones that provide space for critical self-examination and the open expression of ideas.[3] Ernesto Verdeja in his essay here on a theory of reparations calls for careful reconceptualization of "historical memory and combating unreflective, 'monumental' understandings of the past that justify crimes." This process of reconceptualization has been taking place in varying degrees in Latin America as democratization has taken hold in the past twenty years. While no single causal analysis is ever sufficient, it is evident that a major contributing factor to the ethnic violence in the former Yugoslavia was the nation's failure, for obvious reasons, to effectuate an open society in the aftermath of the Second World War. The ethnic violence and genocides that have marred Africa are a reflection of the failures of democratization in the postcolonial period. In contrast, German reconciliation with the victims of the Holocaust can be seen as a positive outgrowth of the success with which a democratic way of life has taken root in Germany.

The German example of reconciliation is worth exploring for the lessons it may hold for the general process of reconciliation between perpetrators and victims of genocide. It was not a given that reconciliation would take place between Germans and Jews at the end of the Second World War. Nazi culture had deep roots in a history of German anti-Semitism. Most Germans viewed the fall of the Nazi regime and the Allied occupation with a deep sense of humiliation. Europe may have been liberated, but in the eyes of most Germans, Germany had not. Many Germans viewed themselves as victims, not victimizers. This sense of

---

[3] Such generalizations are of course open to easy counterexamples. William Bradford, a contributor to this volume, may well cite the treatment of American Indians as the most obvious counterexample. My qualification of "healthy" is a reflection of this worry.

victimization was reinforced by the influx of some thirteen million refugees, mostly of German descent (*Volksdeutsche*) from Central and Eastern Europe. Elazar Barkan captures well the public attitude of most Germans at the end of the war:

> Following the war, it was the German victims, not the victims of Germany, who occupied public attention. German animosity for the inflicted suffering was initially directed against the Western occupying forces, which, together with the Soviets, were viewed as the villains. . . . In contrast, the Nazi regime and German guilt were ignored and willfully erased from memory. During the fifties and into the seventies, German memory focused on German suffering during the war and its aftermath. . . . In the West German political and cultural system Germans were the victims of war. (Barkan 2000, 10)

Some have referred to these postwar attitudes as the "second wound of silence." In ignoring what was done to the victims of genocide, one further injures the victims. Trudy Govier writes: "To ignore the wrong is to imply that it, and the suffering resulting from it, do not really matter. Truly this is adding the wound of insult to the wound of injury. Acknowledgement by relevant individuals and institutions may help to heal the second wound of silence" (2003, 83).

Sixty years on, there has been a significant shift in German public opinion about the war and the Holocaust. The healing has begun. What brought about this shift in these deeply rooted perceptions of the Third Reich? Historians, both German and non-German, have grappled with making sense of the complex factors behind this shift. The denazification program imposed by the victorious Allies is judged by most historians to have been a failure. Nor were the propaganda efforts of both the West and the Soviets to inculcate the "official" history of the Nazi era very successful. As I remarked earlier, the seeds for reconciliation were planted when a conscious decision was made by German society and its leaders to choose the path of an open and democratic way of life. The founding of the Federal Republic of Germany provided the necessary space within which this democratic way of life could grow. Oshana in her essay argues that "taint produces a moral burden to make restitution to others and to authenticate one's identity as a moral agent." While not universally shared by the German public at the time, this moral burden was recognized by the new postwar German leadership. Barkan writes: "The process [of restitution to Jewish victims] began in the early 1950s, shaped by Chancellor Konrad Adenauer and a group of leading German politicians who viewed it as a moral obligation, as well as a pragmatic policy, that would facilitate the acceptance of Germany by the world community" (2000, 8). In August 1952 a formal restitution agreement was concluded between the Federal Republic and Israel, but the process of reconciliation had only begun. The decades that followed were marked by a slow progress toward reconciliation. Starting in the 1960s, Holocaust education became a component in German secondary-school education. While the extent and success of such education is open to debate, the fact that it is officially recognized in the curriculum is important.

Still, it wasn't until the 1970s that the horrors of the Nazi era became the subject of open debate in the public sphere.[4] The "historians' debate" (*Historikerstreit*) of the mid-1980s to the 1990s provided a space for an open and critical reexamination of twentieth-century German history. Both Ernesto Verdeja and William Bradford emphasize in their essays the importance of symbolic public recognition of genocides and crimes against humanity. For Germans the opening in Berlin of the Monument to the Murdered Jews of Europe in May of 2005 marked an important public moment of acknowledgment and hence of reconciliation.

There are important parallels and significant differences between the processes of reconciliation in postwar Germany and postwar Japan. One would think that because democracy has taken root in Japan in the past sixty years there would be a degree of Japanese progress with regard to reconciliation similar to that in Germany, but this is not necessarily the case. The Nanking massacres, the "comfort women" (sexual slaves) from Korea, China, and other Asian nations, as well as numerous other atrocities of the 1937–1945 period have not been faced in a forthright manner by many in the Japanese political elite and among much of the general public. Visits by Japanese prime ministers to the Yasukuni Shrine in which Japan's war dead are venerated, including fourteen convicted class A war criminals, one of whom was the wartime prime minister General Hideki Tojo, have fueled resentment by many of Japan's Asian neighbors.[5] In contrast to German school curricula and textbooks, Japanese educational materials offer students little exposure to the atrocities committed by the Imperial Japanese army in the 1930s and 1940s. The extent and depth of reconciliation in Japan is hard to judge, but it is clear that more progress needs to be made.

Before concluding, I must return to where I began and ask: What are the prospects of genuine reconciliation between the descendants of perpetrators and victims of the Armenian genocide? I am the child of genocide survivors. My Turkish graduate student, I would venture to say, is two or three generations removed from the events of the 1915–1923 period. I earlier agreed with the work of Kovach, Oshana, and May

---

[4] A useful source for understanding the present state of Holocaust education and public discourse in Germany is an online interview with Lars Rensmann, professor of political science in Munich and Potsdam, www.pbs.org/wgbh/pages/frontline/shows/germans/germans/education.html (accessed October 10, 2006).

[5] The symbolic meaning of such visits is explained in a BBC News account of the Shrine: "Within the shrine, the souls of the dead are worshipped rather than just remembered. According to Japan's national Shinto religion, humans are transformed into 'kami' or deities when they die, and as such are worshipped by their descendants. The kami of remarkable people are enshrined"; news.bbc.co.uk/2/hi/asia-pacific/1330223.stm (accessed October 10, 2006).

regarding the importance of the need for individual moral self-assessment in light of the history one shares as a member of an ethnic community implicated in genocide. I was particularly concerned with those aspects of ethnic self-identity that may lead to new acts of violence. As I remarked earlier, the Armenian genocide is a highly controversial topic in present-day Turkey. The official position of the modern state of Turkey with regard to the Armenian genocide is one of denial.[6] As a result, it is hard to draw easy lessons from the reconciliation processes in postwar Germany and Japan. As Haig Khatchadourian explains in his essay, the government of Turkey, its semi-official organs, and many in the political and intellectual elite are actively involved in a campaign of genocide denial. Claims of denial that are commonly made while most genocides are being perpetrated (including the genocide currently taking place in Darfur)— vociferous public denials, alternative explanations, minimizations, and the maintenance of a high degree of secrecy as to the command structure of the slaughter process—have been and continue to be made for the Armenian genocide ninety years after the fact.[7] This is not to say that the wall of silence and denial has not been breached. The taboo within Turkey against any public discussion of these events was broken when an academic conference was held at Istanbul's Bilgi University in September 2005. Even holding this conference was no simple matter, given the fact that initial government and then judicial opposition resulted in two postponements and a last-minute change of venue.[8] As I argued earlier,

---

[6] For a balanced treatment of the campaign of Armenian genocide denial see chapter 6, "Epilogue: The Geopolitics of Memory," in Donald Bloxham, *The Great Game of Genocide: Imperialism, Nationalism, and the Destruction of the Ottoman Armenians* (Oxford: Oxford University Press, 2005).

[7] A typical example of denial by way of an alternative explanation, one that seeks to minimize the scope of the Armenian genocide, can be found in the following quote from an article by Demir Delan written in a publication of the Federation of Canadian Turkish Associations: "It is a fact that approximately 700,000 Armenians were killed or died of starvation and disease during the First World War in eastern Anatolia. It is also a fact that more than 2 million Turks and Muslims were massacred by the Armenians at the turn of the century or died during the First World War in eastern Anatolia, fighting Armenians and Russians. These were tragic events from which lessons should be learned, so that similar incidents of ultra-nationalism that result in the total uprooting and devastation of communities are not allowed to occur again. The Turkish community in Canada and the U.S, as well as the Turks in Turkey recognize the Armenian deaths and suffering during this period. What they deeply object to is the propaganda and distortion of facts by Armenian activists who are misleading the public in order to further their political agenda by crying 'genocide,' while ignoring the death and suffering of more than twice as many Turks." "Perpetuating the Genocide Myth," www.ataa.org/ataa/ref/arm_fcta.html (accessed October 22, 2006).

[8] For an account of this conference see Aisha Labi, "Controversial Conference on Genocide Held in Turkey," *Chronicle of Higher Education*, October 7, 2005, 48. The importance of this event for the democratic opening taking place in Turkey is captured in an opinion piece by Ilnur Cevik, "So did the Armenian conference hurt our country's interests?" *New Anatolian*, September 26, 2005. www.turkishweekly.net/comments. php?id = 1763 (accessed October 23, 2006).

if genuine reconciliation is to take place, perpetrator societies must adopt a democratic way of life in which no subject matter is taboo. The democratization process in Turkey has been long in coming and has only of late gained some momentum, spurred on in part by Turkey's desire to join the European Union. One of the participants in the Bilgi conference, the Turkish historian Taner Akçam, has clearly articulated the importance of breaking such taboos: "If Turkey is to develop from an authoritarian, bureaucratic state into a standard Western democracy, it must come to terms with history and take a critical approach towards the problems surrounding its national identity. For this to occur, Turkish society must take an active role in opening a debate on the Armenian Genocide. . . . The dominance of the denial syndrome must be overcome, and direct interaction between Turkish and Armenian societies must take place" (Akçam 2004, 9). These words were written almost two years before the Bilgi conference and serve as part of a growing call for change.

While still in its nascent stage, this open debate is being fostered by such Turkish writers as Orhan Pamuk, whose recent award of the Nobel Prize in literature was a matter both of pride and of controversy in his home country. Nationalists in Turkey have condemned him as a traitor, and they forced an ultimately unsuccessful prosecution against him for insulting Turkish identity. He had stated in a Swiss magazine interview that a million Armenians and thirty thousand Kurds were killed, yet no one dares speak of it. While Pamuk stops short of referring to the killings of a million Armenians as genocide, he has questioned the wall of silence that has prevailed in modern Turkey about aspects of its own history. In his writings, both fiction and nonfiction, he has grappled with issues surrounding what it means to be a Turk in a nation that aspires to become an open, liberal, democratic state. Kovach argues that one's alignment with the "idea of the group" is crucial for assessing the moral burdens one bears as a member of an ethnic group tainted by genocide. Individuals, such as Pamuk, who question the "official" historical narrative of the dissolution of the Ottoman Empire, the founding of the Turkish Republic, and the treatment of minorities (Kurds in particular) are remodeling notions of what it means to be a Turk. This is a process of moral self-assessment built upon a critical examination of one's relationships with one's ethnic community and the ancestral legacy this entails.

I asserted earlier that a healthy democratic way of life facilitates reconciliation between the descendants of the victims of genocide and the descendants of genocide perpetrators. This was certainly the case for Germany. Modern-day Turkey is only now on the threshold of shedding its authoritarian structures. Earlier attempts at liberalization in the 1960s, 1970s, and 1980s led to three successive military coups. The National Security Council dominated by the military forms a parallel government that exerts considerable control over Turkish civil society.[9] The hold of nationalist ideology on various levels of Turkish society makes the task of reconciliation for Turks and Armenians considerably more difficult than the current process of German reconciliation with the victims of the Holocaust. While there never was a postwar state-sponsored denial of the Holocaust, parallels can be drawn between Turkey today and the Germany of the postwar period. The moral leadership of such individuals as Chancellor Adenauer, who faced considerable obstacles in his chosen path of reconciliation, stands out *precisely because* of the silence that dominated the general public attitude toward the Holocaust.

Setting aside for the moment the question of the official government denial of the Armenian genocide, what are some of the lessons to be learned from the silences of postgenocide Germany and Turkey? Both peoples faced great traumas in their defeats in the World Wars. It is a well-established psychological phenomenon that for those who have been traumatized a response of selective memory or silence is common. A defensive wall of forgetting is often erected. The hardships of rebuilding one's life and the life of the nation require devoting considerable energy to the present, often reinforcing the silence surrounding the events of the past. When you add to this the widespread involvement of hundreds of thousands of individuals in the mechanisms of genocide, there is an added impetus for silence lest one's culpability be exposed.[10]

Over decades of authoritarian rule and with no strong international voice to press the case for Armenian restitution, the attitudes of the Turkish public toward the Armenian massacres became more and more diffuse, yet more and more sedimented. The strong Allied presence in postwar Germany and the birth of the state of Israel were a counterbalance to German forgetting. The failures of the international community in dealing with the aftermath of the First World War with regard to both Germany and Ottoman Turkey are well documented. There was no viable Armenian state to press the case for restitution, and geopolitical and economic interests dictated eventual Western support for the new Turkish state. After the Second World War American and NATO coldwar strategy continued this policy. The geopolitics of the Middle East now plays a major role in American state collusion with genocide

---

[9] The hindrances to democracy in Turkey are discussed in Akçam 2004 (especially 1–4).

[10] Akçam has persuasively argued that many members of the Committee of Union and Progress (the Young Turks) who were directly involved in the Armenian genocide played an active role in the founding of the modern Turkish republic in 1923. See especially Akçam 2004, 237–41.

denial.[11] Many factors have contributed to the current Turkish public attitude toward the Armenian genocide, the complexities of which are beyond the scope of my remarks here. This public attitude is effectively captured by Akçam, who has written extensively on the issue: "When one speaks of the attitude of Turkish society on this subject [the Armenian genocide], I suggest that it be portrayed as ignorance, apathy, fatalism, reticence and silence rather than denial" (2004, 227).

As Akçam goes on to point out, there is no monolithic attitude toward the Armenian genocide, with various subgroups displaying a range of responses. For those who display ignorance, Akçam places some of the blame on the educational system: "State-sponsored education, consisting of nationalistic historiography, is the reason for this ignorance and this attitude. In recent years, this situation of not knowing and not caring has slowly begun to give way to an interest in learning what really happened" (228). Strengthening an independent educational system, one in which all topics are open to critical and unbiased investigation, is crucial to the process of reconciliation. Akçam, who is keenly aware of the literature on Germans and the Holocaust, has argued that unlike many Germans who were unwilling to acknowledge their support for the Nazi regime ("We didn't know, we weren't aware"), many Turks discuss the subject of the Armenian massacres, but only in the private sphere: "The official position of the state is justified in the public sphere, but its errors are freely discussed in the private sphere. Turkish reality is that, in the public arena, the official state narrative appears to be embraced, while in private, markedly different opinions are voiced and defended ... this has led to a schizophrenic situation" (229).

What will it take to cure this schizophrenia? Or to use the language of Oshana and May, how does one achieve "authenticity with regard to one's self-conception" and diminish the gap between the private self and the public self? Oshana and others have described the process by which one removes the moral taint of genocide as "atonement." Whatever we may choose to call it, there are no easy answers to these questions. But the examples set by such individuals as Pamuk, Akçam, and the organizers of the Bilgi conference can all point the way. They and many more like them are engaging in a process of open and frank dialogue among themselves as to what it means to be a Turk who is willing to acknowledge, understand, condemn, and praise aspects of his or her ethnic heritage.

---

[11] The recent recall of the American ambassador to Armenia for having uttered the "genocide" word in describing the Armenian massacres of 1915–1918 is a sorry reflection of this collusion. For an account of American complicity in the denial of the Armenian genocide see "Epilogue: Turkish Denial of the Armenian Genocide and U.S. Complicity," in Peter Balakian, *The Burning Tigris: The Armenian Genocide and America's Response* (New York: HarperCollins, 2003).

I have not even broached the issue as to the kind of work that needs to be done on the part of the descendents of genocide victims in order to facilitate reconciliation. Certainly, adopting a victim's history is not very useful to understanding the causes of one's victimization. Understanding the Armenian genocide from the perpetrators' perspective is important not only for those Turks, such as Akçam, who are genuinely concerned with the tendencies toward ethnic violence in Turkey today, especially toward the Kurds, but also for Armenians who must engage in a dialogue with Turks if the goal of reconciliation is ever to be achieved.[12]

I began this epilogue with a description of an incident that occurred during a workshop of Turkish and Armenian scholars.[13] These workshop participants have been meeting on a regular basis to grapple with many of the hard issues I have described above. In exploring their shared history from each other's perspective they have taken the first tentative steps toward reconciliation. Karen Kovach concluded her essay in this volume by describing the moral work that needs to be done in the aftermath of genocide. While the work being done by these scholars would normally be described under the disciplinary categories of history, sociology, political science, and philosophy, there is an important sense in which it can be described as the work of morality. Kovach's words are quite fitting in this regard:

> The competent moral agent does not spend much time trying to wish away the difficult, unpleasant, or inconvenient realities that shape the context in which she must act. She looks them in the face, acknowledging that it is *with them* that she must work. Much of the work involved in the restoration or creation of morally responsible relations between groups after genocide will be carried out by generations of group members who were not yet born when the killing took place, but whose lives will be substantially shaped by it all the same.

I fervently hope that the essays contained in this volume will contribute in some small measure to the moral work that needs to be done in the aftermath of genocide.

---

[12] Akçam warns: "At present, another wave of nation building is under way in Anatolia. At the time of the first wave [during the period of the Armenian Genocide], Turks embraced their national identity in a violent manner that would form the foundation for future political organization of the country. It is no exaggeration to say that the potential for the same violent embrace of their national identity exists in the Turkish nation today" (150). See also his discussion of the importance of understanding the perpetrator perspective in Akçam, 41–44.

[13] More information about the Workshop for Armenian/Turkish Scholarship (WATS) can be obtained at the website: www.armturkworkshop.org.

References

Akçam, Taner. 2004. *From Empire to Republic: Turkish Nationalism and the Armenian Genocide*. London: Zed Books.

Barkan, Elazar. 2000. *The Guilt of Nations: Restitution and Negotiating Historical Injustices*. New York: W. W. Norton.

Govier, Trudy. 2003. "What is Acknowledgement and Why Is It Important?" In *Dilemmas of Reconciliation: Cases and Concepts*, edited by Carol A. L. Prager and Trudy Govier, 65–89. Waterloo, Canada: Wilfrid Laurier University Press.

May, Larry. 1991. "Metaphysical Guilt and Moral Taint." In *Collective Responsibility: Five Decades of Debate in Theoretical and Applied Ethics*, edited by Larry May and Stacey Hoffman, 239–54. Savage, Md.: Rowan & Littlefield.

INDEX